PENGUIN

SPUNYARN: SEA PO

JOHN MASEFIELD was born in Ledbury, Herefordshire, in 1878. He was orphaned at an early age, and attended Warwick School before joining the school ship HMS *Conway*. At the age of fifteen he embarked on a career at sea with a voyage to Chile, via Cape Horn, but was invalided back to England. Wishing to become a writer, he failed to report for a new position on a ship in New York and became a homeless vagrant before finding work in a bar and then a carpet factory. Returning to England in 1897, he published his first poem in a periodical two years later. His first volume of poetry, *Salt-Water Ballads*, was issued in 1902 and his last volume, *In Glad Thanksgiving*, in 1967. Masefield became a best-selling author, with an output that included novels, children's books, plays and works of contemporary history. Appointed Poet Laureate in 1930, he was awarded the Order of Merit in 1935. He died in 1967 after a distinguished literary career. His two fantasy novels for children, *The Midnight Folk* and *The Box of Delights*, have been acclaimed as 'two of the greatest children's books ever written' by *The Times* and his poems 'Sea-Fever' and 'Cargoes' were described by John Betjeman as 'two lyrics which will be remembered as long as the language lasts'.

PHILIP W. ERRINGTON is a Director in the Department of Printed Books and Manuscripts at Sotheby's. After completing a doctoral thesis on Masefield, he was appointed a visiting research fellow of the University of London in 2000 and honorary research fellow of University College London in 2005. His bibliography *John Masefield – The 'Great Auk' of English Literature* was published by the British Library in 2004. He has edited numerous volumes of Masefield, including *Sea-Fever: Selected Poems of John Masefield* and *Reynard the Fox* for Carcanet, *John Masefield's Great War* for Pen and Sword, and *The Midnight Folk* and *The Box of Delights* for Egmont.

JOHN MASEFIELD

Spunyarn

Sea Poetry and Prose

Edited with an Introduction and Notes by
PHILIP W. ERRINGTON

PENGUIN BOOKS

I dedicate my share of this book
to the memory of David Lankey

PENGUIN CLASSICS

Published by the Penguin Group
Penguin Books Ltd, 80 Strand, London WC2R 0RL, England
Penguin Group (USA) Inc., 375 Hudson Street, New York, New York 10014, USA
Penguin Group (Canada), 90 Eglinton Avenue East, Suite 700, Toronto, Ontario,
Canada M4P 2Y3 (a division of Pearson Penguin Canada Inc.)
Penguin Ireland, 25 St Stephen's Green, Dublin 2, Ireland (a division of Penguin Books Ltd)
Penguin Group (Australia), 250 Camberwell Road, Camberwell, Victoria 3124, Australia
(a division of Pearson Australia Group Pty Ltd)
Penguin Books India Pvt Ltd, 11 Community Centre, Panchsheel Park, New Delhi – 110 017, India
Penguin Group (NZ), 67 Apollo Drive, Rosedale, Auckland 0632, New Zealand
(a division of Pearson New Zealand Ltd)
Penguin Books (South Africa) (Pty) Ltd, 24 Sturdee Avenue, Rosebank, Johannesburg 2196, South Africa

Penguin Books Ltd, Registered Offices: 80 Strand, London WC2R 0RL, England

www.penguin.com

This collection first published in Penguin Classics 2011
1

Copyright © The Estate of John Masefield, 2011
Introduction, selection and editorial matter © Philip W. Errington, 2011
All rights reserved

The moral right of the editor has been asserted

Set in 10.25/12.25 pt PostScript Adobe Sabon
Typeset by Jouve (UK), Milton Keynes
Printed in England by Clays Ltd, St Ives plc

ISBN: 978-0-141-19160-7

www.greenpenguin.co.uk

Penguin Books is committed to a sustainable future
for our business, our readers and our planet.
The book in your hands is made from paper
certified by the Forest Stewardship Council.

Contents

SPUNYARN: SEA POETRY
AND PROSE

Poetry

Short Stories

Other Prose

Extracts from Novels

Acknowledgements

I am extremely grateful to all those who have assisted in the preparation of this volume. For their special assistance I thank Dr Peter Beal, Robin Bussell, Jeremy Crow, Eileen Errington, Dr William Errington, David Fletcher-Rogers, Helen Fletcher-Rogers, Elizabeth Haylett-Clark, Sarah Hyde, Professor Susan Irvine, John Wyse Jackson, Dr David Jenkins of the National Waterfront Museum in Swansea, Katharine Lankey, Richard Masefield, Delphie Masefield Hall, Kathryn Metzenthin, Tessa Milne, Dr Simone Murray, Chris Noël, Roy Palmer, Kate Parker, Polly Parry and her colleagues at the Natural History Museum, Dr Stephen Roe, Mary Roe, Henry Roe, Bob Sanders, my colleagues within the Department of Printed Books and Manuscripts at Sotheby's, Bob Vaughan, Alfie Windsor, Joan Winterkorn, Sheila Woolf and Professor Henry Woudhuysen. As ever, I thank my wife, Liz Errington, for her support.

In addition I wish to record my thanks to W. H. Masefield for his help and permission to consult restricted manuscript material located at the Bodleian Library. I am also grateful to the Harry Ransom Humanities Research Center, the University of Texas, for two fellowships to enable me to consult their Masefield papers in 2002 and 2008.

Chronology

'When I am buried, all my thoughts and acts
Will be reduced to lists of dates and facts . . .'
'Biography', 1914

1878   Born in Ledbury, Herefordshire.
1885   Death of Masefield's mother.
1888   Attends Warwick School.
1890   Leaves Warwick School.
1891   Death of Masefield's father. Masefield's uncle and aunt,
        William and Kate Masefield, become full guardians of the six
        Masefield children. Joins HMS *Conway*.
1894   Leaves HMS *Conway*. Apprenticed to the *Gilcruix* and
        sails from Cardiff to Iquique in Chile via Cape Horn. Dis-
        charged from crew and returns to England classified as a
        'Distressed British Sailor'.
1895   Crosses the Atlantic to join the *Bidston Hill* but deserts
        ship to become a homeless vagrant in America. Obtains bar-
        work in Greenwich Village, New York, then employed at a
        carpet factory in Yonkers.
1896   Reads Geoffrey Chaucer for the first time.
1897   Returns to England and finds work as a junior clerk in
        London.
1898   Starts work as a bank clerk.
1899   First poem, 'Nicias Moriturus', published in *The Outlook*.
1900   First meets W. B. Yeats.
1901   Abandons job at the bank and becomes a freelance
        writer.
1902   Secretary to Wolverhampton Art and Industrial Exhib-
        ition. Publication of *Salt-Water Ballads* (poems).
1903   First meets J. M. Synge. Engaged and married to
        Constance de la Cherois Crommelin (1867–1960). Publica-
        tion of *Ballads*.

1904   Birth of Judith Masefield (1904–88). Moves to Dia-
mond Terrace, Greenwich, London. Stays in Manchester to
work on *Manchester Guardian*.

1905   Leaves Manchester. Stays at Coole with Lady Gregory.
Publication of *A Mainsail Haul* (short stories).

1906   Introduced to Harley Granville Barker.

1907   First production of *The Campden Wonder* at the Court
Theatre, London. Publication of *A Tarpaulin Muster* (short
stories). Moves from Greenwich to Maida Hill West, Pad-
dington.

1908   First production of *Nan* at the New Royalty Theatre,
London. Publication of first novel, *Captain Margaret*.

1909   First letters to Elizabeth Robins, the actress, writer and
suffragist.

1910   Lecture on women's suffrage at the Queen's Hall. Birth
of Lewis Masefield (1910–42). Termination of correspond-
ence with Elizabeth Robins. Publication of third volume of
poetry, *Ballads and Poems* (largely comprising verse from his
first two volumes). First production of *The Tragedy of Pom-
pey the Great* at the Aldwych Theatre, London.

1911   Publication of *The Everlasting Mercy* (long narrative
poem).

1912   Visited by Rupert Brooke. Publication of *The Widow in
the Bye Street* (long narrative poem). Awarded Edmond de
Polignac Prize for *The Everlasting Mercy*. Moves from Pad-
dington to Well Walk, Hampstead.

1913   Publication of *The Daffodil Fields* and *Dauber* (long
narrative poems).

1914   Publication of 'August, 1914' (poem). First production
of *Philip the King* at the Theatre Royal, Bristol.

1915   Works as a hospital orderly at Arc-en-Barrois, Haute
Marne. Inspects military hospitals in France. Commands
ambulance boat in Dardanelles. First production of *The
Faithful* at the Birmingham Repertory Theatre.

1916   Lecture and propaganda tour of America (three
months). Publication of *Gallipolli* (history). Inspects Ameri-
can Red Cross hospitals in France. Meets Sir Douglas Haig.

1917   Research on Somme battlefield. First production of

Good Friday at the Garrick Theatre, London. Moves from Hampstead to Boars Hill, near Oxford.

1918   Lecture and propaganda tour of America (seven months). Honorary degrees from universities of Yale and Harvard. Visited by Siegfried Sassoon. Works with 'Department of Hospitality to American Forces'.

1919   Publication of *Reynard the Fox* (long narrative poem). First of Masefield's amateur theatricals, including Yeats's *The Pot of Broth* at the Recreation Room, Wootton.

1922   Honorary degree from University of Oxford.

1923   First production of *Melloney Holtspur* at St Martin's Theatre, London. Organizes first of an annual verse-speaking festival (the 'Oxford Recitations'). Publication of *Collected Poems*. Honorary degree from University of Manchester.

1924   Lays foundation stone for the 'Music Room' theatre in his garden at Boars Hill. First radio broadcast, reading from his own works for the British Broadcasting Corporation. Delivers the Romanes lecture on Shakespeare at the Sheldonian Theatre, Oxford. Publication of *Sard Harker* (novel). First performance of Masefield's amateur theatricals within the Music Room (production of Laurence Binyon's *The Young King*).

1925   First production of *The Trial of Jesus* at the Music Room; attended by George Bernard Shaw.

1926   Visits America. Presented to President Coolidge.

1927   First production of *Tristan and Isolt* at the Century Theatre, London. Publication of *The Midnight Folk* (children's novel).

1928   Production of *The Coming of Christ* in Canterbury Cathedral (music by Gustav Holst and costumes by Charles Ricketts).

1930   Appointed Poet Laureate. Holds Yeats festival at the Music Room. Honorary degrees from universities of Liverpool and St Andrews. Receives Freedom of the City of Hereford.

1931   Delivers lecture entitled 'Poetry' at the Queen's Hall. Honorary degree from University of Cambridge.

1932   Honorary degree from University of Wales.

1933   Visit to America. Moves from Oxford to Pinbury Park,

near Cirencester. Announces creation of Royal Medal for Poetry. Publication of *The Bird of Dawning* (novel).

1935   Order of Merit conferred. Publication of *The Box of Delights* (children's novel).

1936   Visits America twice, including participation in Harvard tercentenary celebrations.

1937   Broadcasts 'Coronation Ode' on television and a radio talk on Coronation Night to America. Elected President of the Society of Authors.

1938   Awarded Hanseatic Shakespeare Prize (Hamburg University).

1939   Final year that Masefield organized the 'Oxford Recitations'. Moves from Cirencester to Burcote Brook, Abingdon.

1941   Publication of *The Nine Days Wonder* (history).

1943   First radio adaptation of *The Box of Delights*.

1944   Delivers the second annual lecture of the National Book Council at Caxton Hall, Westminster.

1946   Honorary degree from University of Sheffield.

1947   Honorary degree from University of London.

1952   Publication of *So Long to Learn* (autobiography).

1958   Eightieth birthday marked by exhibition at *The Times* Bookshop.

1959   Publication on LP record of *The Story of Ossian* (long narrative poem).

1961   Receives Royal Society of Literature Companionship of Literature. Awarded William Foyle Poetry Prize.

1964   First recipient of an award from the National Book League.

1967   Publication of *In Glad Thanksgiving* (poetry). Death of John Masefield and memorial service at Westminster Abbey.

Introduction

John Masefield claimed that 'the sea creates stories' and 'in a
ship the spinning of yarns was almost a part of the craft'.[1] The
future Poet Laureate had been educated aboard the training
ship HMS *Conway* between September 1891 and March 1894,
and then apprenticed aboard a four-masted barque from April
1894 until he was discharged, classified as a 'Distressed British
Sailor', four months later. His career at sea was short yet it
is only Joseph Conrad who, in the late nineteenth and early
twentieth centuries, can compare with him. Masefield is our
native-born writer of the sea and when John Betjeman con-
fidently stated that the poems 'Sea-Fever' and 'Cargoes' (see
pp. 6 and 24) would be 'remembered as long as the language
lasts'[2] he identified six stanzas from Masefield's vast output
that are an intrinsic part of our literature. Masefield, however,
enjoyed a career that spanned almost seven decades in which
he had been a best-selling novelist, an innovative playwright, a
prodigious reviewer, a respected lecturer, an essayist, a writer
of fantasy for children, a historian, a literary critic, a govern-
ment propaganda agent and, as predicted by W. B. Yeats, 'a
popular poet'.[3] In other words, there is more to Masefield than
just 'Sea-Fever' and 'Cargoes'.

John Edward Masefield was born in June 1878 in Ledbury,
Herefordshire, to George and Caroline Masefield and enjoyed
an idyllic childhood until the age of six when his mother died.
A 'vulgar woman' became governess for the six Masefield chil-
dren and the rebellious John once stabbed her with a fork in
the arm.[4] When Masefield's father, a lawyer in the family firm
of solicitors, died in an asylum in 1891, the children came

under the charge of their uncle and aunt, William and Kate Masefield. Aunt Kate took exception to John's aspirations to become a writer and, at the age of thirteen, he was sent to HMS *Conway* in Liverpool. Masefield later wrote that 'as a ship she was obsolete and rotten, as a school she was infamous, and as a training place for officers, she was despicable . . . I was the youngest boy there for a full year. The tone of the ship was infamous. Theft, bullying, barratry, sodomy, and even viler vice were rampant . . .'[5]

At the age of fifteen he was apprenticed on a ship sailing round Cape Horn to Chile. He experienced acute seasickness shortly after leaving Cardiff Docks, and then the Horn subjected him to 'thirty-two days of such storm and cold as I hope never to see again'.[6] Upon his arrival in Chile, sunstroke combined with exhaustion and Masefield was hospitalized in Valparaiso before he returned to England. Back home in Ledbury, Aunt Kate insisted that her nephew must return to sea and a new position was found aboard a ship then in New York. Although Masefield crossed the Atlantic, he failed to report for duty. He later wrote: 'I deserted ship . . . and cut myself adrift from her and from my home. I was going to be a writer, come what might.'[7]

At the age of sixteen Masefield became a vagrant in America. He 'tramped, and cut wood, and did chores, and starved, and slept out'.[8] Presently he secured a position as a junior bar-tender in New York before working in a Yonkers carpet factory for two years. The job allowed the aspiring writer to read voraciously and practise his craft. On 6 September 1896 he read Geoffrey Chaucer for the first time[9] and 'felt the real delight of poetry'.[10] At a time of economic depression his job was precarious, however, and when the factory was forced into temporary closure, Masefield nearly returned to the sea. Then in 1897 he had an argument with his boss, left Yonkers and worked his way home across the Atlantic as a steerage steward.[11] He landed in Liverpool with six pounds and a revolver. He later wrote: 'I was going to try to get a job as a clerk (I knew nothing of business). Failing that, I was going to shoot myself. I was desperately ill and sick. I hadn't the strength to face more hardships.'[12]

Such were the experiences of the young Masefield. Accounts of his life, by himself and others, show him as a person of contrasts and complexity. As a writer he would innovate and experiment. He would experience sensational popular success and complete critical indifference. As a man he would remain married for fifty-six years until the death of his wife yet also gather a number of young ladies for extra-marital liaisons. Of all the contrasts, early critics and commentators were particularly intrigued by Masefield's early years. Prior to publication of his first novel in 1908, he wrote to his publisher:

> May I ask you, before my novel comes out, to do something for me? I want you not to mention my unhappy past, in America and elsewhere, to people connected with the press. Those squalid hours, and my early work based upon them, have given me a picaresque reputation which is in the way of the serious reputation I now seek . . .[13]

It is not entirely clear whether Masefield includes his sea career in the 'unhappy past', yet the statement identifies a further contradiction. Masefield could not, ultimately, reinvent his early life and would later publish book-length accounts of his first term on board HMS *Conway* and his time in the carpet factory.[14] In Masefield's work there is a longing to understand the past and define a sense of home. In depicting long sea voyages, in evoking exotic locations and in describing communities aboard ship, Masefield writes of homesickness. The act of going to sea is, essentially, both a rejection of home and the embracing of a life of isolation. It should therefore be no surprise that the teenager would turn to the life of a homeless tramp. For the confused and alienated Masefield the desired homecoming was, perhaps, to a parental home that was denied him. His early poetry frequently dwells on death, which may have been the young writer's perception of the only true homecoming. The experiences of his youth would, despite his reservations and anguish about them, provide material for works throughout his career.

That literary career began in earnest in 1899 with publication of a poem, 'Nicias Moriturus', in a periodical and it was with this one ballad to his name that he approached W. B. Yeats in the late autumn of 1900. Invitations to the Irish poet's Monday evening gatherings enabled Masefield to meet such luminaries as Lady Gregory, J. M. Synge, George Russell ('AE'), Ernest Rhys, Arthur Symons, William Strang and Laurence Binyon. It appears that some members of the circle took considerable interest in their new acquaintance. Masefield was then working as a bank clerk and Binyon was instrumental in Masefield abandoning his job and in securing his services as exhibition secretary for the 1902 Wolverhampton Art and Industrial Exhibition, in addition to work on an edition of John Keats for which Masefield provided footnotes. While Masefield was in Wolverhampton the publisher Grant Richards invited him to collect the numerous poems which had, by then, appeared in newspapers and periodicals. Under the title of *Salt-Water Ballads*, Masefield's first volume was published in November 1902.

The volume – which contained 'Sea-Fever' – met with little notice and Masefield, who had married in July 1903, threw himself into the life of a literary hack. Between 1902 and 1911 he published eighteen volumes of his own work (of which only three were books of poetry), edited or introduced seventeen others (of which ten were of a literary nature and seven were on historical naval topics) and contributed to, or was associated with, seven other books. This was in addition to work for around twenty-six newspapers or periodicals, totalling in excess of 580 contributions.[15] His play *Nan*, first staged in 1908 and directed by Harley Granville Barker, was, in Yeats's opinion, 'a wonderful play – the best English play since the Elizabethans'[16] and his first six novels had been generally well received. Despite these successes the period was one of experiment combined with a desperate attempt to find financial security. In later life he recalled 'a very real blackness of despair' and noted that 'my work was not what I had hoped'.[17]

This changed in 1911 with publication of *The Everlasting Mercy*, a long narrative poem telling of the spiritual enlightenment of a drunken poacher. It was followed by *The Widow in*

the Bye Street (1912) and *Dauber* (1913). The first two narra-
tives are set in the countryside of Masefield's youth while the
third tells of an aspiring artist who goes to sea in order to fund
his studies at art school. His aim is to capture life at sea in his
paintings: 'It's not been done, the sea, not yet been done, / From
the inside, by one who really knows . . .'[18] but he is a poor painter
and a worse seaman and is treated with contempt by his fellow
sailors. Just as he starts to demonstrate sailor qualities and earn
the respect of the crew, he falls to his death during a storm. The
character would resonate throughout Masefield's work.

With the outbreak of war, Masefield became an orderly at a
military hospital in France. He then took charge of a motor-
boat ambulance service at Gallipoli in 1915 before a propaganda
tour of the United States in 1916. His best-selling prose work
on the Gallipoli campaign led to an official invitation from Sir
Douglas Haig to chronicle the Battle of the Somme, although
Masefield's full plan was never completed owing to govern-
ment bureaucracy. A lecture tour of the United States followed
in 1918 and, as the war ended, Masefield was working for the
'Department of Hospitality to American Forces' in England.[19]
Masefield was now forty and, mirroring what Yeats had done
for him, he supported emerging talent. Siegfried Sassoon paid a
number of visits and Robert Graves took up residence in a cot-
tage within the grounds of Masefield's house at Boars Hill near
Oxford. His own work included further long narrative poems.
The epic *Reynard the Fox* (1919) describes an English commu-
nity and an exhilarating hunt. It was Masefield's poetic response
to the Great War: in his fox he identified 'something primitive,
wild, beautiful and strange in the Spirit of Man [that] had been
pursued through most of Europe with the threat of death'.[20]

By the early 1920s Masefield's attentions had turned again
to drama. Following experiments in the presentation of plays
using community and university talent, he built a theatre (the
'Music Room') in the grounds of his house and produced a
wide range of works, including plays by William Shakespeare,
Jean Racine (in translation), W. B. Yeats and Thomas Hardy.
This period also saw Masefield returning to the novel, with
Sard Harker in 1924 and *Odtaa* in 1926. *Sard Harker*,

considered by Graham Greene as a work that 'would have been the greatest adventure story in the language if it hadn't got the absurd ending',[21] has a sailor as the central character, but the setting is, 'the swamps and mountains of a blood-soaked South American dictatorship' (as noted by the publisher's blurb to the 1963 Penguin edition). Over the next decade the novels *The Bird of Dawning* (1933), *The Taking of the Gry* (1934) and *Victorious Troy* (1935) were to be set at sea and include sailors as their central characters.

With the death of Robert Bridges in 1930, Masefield was offered the position of Poet Laureate. He immediately suggested that he might be unsuitable, noting that 'I am not now a ready writer; and can write verse only rarely, in moments of deep feeling.'[22] The prime minister, Ramsay MacDonald, nevertheless submitted his name to George V and Masefield was appointed as a member of the royal household of the 'Sailor King'. The writer had come far from a failed sailor and homeless vagabond. It took four years and the Laureate's third official verse to find a sea theme: in 1934 Masefield provided a verse for the launch of the *Queen Mary*.[23] It is significant that Masefield's 'Queen Mary' was a ship and not a member of the royal family.

As Poet Laureate, Masefield created the Royal Medal for Poetry in 1933. Each year he would head a committee to read new volumes of verse and, during thirty years of Masefield's tenure, recipients of the medal included W. H. Auden, John Betjeman, Siegfried Sassoon and Christopher Fry.[24] The middle years of the 1930s also saw publication of his second fantasy novel for children: *The Box of Delights* (1935). This sequel to *The Midnight Folk* (1927) is a significant landmark in children's literature and a perennial favourite for broadcast adaptations. Masefield also developed verse festivals and in 1939 he called upon the services of a young professor of Middle English to recite Chaucer's 'The Reeve's Tale' as part of the Oxford Summer Diversions. J. R. R. Tolkien threw himself into the task and appeared in Chaucerian costume to further delight the audience. Other successful novels appeared in the 1940s (including the *Ned* trilogy) and there was also a productive collaboration with the painter Edward Seago on three volumes of poetry. In 1941 the chronicler of Gallipoli repeated his success with an account of the Dunkirk evacuation, published, following resolution of censorship problems, as *The Nine Days Wonder*. Poor health brought silence in the 1950s but Masefield returned in the 1960s, embracing new media (his recording of *The Story of Ossian* was acclaimed by the *Gramophone* as 'the most important record ever issued in the history of the gramophone')[25] and producing a flurry of works. His last volume appeared a couple of months before his death in May 1967. In a memorial address at Westminster Abbey, Robert Graves claimed that in Masefield 'the fierce flame of poetry had truly burned'.[26]

In his 1914 poem 'Biography', Masefield complains that 'When I am buried, all my thoughts and acts / Will be reduced to lists of dates and facts'[27] and in my brief biographical sketch the complex antagonisms in Masefield's character are lost. Two of the most crucial of these were his feelings towards the sea and, later in his career, his attitude to his early work. Both are of significance to this present volume.

In 1904 Masefield wrote to Yeats that 'it is a pity I ever left the sea; there is nothing like it.'[28] Many years later he acknowledged in *New Chum* (1944) that within naval life 'something was very much amiss somewhere . . . and I knew very well . . . that I did not want to belong to it.'[29] It is in these two views that we find one of the essential contradictions in Masefield. He was the seasick sailor who yearned for the sea, he loathed the crude nature of sailors yet celebrated their craft, and he was fascinated by the beauty of the water but aware of the threat of death.

The early work of Masefield is a deliberate attempt to portray sailors and the mythology of the sea. He sets out to depict the mythology of the sea and seafaring in all its allure while at the same time distancing himself from his subject: the writer in the guise of the narrator is frequently present as a conspicuous figure. In several of his short stories he retells a sailor's yarn but is eager to frame the tale within the situation in which it was told and reports it as speech. Such speech was often coarse or racist and Masefield is frequently an uncomfortable narrator.

By contrast, the yarn as a piece of short fiction sat comfort-
ably with its original form of publication. As a struggling writer
Masefield turned to his pen for money. In 1903 he wrote to
Jack B. Yeats's wife Cottie that 'I am now going to grind out
work like a barrel-organ on the August Bank' and, with refer-
ence to his marriage plans, he confessed: 'it's mostly a question
now, alas, of dollars.'[30] Work for *The Speaker* and the *Man-
chester Guardian* required book reviews and the creation of a
'Miscellany' column. It also provided a forum for poetry and
short stories. Masefield's first three published volumes, *Salt-
Water Ballads* (1902), *Ballads* (1903) and *A Mainsail Haul*
(1905), all relied heavily on material previously published in
periodicals and newspapers. Masefield was, however, a revising
author who was both fastidious and sloppy at times throughout
his career. Asked about the first line of 'Sea-Fever', for example
('I must down' or 'I must go down'), he merely responded that
'the word "go" seems to have crept in.'[31]

Nevertheless, original manuscripts tend to reveal Masefield
as a careful and deliberate craftsman at this stage of compos-
ition. The first drafts of 'Sea-Fever' show, for example, a
considered sequence of development from 'I must out on the
roads again' through 'I must down to the roads again' to 'I
must down to the seas again'.[32] Throughout his career Mase-
field would produce numerous drafts, which would then be cut
and pasted in notebooks and further revised. Masefield appears
to have regarded periodicals as ephemeral publications and
most texts were revised, if only slightly, for their first publica-
tion in volume format.

In addition to the revision of texts for book publication there
is also a changing attitude to his canon. His first three books
would all undergo revisions and these distort our perception of
Masefield's early work as well as revealing his changing attitude
to it. Most of the material collected in this volume is early Mase-
field in an original form. Much has an attractive roughness in the
writing that the mature author would revise or suppress. This
work is contemporary with 'Sea-Fever' (1902) and 'Cargoes'
(1903) and, as posterity has such a fondness for these two poems,
I believe we should be excused for stripping away the layers of

Masefield's revisions and distortions to look again at his early output in the form that it first appeared. The early works include his only volume of predominantly sea poetry and only two volumes of short stories. They reveal a new and distinctive voice. A contemporary reviewer of *A Mainsail Haul* wrote, for example, that 'in his prose he is alone, with a style that can attain strength and wildness and exuberance and tenderness and combine the moods of an active sailor and a contemplative landsman wonderfully.'[33] Naturally Masefield did not write exclusively of the sea but it is, perhaps, in sea literature that he achieved his enduring success and first innovation.

Writing to his brother-in-law, Masefield noted that *Salt-Water Ballads* 'deserves the recognition of a maritime people. It is something new said newly . . . I feel that, in any case, I've said a straight word sure to be recognized as such by some few . . .'[34] Kipling had introduced the vernacular in his *Barrack-Room Ballads* (1892) but Masefield applied the concept to a nautical environment and also introduced a range of technical terms. The freshness and authenticity of diction was, however, a concern for his publisher, Grant Richards. Masefield provided a glossary for *Salt-Water Ballads* but noted to Richards that 'I'm afraid that these sea-terms will prove great stumbling blocks to most.'[35] One reviewer, nevertheless, was convinced and noted that Masefield's verses were 'hearty and strong with the tarry vocabulary of sailor-folk'.[36] Of particular concern to Richards was Masefield's use of the word 'bloody' (which was, largely, retained).

Nine years later Masefield was to create a sensation with his use of colloquial diction in *The Everlasting Mercy* (although the 'offensive' word was blanked out of the *English Review*'s publication in October 1911). Lord Alfred Douglas branded Masefield's narrative 'nine tenths sheer filth'[37] although, in contrast, J. M. Barrie described it as 'incomparably the finest literature'[38] and Robert Graves later claimed that Masefield's innovation had emboldened Bernard Shaw to make the word his dramatic climax of *Pygmalion* (1913).[39] This, however, was all to come. In 1902 Grant Richards asked for a discussion – little thinking that he would later encounter similar issues with

James Joyce and *Dubliners*.[40] A letter to Richards reveals Masefield's concern, but also typical humour:

> . . . I have been thinking over the word 'bloody' and have decided to use it sparingly, feeling that it is not a very popular adjective at sea; marine taste preferring a coarser and more expressive word, an equivalent to tell the truth, for 'copulating.' I want to ask you, also, if, in your opinion, a freedom of the kind would militate in any way against the book's chances. Personally I don't think it would but I should like to be guided by your experience . . .[41]

Such diction was largely rejected by the older writer, however. When in 1945 his publishers suggested a revised edition of his *Collected Poems* (first published in 1923), Masefield was enthusiastic and wrote that 'there are many pages of early work that I would gladly scrap.'[42] Of the fifty-two poems which were present in the 1902 first edition of *Salt-Water Ballads*, only four were included in the 1946 edition of *Poems* (the omission of 'Collected' was entirely justified). Masefield even came to dislike 'Sea-Fever'. In 1925 he was asked whether he would sign an illustrated edition of the poem. He responded that 'I loathe the verses sufficiently to hate the thought of signing them.'[43]

Masefield had once used a literary agent. However, upon the death of C. F. Cazenove during the First World War, he tended to deal with publishers directly (although using the Society of Authors for legal advice and the creation of contracts). It was an arrangement that – copyrights permitting – allowed Masefield an unchallenged position and resulted in decisions which may seem with hindsight surprising or misguided. (A proposed film version of his play *Good Friday* was to have starred Richard Burton, for example, but Masefield appears not to have co-operated.)[44] As the public clamoured for reprints of his early books, they received revised editions. Despite early attempts to reprint *Salt-Water Ballads* in 1906, it was not until 1913 that a second edition was published. The text was revised (together with an apology stating 'some of this book was written in my boyhood, all of it in my youth').[45] It was that edition which was reprinted through many different impressions. The history of

A Mainsail Haul, his first volume of short stories, is more extreme.

The first edition was published in 1905. The second edition was 'revised and much enlarged' in 1913 and this changed the volume from a book of tales and reminiscences (often in the first person) to a more distanced collection including several historical sketches. Subsequent editions and reprints used the revised text. In the early 1950s the Poet Laureate was asked whether he would allow a new edition of *A Mainsail Haul*. Masefield saw an opportunity to publish a single volume consisting of the best of his two short-story collections, *A Mainsail Haul* and *A Tarpaulin Muster*. He found, however, that the Richards Press were protective of their rights in *A Tarpaulin Muster* (first published in 1907). They requested a hundred pounds and Masefield replied that he would 'not offer more than twenty'.[46] He was eventually to pay the asking price but the business was completed too late for any of the stories from *A Tarpaulin Muster* to be added to the new edition of *A Mainsail Haul*.[47] (This present volume is the first to bring together material from these two sources.) When the 1954 edition of *A Mainsail Haul* appeared, it bore little resemblance to the original edition of almost half a century earlier. When a publishing contract was being discussed, Masefield stated he was 'rather against asking for an advance' against royalties, on the grounds that 'it is a horrid little book.'[48] In revising and reissuing, the aged Poet Laureate had moved a long way from the rough and attractive immediacy of his early work. It is a move we can reverse with advantage.

In assembling this new collection I have gathered material from the original editions in addition to pieces that were printed only in newspapers or periodicals. I have also taken the opportunity to include some entirely new texts from manuscript sources. I have rejected the alterations of the older writer, sometimes separated from the creation of his work by several decades. I have also chosen to concentrate on short-story yarns rather than historical sketches. The yarns derive from the time that Masefield was at sea rather than the period in which, when he wasn't holding the door for Lenin,[49] he undertook 'an unsystematic greedy study of the literature of the sea'[50] in the British Museum.

This is the first collection of both poetry and prose in a single volume concerning Masefield's writing on the sea. As early as 1910 he suggested to his literary agent a volume combining some of *Salt-Water Ballads* with *A Tarpaulin Muster* but the plan was, ultimately, abandoned.[51] In producing a volume once denied to the author, it also seems appropriate to allow Masefield a title on which he had once 'set [his] heart'.[52] In August 1902 Masefield wrote to Richards suggesting that 'as for a title I find that the one I set my heart on has been already collared.'[53] (It is assumed that Masefield had been studying the British Library catalogue.) The definition of 'spunyarn' as provided in *Salt-Water Ballads* is 'a three-strand line spun out of old ropeyarns knotted together ... the spinning of such yarn is a favourite occupation ...'[54] It therefore seems fitting to construct this volume from different strands of Masefield's work: poetry, short stories, other prose pieces and some short extracts from novels. The majority date from Masefield's early period of creativity before *The Everlasting Mercy* in 1911. A few later poems and extracts from his mature novels have been included to provide a comparison and balance.

The poetry ranges from Masefield's first published poem in 1899 to a verse from the last volume of poetry issued during the author's lifetime, in 1967. The majority of pieces, however, come from Masefield's early career and include twenty items from *Salt-Water Ballads* (1902) and seven items from *Ballads* (1903). There are also ten poems that Masefield chose not to collect: three from manuscript sources and seven from periodicals. In correspondence with the Society of Authors, Masefield was fond of quoting Yeats on the matter of discarded work:

Please let me quote to you some lines by Mr Yeats.

> Accurst, who bring to light of day
> The writings I have cast away,
> But blest be he who prints them not
> And lets the kind worm take the lot.

Trebly blest be she who thus gives the kind worm a chance.[55]

Given that Masefield was not always the best self-critic, and that the kind worm is, now, a little defeated by microfilm and digital scans, I am including these rarities, which will not damage Masefield's reputation. The range of work, written over sixty-eight years, shows Masefield relishing the coarse life, tall stories and brutality of sea life before a more distanced voice becomes nostalgic for a lost age of sailing-ships. As Masefield aged, his sea poems became focused on lost vessels of beauty and his sense of naval history. He suppressed the harsh yet attractive realities of the life he had experienced.

This change from experience to nostalgia can also be seen in Masefield's use of the short-story form. In his vast canon of work there are only two collections of short stories, which date from the beginning of his career. As has been noted, revisions of the first collection saw the replacement of yarns with historical essays. The twenty-eight examples provided here are sailor's yarns and Masefield's musings on sea life. Seven stories come from *A Mainsail Haul* (1905), sixteen from *A Tarpaulin Muster* (1907) and one from the revised *A Mainsail Haul* (1913). There are also four previously uncollected examples. Of these, three are fascinating autobiographical episodes from the usually reticent Masefield.

A selection of other prose provides an opportunity to print an autobiographical sketch for the first time. The existence of an early autobiography of Masefield's time at sea was first noted in 1978 in Babington Smith's biography. It reveals a fictionalized account of Masefield's apprenticeship in the *Gilcruix* and is a major contribution to the author's sea literature. Masefield's book reviews are a rich, and neglected, area of his output and I have included in this volume all three of Masefield's reviews on works by Joseph Conrad. To broaden our view of Masefield's writing on other great sea writers, I have also selected short essays on Captain Frederick Marryat, Herman Melville and R. H. Dana. All of these have remained uncollected until now, and, in a few examples, are entirely unknown to Masefield scholarship. I have also included Masefield's essay entitled 'Chanties', which marked a turning-point in his career. As an expert in the field, the author was invited to advise Harley

Granville Barker on sea chanties for a production of Shaw's *Captain Brassbound's Conversion*.[56] Masefield was therefore introduced to the 'new drama' of the early twentieth century. 'On the Sea and Sailors' represents another valuable contribution from a periodical and 'Sailing-Ships' provides text from an abandoned collaboration between Masefield and the photographer Alvin Langdon Coburn.

The final strand of *Spunyarn* comprises five extracts from Masefield's novels. *Lost Endeavour* is a comparatively youthful work from 1910. The others all date from the 1930s and Masefield's maturity as a novelist. Once again we encounter nostalgic visions of tea-clipper races or a historical novel set aboard a late eighteenth-century slave ship. I have also included an episode from *The Box of Delights*. Kay and his friends playing with toy ships demonstrate Masefield recycling his own experiences of sailing boats with Jack Yeats in 1903.[57] Masefield's nostalgia frequently included self-nostalgia.

Today we largely regard Masefield as a poet and, moreover, as a poet of the sea. In 1978 Ronald Hope introduced a volume of Masefield's sea verse and noted that the author was 'the finest English poet of the sea and the only seafaring poet of any stature'.[58] The title of 'poet' would, however, have been one that Masefield failed to recognize. In his autobiographical account of his literary development, *So Long to Learn* (1952), he described storytelling as 'the law of my being'[59] and he saw himself as a writer of stories. In the author's concern with narrative lay the seeds for critical rejection, however. In 1958 Masefield observed that from 300 million readers of English, three read his work and four criticized it.[60] The writer who had once been at the cutting edge of literature became, in the view of one commentator, 'a Georgian relic in the Nuclear Age'.[61] Masefield had ceased to be a radical. The first version of *Collected Poems* sold over 100,000 copies between 1923 and 1930[62] but poor decisions and damaging revisions contributed to a declining reputation. There were those who understood when this decline started. In 1953 J. Donald Adams noted in the *New York Times* that:

... the name of John Masefield, I venture to say, will long outlast
in English poetry many of those who have overshadowed him
during the years of his reputation's decline. For much too long a
time now he has been in disfavor with the self-appointed arbiters
of taste and with those living idols whom they have set up for our
worship. But unless I am grievously deceived, posterity will sal-
vage and cherish, out of his work, both in poetry and prose, a
remnant not too small which stands firmly in the great tradition
of the English tongue ...[63]

Masefield simply became unfashionable. He was an access-
ible writer of narrative and not an intellectual or modernist.
Yet he is far from a simplistic writer: reading Masefield is a
highly rewarding and entertaining experience. With this first
collection to gather his work in different genres within the same
subject area, we can see his writing on the sea come into a new
focus. Writing to the dedicatee of *A Tarpaulin Muster* in 1907
Masefield noted:

You must tell your friends that I am, quite frankly, a fraud, and
that I have very little sea-experience; but you must tell them, also,
that an artist is only hampered by experience; and that it is no
more necessary to be a sailor, to write about the sea, than it was
necessary for Shakespeare to keep a brothel, or to poison his
father, in order to write parts of *Hamlet* and of *Measure for
Measure* ...[64]

But in that statement is the mystery of creative imagination.
John Masefield was a writer of experience *and* imagination
whose motive was usually to spin a good yarn.

However hard Masefield tried to distance himself from the
sea, it had created him and defined him. On 5 March 1910
he delivered a speech to the 'Essay Society' of New College,
Oxford. He commenced:

A few days ago I asked a young friend ... what sort of address
you would expect from me. I told him that I had only two subjects

for which I cared intensely – Woman's Suffrage and Religion. Would you be likely to care for either of these? He didn't answer my question, but was understood to say that you would be much more likely to like 'something about the sea'.

Well, I'm not going to tell you about the sea. The truth about the sea was expressed, four centuries ago, by Hernando Cortés, during his march on Mexico. The troops of Cortés at the moment were short of food. They were suffering from fever. They hadn't any clothes to speak of. And they had been fighting night and day for some while. They wanted to go back to the sea and the island of Cuba. Cortés remarked, 'You're here to fight. Don't you think about the sea. The sea's no good to you.'

So I won't tell you about the sea. The sea's always there for you when you want it. But I shan't be always here . . .[65]

Although Masefield frequently tried to dismiss his sea experiences, he could not, ultimately, spurn this essential strand of his life and writing. Perhaps the most revealing contribution in this volume is the author's short story 'In the Roost' from 1906. The existence of an ill-fated painter had previously made an appearance in Masefield's 1901 autobiographical sketch. In 1912 Masefield used the tale again for his long narrative poem *Dauber*. In 1962 he chose that work as one of two narrative poems, with *Reynard the Fox*, to present together in a single volume.[66] The same year saw the issue of a long-playing record entitled *The Fortune of the Sea and The Wanderer's Image*, which included excerpts from *Dauber*.[67] Masefield wrote that 'To myself Dauber remains an image of one who knows the law of his being, and obeys that law, cost what it may, through misery to early death if necessary. If the star in the mind shine bright, what does other darkness matter?'[68] In many respects the character of Dauber includes a significant autobiographical angle. Masefield did not suffer an early death but he had obeyed 'the law of his being'. He rejected the sea to become a writer 'come what might'. Try as he might, however, the writer could not reject the sea.

NOTES

1. John Masefield, *So Long to Learn* (London: William Heinemann, 1952), p. 72.
2. John Betjeman, 'Preface' to John Masefield, *Selected Poems* (London: William Heinemann, 1978), p. vii.
3. Yeats's comment was recorded by Lady Gregory (see Daniel J. Murphy (ed.), *Lady Gregory's Journals*, Vol. 1 (Gerrards Cross: Smythe, 1978), p. 385).
4. Masefield admitted his crime in an autobiographical sketch written for Elizabeth Robins in January 1910 (Berg Collection, New York Public Library).
5. Autobiographical sketch written for Elizabeth Robins (Berg Collection, New York Pubic Library).
6. Ibid.
7. Ibid.
8. Ibid.
9. Masefield was so struck with his entering 'into a world of poetry until then unknown to me' (see John Masefield, *In the Mill* (London: William Heinemann, 1941), p. 97) that he noted the date and time of reading in the margin of his book (see John Masefield, letter to Elizabeth Robins, 4 April 1910 (Berg Collection, New York Public Library)).
10. John Masefield, 'Preface' to *Poems* (New York: Macmillan, 1935), p. v. In this preface, only published in America, Masefield stated: 'I first felt the real delight of poetry in a room in Yonkers, New York. It was there that I decided that I had rather write verse than do anything else in the world.'
11. See 'A Steerage Steward' in this collection.
12. Autobiographical sketch written for Elizabeth Robins (Berg Collection, New York Public Library).
13. John Masefield, letter to Grant Richards, 21 April 1908 (Fales Library, Elmer Holmes Bobst Library, New York University).
14. See John Masefield, *New Chum* (London: William Heinemann, 1944) and *In the Mill* (London: William Heinemann, 1941).
15. See Philip W. Errington, *John Masefield – The 'Great Auk' of English Literature – A Bibliography* (London: British Library, 2004).
16. W. B. Yeats's opinion was recorded by J. M. Synge in a letter to Molly Allgood, 11 January 1908 (see Ann Saddlemyer (ed.), *The*

Collected Letters of John Millington Synge, Vol. 2 (Oxford: Oxford University Press, 1984), p. 129).

17. John Masefield, *So Long to Learn* (London: William Heinemann, 1952), p. 185.

18. John Masefield, *Dauber* (London: William Heinemann, 1913), p. 4. The length of the poem, at over 15,000 words, unfortunately necessitates its exclusion from the present volume.

19. Masefield's First World War experiences are summarized within the introduction to Philip W. Errington (ed.), *John Masefield's Great War* (Barnsley: Pen and Sword, 2007).

20. John Masefield, 'Introduction' to 'Reynard the Fox', *Dauber & Reynard the Fox* (London: William Heinemann, 1962), p. 78.

21. Quoted within Norman Sherry, *The Life of Graham Greene* (London: Jonathan Cape, 1989), p. 312.

22. John Masefield, letter to Ramsay MacDonald, 30 April 1930 (PRO30/69 676, f. 629, National Archives).

23. See 'Number 534' in this collection.

24. Awarded in 1937, 1957, 1960 and 1962 respectively.

25. *Gramophone*, June 1959, p. 27.

26. Robert Graves, 'Address ... at the Memorial Service to John Masefield, June 20th, 1967', *Westminster Abbey Occasional Paper No. 18* (London: Westminster Abbey, 1967), p. 17.

27. John Masefield, 'Biography', *Philip the King and Other Poems* (London: William Heinemann, 1914), p. 76.

28. John Masefield, letter to W. B. Yeats, 24 August 1904 (Berg Collection, New York Public Library).

29. John Masefield, *New Chum* (London: William Heinemann, 1944), p. 186.

30. John Masefield, letter to Mary Cottenham Yeats, *c.* May 1903 (Yeats Archive, L. Mas. 1, National Gallery of Ireland).

31. See Linda Hart, 'A First Line Mystery', *The Journal of the John Masefield Society*, Vol. 2 (Ledbury: John Masefield Society, 1993), pp. 11–14.

32. The working drafts for *Salt-Water Ballads* are in the Berg Collection, New York Public Library.

33. See *The Academy*, 5 August 1905, p. 808.

34. John Masefield, letter to Harry Ross, 1 December 1902 (uncatalogued Magnus deposit, box 3, Bodleian Library).

35. John Masefield, letter to Grant Richards, 17 September 1902 (Berg Collection, New York Public Library).

36. *Academy and Literature*, 13 December 1902, p. 652.

37. Lord Alfred Douglas's comment is noted by Muriel Spark (see

Muriel Spark, *John Masefield* (London: Peter Nevill, 1953), p. 5). I have been unable to trace the original source.

38. Barrie stated his opinion while awarding a Royal Society of Literature prize in 1912 (see *The Times*, 29 November 1912, p. 6).

39. Robert Graves, 'Address ... at the Memorial Service to John Masefield, June 20th, 1967', *Westminster Abbey Occasional Paper No. 18* (London: Westminster Abbey, 1967), p. 17.

40. In 1906 Richards's printer refused to set parts of *Dubliners* on grounds of immorality. Joyce's use of the word 'bloody' was only one aspect and, on this, Joyce was relatively accommodating. During April 1906 he wrote to Richards that 'I cannot ... suggest any other word than the word "bloody" for the story *Grace*.' However, during June 1906, he wrote: 'I shall delete the word "bloody" wherever it occurs except in one passage' (see Stuart Gilbert (ed.), *Letters of James Joyce, Volume One* (London: Faber and Faber, 1957), pp. 60–64). Richards did not publish the work until 1914.

41. John Masefield, letter to Grant Richards, 7 September 1902 (Houghton Library, *61M-93, Harvard University).

42. John Masefield, letter to Louisa Callender, *c.* April 1945 (Archives of William Heinemann).

43. John Masefield, letter to G. H. Thring, 20 January 1925 (Department of Manuscripts, Add. Ms. 56581, ff. 16–17, British Library).

44. See Edna M. Cahill, letter to John Masefield, 16 December 1958 (Harry Ransom Humanities Research Center, MS (Masefield, J.) Recip Baker (Walter H.) Company, University of Texas).

45. John Masefield, untitled note, *Salt-Water Ballads* (London: Elkin Mathews, 1913), p. v.

46. John Masefield, letter to Anne Munro-Kerr, 6 June 1953 (Department of Manuscripts, Add. Ms. 56624, f. 110, British Library).

47. For full details of the intricate wrangling, see Philip W. Errington, *John Masefield – The 'Great Auk' of English Literature – A Bibliography* (London: British Library, 2004), pp. 20–21.

48. John Masefield, letter to Anne Munro-Kerr, 20 June 1953 (Department of Manuscripts, Add. Ms. 56624, f. 120, British Library).

49. In *So Long to Learn* (London: William Heinemann, 1952, pp. 158–9) Masefield recalls noticing 'a most unusual man' in the British Museum Reading Room and 'felt the extraordinary attraction of his strangeness'. He continues:

    ... I was very young; it was not for me to begin a conversation, but sometimes I wished that the strange man would speak to me. Once,

as it fell, he did speak to me. I was leaving the Room, and found
that he was following. I held open the door so that he might pass;
his face lit up with a smile to me, as he thanked me and passed on.
Later, I knew that this strange being was Lenin . . .

See also Corliss Lamont, *Remembering John Masefield* (London:
Kaye and Ward, 1972), pp. 83–4.

50. John Masefield, *So Long to Learn* (London: William Heinemann,
1952), p. 160.

51. In a letter to his agent, C. F. Cazenove, Masefield mentions a plan
to let a publisher 'reprint the *Salt-Water Ballads* . . . on condition
that he print with them . . . the best of the *Tarpaulin Muster* sea
tales, say half a dozen, with the one or two new ones from the
Guardian, and one or two new ballads' (John Masefield, letter to
C. F. Cazenove, 25 May 1910, Private Collection).

52. John Masefield, letter to Grant Richards, 29 August 1902 (Berg
Collection, New York Public Library).

53. Ibid.

54. John Masefield, 'Glossary' to *Salt-Water Ballads* (London: Grant
Richards, 1902), p. 111.

55. John Masefield, letter to to S. M. Perry, *c.* February 1948 (Depart-
ment of Manuscripts, Add. Ms. 56620, f. 169, British Library).

56. See Theodore Stier, *With Pavlova Round the World* (London:
Hurst and Blackett, 1927), p. 265, and C. B. Purdom, *Granville
Barker* (London: Rockliff, 1955), p. 56.

57. Masefield and Jack B. Yeats constructed toy boats and sailed
them on the River Gara in April 1903. See also 'The Gara Brook'
and the 'The Gara River' in this collection.

58. Ronald Hope, 'Introduction' to John Masefield, *The Sea Poems*
(London: William Heinemann, 1978), p. vii.

59. John Masefield, *So Long to Learn* (London: William Heinemann,
1952), p. 3.

60. John Masefield, letter to Audrey Naper-Smith, *c.*1958 (see John
Masefield, *Letters to Reyna* (London: Buckan and Enright,
1983), p. 197).

61. Sanford Sternlicht, *John Masefield* (Boston, MA: Twayne Pub-
lishers, 1977), p. 147.

62. William Buchan, 'Introduction' to John Masefield, *Letters to
Reyna* (London: Buchan and Enright, 1983), p. 26.

63. J. Donald Adams, 'Speaking of Books', *New York Times Book
Review*, 31 May 1953, p. 2.

64. John Masefield, letter to Harley Granville Barker, 30 March

1907 (Department of Manuscripts, Add. Ms. 47897, f. 13, British Library).

65. John Masefield, speech to the 'Essay Society' of New College, Oxford (Berg Collection, New York Public Library).

66. John Masefield, *Dauber & Reynard the Fox* (London: William Heinemann, 1962).

67. A recording made by the Argo Record Company in 1959 was released in 1962 as RG230.

68. John Masefield, *Dauber & Reynard the Fox* (London: William Heinemann, 1962), pp. 2–3.

Further Reading

BIOGRAPHICAL AND AUTOBIOGRAPHICAL

Babington Smith, Constance, *John Masefield – A Life* (Oxford: Oxford University Press, 1978; republished Stroud: History Press, 2008)

Masefield, John, *In the Mill* (London: William Heinemann, 1941)

——, *New Chum* (London: William Heinemann, 1944; expanded editions in 1947 and 1948)

——, *So Long to Learn* (London: William Heinemann, 1952)

——, *Grace Before Ploughing* (London: William Heinemann, 1966)

BIBLIOGRAPHICAL

Errington, Philip W., *John Masefield – The 'Great Auk' of English Literature – A Bibliography* (London: British Library, 2004)

CRITICAL STUDIES

Drew, Fraser, *John Masefield's England* (Rutherford, NJ: Fairleigh Dickinson University Press, 1973)

Dwyer, June, *John Masefield* (New York: Ungar, 1987)

Masefield Society, *The Journal of the John Masefield Society*, Vols. 1– (Ledbury: John Masefield Society, 1993–)

Spark, Muriel, *John Masefield* (London: Peter Nevill, 1953; revised edition London: Hutchinson, 1992)

Sternlicht, Sanford, *John Masefield* (Boston, MA: Twayne Publishers, 1977)

Strong, L. A. G., *John Masefield* (London: Longmans, Green & Co., 1952; corrected edition, 1964)

SELECTED WORKS BY MASEFIELD

With over 178 individual titles of books and pamphlets by Masefield, the following list represents only recent editions.

Arthurian Poets – John Masefield, edited and introduced by David Llewellyn Dodds (Cambridge: D. S. Brewer, 1994)

The Box of Delights, newly corrected from the manuscript (London: Egmont, 2008)

John Masefield's Great War: Collected Works, edited with an introduction by Philip W. Errington (Barnsley: Pen and Sword, 2007)

The Midnight Folk, newly corrected from the manuscript (London: Egmont, 2008)

Reynard the Fox, edited with an introduction by Philip W. Errington (Manchester: Carcanet Press, 2008)

Sea-Fever: Selected Poems, edited with an introduction by Philip W. Errington (Manchester: Carcanet Press, 2005)

Sea Life in Nelson's Time (Barnsley: Pen and Sword, 2002)

The Twenty-Five Days, with an introduction by Jon Cooksey (Barnsley: Pen and Sword, 2004)

A Note on the Text

Within each section, individual texts are arranged in chronological sequence of composition.

As noted in the Introduction, Masefield was an author who frequently revised his texts. As a general rule, I have chosen the version which appeared in the first edition of a Masefield volume as my copy-text. These texts have been collated against earlier periodical publications and other relevant sources. The first edition texts reveal slightly polished versions from those in journal or newspaper.

Current style has been applied to punctuation: serial commas have been omitted in a list of three or more items within the prose; double quotation marks have become single; and closing quotation marks have, in some cases, been moved to precede other punctuation. Full points have been kept in some less familiar abbreviations but, otherwise, Masefield's punctuation has been retained. In a few circumstances I have chosen to add punctuation for texts that were previously unpublished or for obvious grammatical lapses.

I have attempted some consistency of spelling and capitalization throughout the entire collection but retained a number of idiosyncrasies, especially in the poetry. Masefield had a fondness for truncating verbs ('burnt' for 'burned', for example) and I have generally retained these. I have also preserved the author's use of phonetic spelling when presenting sailors' speech. Manuscript evidence suggests that Masefield wrote prose with the precision of a poet and I hope to have preserved as much authorial intention as possible.

Finally I have yet to find an example of Masefield using the word 'shanty'. His preferred spelling of 'chanty' has been used throughout.

POETRY

Nicias Moriturus[1]

An' Bill can have my sea-boots, Nigger Jim can have
    my knife,
You can divvy up the dungarees an' bed,
An' the ship can have my blessing, an' the Lord can
    have my life,
An' sails an' fish my body when I'm dead.

An' dreaming down below there in the tangled greens
    an' blues,
Where the sunlight shudders golden round about,
I shall hear the ships complainin' an' the cursin' of
    the crews,
An' be sorry when the watch is tumbled out.

I shall hear them hilly-hollying[2] the weather crojick brace,
And the sucking of the wash about the hull;
When they chanty up the topsail I'll be hauling in my place,
For my soul will follow seawards like a gull.

I shall hear the blocks a-grunting in the bumpkins over-side,
An' the slatting of the storm-sails on the stay,
An' the rippling of the catspaw[3] at the making of the tide,
An' the swirl and splash of porpoises at play.

An' Bill can have my sea-boots, Nigger Jim can have
    my knife,
You can divvy up the whack I haven't scofft,
An' the ship can have my blessing and the Lord can have
    my life,
For it's time I quit the deck and went aloft.

Trade Winds

In the harbour, in the island, in the Spanish Seas,
Are the tiny white houses and the orange-trees,
And day-long, night-long, the cool and pleasant breeze
Of the steady Trade Winds blowing.

There is the red wine, the nutty Spanish ale,
The shuffle of the dancers, the old salt's tale,
The squeaking fiddle, and the soughing[1] in the sail
Of the steady Trade Winds blowing.

And o' nights there's fire-flies and the yellow moon,
And in the ghostly palm-trees the sleepy tune
Of the quiet voice calling me, the long low croon
Of the steady Trade Winds blowing.

Cardigan Bay

Clean, green, windy billows[1] notching out the sky,
Grey clouds tattered into rags, sea-winds blowing high,
And the ships under topsails, beating, thrashing by,
And the mewing of the herring gulls.

Dancing, flashing green seas shaking white locks,
Boiling in blind eddies over hidden rocks,
And the wind in the rigging, the creaking o' the blocks,
And the straining of the timber hulls.

Delicate, cool sea-weeds, green and amber-brown,
In beds where shaken sunlight slowly filters down
On many a drowned seventy-four,[2] many a sunken town,
And the whitening of the dead men's skulls.

Bill

He lay dead on the cluttered deck and stared at the
    cold skies,
With never a friend to mourn for him nor a hand to close
    his eyes:
'Bill, he's dead,' was all they said; 'he's dead, 'n' there he lies.'

The mate came forrard at seven bells and spat across the rail:
'Just lash him up wi' some holystone in a clout[1] o' rotten sail,
'N', rot ye, get a gait on[2] ye, ye're slower'n a bloody snail!'

When the rising moon was a copper disc and the sea was a
    strip of steel,
We dumped him down to the swaying weeds ten fathom
    beneath the keel.
'It's rough about Bill,' the fo'c's'le said, 'we'll have to stand
    his wheel.'

[Bidding Goodbye]

Over the dim blue rim of the sea
Swims the dim yellow ball of the moon;
The topsail slats as we pass the quay
And the yard goes up with a tune.

I have bidden goodbye to the streets and the shops
And the inns with the twisted signs,
To the red ridged-roofs and the chimney tops
And the country maids and the wines.

The dim grey wreaths of the wet sea-mist
Blot the dull brown lie of the land,
And we are at sea with the ropes to fist
And the wet white sails to hand.

I have bidden goodbye to the harbour light
And the warm red lips of my dear
And the bells will ring in the town tonight
And the men in the inns will hear.

Sea-Fever

I must down[1] to the seas again, to the lonely sea and
     the sky,
And all I ask is a tall ship and a star to steer her by,
And the wheel's kick and the wind's song and the white
     sail's shaking,
And a grey mist on the sea's face and a grey dawn
     breaking.

I must down to the seas again, for the call of the
     running tide
Is a wild call and a clear call that may not be denied;
And all I ask is a windy day with the white clouds flying,
And the flung spray and the blown spume, and the seagulls
     crying.

I must down to the seas again, to the vagrant gypsy life,
To the gull's way and the whale's way where the wind's
     like a whetted knife;
And all I ask is a merry yarn from a laughing fellow-rover,
And quiet sleep and a sweet dream when the long
     trick's over.

Burial Party

'He's deader 'n nails,' the fo'c's'le said, ''n' gone to his long
   sleep';
''N' about his corp,'[1] said Tom to Dan, 'd'ye think his
   corp'll keep
Till the day's done, 'n' the work's through, 'n' the ebb's
   upon the neap?'[2]

'He's deader 'n nails,' said Dan to Tom, ''n' I wish his
   sperrit j'y;
He spat straight 'n' he steered true, but listen to me, say I,
Take 'n' cover 'n' bury him now, 'n' I'll take 'n' tell you why.

'It's a rummy rig of a guffy's yarn,[3] 'n' the juice of a rummy
   note,[4]
But if you buries a corp at night, it takes 'n' keeps afloat,
For its bloody[5] soul's afraid o' the dark 'n' sticks within the
   throat.

''N' all the night till the grey o' the dawn the dead 'un has
   to swim
With a blue 'n' beastly Will o' the Wisp[6] a-burnin' over him,
With a herring, maybe, a-scoffin' a toe or a shark a-chewin'
   a limb.

''N' all the night the shiverin' corp it has to swim the sea,
With its shudderin' soul inside the throat (where a soul's no
   right to be),
Till the sky's grey 'n' the dawn's clear, 'n' then the sperrit's
   free.

'Now Joe was a man was right as rain. I'm sort of sore for
   Joe,
'N' if we bury him durin' the day, his soul can take 'n' go;
So we'll dump his corp when the bell strikes 'n' we can get
   below.

'I'd fairly hate for him to swim in a blue 'n' beastly light,
With his shudderin' soul inside of him a-feelin' the
     fishes bite,
So over he goes at noon, say I, 'n' he shall sleep tonight.'

Sorrow o' Mydath[1]

Weary the cry of the wind is, weary the sea,
Weary the heart and the mind[2] and the body o' me.
Would I were out of it, done with it, would I could be
A white gull crying along the desolate sands!

Outcast, derelict soul in a body accurst,
Standing drenched with the spindrift,[3] standing athirst,
For the cool green waves of death to arise and burst
In a tide of quiet for me on the desolate sands.

Would that the waves and the long white hair o' the spray
Would gather in splendid terror and blot me away
To the sunless place o' the wrecks where the waters sway
Gently, dreamily, quietly over desolate sands!

Mother Carey
(As Told Me by the Bo'sun)

Mother Carey? She's the mother o' the witches
'N' all *them* sort o' rips;[1]
She's a fine gell to look at, but the hitch is,
She's a sight too fond of ships.
She lives upon a iceberg to the norred,[2]
An' her man he's Davy Jones,
'N' she combs the weeds upon her forred[3]
With pore drowned sailors' bones.

She's the mother o' the wrecks, 'n' the mother
Of all big winds as blows;
She's up to some deviltry or other
When it storms, or sleets, or snows.
The noise of the wind's her screamin',
'I'm arter a plump, young, fine,
Brass-buttoned, beefy-ribbed young seam'n
So as me 'n' my mate kin[4] dine.'

She's a hungry old rip[5] 'n' a cruel
For sailor-men like we,
She's give a many mariners the gruel
'N' a long sleep under sea.
She's the blood o' many a crew upon her
'N' the bones of many a wreck,
'N' she's barnacles a-growin' on her
'N' shark's teeth round her neck.

I ain't never had no schoolin'
Nor read no books like you,
But I knows 't ain't healthy to be foolin'
With that there gristly[6] two.
You're young, you thinks, 'n' you're lairy,[7]
But if you're to make old bones,
Steer clear, I says, o' Mother Carey
'N' that there Davy Jones.

Fever-Chills

He tottered[1] out of the alleyway with cheeks the colour of
    paste,
And shivered a spell and mopped his brow with a clout[2]
    of cotton waste:
'I've a lick[3] of fever-chills,' he said, ''n' my inside it's green,
But I'd be as right as rain,' he said, 'if I had some
    quinine,[4] –
But there ain't no quinine for us poor sailor-men.

'But them there passengers,' he said, 'if they gets
    fever-chills,[5]
There's brimmin' buckets o' quinine for them, 'n' bulgin'
    crates o' pills,
'N' a doctor with Latin 'n' drugs 'n' all – enough to sink
    a town,
'N' they lies quiet in their blushin' bunks 'n' mops their
    gruel down, –
But there ain't none o' them fine ways for us poor
    sailor-men.

'But the Chief[6] comes forrard 'n' he says, says he, "I gives
    you a straight tip:
Come none o' your Cape Horn fever lays[7] aboard o' this
    yer ship.
On wi' your rags o' duds,[8] my son, 'n' aft, 'n' down
    the hole:
The best cure known for fever-chills is shovelling bloody
    coal."[9]
It's *hard,* my son, that's what it is, for us poor sailor-men.'

'Port o' Many Ships'

'It's a sunny pleasant anchorage, is Kingdom Come,
Where crews is always layin' aft for double-tots o' rum,
'N' there's dancin' 'n' fiddlin' of ev'ry kind o' sort,
It's a fine place for sailor-men is that there port.
    'N' I wish –
    I wish as I was there.

'The winds is never nothin' more than jest light airs,
'N' no-one gets belayin'-pinned, 'n' no-one never swears,
Yer free to loaf an' laze around, yer pipe atween yer lips,
Lollin' on the fo'c's'le, sonny, lookin' at the ships.
    'N' I wish –
    I wish as I was there.

'For ridin' in the anchorage the ships of all the world
Have got one anchor down 'n' all sails furled.
All the sunken hookers 'n' the crews as took 'n' died
They lays there merry, sonny, swingin' to the tide.
    'N' I wish –
    I wish as I was there.

'Drowned old wooden hookers green wi' drippin' wrack,[1]
Ships as never fetched to port, as never came back,
Swingin' to the blushin' tide, dippin' to the swell,
'N' the crews all singin', sonny, beatin' on the bell.
    'N' I wish –
    I wish as I was there.'

D'Avalos'[1] Prayer

When the last sea is sailed and last shallow charted,
When the last field is reaped and the last harvest stored,
When the last fire is out and the last guest departed,
Grant the last prayer that I shall pray, Be good to me,
    O Lord!

And let me pass in a night at sea, a night of storm and
    thunder,
In the loud crying of the wind through sail and rope
    and spar;
Send me a ninth great peaceful wave to drown and roll me
    under[2]
To the cold tunny-fishes'[3] home where the drowned
    galleons are.

And in the dim green quiet place far out of sight
    and hearing,
Grant I may hear at whiles the wash and thresh[4] of the
    sea-foam
About the fine keen bows of the stately clippers steering
Towards the lone northern star and the fair ports of home.

One of the Bo'sun's Yarns

Loafin' around in Sailor Town, a-bluin'[1] o' my advance,
I met a derelict donkeyman who led me a merry dance,
Till he landed me 'n' bleached me fair[2] in the bar of a
    rum-saloon,
'N' there he spun me a juice of a yarn to this-yer brand
    of tune.

'It's a solemn gospel, mate,' he says, 'but a man as ships
    aboard
A steamer-tramp, he gets his whack of the wonders of the
    Lord –
Such as roaches crawlin' over his bunk, 'n' snakes inside
    his bread,
And work by night and work by day enough to strike
    him dead.

'But that there's by the way,' says he; 'the yarn I'm goin'
    to spin
Is about myself 'n' the life I led in the last ship I was in,
The *Esmeralda*, casual tramp, from Hull towards
    the Hook,[3]
Wi' one o' the brand o' Cain[4] for mate 'n' a human
    mistake for cook.

'We'd a week or so of dippin' around in a wind from
    outer hell,
With a fathom or more of broken sea at large in the
    forrard well,
Till our boats were bashed and bust and broke and gone
    to Davy Jones,
'N' then come white Atlantic fog as chilled us to
    the bones.

'We slowed her down and started the horn and watch
    and watch about,
We froze the marrow in all our bones a-keepin' a good
    look-out,
'N' the ninth night out, in the middle watch, I woke from
    a pleasant dream,
With the smash of a steamer ramming our plates a point
    abaft the beam.

' 'Twas cold and dark when I fetched the deck, dirty 'n'
    cold 'n' thick,
'N' there was a feel in the way she rode as fairly turned
    me sick; –
She was settlin', listin' quickly down, 'n' I heard the
    mates a-cursin',
'N' I heard the wash 'n' the grumble-grunt of a steamer's
    screws reversin'.

'She was leavin' us, mate, to sink or swim, 'n' the words
    we took 'n' said
They turned the port-light grassy-green 'n' the starboard
    rosy-red.
We give her a hot perpetual taste of the singeing curse of
    Cain,
As we heard her back 'n' clear the wreck 'n' off to her
    course again.

'Then the mate came dancin' on to the scene, 'n' he says,
    "Now quit yer chin,[5]
Or I'll smash yer skulls, so help me James, 'n' let some
    wisdom in.
Ye dodderin'[6] scum o' the slums," he says, "are ye drunk
    or blazin' daft?
If ye wish to save yer sickly hides, ye'd best contrive
    a raft."

'So he spoke us fair and turned us to, 'n' we wrought wi'
    tooth and nail
Wi' scantling, casks, 'n' coops 'n' ropes, 'n' boiler-plates
    'n' sail,
'N' all the while it were dark 'n' cold 'n' dirty as it
    could be,
'N' she was soggy 'n' settlin' down to a berth beneath
    the sea.

'Soggy she grew, 'n' she didn't lift, 'n' she listed more 'n'
    more,
Till her bell struck 'n' her boiler-pipes began to wheeze
    'n' snore;
She settled, settled, listed, heeled,[7] 'n' then may I be cust,
If her sneezin', wheezin' boiler-pipes did not begin to bust!

' 'N' then the stars began to shine, 'n' the birds began
    to sing,
'N' the next I knowed I was bandaged up 'n' my arm
    were in a sling,
'N' a swab in uniform were there, 'n' "Well," says he, " 'n'
    how
Are yer arms, 'n' legs, 'n' liver, 'n' lungs, 'n' bones a-feelin'
    now?"

' "Where am I?" says I, 'n' he says, says he, a-cantin' to the
    roll,
"You're aboard the RMS *Marie* in the after Glory-Hole,
'N' you've had a shave, if you wish to know, from the
    port o' Kingdom Come.
Drink this," he says, 'n' I takes 'n' drinks, 'n' s'elp me, it
    was rum!

'Seven survivors seen 'n' saved of the *Esmeralda*'s crowd,
Taken aboard the sweet *Marie* 'n' bunked 'n' treated proud,
'N' D.B.S.'d[8] to Mersey Docks ('n' a joyful trip we made),
'N' there the skipper were given a purse by a grateful
    Board of Trade.

'That's the end o' the yarn,' he says, 'n' he takes 'n' wipes
    his lips,
'Them's the works o' the Lord you sees in steam 'n' sailin'
    ships, –
Rocks 'n' fogs 'n' shatterin' seas 'n' breakers right ahead,
'N' work o' nights 'n' work o' days enough to strike you
    dead.'

Sea-Change[1]

'Goneys an' gullies[2] an' all o' the birds o' the sea,
They ain't no birds, not really,' said Billy the Dane.
'Not mollies,[3] nor gullies, nor goneys at all,' said he,
'But simply the sperrits of mariners livin' again.

'Them birds goin' fishin' is nothin' but souls o' the
    drowned,
Souls o' the drowned an' the kicked as are never
    no more;
An' that there haughty old albatross cruisin' around,
Belike he's Admiral Nelson or Admiral Noah.

'An' merry's the life they are living. They settle and dip,
They fishes, they never stands watches, they waggle their
    wings;
When a ship comes by, they fly to look at the ship
To see how the nowaday mariners manages things.

'When freezing aloft in a snorter,[4] I tell you I wish –
(Though maybe it ain't like a Christian) – I wish
    I could be
A haughty old copper-bound[5] albatross dipping for fish
And coming the proud over all o' the birds o' the sea.'

One of Wally's[1] Yarns

The watch was up on the topsail yard a-making fast the sail,
'N' Joe was swiggin'[2] his gasket taut, 'n' I felt the stirrup *give*,
'N' he dropped sheer from the tops'l-yard 'n' barely cleared
     the rail,
'N' o' course, we bein' aloft, *we* couldn't do nothin' –
We couldn't lower a boat and go a-lookin' for him,
For it blew hard 'n' there was sech a sea runnin'
That no boat wouldn't live.[3]

I seed him rise in the white o' the wake, I seed him lift a hand
('N' him in his oilskin suit 'n' all), I heard him lift a cry;
'N' there was his place on the yard 'n' all, 'n' the stirrup's
     busted strand.
'N' the old man said there's a cruel old sea runnin',
A cold green Barney's Bull[4] of a sea runnin';
It's hard, but I ain't agoin' to let a boat be lowered:
So we left him there to die.

He couldn't have kept afloat for long an' him lashed up 'n' all,
'N' we couldn't see him for long, for the sea was blurred with
     the sleet 'n' snow,
'N' we couldn't think of him much because o' the snortin',
     screamin' squall.
There was a hand less at the halliards 'n' the braces,
'N' a name less when the watch spoke to the muster-roll,
'N' a empty bunk 'n' a pannikin as wasn't wanted
When the watch went below.

Cape Horn Gospel – I

'I was on a hooker once,' said Karlssen,
'And Bill, as was a seaman, died,
So we lashed him in an old tarpaulin
And tumbled him across the side;

And the fun of it was that all his gear was
Divided up among the crew
Before that blushing human error,
Our crawling little captain, knew.

'On the passage home one morning
(As certain as I prays for grace)
There was old Bill's shadder a-hauling
At the weather mizzen-topsail brace.
He was all grown green with sea-weed,
He was all lashed up and shored;[1]
So I says to him, I says, "Why, Billy!
What's a-bringin' of you back aboard?"

' "I'm a-weary of them there mermaids,"
Says old Bill's ghost to me;
"It ain't no place for a Christian
Below there – under sea.
For it's all blown sand and shipwrecks,
And old bones eaten bare,
And them cold fishy females
With long green weeds for hair.

' "And there ain't no dances shuffled,
And no old yarns is spun,
And there ain't no stars but star-fish,
And never any moon or sun.
I heard your keel a-passing
And the running rattle of the brace,"
And he says "Stand by," says William,
"For a shift towards a better place."

'Well, he sogered[2] about decks till sunrise,
When a rooster in the hen-coop crowed,
And as so much smoke he faded
And as so much smoke he goed;

And I've often wondered since, Jan,[3]
How his old ghost stands to fare
Long o' them cold fishy females
With long green weeds for hair.'

Cape Horn Gospel – II

Jake was a dirty Dago lad, an' he gave the skipper chin,[1]
An' the skipper up an' took him a crack with an iron
    belaying-pin
Which stiffened him out a rusty corp,[2] as pretty as you
    could wish,
An' then we shovelled him up in a sack an' dumped him
    to the fish.
That was jest arter we'd got sail on her.

Josey slipped from the tops'l-yard an' bust his bloody back
(Which comed from playing the giddy goat an' leavin' go
    the jack);
We lashed his chips in clouts[3] of sail an' ballasted him with
    stones,
'The Lord hath taken away,' we says, an' we give him to
    Davy Jones.
An' that was afore we were up with the Line.[4]

Joe were chippin' a rusty plate a-squattin' upon the deck,
An' all the watch he had the sun a-singein' him on
    the neck,
An' forrard he falls at last, he does, an' he lets his
    mallet go,
Dead as a nail with a calenture,[5] an' that was the end
    of Joe.
An' that was just afore we made the Plate.[6]

All o' the rest were sailor-men, an' it come to rain
an' squall,
An' then it was halliards, sheets, an' tacks 'clue up, an'
let go all.'
We snugged her down an' hove her to, an' the old
contrairy cuss[7]
Started a plate,[8] an' settled an' sank, an' that was the
end of us.

We slopped around on coops an' planks in the cold an'
in the dark,
An' Bill were drowned, an' Tom were ate by a swine of a
cruel shark,
An' a mail-boat reskied[9] Harry an' I (which comed of
pious prayers),
Which brings me here a-kickin' my heels in the port of
Buenos Ayres.

I'm bound for home in the *Oronook*, in a suit of looted
duds,[10]
A D.B.S.[11] a-earnin' a stake by helpin' peelin' spuds,
An' if ever I fetch to Prince's Stage[12] an' sets my feet
ashore,
You bet your hide that there I stay, an' follers the sea
no more.

A Ballad of John Silver[1]

We were schooner-rigged and rakish, with a long
and lissome[2] hull,
And we flew the pretty colours of the cross-bones and
the skull;
We'd a big black Jolly Roger flapping grimly at the fore,
And we sailed the Spanish Water in the happy days
of yore.

We'd a long brass gun amidships, like a well-conducted
      ship,
We had each a brace of pistols and a cutlass at the hip;
It's a point which tells against us, and a fact to be
      deplored,
But we chased the goodly merchant-men and laid
      their ships aboard.

Then the dead men fouled the scuppers and the wounded
      filled the chains,
And the paint-work all was spatter-dashed with other
      people's brains,
She was boarded, she was looted, she was scuttled till
      she sank,
And the pale survivors left us by the medium of the plank.

O! then it was (while standing by the taffrail on the poop)
We could hear the drowning folk lament the absent
      chicken-coop;
Then, having washed the blood away, we'd little else
      to do
Than to dance a quiet hornpipe as the old salts taught
      us to.

O! the fiddle on the fo'c's'le, and the slapping naked soles,
And the genial 'Down the middle, Jake, and curtsy when
      she rolls!'
With the silver seas around us and the pale moon overhead,
And the look-out not a-looking and his pipe-bowl
      glowing red.

Ah! the pig-tailed, quidding³ pirates and the pretty pranks
      we played,
All have since been put a stop-to by the naughty Board
      of Trade;
The schooners and the merry crews are laid away to rest,
A little south the sunset in the Islands of the Blest.

Lyrics from *The Buccaneer*

I

We are far from sight of the harbour lights,
Of the sea-ports whence we came,
But the old sea calls and the cold wind bites,
And our hearts are turned to flame.

And merry and rich is the goodly gear
We'll win upon the tossing sea,
A silken gown for my dainty dear,
And a gold doubloon[1] for me.

It's the old old road and the old old quest
Of the cut-throat sons of Cain,[2]
South by west and a quarter west,
And hey for the Spanish Main.[3]

II

There's a sea-way somewhere where all day long
Is the hushed susurrus of the sea,
The mewing of the skuas,[4] and the sailor's song,
And the wind's cry calling me.

There's a haven somewhere where the quiet o' the bay
Is troubled with the shifting tide,
Where the gulls are flying, crying in the bright white spray,
And the tan-sailed schooners ride.

III

The toppling rollers[5] at the harbour mouth
Are spattering the bows with foam,
And the anchor's catted, and she's heading for the south
With her topsails sheeted home.

And a merry measure is the dance she'll tread
(To the clanking of the staysail's hanks)
When the guns are growling and the blood runs red,
And the prisoners are walking o' the planks.

IV

We slew him there in the blue lagoon
Where fierce mosquitoes hum,
His soul mewed when his throat was cut
And passed to kingdom come.

We buried him in the blue lagoon
When he was cold and dead;
In the pale light of the misty moon
Our snickersnees[6] were red.

There is blood on thy snickersnee, brother,
There is red blood on mine,
But the clotted gore o' the man that's no more
Is sweeter to me than wine.

Spunyarn[1]

Spunyarn, spunyarn, with one to turn the crank,
And one to slather[2] the spunyarn, and one to knot
    the hank;
It's an easy job for a summer watch, and a pleasant job
    enough,
To twist the tarry lengths of yarn to shapely sailor stuff.

Life is nothing but spunyarn on a winch in need of oil,
Little enough is twined and spun but fever-fret and moil.[3]
I have travelled on land and sea, and all that I have found
Are these poor songs to brace[4] the arms that help the
    winches round.

Personal

Tramping at night in the cold and wet, I passed the
    lighted inn,
And an old tune, a sweet tune, was being played within.
It was full of the laugh of the leaves and the song the
    wind sings;
It brought the tears and the choked throat, and a catch
    to the heart-strings.

And it brought a bitter thought of the days that now were
    dead to me,
The merry days in the old home before I went to sea –
Days that were dead to me indeed. I bowed my head to
    the rain,
And I passed by the lighted inn to the lonely roads again.

[An Inscription for *Salt-Water Ballads*]

Enclosed, I pray thee, Skipper,[1] find
Some tarry whiffs of Channel wind,
Some ballads seven times refined
By careful study.
The author hopes you will not mind
His use of 'bloody'.

Some critic folk who know the trick
To spread the purple patches thick
Complain my language makes 'em sick:
'So coarse!' 'So brutal!'
Say did ye ever hear avick[2]
Such utter footle?[3]

Critics should go to sea in ships
Wi' drunken mates a score o'trips
Wi' men from whom the 'bloody' drips

As smooth as laughter.
Damns would be tumbling from their lips
A twelve-year after.

But there we'll let the critics be.
I do not care a tinker's D[4]
However they try to worry me
In mag and journal.
Critics are mere ephemeral:
The sea's eternal.

I sing the Sailor – I'm the Bard
To dramatize the Compass Card,[5]
Write epics on a topsail yard
In a ship's honour,
To glorify the tanned and tarred
Old seamen on her.

Cargoes

Quinquireme of Nineveh from distant Ophir,[1]
Rowing home to haven in sunny Palestine,[2]
With a cargo of ivory,
And apes and peacocks,[3]
Sandalwood, cedarwood,[4] and sweet white wine.

Stately Spanish galleon coming from the Isthmus,[5]
Dipping through the tropics by the palm-green shores,
With a cargo of diamonds,
Emeralds, amethysts,
Topazes, and cinnamon, and gold moidores.[6]

Dirty British coaster with a salt-caked smokestack,
Butting[7] through the Channel in the mad March days,
With a cargo of Tyne coal,[8]
Road-rails, pig-lead,[9]
Firewood, ironware, and cheap tin trays.

Blind Man's Vigil

Mumblin' under the gallows, hearin' the clank o' the chain,
Hearin' the suck o' the sea as the tide goes by the stair,
I fiddles a lilt o' tune to the bones o' the men o' the Main,[1]
Who dangle, rattle and dance in the rusty chains on air.

Poor old mariners' bones, a mark for cobbles and hoys,
As they go about in the Reach[2] when the dingy tide's
    at flood.
Bones of Billy's old shipmates, bones o' the merry boys,
Whose faults were dollars and girls, and a too quick tick
    o' the blood.

They wasn't the lads to rest in a patch of Christian mould,
Under a marble slab with a verse o' Scripter to 't.
They asked for liquor, an' fun, an' a friend to share
    the gold,
An' a dance in hemp[3] at last wi' nothin' but air to foot.

I fiddles 'em bits o' tunes, an' ballads, an' songs, an' rhymes,
Of the sort that brought the anchor home, an' the yard to
    the masthead;
An' I think they likes to hear, for it makes 'em mind
    the times,
When the blood was hot, an' the throat was dry, an' a
    woman's lips were red.

Fiddlin' under the gallows I mumbles tunes an' words
To the danglin', janglin' rags an' bones that once were
    lads I knew;
(An' I think they likes to hear), an' it scares away the birds,
From the men who go where the wind blows, an' went
    where the wind blew.

Spanish Waters

Spanish waters, Spanish waters, you are ringing in
    my ears,[1]
Like a sweet quaint piece of music from the grey
    forgotten years;
Telling tales, and weaving runes, and bringing weary
    thoughts to me
Of the sandy beach at Muertos,[2] where I would that
    I could be.

Oh the sunny beach at Muertos, and the windy spit[3]
    of sand,
Off of which we came to anchor while the shipmates
    went a-land;
Where the blue laguna emptied over snags of rotting trees,
And the golden sunlight quivered on the brilliant
    colibris.[4]

We came to port at Muertos when the dipping sun
    was red,
And we moored her half-a-mile to sea, to west of Nigger
    Head;
And before the mist was on the Key,[5] before the day
    was done,
We put ashore to Muertos with the gold that we had won.

We bore it through the marshes in a half-score
    battered chests,
Sinking, staggering in the quagmire till the lush weed
    touched the breasts,
While the slithering feet were squelching in the pulp
    of fallen fruits,
And the cold and clammy leeches bit and sucked us
    through the boots.

The moon came white and ghostly as we laid the treasure
    down,
All the spoil of scuttled carracks, all the loot of Lima Town.[6]
Copper charms and silver trinkets from the chests of perished
    crews,
Gold doubloons and double moidores, louis d'ors and
    portagues.[7]

Clumsy yellow-metal earrings[8] from the Indians of Brazil,
Emerald ouches out of Rio, silver bars from Guayaquil,[9]
Silver cups and polished flagons,[10] censers wrought in
    flowered bronze,
And the chased enamelled sword hilts of the courtly Spanish
    Dons.

We smoothed the place with mattocks,[11] and we took and
    blazed the tree,
Which marks you where the gold is hid that none will ever
    see,
And we laid aboard the brig again, and south-away we steers,
Through the loud white surf of Muertos which is beating in
    my ears.

I'm the last alive that knows it. All the rest were took and
    swung
In chains at Execution Dock,[12] where thieves and such are
    hung,
And I go singing, fiddling, old and starved and castaway,
And I know where all the gold is that we won with
    L'Ollonais.[13]

Well, I've had a merry life of it. I'm old and nearly blind,
But the sun-dried swinging shipmates' chains are clanking in
    my mind;
And I see in dreams, awhiles, the beach, the sun's disc dipping
    red,
And the tall brig, under topsails, swaying in past Nigger
    Head.

I'd be glad to step ashore there. Glad to take a pick and go
To the lone blazed coco-palm tree in the place no others
    know,
And lift the gold and silver that has mouldered there
    for years
By the loud white surf of Muertos which is beating in
    my ears.

Roadways

One road leads to London,
One road runs to Wales,[1]
My road leads me seawards
To the white dipping sails.
One road leads to the river,
As it goes singing slow;
My road leads to shipping,
Where the bronzed sailors go.

Leads me, lures me, calls me
To salt green tossing sea;
A road without earth's road-dust
Is the right road for me.
A wet road heaving, shining,
And wild with seagulls' cries,
A mad salt sea-wind blowing
The salt spray in my eyes.

My road calls me, lures me
West, east, south and north;
Most roads lead men homewards,
My road leads me forth
To add more miles to the tally
Of grey miles left behind,
In quest of that one beauty
God put me here to find.[2]

Captain Stratton's Fancy

Oh some are fond of red wine, and some are fond
    of white,
And some are all for dancing[1] by the pale moonlight,
But rum alone's the tipple, and the heart's delight
Of the old bold mate of Henry Morgan.[2]

Oh some are fond of Spanish wine, and some are fond
    of French,
And some'll swallow tay[3] and stuff fit only for a wench,
But I'm for right Jamaica[4] till I roll beneath the bench,
Says the old bold mate of Henry Morgan.

Oh some are for the lily, and some are for the rose,
But I am for the sugar-cane that in Jamaica grows.
For it's that that makes the bonny drink to warm
    my copper nose,
Says the old bold mate of Henry Morgan.

Oh some are fond of fiddles, and a song well sung,
And some are all for music for to lilt upon the tongue;
But mouths were made for tankards, and for sucking at
    the bung,[5]
Says the old bold mate of Henry Morgan.

Oh some are fond of dancing, and some are fond of dice,
And some are all for red lips, and pretty lasses' eyes;
But a right Jamaica puncheon[6] is a finer prize
To the old bold mate of Henry Morgan.

Oh some that's good and godly ones they hold that it's
    a sin,
To troll[7] the jolly bowl around, and let the dollars spin;
But I'm for toleration, and for drinking at an inn,
Says the old bold mate of Henry Morgan.

Oh some are sad and wretched folk that go in
 silken suits,
And there's a mort[8] of wicked rogues that live in
 good reputes;
So I'm for drinking honestly, and dying in my boots,
Like an old bold mate of Henry Morgan.

St Mary's Bells

It's pleasant in Holy Mary
By San Marie Lagoon,[1]
The bells they chime and jingle
From dawn to afternoon.
They rhyme and chime and mingle,
They pulse and boom and beat,
And the laughing bells are gentle
And the mournful bells are sweet.

Oh, who are the men that ring them,
The bells of San Marie,
Oh, who but sonsie[2] seamen
Come in from over sea,
And merrily in the belfries
They rock and sway and hale,
And send the bells a-jangle,
And down the lusty ale.

It's pleasant in Holy Mary
To hear the beaten bells
Come booming into music,
Which throbs, and clangs, and swells,
From sunset till the daybreak,
From dawn to afternoon.
In port of Holy Mary
On San Marie Lagoon.

The Emigrant

Going by Daly's shanty I heard the boys within
Dancing the Spanish hornpipe to Driscoll's violin,
I heard the sea-boots shaking the rough planks of the floor,
But I was going westward, I hadn't heart for more.

All down the windy village the noise rang in my ears,
Old sea-boots stamping, shuffling, bringing the bitter tears,
The old tune piped and quavered, the lilts[1] came clear and
    strong,
But I was going westward, I couldn't join the song.

There were the grey stone houses, the night wind blowing keen,
The hill-sides pale with moonlight, the young corn springing
    green,
The hearth nooks lit and kindly, with dear friends good to see,
But I was going westward, and the ship waited me.

Christmas, 1903

O, the sea breeze will be steady, and the tall ship's going trim,
And the dark blue skies are paling, and the white stars
    burning dim;
The long night-watch is over, and the long sea-roving done,
And yonder light is the Start Point light,[1] and yonder comes
    the sun.

O, we have been with the Spaniards, and far and long on the sea;
But there are the twisted chimneys, and the gnarled old inns
    on the quay.
The wind blows keen as the day breaks, the roofs are white
    with the rime,[2]
And the church-bells ring as the sun comes up to call men in
    to Prime.[3]

The church-bells rock and jangle, and there is peace on the
    earth.
Peace and good will and plenty and Christmas games and
    mirth.
O, the gold glints bright on the wind-vane as it shifts above
    the squire's house,
And the water of the bar of Salcombe[4] is muttering about the
    bows.

O, the salt sea tide of Salcombe, it wrinkles into wisps of
    foam,
And the church-bells ring in Salcombe to ring poor sailors
    home.
The belfry rocks as the bells ring, the chimes are merry as
    a song,
They ring home wandering sailors who have been homeless
    long.[5]

An Old Song Re-sung

I saw a ship a-sailing, a-sailing, a-sailing,
With emeralds and rubies and sapphires in her hold;[1]
And a bo'sun in a blue coat bawling at the railing,
Piping through a silver call that had a chain of gold;
The summer wind was failing and the tall ship rolled.

I saw a ship a-steering, a-steering, a-steering,
With roses in red thread worked upon her sails;
With sacks of purple amethysts, the spoils of buccaneering,
Skins[2] of musky yellow wine, and silks in bales,
Her merry men were cheering, hauling on the brails.

I saw a ship a-sinking, a-sinking, a-sinking,
With glittering sea-water splashing on her decks,
With seamen in her spirit-room singing songs and drinking,
Pulling claret bottles down, and knocking off the necks,
The broken glass was chinking as she sank among the wrecks.

A Song

I yarned with ancient shipmen beside the galley range,
And some were fond of women, but all were fond of change;
They sang their quavering chanties, all in a fo'c's'le drone,
And I was finely suited, if I had only known.

I rested in an ale-house that had a sanded floor,
Where seamen sat a-drinking and chalking up the score;[1]
They yarned of ships and mermaids, of topsail sheets and
     slings,
But I was discontented: I looked for better things.

I heard a drunken fiddler, in Billy Lee's Saloon,
I brooked[2] an empty belly with thinking of the tune:
The beer-mugs clanked approval, the drunkards rose to dance,
And now I know the music was life and life's romance.[3]

The Gara Brook[1]

Babbling and rippling as over the pebbles it bubbles
Slips the cold brook from the dripping wet woods to the piers,
Passing the acres in stook and the dull yellow stalks of the
     stubbles,[2]
On to the sea and the ships and the sailors with rings in their
     ears.

Over the tremulous grasses it gurgles and gushes,
Leaving the fields that are sweet with the smell of the fruit,
Lapping the hooves of the kine[3] and the green, rusty bunches
     of rushes,
Washing the heavy red clay from the twists of the alder-tree
     root.

Babbling and rippling, it sings past the bend, past the
    boulders,
On to the sea and the ships and the songs of the men on
    the quay –
Men who are tanned in the cheeks and strong in the arms
    and the shoulders,
Men with the swaggering walk and the tarry, salt ways
    of the sea.

Would I could follow the brook to the pier where the
    schooners are lying,
Drying brown sails in the sun, while the mariners drink
    at the inn;
Would I could drift with the stream to the bay where the
    gannets are crying,
There where the shore dies away and the merry adventures
    begin.

A Whaler's Song

There are some that are fond of the galley, the beaked
    bitter snake of the seas
Which rings with the cries of the rowers chained fast to the
    bench by the knees,
And beaten and flogged by the soldiers, and chained by the
    wrists to the oar,
As they row through the salt of the spindrift[1] that breaks
    white and bright by the shore.

Ah! life it is hell on the galley; but, ah! she is swift, she is
    swift,
For the long yellow blades swing and quiver and tatter the
    seas into drift;[2]
And the red-coats[3] fire the cannon, and the oar-blades slash
    at the sea,
But the whips crack quick at the flogging – oh! never the
    galley for me.

There are some that are fond of a schooner that sweeps
    through the sea like a deer,
With a flapping black banner above her, and swarthy
    sea-dogs[4] at her gear,
A straining white topsail and stunsail, a wicked brass
    pivoted gun,
And little red stains on her planking to mark where the
    murders were done.

But it's dreary afloat on a schooner, adrift in the sweltering
    calms,
Giving ear to the roar of the rollers[5] that burst at the roots
    of the palms;
With the water grown foul, and the rum gone, the tongue
    of you blackened with thirst,
And the gallows, at last, in Jamaica – I reckon the schooner
    accurst.

There's many are fond of the frigate, black-hulled, with a
    ribbon of white,
All pierced for the muzzles of cannon that jolly blue-jackets[6]
    keep bright;
Her spars tower one on the other, her royals are dimmed in
    the clouds,
And never a harp made the music one hears from the wind
    in her shrouds.

But her little blue-coated lieutenants they lead you the life
    of a dog,
They give you the cat at the gangway: they're handy at
    stopping your grog;
They've brass-work, and gun drill, and sail drill to worry
    and harry[7] and wear,
So I'll keep away from the frigate as long as lieutenants are
    there.

And some have a word for the geordie, the blackened old
    brig from the Tyne,
Grimed over with soot from the coal wharves and scurfed
    to the tops with the brine,[8]
And sluicing her decks as she squatters, and springing her
    spars as she sends,[9]
And wallowing south to the Medway[10] with barnacles
    crusting her bends.

But the best of all ships is the whaler that staggers due
    south full and by
To the lonely blue seas where the whales go a-blowing
    bright sprays at the sky,
Alone with the screaming grey seagulls, the rolling great
    kings of the sea –
Oh! ship me to sail on a whaler, a whaler's the hooker
    for me.

The Greenwich Pensioner[1]

'I'll go no more a roving by the light of the moon,[2]
My feet are tired of roving; my heart is out of tune,
My heart is out of tune, it will neither sing nor sound,
And the men that I was mates with are under sod[3] or
    drowned.

'I'll go no more a roving by land or by the sea;
The mates are done with roving that hauled the ropes
    with me,
Or sang the country songs as we wandered through
    the shire;
And I must come to moorings and gather to the fire.'

Posted as Missing

Under all her topsails she trembled like a stag,
The wind made a ripple in her bonny red flag;
They cheered her from the shore and they cheered her
    from the pier,
And under all her topsails she trembled like a deer.

So she passed swaying, where the green seas run,
Her wind-steadied topsails were stately in the sun;
There was a glitter on the water from her red port-light,
So she passed swaying, till she was out of sight.

Long and long ago it was, a weary time it is,
The bones of her sailor-men are coral plants by this;
Coral plants, and shark-weed,[1] and a mermaid's comb,
And if the fishers net them they never bring them home.

It's rough on sailors' women. They have to mangle[2] hard,
And stitch at dungarees till their finger-ends are scarred,
Thinking of the sailor-men who sang among the crowd,
Hoisting of her topsails when she sailed so proud.

Campeachy[1] Picture

The sloop's sails glow in the sun; the far sky burns,
Over the palm-tree tops wanders the dusk,
About the bows a chuckling ripple churns;
The land wind from the marshes smells of musk.
A star comes out; the moon is a pale husk;
Now, from the galley-door, as supper nears,
Comes a sharp scent of meat and Spanish rusk[2]
Fried in a pan. Far aft, where the lamp blears,
A seaman in a red shirt eyes the sails and steers.

Soon he will sight that isle in the dim bay
Where his mates saunter by the camp-fire's glow;
Soon will the birds scream, scared, and the bucks bray,
At the rattle and splash as the anchor is let go;
A block will pipe,[3] and the oars grunt as they row,
He will meet his friends beneath the shadowy trees,
The moon's orb like a large lamp hanging low
Will see him stretched by the red blaze at ease,
Telling of the Indian girls, of ships, and of the seas.

A Pleasant New Comfortable Ballad Upon
the Death of Mr Israel Hands,[1]
Executed for Piracy
To the Tune of 'I Wail in Woe'[2]

My name is Mr Israel Hands
That here upon the breezes stands,
I was a Pyrat on the Sea,
So, citizens, be warned by me,
O Grief!

O citizens! be warned by me,
I took a ship upon the sea,
I killed the captain with a knife,
Now I must end my wicked life,
O Grief!

'The prigs and cullies[3] on the lay
They do rejoice now at this day,'
Because that I on Tyburn tree[4]
Do end my life by treachery.
O Grief!

Third Mate

All the sheets are clacking,[1] all the blocks are whining,
The sails are frozen stiff and the wetted decks are shining;
The reef's in the topsails, and it's coming on to blow,
And I think of the dear girl I left long ago.

Grey were her eyes, and her hair was long and bonny,
Golden was her hair, like the wild bees' honey.
And I was but a dog, and a mad one to despise,
The gold of her hair and the grey of her eyes.

There's the sea before me, and my home's behind me,
And beyond there the strange lands where nobody
        will mind me,
No one but the girls with the paint upon their cheeks,
Who sell away their beauty to whomsoever seeks.

There'll be drink and women there, and songs and
        laughter,
Peace from what is past and from all that follows after;
And a fellow will forget how a woman lies awake,
Lonely in the night-watch crying for his sake.

Black it blows and bad and it howls like slaughter,
And the ship she shudders as she takes the water.
Hissing flies the spindrift[2] like a wind-blown smoke,
And I think of a woman and a heart I broke.

Truth

Man with his burning soul
Has but an hour of breath
To build a ship of truth
In which his soul may sail –

Sail on the sea of death,
For death takes toll
Of beauty, courage, youth,
Of all but truth.

Life's city ways are dark,
Men mutter by; the wells
Of the great waters moan.
O death! O sea! O tide!
The waters moan like bells;
No light, no mark,
The soul goes out alone
On seas unknown.

Stripped of all purple robes,
Stripped of all golden lies,
I will not be afraid,
Truth will preserve through death.
Perhaps the stars will rise –
The stars like globes;
The ship my striving made
May see night fade.

Ships

I cannot tell their wonder nor make known
Magic that once thrilled through me to the bone,
But all men praise some beauty, tell some tale,
Vent a high mood which makes the rest seem pale,
Pour their heart's blood to nourish[1] one green leaf,
Follow some Helen[2] for her gift of grief,
And fail in what they mean, whate'er they do:
You should have seen, man cannot tell to you
The beauty of the ships of that my city.[3]

That beauty now is spoiled by the sea's pity:
For one may haunt the pier a score of times
Hearing St Nicholas' bells[4] ring out the chimes,
Yet never see those proud ones swaying home,
With mainyards backed and bows a cream of foam,
Those bows so lovely-curving, cut so fine
Those coulters[5] of the many-bubbled brine,
As once, long since, when all the docks were filled
With that sea beauty man has ceased to build.

Yet though their splendour may have ceased to be,
Each played her sovereign part in making me;
Now I return my thanks with heart and lips
For the great queenliness of all those ships.

And first the first bright memory, still so clear,
An autumn evening in a golden year,
When in the last lit moments before dark
The *Chepica*, a steel-grey lovely barque,
Her trucks aloft in sun-glow red as blood,
Came to an anchor near us on the flood.
Then come so many ships that I could fill
Three docks with their fair hulls remembered still,
Each with her special memory's special grace,
Riding the sea, making the waves give place
To delicate high beauty; man's best strength,
Noble in every line in all their length.
Ailsa, *Genista*, ships, with long jib-booms,
The *Wanderer*[6] with great beauty and strange dooms,
Liverpool (mightiest then) superb, sublime,
The *California* huge, as slow as Time.
The *Cutty Sark*,[7] the perfect *J. T. North*,
The loveliest barque my city has sent forth.
Dainty *Redgauntlet*,[8] well remembered yet,
The splendid *Argus* with her skysail set,
Stalwart *Drumcliff*, white-blocked majestic *Sierras*,
Divine bright ships, the water's standard bearers.
Melpomene, *Euphrosyne*, and their sweet

Sea-troubling sisters of the Fernie Fleet.[9]
Corunna (in whom my friend died) and the old
Long since loved *Esmeralda* long since sold.
Centurion passed in Rio, *Glaucus* spoken,[10]
Aladdin burnt, the *Bidston* water-broken,
Yola in whom my friend sailed, *Dawpool* trim,
Fierce-bowed *Egeria* plunging to the swim,
Stanmore wide-sterned, sweet *Cupica*, tall *Bard*
Queen in all harbours with her moonsail yard.

Though I tell many there must still be others,
McVickar Marshall's ships and Fernie Brothers'[11]
Lochs, *Counties*, *Shires*, *Drums*, the countless lines
Whose house-flags all were once familiar signs
At high main trucks on Mersey's windy ways
When sun made all the wind-white water blaze.
Their names bring back old mornings when the docks
Shone with their house-flags and their painted blocks,
Their raking masts below the Custom House
And all the marvellous beauty of their bows.

Familiar steamers, too, majestic steamers,
Shearing Atlantic roller-tops[12] to streamers
Umbria, *Etruria*, noble, still at sea,
The grandest, then, that man had brought to be.
Majestic, *City of Paris*, *City of Rome*
Forever jealous racers, out and home.
The Alfred Holt's blue smokestacks[13] down the stream,
The fair *Arabian*[14] with her bows a-cream.
Booth liners, Anchor liners, Red Star liners,[15]
The marks and styles of countless ship designers.
The *Magdalena*, *Puno*, *Potosi*,
Lost *Cotopaxi*, all well-known to me.

These splendid ships, each with her grace, her glory,
Her memory of old song or comrade's story,
Still in my mind the image of life's need,
Beauty in hardest action, beauty indeed.

'They built great ships and sailed them' sounds most brave,
Whatever arts we have or fail to have;
I touch my country's mind, I come to grips
With half her purpose thinking of these ships.

That art untouched by softness, all that line
Drawn ringing hard to stand the test of brine;
That nobleness and grandeur, all that beauty
Born of a manly life and bitter duty;
That splendour of fine bows which yet could stand
The shock of rollers never checked by land.
That art of masts, sail-crowned, fit to break,
Yet stayed to strength, and back-stayed into rake,[16]
The life demanded by that art, the keen
Eye-puckered, hard-case seamen, silent, lean,
They are grander things than all the art of towns,
Their tests are tempests and the sea that drowns.
They are my country's line, her great art done
By strong brains labouring on the thought unwon,
They mark our passage as a race of men,
Earth will not see such ships as those again.

The Gara River[1]

Oh give me back my ships again,
Lonesome Gara, babbling Gara,
My gilded galleons of Spain
Your blue waves sunk, oh bonny Gara.
Give me again the *Monte*[2] bold,
The beaks[3] that dipped, the beams that rolled,
The green hulled holy ships of old
That you have foundered, babbling Gara.

Give me my youth to have again,
Lonesome Gara, hurried Gara,
Link upon link, a golden chain
That Time has plundered, merry Gara.

The green sweet combes,[4] the setting sun,
The fires we lit, the yarns we spun,
The stately ships launched one by one
And one by one, lost, sunny Gara.

The Pathfinder

She lies at grace, at anchor, head to tide,
The wind blows by in vain: she lets it be.
Gurgles of water run along her side,
She does not heed them: they are not the sea.
She is at peace from all her wandering now,
Quiet is in the very bones of her;
The glad thrust of the leaning of her bow
Blows bubbles from the ebb but does not stir.

Rust stains her side, her sails are furled, the smoke
Streams from her galley-funnel and is gone;
A gull is settled on her skysail truck.
Some dingy seamen, by her deck-house, joke;
The river loiters by her with its muck,
And takes her image as a benison.[1]

The Wanderer[1]

You swept across the waters like a Queen,
Finding a path where never trackway showed,
Daylong you coultered the ungarnered[2] clean
Casting your travelling shadow as you strode.

And in the nights, when lamps were lit, you sped
With gleams running beside you, like to hounds,
Swift, swift, a dappled glitter of light shed
On snatching sprays above collapsing mounds.

And after many a calm and many a storm,
Nearing the land, your sailors saw arise
The pinnacles of snow where streamers form,
And the ever-dying surf that never dies.

Then, laden with Earth's spoils, you used to come
Back, from the ocean's beauty to the roar
Of all the hammers of the mills of home,
Your wandering sailors dragged you to the shore,

Singing, to leave you muted and inert,
A moping place for seagulls in the rain
While city strangers trod you with their dirt,
And landsmen loaded you for sea again.

The Crowd

They had secured their beauty to the dock,
First having decked her to delight the eye.
After long months of water and the sky
These twenty saw the prison doors unlock;

These twenty men were free to quit the ship,
To tread dry land and slumber when they chose,
To count no bells that counted their repose,
To waken free from python Duty's grip.

What they had suffered and had greatly been
Was stamped upon their faces; they were still
Haggard with the indomitable will
That singleness of purpose had made clean.

These twenty threadbare men with frost-bit ears
And canvas bags and little chests of gears.

Posted

Dream after dream I see the wrecks that lie
Unknown of man, unmarked upon the charts,
Known of the flat-fish with the withered eye,
And seen by women in their aching hearts.

World-wide the scattering is of those fair ships
That trod the billow tops till out of sight:
The cuttle mumbles[1] them with horny lips,
The shells of the sea-insects crust them white.

In silence and in dimness and in greenness
Among the indistinct and leathery leaves
Of fruitless life they lie among the cleanness.
Fish glide and flit, slow under-movement heaves:

But no sound penetrates, not even the lunge
Of live ships passing, nor the gannet's plunge.

If[1]

If it could be, that in this southern port
They should return upon the south-west gale
To make again the empty bay their court
Queen beyond queen, at rest or under sail.

And if, from every ship, the songs should rise
From those strong throats, and all be as before,
Should we not all be changed and recognize
Their inner power and exalt them more?

Not so, we should not, we should let them be,
Each age must have its unregarded use,
That is but of its time, on land and sea,
Things have their moment, not a longer truce.

Each darkness has her stars, and when each sets
The dawn, that hardly saw her, soon forgets.

I Saw Her Here

All tranquil is the mirror of the bay,
Empty the anchorage from shore to shore;
A seagull rides the water where she lay
The ships are gone, they come not any more.

Smoke rises from the town, not any noise
Save from the gulls that mew about the pier,
The shadows in the water stand at poise,
All different from the day when she was here.

For she was here when the tumultuous west
Roared on this granite coast for days together,
And billows rode the Channel under crest
While all the hurt swans sheltered from the weather,

And maddened water seethed along her sides
Here, in this quiet, where the seagull rides.

After Forty Years[1]

Let us walk round: the night is dark but fine,
And from the fo'c's'le we shall surely see
The lights of steamers passing to the sea,
And all the city lamplight, line on line.

There on the flood the trampled trackways shine
With hasting[2] gleamings shaken constantly,
The River is the thing it used to be
Unchanged, unlike those merry mates of mine.

This is the very deck, the wind that blows
Whines in the self-same rigging: surely soon
Eight bells will strike, and to his fading tune
Will come the supper-call from Wally Blair:[3]
And then alive, from all the graves none knows,
Will come the boys we knew, the boys we were.

A Seaman's Prayer

Our lives are passed away from any land
In waters, in the hollow of Thy hand.

Our ways are found by sun and moon and star
But ever in Thy hand our fortunes are.

Thy dangers hem us in, of every kind,
The seas that shatter, and the fogs that blind.

The wind that heaps the sea; the rock; the shoal;
Collision and fire, those daunters of the soul.

Save us from these, yet if that may not be
Grant us the manhood fitting to Thy sea.

Number 534[1]

For ages you were rock, far below light,
Crushed, without shape, earth's unregarded bone.
Then Man in all the marvel of his might
Quarried you out and burned you from the stone.

Then, being pured to essence, you were naught
But weight and hardness, body without nerve;
Then Man in all the marvel of his thought
Smithied you into form of leap and curve;

And took you, so, and bent you to his vast,
Intense great world of passionate design,
Curve after changing curving, braced and masst[2]
To stand all tumult that can tumble brine,

And left you, this, a rampart of a ship,
Long as a street and lofty as a tower,
Ready to glide in thunder from the slip
And spear the sea with majesty of power.

I long to see you leaping to the urge
Of the great engines, rolling as you go,
Parting the seas in sunder in a surge,
Shredding a trackway like a mile of snow

With all the wester[3] streaming from your hull
And all gear twanging shrilly as you race,
And effortless above your stern a gull
Leaning upon the blast and keeping place.

May shipwreck and collision, fog and fire,
Rock, shoal and other evils of the sea,
Be kept from you; and may the heart's desire
Of those who speed your launching come to be.

The Eyes

I remember a tropic dawn before turn-to,
The ship becalmed, the east in glow, a dimness,
Dark still, of fleece clouds mottled to the zenith,
The seamen as men dead upon the deck,
Save three who watched, dark statues they, dark bronze.

All things were silent save uneasy gear,
So silent that one heard the flying fish
Startling in frisk and plopping in the sea,
So many that we knew that multitudes
Of living things were near us though unseen.

Marvellously the fleece clouds changed from dim
Through every lovely colour into gold,
And then through every light to intense gleam,
Until a miracle of burning eyes
Looked down upon our thirty distinct souls.

Each of us and the fishes in the deeps,
And every flitting sprite that leapt and sped,
Those watchers knew and called each by his name.

Canal Zone[1]

Among these hills, twelve generations since,
The skirt-of-fortune-plucker, Francis Drake,[2]
Saw from the watch-tree with the Indian prince
The bright Pacific basking like a snake.

Eastward and Westward lay the scenes achieved,
Southward, the deed to do, to Northward, foam
Lapsed on the grave, that waited, as it heaved,
The guest with darings done, not going home.

Now, new adventures hold. Across the track
Where once he stopped the treasure-mules, a 'plane
Roars to the air-base, bringing tourists back;
The spill-way thunders from the inland sea;
But quiet are the bonnet and the bee:[3]
The Dragon slumbers beside sleeping Spain.

To the Seamen

You seamen, I have eaten your hard bread
And drunken from your tin, and known your ways;
I understand the qualities I praise
Though lacking all, with only words instead,

I tell you this, that in the future time
When landsmen mention sailors, such, or such,
Someone will say 'Those fellows were sublime
Who brought the Armies from the Germans' clutch.'

Through the long time the story will be told;
Long centuries of praise on English lips,
Of courage godlike and of hearts of gold
Off Dunquerque beaches in the little ships.

And ships will dip their colours in salute
To you, henceforth, when passing Zuydecoote.[1]

Crews Coming Down Gangways

After long watching of the fatal sea,
And anxious peering at the deadly air,
The peril ends, the mariners are free,
They step with baggage down the narrow stair.

There is no danger seamen have not run:
Tempests have drowned them since the world began,
They have dared shipwreck, frostbite and the sun,
But these have dared a greater horror: Man.

Give Way

'Give way, my lads,' the coxswains used to say
Bossing the crew and thinking themselves clever,
'So toss her up and splash me not with spray . . .
Give way.'

Then, out across the Sloyne[1] or down the bay
The cutter made the water walls dissever,[2]
The seagulls mewed above us in their play.

All earthly ill surrenders to endeavour,
Every tomorrow is another day,
All irons that seem barriers for ever
Give way.

SHORT STORIES

Sea Superstition

One moonlit night in the tropics, as my ship was slipping south under all sail, I was put to walking the deck on the lee side of the poop, with orders to watch the ship's clock and strike the bell at each half-hour. It was a duty I had done nightly for many nights, but this night was memorable to me. The ship was like a thing carved of pearl. The sailors, as they lay sleeping in the shadows, were like august things in bronze. And the skies seemed so near me, I felt as though we were sailing through a cave, the roof of which was wrought of dim branches, as of trees, that bore the moon and the stars like shining fruits.

Gradually, however, the peace in my heart gave way to an eating melancholy, and I felt a sadness, such as has come to me but twice in my life, that was like a dark cloak over my mind. With the sadness there came a horror of the water and of the skies, till my presence in that ship, under the ghastly corpse-light of the moon, among that sea, was a terror to me past power of words to tell. I went to the ship's rail, and shut my eyes for a moment, and then opened them to look down upon the water rushing past. I had shut my eyes upon the sea, but when I opened them I looked upon the forms of the sea-spirits. The water was indeed there, hurrying aft as the ship cut through; but in the bright foam for far about the ship I saw multitudes of beautiful, inviting faces that had an eagerness and a swiftness in them unlike the speed or the intensity of human beings. I remember thinking that I had never seen anything of such passionate beauty as those faces, and as I looked at them my melancholy fell away like a rag. I felt a longing to fling myself over the rail, so as to be with that inhuman beauty. Yet even as I looked that beauty became terrible, as the night had been terrible but a few seconds before. And with the changing of my emotions the faces changed. They became writhelled and hag-like: and in the leaping of the water, as we rushed, I saw malevolent white hands that plucked and snapped at me. I remember I was afraid to go near the rail again before the day dawned.

Not very long after that night, when I was sitting in a tavern garden with a Danish sailor who was all broken on the wheel of his vices and not far from his death, I talked about the sea-spirits and their beauty and their wildness, feeling that such a haunted soul as my companion's would have room in its crannies for such wild birds to nest. He told me much that was horrible about the ghosts who throng the seas. And it was he who gave me the old myth of the seagulls, telling me that the souls of old sailors follow the sea, in birds' bodies, till they have served their apprenticeship or purged their years of penitence. He told me of two sailors in a Norway barque, though I believe he lied when he said that he was aboard her at the time, who illustrated his sermon very aptly. The barque was going south from San Francisco, bound home round the Horn,[1] and the two men were in the same watch. Somehow they fell to quarrelling as to which was the better dancer, and the one killed the other and flung him overboard during one of the night-watches. The dead body did not sink, said my friend, because no body dares to sink to the under-sea during the night-time; but in the dawn of the next day, and at the dawn of each day till the barque reached Norway, a white gull flew at the slayer, crying the lorn cry of the gulls. It was the dead man's soul, my friend said, getting her revenge. The slayer gave himself up on his arrival at the home port, and took poison while awaiting trial.

When he had told me this tale, the Dane called for a tot of the raw spirits of that land, though he must have known, he being so old a sailor, that drink was poison to him. When he had swallowed the liquor, he began a story of one of his voyages to the States. He said that he was in a little English ship coming from New York to Hamburg, and that the ship – the winds being westerly – was making heavy running, under upper-topsails, nearly all the voyage. When he was at the wheel with his mate (for two men steered in the pitch and hurry of that sailing) he was given to looking astern at the huge comber[2] known as 'the following sea', which topples up, green and grisly, astern of every ship with the wind aft. The sight of that water has a fascination for all men, and it fascinated him, he said, till he thought he saw in the shaking wave the image of an old halt[3] man who came limping, bent on a crutch, in the white wake of the clipper. So vivid was the image of that cripple, he leaned across the wheel-box to his mate, bidding him to look at the quaint thing; and his mate looked, and immediately went white to the lips, calling to the saints to preserve him. My friend then told me that the cripple only appears to ships foredoomed to shipwreck, 'and,' he said, 'we were run down in the Channel and sunk in ten minutes' by a clumsy tramp dipping out from London.

After a while I left that country in a steamer whose sailors were of nearly every nation under the sun, and from a Portuguese aboard her I got another yarn. In the night-watches, when I was alone on the poop, I used to lean on the taffrail to see the bright water reeling away from the screws. While loafing in this way one night, a little while before the dawn, I was joined by the Portuguese, an elderly, wizened fellow, who wore earrings. He said he had often seen me leaning over the taffrail, and had come to warn me that there was danger in looking upon the sea in that way. Men who looked into the water, he told me, would at first see only the bubbles, and the eddies, and the foam. Then they would see dim pictures of themselves and of the ship. But at the last they always saw some unholy thing, and the unholy thing would lure them away to death. And it was a danger, he said, no young man should face, for though the other evil spirits, those of the earth and air, had power only upon the body, the evil spirits of the sea were deadly to the

soul. There was a lad he had known in Lisbon who had gone
along the coast in a brig, and this lad was always looking into
the sea, and had at last seen the unholy things and flung his
body to them across the rail. The brig was too near the coast,
and it blew too freshly inshore, for the sailors to round-to to
pick him up. But they found the lad in Lisbon when they got
home. He said he had sunken down into the sea, till the sea
opened about him and showed him a path among a field of
green corn. He had gone up the path and come at last to a
beautiful woman, surrounded by many beautiful women, but
the one seemed to him to be the queen. She was so beautiful, he
said, the sight of her was like strong wine; but she shook her
head when she saw him, as though she could never give him her
love, and immediately he was at the surface, under the skies,
struggling towards some rocks a little distance from him. He
reached the shore and went home to Lisbon in a fisher-boat,
but he was never quite sane after seeing that beauty beneath the
sea. He became very melancholy, and used to go down the
Tagus[4] in a row-boat, singing to himself and looking down into
the water.

Before I left that ship I had to help clean her for her decent
entry to the Mersey. I spent one afternoon with an old man
from the Clyde doing up some ironwork, first with rope-yarn
and paraffin, then with red-lead.[5] The mate left us to ourselves
all the watch, because the old man was trusty, and we had a
fine yarn together about the things of the sea. He said that there
were some who believed in the white whale, though it was all
folly their calling him the king of all the fishes. The white whale
was nothing but a servant, and lay low, 'somewhere nigh the
Poles', till the last day dawned. And then, said the old man,
'he's a busy man raising the wrecks.' When I asked him who
was the king of all the fishes, he looked about to see that there
were no listeners, and said, in a very earnest voice, that the king
of the fish was the sea-serpent. He lies coiled, said the old man,
in the hot waters of the Gulf, with a gold crown on his head,
and a 'great sleep upon him', waiting till the setting of the last
sun. 'And then?' I asked. 'Ah, then,' he answered, 'there'll be
fine times going for us sailors.'

A Sailor's Yarn

Down the jetty, where the tide ran, where the wet green weed lay, there used to come the schooners, with tanned sails, to load gravel for the Welsh seaports. A strong smell of tar and sea-weed hung about the jetty end, and on a Sunday the old men of the sea would take their tobacco there, among the nets and the lobster creels, and the scraps of dunnage. It was fine to be at the jetty end when the yarns were going, for among those old men, those earringed, gnarled sailors, were some who had gone in famous clippers in the days of the Black Ball line.[1] One of these told me the following yarn as I rocked alongside the jetty end in the ship's dinghy I had brought in with the mail:

'Once upon a time there was a clipper-ship called the *Mary*, and she was lying in Panama waiting for a freight. It was hot, and it was calm, and it was hazy, and the men aboard her were dead sick of the sight of her. They had been lying there all the summer, having nothing to do but to wash her down, and scrape the royal masts with glass, and make the chain cables bright. And aboard of her was a big A.B.[2] from Liverpool, with a tattooed chest on him and an arm like a spar. And this man's name was Bill.

'Now, one day, while the captain of this clipper was sunning in the club, there came a merchant to him offering him a fine freight home and "despatch" in loading. So the old man went aboard that evening in a merry temper, and bade the mates rastle[3] the hands aft. He told them that they could go ashore the next morning for a "liberty-day" of four-and-twenty-hours, with twenty dollars pay to blue,[4] and no questions asked if they came aboard drunk. So forward goes all hands merrily, to rout out their go-ashore things, their red handkerchiefs, and "sombre-airers",[5] for to astonish the Dons. And ashore they goes the next morning, after breakfast, with their silver dollars[6] in their fists, and the jolly-boat to take them. And ashore they steps, and "So long!" they says to the young fellows in the boat, and so up the Mole[7] to the beautiful town of Panama.

'Now the next morning that fellow Bill I told you of was

tacking down the city to the boat, singing some song or another.
And when he got near to the jetty he went fumbling in his
pocket for his pipe, and what should he find but a silver dollar
that had slipped away and been saved. So he thinks, "If I go
aboard with this dollar, why the hands'll laugh at me; besides
it's a wasting of it not to spend it." So he cast about for some
place where he could blue it in.

'Now close by where he stood there was a sort of a great
store, kept by a Johnny Dago.[8] And if I were to tell you of the
things they had in it, I would need nine tongues and an oiled
hinge to each of them. But Billy walked into this store, into the
space inside, into like the 'tween-decks, for to have a look about
him before buying. And there were great bunches of bananas
a-ripening against the wall. And sacks of dried raisins, and bags
of dried figs, and melon seeds, and pomegranates enough to
sink you. Then there were cotton bales, and calico, and silk of
Persia. And rum in puncheons,[9] and bottled ale. And all man-
ner of sweets, and a power of a lot of chemicals. And anchors
gone rusty, fished up from the bay after the ships were gone.
And spare cables, all ranged for letting go. And ropes, and sails,
and balls of marline stuff. Then there was blocks of all kinds,
wood and iron. Dunnage there was, and scantling, likewise sea-
chests with pictures on them. And casks of beef and pork, and
paint, and peas, and peter-olium. But for not one of these things
did Billy care a handful of bilge.

'Then there were medical comforts, such as ginger and
calavances.[10] And plug tobacco, and coil tobacco, and tobacco
leaf, and tobacco clippings. And such a power of a lot of bulls'
hides as you never saw. Likewise there was tinned things like
cocoa, and boxed things like China tea. And any quantity of
blankets, and rugs and donkey's breakfasts.[11] And oilskins
there was, and rubber sea-boots, and shore shoes, and Crimee
shirts.[12] Also dungarees, and soap, and matches, so many as
you never heard tell. But no, not for one of these things was Bill
going for to bargain.

'Then there were lamps and candles, and knives and nutmeg-
graters, and things made of bright tin and saucers of red clay;
and rolls of coloured cloth, made in the hills by the Indians.

Bowls there were, painted with twisty-whirls by the folk of old time. And flutes from the tombs (of the Incas), and whistles that looked like flower-pots. Also fiddles and beautiful melode-ons. Then there were paper roses for ornament, and false white flowers for graves; also paint-brushes and coir-brooms.[13] There were cages full of parrots, both green and grey; and white cockatoos on perches a-nodding their red crests; and Java love-birds a-billing, and parakeets a-screaming, and little kittens for the ships with rats. And at the last of all there was a little mon-key, chained to a sack of jib-hanks, who sat upon his tail a-grinning.

'Now Bill he sees this monkey, and he thinks he never see a cuter little beast, not never. And then he thinks of something, and he pipes up to the old Johnny Dago, and he says, pointing to the monkey:

' "Hey-a Johnny! How much-a that-a little munk?"

'So the old Johnny Dago looks at Bill a spell, and then says:

' "I take-a five-a doll' that-a little munk."

'So Billy planks down his silver dollar, and says:

' "I give-a one doll', you cross-eyed Dago."

'Then the old man unchained the monkey, and handed him to Bill without another word. And away the pair of them went, down the Mole to where the boats lay, where a lanchero[14] took them off to the *Mary*.

'Now when they got aboard all hands came around Bill, say-ing: "Why, Bill, whatever are you going to do with that there little monkey?" And Bill he said: "You shut your heads about that there little monkey. I'm going to teach that there little monkey how to speak. And when he can speak I'm going to sell him to a museum. And then I'll buy a farm. I won't come to sea any more." So they just laugh at Bill, and by and by the *Mary* loaded, and got her hatches on, and sailed south-away, on the road home to Liverpool.

'Well, every evening, in the dogwatch, after supper, while the decks were drying from the washing-down, Bill used to take the monkey on to the fo'c's'le-head, and set him on the capstan. "Well, ye little divvle," he used to say, "will ye speak? Are ye going to speak, hey?" and the monkey would just grin and

chatter back at Billy, but never no Christian speech came in
front of them teeth of his. And this game went on until they
were up with the Horn,[15] in bitter cold weather, running east
like a stag, with a great sea piling up astern. And then one
night, at eight bells, Billy came on deck for the first watch,
bringing the monkey with him. It was blowing like sin, stiff and
cold, and the *Mary* was butting through, and dipping her
fo'c's'le under. So Bill takes the monkey, and lashes him down
good and snug on the drum of the capstan, on the fo'c's'le-
head. "Now, you little divvle," he said, "will you speak? Will
you speak, eh?" But the monkey just grinned at him.

'At the end of the first hour he came again. "Are ye going
to speak, ye little beggar?" he says, and the monkey sits and
shivers, but never a word does the little beggar say. And it was
the same at four bells, when the look-out man was relieved. But
at six bells Billy came again, and the monkey looked mighty
cold, and it was a wet perch where he was roosting, and his
teeth chattered; yet he didn't speak, not so much as a cat. So
just before eight bells, when the watch was nearly out, Billy
went forward for the last time. "If he don't speak now," says
Billy, "overboard he goes for a dumb animal."

'Well, the cold green seas had pretty nearly drowned that
little monkey. And the sprays had frozen him over like a jacket
of ice, and right blue his lips were, and an icicle was a-dangling
from his chin, and he was shivering like he had an ague. "Well,
ye little divvle," says Billy, "for the last time, will ye speak? Are
ye going to speak, hey?" And the monkey spoke. "*Speak* is it?
Speak is it?" he says. "It's so cold it's enough to make a little
fellow *swear*."

'It's the solemn gospel truth that story is.'

Port of Many Ships

Sometimes in the afternoons, when I was a lad, I had the chance
to learn sailor-craft on board an old wooden frigate. She was
come down in the world, and lay at moorings in a grimy har-

bour; but at one time she had carried seven hundred sailors and the blue flag of an admiral, and had dipped her blunt nose into all the salt water of the world. It was strange to sit there, on the sunny lower-deck, with the ports all open, looking out upon the shipping, and to picture, from the great ruts worn by the cannon, the busy, stamping, hurrying life that had once gone thronging there, along the long space now so quiet. I used to sit there for hours at a time, propped against a gun, with a mass of rope or strands of rope before me, and an old sailor at my side showing me the knots and the splices. Old, beautiful sea-knots he taught me – the man rope, the Matthew Walker, the crown, the Spanish rose. Delicate plaits he showed to me, things of dainty intricacy – the Turk's head, the diamond, French sennit and Flemish point.[1] He had been a mariner in a Black Ball clipper,[2] and he was one of that old sort of sailor whose hair – so the legend says – was rope-yarn, whose fingers were so many marline-spikes, and whose blood was good 'Stockhollum tar'.[3] He told me many stories of the sea, for his kind old mind was full of coloured threads, each thread a bright tangle of romance. The idle lad to whom he told them has forgotten many, and perhaps those that I set down are not the best. I think he was the last of his tribe, and now that he is dead that old tradition of the sea is dead too, or sounding only in that sad crying of the gulls which is, he said, the talking of old drowned mariners.

One afternoon in the winter I had been more than usually stupid, and the old man, perhaps in despair of making me a sailor, had begun to tell me stories of the swift clipper-ships he had once sailed aboard. The sun was setting as he ended, and the red light in the sky brought into vivid colour that thread of poetry tangled in the heart of every sailor. He called my attention to a mass of glowing cirro-cumulus,[4] with the remark that he wished he could paint so as to fix in burning colour a beauty so perfect and so transient. He fell then to his more beautiful stories, and told me this tale, or myth, in words which I have forgotten, though I know they were simple and forceful, and like a ballad poem in the telling.

'Down in the sea,' he said, 'very far down, under five green miles of water, somewhere in the simmering Gulf of Mexico,

there is a vast sea cave, all roofed with coral. There is a bright-
ness in the cave, although it is so far below the sea. And in the
dim light there the great sea-snake is coiled in immense blue
flashing coils, with a crown of gold upon the horned head of
him. He sits there very patiently from year to year, making the
water tremulous with the threshing of his gills. And about him
at all times swim the goggle-eyed dumb creatures of the sea. He
is the king of all the fishes, the great lord over all the waters.
And he waits there, said the old man, until the judgment day,
when the waters shall pass away for ever and the dim kingdom
disappear. At times the blue coils of his body wreathe them-
selves into new foldings, and then the waters above him burst
into heavy-running seas, the roaring, bursting seas of cyclones.
One folding of his coil will cover a sea with shipwreck; and so
it must be, said the sailor, until the sea and the ships come to an
end together in that fearful storm caused by the serpent's death-
throe.

'Now in that storm,' said the old sailor, 'the fishes in the sea
will die – all except the whales, for the whales are holy fish.
That is why one of them took the prophet Jonah when his ship-
mates threw him overboard. And when that storm is at its
worst, and the snake is dying, there will come a lull and a hush,
like when the boatswain pipes.[5] And in that time of quiet you
will hear a great beating of ship's bells, for in every ship sunken
in the sea the life will go leaping to the white bones of the
drowned. And every drowned sailor, with the green weeds
upon him, will spring alive again; and he will start singing and
beating on the bells, as he did in the sunshine when starting out
upon a cruise. And so great and sweet will be the music that
they make that you will think little of harps from that time on,
my son.

'Now the blue coils of the snake will stiffen out, like a rope
stretched taut for hauling. His long knobbed horns will droop.
His golden crown will roll from his old, tired head. And he will
lie there as dead as herring, while the sea will fall calm, like it
was before the land appeared, with never a white breaker in all
the breadth of her. Then the great white whale, old Moby Dick,
the king of all the whales, will rise up from his quiet in the sea,

and go bellowing to his mates. And all the whales in the world –
the sperm-whales, the razor-back, the black-fish, the rorque, the
right, the forty-barrel Jonah, the narwhal, the hump-back, the
grampus and the thrasher[6] – will come to his "fin-out", blow-
ing their spray to the heavens. Then Moby Dick will call the
roll of them, and from all the parts of the sea, from the north,
from the south, from Callao to Rio,[7] not one whale will be
missing. Then Moby Dick will trumpet, like a man blowing a
horn, and all that sea-company of whales will "sound" (that is,
dive), for it is they that have the job of raising the wrecks from
the red coral beds and the star-fish, down below in the green
water, far from any glint of the sun.

'Then when they come up,' said the old man, as he lit his
wooden pipe and sent the grey smoke curling in the stillness,
'the sun will just be setting in the sea, far away to the west, like
a ball of red fire. And just as the curve of it goes below the sea,
it will stop sinking and lie there like a door. And the stars and
the earth and the wind will stop. And there will be nothing but
the sea, and this red arch of the sun, and the whales with the
wrecks, and a stream of light upon the water. Each whale will
have raised a wreck from among the coral, and the sea will
be thick with them – row-ships and sail-ships, and great big
seventy-fours,[8] and big White Star boats,[9] and battleships, all
of them green with the ooze, but all of them manned by singing
sailors. And ahead of them will go Moby Dick, towing the ship
our Lord was in, with all the sweet apostles aboard of her. And
Moby Dick will give a great bellow, like a foghorn blowing,
and stretch "fin-out" for the red sun away in the west. And all
the whales will bellow out an answer. And all the drowned
sailors will sing their chanties, and beat the bells into a music
passing harps. And the whole fleet of them will start towing at
full speed towards the red sun's globe, at the edge of the sky
and water. I tell you they will make white water, those ships
and fishes.'

'And where will they go to, Mr Blair?'[10] said I. 'Ah,' he
answered, 'when they have flurried west to where the sun is,
the red ball will swing open like a door, and Moby Dick, and
all the whales, and all the ships will rush through it into a grand

anchorage in Kingdom Come. It will be a great calm piece of water, with land close aboard, where all the ships of the world will lie at anchor, tier upon tier, with the hands gathered forward, singing. They'll have no watches to stand, no ropes to coil, no mates to knock their heads in. Nothing will be to do except singing and beating on the bell. And all the poor sailors who went in patched rags, my son, they'll be all fine in white and gold. And ashore, among the palm-trees, among the lilies, there'll be fine inns for the seamen, where you and I, maybe, will meet again, and I spin yarns, maybe, with no cause to stop until the bell goes.'

A Spanish Sailor's Yarn

Some years ago I was on board a schooner plying between St James and the Havana, and we were close in shore, almost within earshot of the Cuban surf. It was a hot July day with little wind, and ashore the green of the palms drooped heavily. We had our tanned, patched topsail set and our decks wetted, and I was lolling in the shadow of the deck-house, tossing a penny-piece for matches with a Spaniard from Wine of the Sea.[1] He had just stopped in his spinning of the coin, and had lit a cigarette. He looked a moment at the long green line of Cuba, with the white water flashing up against its cliff, and 'See,' he said, pointing a skinny hand towards a creek. 'See, that is Coxe's Hole.' I could see a dim dent in the line of Cuba where the sea ran up into a thickly wooded channel, and at the very mouth of this channel a little bare hillock jutted up, with a few grey stones upon its top. 'Coxe's Hole,' repeated the Spaniard. 'Coxe's Hole. Let me tell you the tale of Coxe.'

'A long time ago,' he said, '(and one may reckon that that "long time" was nearly two centuries), a Bristol sailor named Englefield (these tales are always precise in detail) had command of the *Happy* frigate, and came to Kingston with a general cargo. He had loaded for home and sailed for Falmouth, and had met with head winds for rather more than a fortnight, when they made the Cuban coast. They were becalmed there, with their planks crying out, their blocks groaning up aloft, and the guns grinding along the decks. Every inch of the old ship quavered in piping sighs as the swell hove her up and dropped her. They were rolling thus when a long "piracqua"[2] from the shore put off under oars with forty armed men in her. She ran up to the *Happy* and hooked on to her mizzen rigging, laying her aboard at once and making her a prize in less than ten minutes. Her captain, Englefield, they shot. But her second mate, Coxe, a young Bristol man, who could find a ship's position, was elected by the pirates as "artist" (navigator) to their company.'

He took the ship westward on a cruise, and went among the turtlers[3] and guarda-costas which ply the waters of the Gulf. He stole south to the little city of St Mary, a little white town on a lagoon, a little city sweet with myrtle, and made a big spoil of it, winning the stored silver in the fort and melting the sacramental vessels from the church. He ran away north to the American coast, where he burned and plundered, making a prize at Newport of a China ship with bales of silk in her, and of the Governor's dockyard with its ropes, tar, blocks, sea-store and gunpowder. He then sailed east to Guinea, where he sacked Whydah,[4] and took the gold and ivory waiting the king's convoy. He filled up his ship's company with negroes and sailed west again, making Cuba, finding, almost by chance, that channel in the coast my friend had shown to me. It was worth coined gold to him, that channel; for it led to a dim lagoon, blue like the sky, where twenty ships might swing abreast. The beach of it shelved gently. A great ship might careen there; while ashore there was a plenty of tall trees to build him huts or to make spars or planking for masts and decks broken by sea cannon.

He cast anchor there, and sent his guns ashore while he careened and resheathed his frigate. He built a storehouse on the beach of the lagoon, and a rough log-house, crudely thatched, for his ship's company to live in when ashore. As with most pirate captains, his authority was not great. He could not command the rough fellows who manned his guns; but while he brought them fortune they were content that his

share should be the lion's share and his life a life of ease, sprawl-
ing on the cabin cushions, with solacements of rum when he
desired them. He seems to have been a cautious, clever rogue,
for in the next five years his band of ruffians had become almost
a tribe. Recruits had reached him from the logwood cutters of
the coast, from the Indians of the woods, from French cattle
hunters and English tobacco convicts. With great labour he
builded a stone fort at the channel entrance on the coast,
mounting eight brass cannon in it. And daily while the sun was
above the sea a black banner flapped there, and a sentry kept
the time upon a ship's bell. Within the lagoon, as his company
increased, a little wooden town arose, with its dockyard and
shipyard, where boats of sixty tons were built. And though the
houses were huts, and roughly built huts, with crazy palm
thatch, within them there were all the riches of the world –
lace, silk and cloth of gold, the worth of a king's ransom in the
meanest.

'It was his custom,' the Spaniard said, 'to have four ships
cruising at a time[5] – two for the riches of the world, one for
ship's stores, and one for all that she could find. So that after
five years of life in the island or at sea, he had great wealth in
the storehouse on the beach – the gold, ivory, silk, silver and
precious jewels of all the countries in the earth. But at the end
of the fifth year,' the Spaniard said, 'he angered the spirit that
gave him all his fortune, and his luck went from him, and he
fell.' 'How was that, señor?' I asked. 'As so,' he answered.
'May we never anger the woman of the sea.'

'One afternoon,' he said, 'Coxe took a sailboat up the chan-
nel, purposing to fish there for the little swift pica-ré, a fish like
a herring, but more toothsome. It was a hot, still afternoon, the
anchorage almost windless, the parrots screaming in the trees,
the surf roaring along the coast in one continual dull thunder.
Coxe cast his hook about a hundred yards from open water,
and, what with the heat, what with the rum he had had, his
head was singing tunes long before he had a fish aboard. He
was lying over the stern, his thread running over the steering-
crutch,[6] and it seemed to him, in a little while, that he had
hooked a great giant fish, for he could see the flash of him

below him. Although his line was mere sail-twine, it did not break. He was fast to a tarpon,[7] as he thought, and being anxious to get clear, he jerked the line towards him to break it. To his astonishment it held. The water lipped into an eddy with a swirl; and there, facing him, rising from the water like some pale, beautiful flower, was one of the sad women of the sea. Her lips were like hibiscus blossom. Her eyes were dark and sad. Her face was of an extreme pure white, like the white of ivory. And "Ah," she said, "you have come for me at last." He noticed then,' said the Spaniard, 'that one of her cool white fingers was pierced through with his hook and bled. "Ah, my beloved," she said, "you have drawn me to you as the moon draws the sea. I have loved you all these years, and followed your ship into all the harbours below the sun. Take pity on me (she was saying); take me with you to your home upon the land."

'But a great terror had fallen upon Coxe, and he snatched the stretcher[8] from the crutch and beat at the pale, pitiful, lovely head till it sank from before him, moaning. He made a great haste to get on shore and to pour green rum down his throat, but for all that day and for the next day that beautiful face was in his head like a menace, and an angry lamenting cry seemed to fill the lagoon. He put to sea in his brigantine at sunset of the second day, and was taken by Captain Rogers, of the king's ship *Thunderer*, who hanged him at his fore-yard-arm. The colony of pirates was rooted out, but that makes a story of itself, señor. May the saints protect us from evil living – from evil living and from the evil spirits of the sea. Amen.'

The Yarn of Lanky Job

When I was in hospital in Valparaiso,[1] I spent my evenings in the garden with an old lame sailor from Coquimbo.[2] He was a very ancient shellback who had fallen down a hatchway, wrenching a muscle of his knee. His wound caused him much suffering; but at twilight, when the heat and the light became

gentle, his pain was always less fierce than in the day, and he
would then yarn to me of the sights and cities he had seen. The
place we chose for our yarns was among lilies, under a thorn
tree which bore a white fragrant blossom not unlike a tiny rose.
When we were seated in our chairs we could see the city far
below us, and that perfect bay with the ships, and Aconcagua[3]
snowy in the distance. A few yards away, beyond a low green
hedge where the quick green lizards darted, was a barren patch,
a sort of rat warren, populous with rats as big as rabbits. I was
getting well of a fever,[4] and my nerves were shaken, and the
sight of these beasts scattering to their burrows was very hor-
rible to me. One day, when my comrade had watched me
shudder as a rat crept through the hedge in search of food, he
asked me had I heard the story of Lanky Job. I told him that I
had not, and he then spun me the following yarn – a yarn unlike
any that I had ever heard.

'I dare say,' said the old man, 'that you know about rats
leaving a sinking ship? Well, it is about that the yarn goes.'

He told me that Lanky Job was a lazy mariner of ancient
days who was so sleepy he couldn't keep awake at dinner, and
often slept between raising the cup and drinking. He was a
Bristol sailor, notorious for his sleepiness throughout the seven
seas. And though many captains had taken him in hand, none
had ever made him 'spryer than a slug', or got more than a
snail's work out of him. Perhaps he would have been more
careful and more wakeful had he not been born with a caul,[5]
which preserved him at sea from any danger of drowning.
Often he had fallen from aloft or from the forecastle rail while
dreaming pleasantly during his work or look-out. But his cap-
tains had always paused to pick him up, loosing sails and spars
in the hurry of the manoeuvre, and to all his captains he had
made a graceful speech of thanks which ended with a snore at
the ninth or tenth word.

One day he was lolling on a bollard on the quay at Bristol as
fast asleep as man could wish. He had fallen asleep in the fore-
noon, but when he woke the sun was setting, and right in front
of him moored to the quay, was the most marvellous ship that
ever went through water. She was bluff-bowed[6] and squat, with

a great castle in her bows and five poops, no less, one above the other, at her starn.[7] And outside her bulwarks there were painted screens, all scarlet and blue and green; with ships painted on them, and burning birds (he meant Phoenixes) and ladies in cloth of gold. And then above them there were rows of hammocks covered with a white piece of linen. And every little poop had a rail round her of pure polished gold. And her buckets were green, and in every bucket there were big red roses growing. And the bitts were of polished ebony inlaid with mother-of-pearl. And the masts were of ebony with mast-rings of silver. And her decks were all done in parquet-work in green and white woods, and the man who did the caulking had caulked the deck-seams with red tar, for he was a master of his trade. And the cabins was all glorious to behold with carving, and sweet to smell, like oranges. And right astern she carried a great gold lantern with a big blue banner underneath it, and an ivory staff to the whole, all carved by a Chinaman.

So Job looks at the ship, and he thinks he never see a finer, so he ups alongside, and along a little golden gangway, and there he sees a little sea captain with a big red hat and feather, and a silver whistle to him, walking on the quarterdeck.

'Good morning, Job,' says the little sea captain, 'and how d'ye like my ship?'

'Sir,' says Job, 'I never see a finer.'

So the little sea captain takes Job forrard and gives him a bite in the forecastle, and then takes him aft and gives him a sup in the cabin.

'And Job,' he says, 'how would ye like to sail aboard this beautiful ship?'

So Job, who was all wide awake with the beauty of her, he says, 'Oh, sir, I'd like it of all things; she be so comely to see.'

And immediately he said that, Job see the little captain pipe his whistle, and a lot of little sailors in red hats ran up and cast her hawsers off. And then the sails sheeted home of themselves and the ship swung away from Bristol, and there was Job nodding on the quarterdeck, a mile out to sea, the ship running west like a deer.

'You'll be in the port watch,' said the little captain to him, 'and woe betide you, Lanky Job, if we catch you asleep in your watch.'

Now Job never knowed much about that trip of his among them little men in red hats, but he knowed he slept once, and they stuck needles in him. And he knowed he slept twice, and they stuck hot pokers in him. And he knowed he slept a third time, and 'Woe betide you, Lanky Job,' they said, and they set him on the bowsprit end, with bread in one hand and a sup of water in the other. 'And stay you there, Lanky Job,' they said, 'till you drop into the sea and drown.'

Now pitiful was his case truly, for if he looked behind there was little red men to prick him, and if he looked before he got giddy, and if he looked down he got sick, and if he looked up he got dazzled. So he looked all four ways and closed his eyes, and down he toppled from his perch, going splash into the wash below the bows. 'And now for a sleep,' he says, 'since there's no water wet enough to drown me.' And asleep he falls, and long does he drift in the sea.

Now, by and by, when he had floated for quite a while, he sees a big ship, black as pitch, with heavy red sails, come sailing past him in the dawn. And although he had a caul and couldn't be drowned, he was glad enough to see that ship, and right glad indeed to clutch her braces as she rolled. She came swooping down on him, and he caught her main brace as she lay down to leeward from a gust. And with her windward roll and a great heave, he just managed to reach her deck before he fell asleep again. He noticed as he scrambled up the side that she was heavily barnacled, and that she had forty boats to a broadside, all swinging on ivory davits.

But when he woke from his sleep, lo and behold, the ship was manned by nothing but great rats, and they were all in blue clothes like sailors, and snarling as they swung the yards. And as soon as they saw Lanky Job they came around him, gnashing their long yellow teeth and twirling their hairy whiskers. And the multitude of them was beyond speech, and at every moment it seemed to Job that a boat came alongside with more of them, till the decks were ropy with their tails. Six or seven of them seized hold of him and dragged him aft to where a big

bone tiller swung, with a helmsman on each side of it, seated in
heavy golden chairs. These helmsmen were half men, half rats,
and they were hairy like rats, and grey like rats, and they had
rats' eyes. But they had the minds of men, and they were the
captains of that hooker, and right grim they were to look at
steadily. Now when he sees those grim things sitting there, Job
knew that he'd come aboard the rat flagship, whose boats row
every sea, picking up the rats as they leave ships going to sink.
And he gave a great scream and punched out at the gang who
held him, and over the side he bounded like a young salmon for
swiftness. And he drifted a day and a night, till the salt-cracks
were all over his body, and he came ashore half dead at Avon-
mouth,[8] having been a week away. But always after that Lanky
Job was a spry sailor, as smart as you could find anywheres.

In Dock – I

My first impressions of a sailor's life were obtained at second
hand from old sailors who wore earrings and chewed, and
whose notions of seafaring were antique and almost beautiful.
I thought those tarry lips dripped truth as well as tobacco juice,
and my error, when it was forced upon me, hurt me like the
rope's end which opened my eyes. I had finished my training
(such as it was). I had received my sea-going kit and my orders
to be on board by noon. And as I went to the Docks I felt, I
remember, strangely at one with the sun, strangely hopeful and
confident, telling myself rosy yarns, and conscious of the nobil-
ity of a sailor's life.

I had heard of my ship, the *Cairngorm*,[1] from lads who had
seen her and sailed in her, and I had a fine picture painted in my
brain of myself in a brass-bound suit walking her quarterdeck.
She lay in mid-dock, and it was a proud moment for me when
I paid the boy who carried my gear, and hailed her from the
grimy pier-head, '*Cairngorm* ahoy!'

A filthy youth in dungarees put in from her gangway in a
dinghy. He was a *Conway* boy of my time and one morning's

work had altered him strangely from the neat midshipman I
had known a month before. He tumbled my gear into the stern-
sheets and I jumped in and took the oars from him and pulled
alongside. He took the opportunity to smoke the fag-end of a
cigarette which had laid crumpled in his trouser pocket since
the morning. When I reached the deck, a little pock-marked
man with a limp and a sallow face came shambling to me. He
was in shirt sleeves and smoked a foot of clay.

'So you're another of 'em?'

He had 'mate' written all over him, so I touched my cap and
said, 'Yes, sir.'

'Go forrard to the half-deck with your gear, shift your duds[2]
and come on deck an' turn-to.'

As I went to the half-deck (the deck-house given over to the
apprentices), the second mate met me. He was a great lion of a
man, lively on his feet, quick in the eye, with a good chest and
grand arms, a holy terror when having trouble with his watch.
He greeted me with curt disapproval. 'So you're another of
them.'

I touched my cap very timidly. 'Yes, sir.'

'Great snakes,' he said. 'Go, shift yourself, and then turn-to
here. You needn't touch your cap to me. I don't stand on cere-
mony. Look lively now. What the divil are ye standing there
for?'

I half expected to be kicked, but it was only his deep-sea
manner gone sour, as it were, from being kept so long in dock.
I jumped for the half-deck at the order, and gave a hand at the
bestowal of my gear.

The old *Cairngorm* was loading patent fuel for Pisagua,[3]
and the black blocks of compressed coal-dust were sliding
down her hatches at the rate of, roughly speaking, 200 tons a
day. One hatch was just abaft the half-deck door, and though
fuel is tolerably clean, it had spread in fine particles through the
closed edges of the skylight and the chinks of the door, till the
half-deck was like a collier's pantry. As I opened the door to
enter, the desolation of the place came over me like a bad
dream, for it was in a state of litter and disorder quite indes-
cribable. It was not a large place (its measurements were twelve

feet square by eight feet high), and the hurried unpacking of
five boys had strewn it two feet deep in clutter and scattered
clothes. Chests and sailor's bags, sea bedding, tin plates, pan-
nikins and dungarees were flung 'all-to-how' under the bunks
and over the floor and on the lockers. I never had seen such a
dissolute sight, and the rough discomfort of the place made me
sick to be there. I shifted into dungarees with all despatch, and
hurried on deck to my duty.

Quick as I had been I had not 'stepped lively' enough for the
second mate's fancy. 'Great snakes, you,' he cried, 'have you
been asleep in there, or how? Get on to the rope here – *here*,
this bit of string. Now sway.' I swayed dutifully till long into
the afternoon. Before we knocked off work for the day a ship-
mate and I were set to putting the half-deck into sailor shape.
When we had finished it looked something as follows:

Two of its sides were fitted with a double tier of bunks (two
bunks in each tier). Its forward wall was fitted with a narrow
table covered with oilskins. Its after wall was pierced with a
door, and fitted with a small water-tank and two lockers (one
of them a wash-hand stand) for the storage of plates and pan-
nikins. Its walls were iron, and painted to resemble polished
maple-wood. The lad who did the painting must have had a
duplicate key to the spirit room. Our six sea-chests were drawn
up in orderly-wise for use as seats, the deck was scrubbed, the
black table laid out with knives, forks and tin plates, and when
it had struck six o'clock, and work had ceased in the docks for
the day, the place, it may be, looked a little strange, but neat
enough for a man to dwell in without actual pain.

It was our custom to wash ourselves before supper, and this
act of virtue we performed on deck, using two dented tin basins
in turn. When we were cleansed we sent one of our number
forward to the galley for 'supper'.

This meal consisted of a sodden mess of 'dry hash', which
fell with a most unreassuring 'plunk' when helped on to a plate.
We had also some broken portions of a loaf, a block of rancid
butter, some moist salt, and a kettleful of ship's 'tea'. Coming
to six hungry lads, who had been doing the hardest kinds of
manual labour all day, and who were fresh from the pleasant

refinements of the *Conway*, this disgusting mess was at once an injury and an insult. Food at sea is bad always, but to give food not so much bad as *vile* when in dock is inexcusable. We could not eat it. The very pigs in the stye refused it. We hove it into the pigs' platter and supped on some Bovril, a few buns, a little jam and some tobacco.

When we had fed and cleared away the relics of the meal, we lit our pipes and turned in to our bunks. One of our number washed the plates in a bucket and dried them with his handkerchief, while one other, who had been two years at sea, summed up the ship and her mates with point, with accuracy, and with prophecy. He then suggested that a 'sing-song' should be held to make the evening pass brightly with something of the refinements of art. We had no songsters in our mess, but we fell in with his suggestion because we all felt, I think, that without some distraction of the kind the hatefulness of life in such a place would burn itself unpleasantly upon the plates of our brains.

Chris, one of my shipmates, applauded loudly.

'Yes, my son,' he said, 'let's have a sing-song. Shut up, you other fellows! Me and Sandy'll sing you a duet.'

'What the — — duet'll we sing?' asked Sandy.

'Why, "McGilligan".'[4]

'Oh, rot! I'm not going to sing that — — slush.'

'Yes you are, man. Shut up, you other fellows. Are you ready, Sandy? Begin, — —'

The duet of 'McGilligan', or as much of it as I remember, goes as follows. I print it exactly as sung:

I backed a horse the other day, that horse he did not win before I back that horse again I'll see him run to

  Alleluia. Keep your seats I am not swearing Alleluia the truth I always tell. Chorus you other fellows McGilligan get your hair cut where did you get that hat Ally Sloper up a tree whiskers for a cat how d'ye like your eggs boiled could you eat a sausage lunch where'er I go the lumbers cry Cairngorms a dollar a ton.

Other ballads followed – 'Sam Hall',[5] for instance, and 'Spanish Ladies'[6] and 'The Long, Long Time Ago'.[7] We were wont to

sing these songs night after night (we had but one or two others)
until the sound of them was nauseous past power of words.
Our one possible amusement after work had ceased, if shore
was forbidden, was to smoke many pipes between songs such
as that given above. On this first night of my new life, these
wretched ballads, heard in the unaccustomed squalor of a half-
deck, gave me a disgusted loathing for the sea and all connected
with it. I was fifteen years old and I had looked to find a life
rough in the main but withal courtly (as in Marryat).[8] Instead I
found a life brutal as that of a convict, a life foul, frowsy, whose
one refinement was that of the low tavern by the dock.

Don Alfonso's Treasure Hunt

Now in the old days,[1] before steam, there was a young Spanish
buck who lived in Trinidad, and his name was Don Alfonso.
Now Trinidad is known, in a way of speaking, among sailor-
men, as Hell's Lid, or Number One Hatch, by reason of its
being very hot there. They've a great place there, which they
show to folk, where it's like a cauldron of pitch. It bubbles
pitch out of the earth, all black and hot, and you see great slimy
workings, all across, like ropes being coiled inside. And talk
about smell there! – talk of brimstone! – why, it's like a cattle-
ship gone derelict, that's what that place is like.

Now by reason of the heat there, the folk of those parts – a
lot of Spaniards mostly, Dagoes[2] and that – they don't do noth-
ing but just sit around. When they turn out of a morning they
get some yellow paper and some leaf tobacco, and they rolls
what they calls cigarellers and sticks them in their ears like
pens. That's their day's work, that is – rolling them yellow cig-
arellers. Well, then, they set around and they smokes – big men,
too, most of them – and they put flowers in their hats – red
roses and that – and that's how they pass their time.

Now this Don Alfonso he was a terror, he was; for they've
got a licker[3] in those parts. If you put some of it on a piece of
paint-work – and this is gospel that I'm giving you – that paint

it comes off like you was using turps. Now Don Alfonso he was a terror at that licker – and that's the sort of Dago-boy Alfonso was.

Now Alfonso's mother was a widow, and he was her only child, like in the play.[4]

Now one time, when Don Alfonso was in the pulperia (that's Spanish for grog-shop), he was a-bluin' down that licker the same as you or I would be bluin' beer. And there was a gang of Dagoes there, and all of them chewing the rag,[5] and all of them going for the vino – that's the Spanish name for wine – v-i-n-o. It's red wine, vino is; they give it you in port to save water.

Now among them fancy Dagoes there was a young Eye-talian who'd been treasure-hunting, looking for buried treasure, in that Blue Nose ship[6] which went among the islands. Looking for gold, he'd been – gold that was buried by the pirates. They're a gay crew, them Blue Nose fellers. What'd the pirates bury treasure for? Not them. It stands to reason. Did yer ever see a shellback go reeving his dollars down a rabbit-warren? It stands to reason. Golden dollar coins indeed. Bury them customs fellers if you like. Now this young Dago, he was coming it proud about that treasure. In one of them Tortugas,[7] he was saying, or off of the Chagres,[8] or if not there among them smelly Samballs,[9] there's whole galley-oons of it lying in a foot of sand with a skellinton on the top. They used to kill a nigger, he was saying, when they burrowed their blunt,[10] so's his ghost would keep away thieves. There's a sight of thieves, ain't there, in them smelly Samballs? An' niggers ain't got no ghosts, not that I ever heard.

Oh, he was getting gay about that buried treasure. Gold there was, and chinking silver dollars[11] and golden jewels, and I don't know what all. 'And I knows the place,' he says, 'where it's all lying,' and out he pulls a chart with a red crost on it, like in them Deadwood Dicky books.[12] And what with the vino and that there licker, may I be spiked if he didn't get them Dagoes strung on a line. So the end of it was that Don Alfonso he come down with the blunt. And that gang of Dagoes they charters a brigantine – she'd a Bible name to her, as is these Dagoes' way – and off they sails a galley-vaunting after galley-oons an' gold

with a skellinton on the top. Now one dusk, just as they was
getting out the lamps and going forward with the kettle, they
spies a land ahead and sings out 'Land, O!' By dark they was
within a mile of shore, hove-to off of a lighthouse that was
burning a red flare. Now the old man he comes to Alfonso, and
he says, 'I dunno what land this may be. There's no land due to
us this week by my account. And that red flare there; there's no
light burning a flare nearer here than Sydney.' 'Let go your
anchor,' says Don Alfonso, 'for land there is, and where there's
land there's rum. And lower away your dinghy, for I'm going in
for a drink. You can take her in, mister, with two of the hands,
and then lay aboard till I whistle.' So they lower the dinghy,
and Don Alfonso takes some cigarellers, and ashore he goes for
that there licker.

Now when he sets foot ashore, and the boat was gone off,
Don Alfonso he walks up the quay in search of a pulperia. And
it was a strange land he was in, and that's the truth. Quiet it
was, and the little white houses still as corfins, and only a lamp
or two burning, and never a sound nor a song. Oh, a glad lad
was Don Alfonso when he sees a nice little calaboosa[13] lying to
leeward, with a red lamp burning in the stoop. So in he goes for
a dram – into the grog-house, into a little room with a fire lit
and a little red man behind the bar. Now it was a caution was
that there room, for instead of there bein' casks like beer or
vino casks, there was only corfins. And the little red man he
gives a grin, and he gives the glad hand to Don Alfonso, and
he sets them up along the bar, and Alfonso lights a cigareller.
So then the Don drinks, and the little red man says, 'Salve.'[14]
And the little red man drinks, and Alfonso says, 'Drink hearty.'
And then they drinks two and two together. Then Alfonso
sings some sort of a Dago song, and the little red man he plays
a tune on the bones, and then they sets them up again and
has more bones and more singing. Then Alfonso says, 'It's time
I was gettin' aboard'; but the little red man says, 'Oh, it's early
days yet – the licker lies with you.' So every time Alfonso
tries to go, the little red man says that. Till at last, at dawn, the
little red man turned into a little red cock and crowed like a
cock in the ox yard. And immejitly the corfins all burst into

skellintons, and the bar broke into bits, and the licker blew up like corpse-lights – like blue fire, the same as in the scripters.[15] And the next thing Don Alfonso knowed he was lying on the beach with a head on him full of mill-wheels and the mill working overtime.

So he gets up and sticks his head in the surf, and blows his whistle for the boat to come. But not a sign of a boat puts in, and not a sign of a hand shows aboard, neither smoke nor nothin'. So when he'd blew for maybe an hour he sees a old skellinton of a boat lying bilged on the sand. And he went off in her, paddling with the rudder, and he got alongside before she actually sank.

Now, when he gets alongside, that there brigantine was all rusty and rotted and all grown green with grass. And flowers were growing on the deck, and barnacles were a foot thick below the water. The gulls had nested in her sails, and the ropes drifted in the wind like flags, and a big red rose-bush was twisted up the tiller. And there in the soft green grass, with daisies and such, were the lanky white bones of all them Dagoes. They lay where they'd died, with the vino casks near by and a pannikin of tin that they'd been using as a dice-box. They was dead white bones, the whole crew – dead of waiting for Don Alfonso while he was drinking with the little red man.

So Don Alfonso he kneels and he prays, and 'Oh,' he says, 'that I might die too, and me the cause of these here whited bones, and all from my love of licker! Never again will I touch rum,' he says. 'If I reach home,' he says – he was praying, you must mind – 'you'll see I never will.' And he hacks through the cable with an axe and runs up the rotten jib by pully-hauly.[16]

Long he was sailing, living on dew and gulls' eggs, sailing with them white bones in that there blossoming old hulk. But at long last he comes to Port of Spain and flies the red wheft[17] for a pilot, and brings up just as sun was sinking. Thirty long years had he been gone, and he was an old man when he brought the whited bones home. But his old mother was alive, and they lived happily ever after. But never any licker would he drink, except only dew or milk – he was that changed from what he was.

In a Fo'c's'le

Ashore, in the towns, men find it easy to amuse themselves, for there is amusement, or at least a satisfaction, in being with a number of one's fellows. With a newspaper and beer and a music-hall it is difficult to be depressed, for no man need suffer much from introspection while opinions, ideals and a sight of the most living of modern arts may be purchased for a few copper coins. But at sea the individual must make his own amusement or become a victim of that brooding melancholy from which so many sailors suffer. A sailing-ship has always reminded me of the Middle Ages, for on board a sailing-ship one meets with the last traces of the medieval temper. One sees in a forecastle or in a half-deck the creation of arts to fill the emptiness of life. There is no newspaper, no beer, and no music-hall when once the ship is out of soundings,[1] so that we find sailors at sea acting precisely as the people of the Middle Ages acted, and as the country-folk of quiet districts act today. In the dogwatches (or at least the second dogwatch), when the day's work about decks is over, and the night-watch is not yet set, the sailors beguile the time just as the old folk beguiled it in the past, in the days when wandering minstrels found a welcome in every tavern. I have seen the most of a ship's company sitting as still as statues listening to a yarn about a ghost, and I remember a young seaman getting 'a bloody coxcomb'[2] for rising from his place while a song was being sung. On one eventful passage I remember how a sailor was 'sent to Coventry'[3] for the whole homeward voyage because he would not subscribe to the joint purchase of an accordion, a musical instrument on which one of the men performed. The crew clubbed together to buy the musician his instrument, so that, like 'Arion on the dolphin's back',[4] he might play to them when work was done. One man refused to subscribe, and his refusal was visited upon him by the displeasure of all hands. I remember the man wandering about like a sort of Ishmael[5] during the night-watches, finding no one to talk with, no one to beg a chew[6] from, and no one to lie beside in the pleasant trade winds when we slept our watches through.

Some of the yarns spun by the fo'c's'le hands are scarcely suited to quotation, and I have heard songs sung by an entire crew in chorus such as no compositor could set without danger to his morals. These yarns and songs are more common now among sailors than some forty years ago, when passages were longer and sailors more of a race apart. They raise a laugh always, but they are always less popular than the old stories, which are more purely folk-tales. Of these the most popular are those which tell of sailors who get the better of the mate, or 'the old man', or the landsman, or the devil. Fanciful and beautiful stories were common enough at one time, though now one must search hard enough to find them. The songs have also deteriorated. The music-hall has sent its lyrics afloat, and beautiful old songs like 'Spanish Ladies',[7] 'Bunclody'[8] and 'The tide is flowing'[9] are now seldom heard. It is, however, something that the art is reverenced even in its decadence. A good singer, a clever story-teller, a nimble dancer, or a musician is always looked upon with reverence. I remember an old sailor who refused to criticize the faulty seamanship of a mate on the ground that 'he sings pretty good', as though any touch of art were sufficient to cover all shortcomings. To the simple mind the 'gifted' man is one to praise or to dread. It is dangerous to speak ill of such a one. 'They have ways of hearing things,' as an old Irish fisherman once remarked to a friend of mine.

One winter night, off the Horn[10] (I was aboard a sailing-ship at that time), a green sea came flooding over the deck-house where I lived, smashing the skylight, and leaving two or three feet of water to wash the chests about. It broke the little 'bogey' stove at which we were accustomed to boil cocoa after our tricks at the wheel and look-out. I therefore took my cocoa tin and pot-hook to the fo'c's'le, where I knew I should find a fire and a welcome. The watch was just come below when I got there, and the space was filled with sailors who were busy taking off their oilskins and wringing the water from their shirts. They gave me leave to use their stove, and I set to work to make my brew, noting how warm, dry, and comfortable the fo'c's'le was, compared to the filthy kennel, knee-deep in water, from which I had come. As I watched my pot, the sailors lit their pipes, hung their wet gear to dry, and fell to sleep or to yarning,

as the fancy took them. 'There was a sailor once,' said one old
man, 'and I think he wasn't much use at it anyway. By dad, I
don't think it. And he went to sea one time in one of them old
tea-clippers, the Thames to Canton River;[11] the *Nancy Strang*
her name was. So when they gets to setting the watch the first
night after leaving the Downs, the mate he comes to this feller.
"What are *you* doing?" he says. "What's *your* name?" "My
name's Jack," he says. "You don't mean it?" says the mate.
"Well, Jack," he says, "just nip aloft there with a can of slush[12]
and grease the main royal mast; the skysail panel don't work
easy." So Jack he greases down the royal mast, and it took him
the best part of an hour, and down he come. "I greased the royal
mast," he says. "Oh, have you, Jack?" says the mate. "Well,
Jack," he says, "just nip up and overhaul them fore-skysail
buntlines." So he do that too, and down he come. "I overhauled
them buntlines," he says. "Have you, Jack?" says the mate.
"Why, then, you'll want a job, Jack," he says; "just nip aloft
again and see if the main topgallant staysail cliphooks is
moused." So he do that too. Well, all that voyage it was "Jack,
just nip aloft and see what's fouling the weather main skysail
brace-block"; or "Jack, shin up that skysail pole and clear the
truck halliards"; or "Jack, aft with you with a scraper and
scrape the end of the gaff." Every nasty little worriting[13] job
they give to him. It was Jack this, and Jack that, and Jack do the
other thing, till he was fairly twisted with it, the same as Bar-
ney's bull.[14] So when they come to Canton River he was all wore
to skin and bone. "Jump in the boat there, Jack," they says,
"and clean her out ready for the old man to go ashore." "I will,
indeed," he says, "when my mother's cows come home,"[15] he
says. And he give a run and jump, and over the side he goes, and
into Canton River, and up the bank into the town. "I'll swallow
the anchor of that there hooker," he says. "I ain't going to be
wore to skin and bone," he says; "having my old iron worked
up," he says. "Jack this, and Jack that, and Jack lay aft till I
ground you into bath-brick. Enough of that," he says. So he lays
low among all them yellow chows,[16] and he watches the *Nancy
Strang* as she sails for the Thames. "A good riddance, you hun-
gry, cruel, sailor's misery," he says. And he goes and ships in a

Yankee packet[17] bound for the Mersey. Well, the first night out
the second mate comes to him. "What's *your* name?" he says.
Well, he'd had enough of Christian names on the trip out, that
fellow had. So he lets on he's a stammerer. So he says, "M M M
M M M M," like he couldn't speak straight. "*What* name?"
says the second mate. "M M M M M," he says. "O snakes!"
says the second mate, "be darned if we haven't got a dumby
aboard. O, set down," he says. "Go and take a set down. You
can give it me in writing in the morning. Here you there, Bill,"
he says. "Up to the main skysail there and unreeve the truck
halliards." So Jack he lies low all the run home, and not a single
stroke did he get called on for, and in a Yankee ship at that.'

Anty Bligh

One night in the tropics I was 'farmer' in the middle watch –
that is, I had neither 'wheel' nor 'look-out' to stand during the
four hours I stayed on deck. We were running down the North-
east Trades, and the ship was sailing herself, and the wind was
gentle, and it was very still on board, the blocks whining as she
rolled, and the waves talking, and the wheel-chains clanking,
and a light noise aloft of pattering and tapping. The sea was all
pale with moonlight, and from the lamp-room door, where the
watch was mustered, I could see a red stain on the water from
the port sidelight. The mate was walking the weather-side of
the poop, while the boatswain sat on the booby-hatch hum-
ming an old tune and making a sheath for his knife. The watch
were lying on the deck, out of the moonlight, in the shadow of
the break of the poop. Most of them were sleeping, propped
against the bulkhead. One of them was singing a new chanty he
had made, beating out the tune with his pipe-stem, in a little
quiet voice that fitted the silence of the night.

> 'Ha! ha! Why don't you blow?
> O ho!
> Come, roll him over . . .'[1]

repeated over and over again, as though he could never tire of
the beauty of the words and the tune.

Presently he got up from where he was and came over to me.
He was one of the best men we had aboard – a young Dane
who talked English like a native. We had had business dealings
during the dogwatch, some hours before, and he had bought a
towel from me, and I had let him have it cheap, as I had one or
two to spare.[2] He sat down beside me, and began a conversa-
tion, discussing a number of sailor matters, such as the danger
of sleeping in the moonlight, the poison supposed to lurk in
cold boiled potatoes, and the folly of having a good time in
port. From these we passed to the consideration of piracy, col-
ouring our talk with anecdotes of pirates. 'Ah, there was no
pirate,' said my friend, 'like old Anty Bligh of Bristol. Dey hung
old Anty Bligh off of the Brazils. He was the core and the
strands of an old rogue, old Anty Bligh was. Dey hung old Anty
Bligh on Fernando Noronha, where the prison is.[3] And he
walked after, Anty Bligh did. That shows how bad he was.'
'How did he walk?' I asked. 'Let's hear about him.' 'Oh, they
jest hung him,' replied my friend, 'like they'd hang anyone else,
and they left him on the gallows after. Dey thought old Anty
was too bad to bury, I guess. And there was a young Spanish
captain on the island in dem times. Frisco Baldo his name was.
He was a terror. So the night dey hung old Anty, Frisco was
getting gorgeous wid some other captains in a kind of a drink-
ing chanty. And de other captains say to Frisco, "I bet you a
month's pay you won't go and put a rope round Anty's legs."
And "I bet you a new suit of clothes you won't put a bowline
around Anty's ankles." And "I bet you a cask of wine you won't
put Anty's feet in a noose." "I bet you I will," says Frisco Baldo.
"What's a dead man anyways," he says, "and why should I be
feared of Anty Bligh? Give us a rope," he says, "and I'll lash
him up with seven turns, like a sailor would a hammock." So
he drinks up his glass, and gets a stretch of rope, and out he
goes into the dark to where the gallows stood. It was a new
moon dat time, and it was as dark as the end of a sea-boot and
as blind as the toe. And the gallows was right down by the sea
dat time because old Anty Bligh was a pirate. So he comes up

under the gallows, and there was old Anty Bligh hanging. And
"Way-ho, Anty," he says. "Lash and carry, Anty," he says. "I'm
going to lash you up like a hammock." So he slips a bowline
around Anty's feet.' . . . Here my informant broke off his yarn
to light his pipe. After a few puffs he went on.

'Now when a man's hanged in hemp,' he said gravely, 'you
mustn't never touch him with what killed him, for fear he
should come to life on you. You mark that. Don't you forget it.
So soon as ever Frisco Baldo sets that bowline around Anty's
feet, old Anty looks down from his noose, and though it was
dark, Frisco Baldo could see him plain enough. "Thank you,
young man," said Anty; "just cast that turn off again. Burn
my limbs," he says, "if you ain't got a neck!⁴ And now climb
up here," he says, "and take my neck out of the noose. I'm as
dry as a cask of split peas." Now you may guess that Frisco
Baldo feller he come out all over in a cold sweat. "Git a gait on⁵
you," says Anty. "I ain't going to wait up here to please you."
So Frisco Baldo climbs up, and a sore job he had of it getting
the noose off Anty. "Get a gait on you," says Anty, "and go
easy with them clumsy hands of yours. You'll give me a sore
throat," he says, "the way you're carrying on. Now don't let
me fall plop," says Anty. "Lower away handsomely," he says.
"I'll make you a weary one if you let me fall plop," he says. So
Frisco lowers away handsomely, and Anty comes to the ground,
with the rope off of him, only he still had his head to one side
like he'd been hanged. "Come here to me," he says. So Frisco
Baldo goes over to him. And Anty he jest put one arm round
his neck and gripped him tight and cold. "Now march," he
says; "march me down to the grog-shop and get me a dram.
None of your six water dollops,⁶ neither," he says; "I'm as dry
as a foul block,"⁷ he says. So Frisco and Anty they go to the
grog-shop, and all the while Anty's cold fingers was playing
down Frisco's neck. And when they got to der grog-shop der
captains was all fell asleep. So Frisco takes the bottle of rum
and Anty laps it down like he'd been used to it. "Ah!" he says,
"thank ye," he says; "and now down to the Mole⁸ with ye," he
says, "and we'll take a boat," he says; "I'm going to England,"
he says, "to say goodbye to me mother." So Frisco he come out

all over in a cold sweat, for he was feared of the sea; but Anty's
cold fingers was fiddling on his neck, so he t'ink he better go.
And when dey come to der Mole there was a boat there – one
of these perry-acks,[9] as they call them – and Anty he says, "You
take the oars," he says. "I'll steer," he says, "and every time
you catch a crab,"[10] he says, "you'll get such a welt as you'll
remember." So Frisco shoves her off and rows out of the har-
bour, with old Anty Bligh at the tiller, telling him to put his
beef[11] on and to watch out he didn't catch no crabs. And he
rowed, and he rowed, and he rowed, and every time he caught
a crab – whack! he had it over the sconce with the tiller. And
der perry-ack it went a great holy big skyoot,[12] ninety knots in
der quarter of an hour, so they soon sees the Bull Point Light
and der Shutter Light,[13] and then the lights of Bristol. "Oars,"
said Anty. "Lie on your oars," he says; "we got way enough."
Then dey makes her fast to a dock-side and dey goes ashore,
and Anty has his arm round Frisco's neck, and "March," he
says; "step lively," he says; "for Johnny comes marching home,"
he says. By and by they come to a little house with a light in the
window. "Knock at the door," says Anty. So Frisco knocks,
and in they go. There was a fire burning in the room and some
candles on the table, and there, by the fire, was a very old, ugly
woman in a red flannel dress, and she'd a ring in her nose and
a black cutty pipe[14] between her lips. "Good evening, mother,"
says Anty. "I come home," he says. But the old woman she just
looks at him but never says nothing. "It's your son Anty that's
come home to you," he says again. So she looks at him again
and, "Aren't you ashamed of yourself, Anty," she says, "com-
ing home the way you are? Don't you repent your goings-on?"
she says. "Dying disgraced," she says, "in a foreign land, with
none to lay you out." "Mother," he says, "I repent in blood,"
he says. "You'll not deny me my rights?" he says. "Not since
you repent," she says. "Them as repents I got no quarrel with.
You was always a bad one, Anty," she says, "but I hoped you'd
come home in the end. Well, and now you're come," she says.
"And I must bathe that throat of yours," she says. "It looks as
though you been hit by something." "Be quick, mother," he
says; "it's after midnight now," he says.

'So she washed him in wine, the way you wash a corpse, and put him in a white linen shroud, with a wooden cross on his chest, and two silver pieces on his eyes, and a golden marigold between his lips. And together they carried him to the perry-ack and laid him in the stern-sheets. "Give way, young man," she says; "give way like glory. Pull, my heart of blood," she says, "or we'll have the dawn on us." So he pulls, that Frisco Baldo does, and the perry-ack makes big southing – a degree a minute – and they comes ashore at the Mole just as the hens was settling to their second sleep. "To the churchyard," says the old woman; "you take his legs." So they carries him to the churchyard at the double. "Get a gait on you," says Anty. "I feel the dawn in my bones," he says. "My wraith'll chase you if you ain't in time," he says. And there was an empty grave, and they put him in it, and shovelled in the clay, and the old woman poured out a bottle on the top of it. "It's holy water," she says. "It'll make his wraith rest easy." Then she runs down to the sea's edge and gets into the perry-ack. And immediately she was hull down beyond the horizon, and the sun came up out of the sea, and the cocks cried cock-a-doodle in the hen-roost, and Frisco Baldo falls down into a swound. He was a changed man from that out.'

'Lee fore brace,' said the mate above us. 'Quit your chin-ning[15] there, and go forward to the rope.'

The Devil and the Deep Sea

Once upon a time, said the old sailor, there was a man with neither luck nor go, whose name was Billy the Spoon.[1] He was by way of being a farmer, but he didn't make much hand of it, and a man who can't make a show at an easy job the like of that, he didn't ought to be about. He used to go around the cowhouse mooning when he ought to have been setting out the cabbages; so he soon run into debt, carrying on in that way. And who would lend money to a lad like him? And when he got into debt he took to hitting the rum. And at last the next

day was rent-day, and he hadn't got not one red cent,[2] nor as
much credit as would put new trousers on a scarecrow. So there
he sets in his room with an empty pipe and a dry pot, like one
of these figureheads they sets up on the Slip. First he thinks of
the rent, and then he thinks of the landlord, and whichever way
it was it seemed pretty fierce. 'Ah,' he says, 'I wish I could sell
my soul to the devil, like the men in the books.' And immejitly
he said that he pops up from the fire, the devil does, and 'Hey,'
he says, 'Billy the Spoon,' he says, 'how would these terms suit
you?' So Billy made a bargain with the devil, and signed it with
his blood, and the agreement was like this. Billy was to have all
his heart's desire in everything for the next twenty years. Not a
thing that he wanted should he want, no matter what it was.
But at the end of the twenty years the devil was to come for
Billy, and then there was to be the fire for Billy from that out.

Well, for nineteen years and nine months Billy had a thun-
dering good time. He ate of the best, he slept in silk, he dressed
in satin and in velvet, and he never drank what was cheaper
than claret wine. But when his time was getting close he became
very solemn in the gills with it, and he got a long face on him
like a mute at a burying. And 'Oh,' he keeps saying, 'whatever
shall I do? Whatever shall I do? Whatever, oh, whatever shall I
do?' till one would have thought the ship was sinking. So at last
he threw up all he had – riches, position, everything – and away
he goes to Liverpool, where he signs on as an ordinary seaman
before the mast. His ship was one of those old China tea-
clippers, the Mersey to Shanghai, and of course he had only to
just wish and any job he was set to he could do. So they cast off
the tug, and away they bowl to the south. Set the skysails, Bill.
Ay, ay, sir. Out studdingsails; let her sink or bear it. They knew
how to sail ships in them days. So at last, when there was only
three days more to run, there they lay becalmed in the Indian
Ocean.

Now that forenoon watch it was Billy's trick at the wheel, so
there he stood on the grating, hanging on to the spokes, blub-
bering like a boy that had his tart stole. 'Oh,' he keeps saying,
'whatever shall I do? Whatever shall I do? Whatever *shall* I
do?' till you'd have longed to hit him one. By and by the old

man came on deck to take the sun, and the mate went below to take the time by the chronometer.

'Hullo!' says the old man, 'what's wrong with *you*, Billy? Have you got the turn-down from your girl?' he says. 'You'd best let me give you a dose of jalap,'[3] he says, 'and that'll set you right. What ails you anyway? Have you anything on your mind?' he says.

'Captain,' he says, 'I sold my soul to the devil. In only three days more the devil will take me to the fire, and there I shall burn,' he says.

'Why, come,' says the old man, 'that's bad, that is. Very bad I call that. But come,' he says, 'did the devil give you no chance, no saving clause, like, in that agreement that you made?'

'Yes, sir,' says Billy. 'If I can give the devil three things to do which he can't do, why then that agreement it ain't worth the paper that it's wrote upon. But what's the good of a chance like that?' he says.

'Never you mind about that,' says the old man, 'you go and have a sleep. I'll fix the devil for you.' And he sends Billy forward to his bunk. And so the time passes till the day the devil was to come.

Early that morning the old man called all hands and told them to clap a handy billy on the main-topsail halliards and to bowse the main-topsail stiff up and down till it set as stiff as a plank. So they do that, and then poured water on the sail till it set without a wrinkle. Then he told them to lower his dinghy down and let her drag alongside. So they do that too. Then he says, 'Rouse out the port cable and range her clear for running.' So they do that too. And the old man shackles a couple of spare anchors and a ton of holystone and a sail full of ballast to the business end. 'Away there to the galley,' he says, 'and fetch them tubs of slush,'[4] he says, 'and slush that chain an inch thick in grease,' he says. So they down on their knees and do that too. 'Now go all hands,' he says, 'all except the carpenter.' 'Chips,' he cries, 'up on the fo'c's'le with you, and stand by to let go anchor when I sing out.' So all hands go below, and Chips goes forward to the fo'c's'le-head, and immediately a great cloud of brimstone comes alongside, with a flash of lightning, and the devil steps aboard.

'Good morning, captain,' says the devil, 'I come for one of your hands. Don't keep me waiting, please. I got a lot to do these times.'

'Ah, Mr Devil,' says the old man, 'supposing I just set you them three jobs to do. It's a pity to wake poor Billy till it's time.'

'Shove ahead,' says the devil, 'ask all you please. Them as don't ask don't want,' he says.

'Well, Mr Devil,' says the old man, 'just nip up to that main-topsail yard and take in three reefs in my main-topsail.'

'Ay, ay, sir,' says the devil, and he nips up aloft and lays out on the yard and reaches over to gather in the slack. Now the sail was stiff up and down, like a board, so of course there wasn't any slack. So the devil hails the deck. 'Lower away your halliards,' he shouts. 'The sail's stiff up and down.'

'I will not lower away my halliards,' says the old man.

'Then come up your sheets,' says the devil. 'How am I to reef a sail that's like a board?'

'You can't do it,' says the old man. 'You can't do it. Neither you nor no one else,' he says. 'Come down from aloft, me son. That's one to me.'

'That's one to you,' says the devil. 'One up and two to play. Let's hear the next.'

So the old man takes him to the rail and shows him the dinghy dragging alongside. 'Get into that there little dinghy,' he says. So the devil jumps in and takes a set down in the stern-sheets. 'Now, Mr Devil,' says the old man, 'take this pretty little salt spoon,' he says 'and bale all the water on this side the boat on to that side the boat with this here pretty little spoon.' And he give he devil a salt spoon to do the baling with. So the devil he look at the old man pretty straight.

'You're a credit, you are,' he says, 'to your profession,' he says. 'One don't get no change out of you,' he says. 'That's two to you,' he says. 'Two up and a third to play. Now what's your next contraption?'

'Now, Mr Devil,' says the old man, 'I'm going to let go my anchor, and as the chain runs out I want you to stopper it with them pretty hands of yours, so as to keep it from running out clear.'

'I am ready,' says the devil.

'Are ye ready forrard, Chips?'

'All ready, sir,' says Chips.

'Then let go your anchor.'

Bang, clip, goes the hammer on the pin, and away goes the anchor, and the ballast and the holystone, rattlety jam, hurrah for Joseph,[5] mind your eye and stand from under. And of course the chain was jumping up and down like Barney's bull,[6] and every time the devil made a grab at it it slipped from his hands and hit him a whang across the gills. So at last, when his hands was all cut to junk, he ran to the great last link of all, which is seized to the heel of the foremast. And he set both his arms through it and held on like grim death. But when the chain was all run out it came to against that link with such a yank that it broke it short off at the seizing, and it took the devil out at the hawseholes, in a shower of sparks like shooting stars. The water bubbled and boiled for a few moments, but the devil never rose. 'Three and game,' says the old man. 'It'll be nice and cooling for him where he is. On deck there, you set of come-day-go-days. Get on deck with you. One of you lay aft to the wheel. Hoist my dinghy inboard, and then lay aft for your lime juice.'

In Dock – II

'Now, turn out here, young fellers! Show a leg and put a stocking on it.'

It was the watchman, a lank, grizzled seaman, giving us the news of daybreak. 'What time is it?'

'Half-past five; so turn out an' get yer coffee. You'll turn-to at six o'clock.'

We turned out of our bunks in a tired, dead-and-alive kind of way, feeling the sleep still rusty in our bones, and our eyes gummy, and our mouths foul. The half-deck had a vile, close smell of stale tobacco in it, and the dawn through the open door looked cheerless as an ashpit. One wanted a cold bath, and a shower bath, and a toothbrush to cleanse away that physical discomfort clinging to us like dirt. But there was no possibility of these things, we knew, until the evening. We turned out dully, and sat on our chests rubbing our drowsy eyes and blinking at each other. 'Go forrard for the coffee, some-one,' said our first-voyager, and I plodded heavily forward with the sixpenny tin kettle in my hand. It is the custom of the sea to drink coffee before turning-to in the morning, and the custom obtains as much in dock as on blue water. The custom is a good custom, and, for a profession so cruel as that of ship-owner, a generous custom, but the coffee is too bad for words. We used to drink it because it was sometimes hot; the only flavour it ever had was a strange twang of tin, 'or metal sick', barely tempered by a taste of ship's molasses. The cook, a sleepy Welshman, red in the eye from his drinkings overnight, filled my kettle sourly, holding a tender nose away from the fumes from the copper.

We drank our coffee hurriedly, eating the last of our shore-buns to take the taste away. We had barely commenced to smoke when the second mate peered in at us from the door. 'Turn-to, here,' he said curtly.

We trooped out on deck just as the clock over the warehouse struck six. It was chilly on deck, and comfortless, but we were not there to think of comfort. We were marched aft to the sail locker in a body, there to 'wrastle out'[1] staysails to bend before breakfast. I was put to bend the main topmast and topgallant staysails, a piece of work which necessitates a nice sense of balance in the performer. The bender goes aloft, say, a hundred and twenty feet, and seats himself astride on a cruel hard wire rope about as thick as a broomstick. He then has to lean gingerly forward and work, with both hands and every muscle above his belt, at a heavy sail dangling underneath him. When you come down from aloft after bending staysails you wonder why you left home. We worked in this way until about half-past seven, when we were called down to get out buckets and brooms and wash the poop down. This was a regular morning task, and had only one unpleasant feature. The water for the washing-down was drawn from the dock. We were high in the water, and every bucket drawn had to be pulled up by hand some twenty feet or more. And this is in a hurry, working navy fashion, like a red streak of sparks, with the third mate's voice in our ears. 'Now, holy Joseph, there, you spill that bucket an' I'll put you scrapin' the sty.'

Before the poop had been cleaned, broomed down and passed by the third mate as 'you' ('that's you', the sea-phrase for any exquisite contentment with labour done), the postman ashore hailed us and I took the boat in for the mail.

Then it was eight o'clock, and we were knocked off for breakfast. This meal was a repetition of the supper of the night before, a tasteless and beastly rendering of old scraps. We talked, while at food, on the probable nature of the coming day's work. We had heard the two mates talking ominously of 'stores', and we knew that, if the ship's stores were coming on board that morning, a stiff day's labour was in pickle for us. For six boys to hoist up and stow fifteen tons of various kinds of stores during one working day is a tolerable achievement. The stores had to be hoisted from the lighter, dragged or carried to the hatch, lowered into the 'tweendecks, dragged or carried to the lazarette, and there stored as the steward wished. When we came on deck again at 8.30 we found, sure enough, a great lighter full of potato sacks coming alongside of us. Our first job was to get them on deck by means of a 'slings and tackle'. Each sack weighed 175 pounds, and had to be carried on the back for a distance of some ten weary yards. 175 pounds is 1,750 pounds after ten yards. Disbelievers may try for themselves. We were only lads, and the sacks were too heavy for us to bear, at any rate, with grace. The mates jeered at us. 'Great snakes there, you, you're shaking like a gory leaf. What the divil's ailin' you? You might be carryin' nitre[2] the way you shape.'

The day went over us, with a short spell for dinner, like an ill dream full of strain. We got at last into a dulled mechanical state in which, at times, we shoved casks, at other times carried boxes or dragged sacks. Voices spoke to us at times and damned us for inattention. The trouble with us was that at half-past three we were all six of us too dead-beat to care a red cent[3] what we did, or how. Lighter after lighter left us, but there were always others ready at hand whenever the grimy bargeman cast loose and waved us farewell. Now it was heavy red-lead[4] in casks, or turps, or oil, or paint, or tar, or new hemp rope, or new blocks, or manilla,[5] or coir. Then it would be food again. 'Prime mess beef', or 'prime mess pork', or split peas, or onions in ropes, or bread in bags, or fancy goods (for the cabin) in boxes.

Our hands were full of splinters, bleeding at the finger-tips, and quite raw down the palm. I don't know how I did what I did that afternoon, but I suppose it was just the sense of duty that had been drilled into me till it was a habit. Soldiers and sailors are like that, I think; they have the collective wisdom of the sheep, the unquestioning mind of the running guinea-pig. Tell them to do a thing, and they will do it, and keep on doing it until they drop. It seems a goodish quality in print; in real life it is goodish only for those who do the telling. When we cast loose the last lighter that afternoon we sank gasping against the fife-rail. 'Great snakes,' roared the second mate, 'what are you knocking off for? You ain't washed down yet. Get the brooms along, and man the head-pump, two of you.'

Towards seven o'clock that evening six utterly tired lads sat upon chests and blinked at each other stupidly in the twilight. They were too dead-fagged to eat, or to wash, or to sing, or to speak, or to undress and turn in. They sat there stupidly for twenty minutes, not saying a word, blinking at each other like owls. They had looked labour in the face, and the exceeding glory of her countenance had smitten them dumb.

A Port Royal Twister

Once upon a time, said the Jamaican in the tavern, there was an English buccaneer who lived in a Port Royal[1] slum. He was a poisonous great ruffian, tattooed with a gallows upon each cheek. The sun had burnt him to the colour of old brandy. He wore a pigtail that was knotted in a strip of bunting. His trousers were of faded scarlet, having been dyed in bullock's blood. He had golden earrings made of double Spanish guineas in his ears. His hat was of fine grey Lima felt, with a brim a yard across and a crown that tapered to a point. He had always a pair of pistols in his belt, a pair of oaths upon his lips, and a pair of deadly sins upon his conscience. Billy Blood was his name, but his shipmates spoke of him as Bloody Bill.

Now Billy came home from a cruise one time with a sack of Spanish gold. He landed from his ship and went to a tavern, as is the custom among sailors. He called for rum and a clean clay pipe. He sat down at a table, with his sack of gold before him. 'You may bring more rum,' he said, 'whenever I bang my pot. If Cut-throat Jake and Jim the Cowboy come here,' he said, 'you'd best tell them where I am.' By and by Jim and Jake arrived at the tavern. 'Oh, happy day,' they said, 'which brings back Bloody Bill. Ramon,' they said, 'Ramon, you barrel-tilter, fetch rum – much rum – that we may welcome home our friend.' So Ramon, the little tavern lad, went and tapped a new cask, and the three friends laughed very heartily when they espied his perspicacity. Then they set to serious drinking in honour of that so fortunate return.

Towards three in the morning, Billy took a bottle of brandy and poured it into a bowl. 'Let us have some burnt brandy,'[2] he remarked. 'Burnt brandy crowns the night,' replied his comrades. 'Ho! bring in a light there, Ramon.' Having lit the brandy they danced solemnly about it as it burned, singing a lyric of the forecastle. Then Billy seized the flaming bowl and drained it down at a gulp. The bowl dropped from his hands and shattered into fragments on the floor. He took a step backwards and a step to one side, and collapsed upon his back like a pole-axed steer.[3] His comrades strove for a moment to revive him by pouring rum down his throat. They then blacked his nose with a piece of burnt cork and rolled away home with a song.

Now, when Billy collapsed upon the floor it seemed to him that he fell and fell and fell, as though he were a pebble going over a precipice. By and by he seemed to be brought up with a round turn, though it was all black about him – as black as so much crape. Presently he thought he saw a sort of a gleam in the blackness, like a slug's track upon a cellar wall or a dead crab in the caves here. Then he thought he heard the ticking of a dropping water-clock,[4] like those you buy in Lima. Then he heard a great whirr of birds, like zips,[5] going by in a covey, and immediately all the birds laughed, like so many people at a pantomime. Then there came a roar and bang, as though he had been fired from a gun, and there he was, blinking like an owl, in a little low room, lit by many candles, with a fire at the one end in an open iron basket. Now, what frightened Billy Blood was the folk who sat there, for there was a table with benches round it, and people sitting at their drink. They weren't nice people either, not in the least like you or me, for though each wore a sort of red cloak, they had the heads of snakes, and they were smoking long clay pipes, and they were laughing in a sort of hissy chuckle. And there was a great Goat-Snake sitting at the head of the table, and whenever he spoke it sent a cold dew along Billy's spine. 'Come here,' he said, 'Billy Blood. Do you know what's going to be done with you?' 'No, sir,' said Billy; 'if you please, sir, I'd rather not.' And directly he said that the room became dark, and it seemed to Billy that he was on the loneliest island of the world – on Desolation Island, to the south of the Diego Ramirez.[6] It was very cold. It snowed in continual little flurries. There was a snarling green sea getting up. There was night and misery rolling in from the south and west. Oh, a bitter place it seemed – a bitter place. Then there came a gull flying past, blowing in the wind like a scrap of dirty paper. 'Wheu, wheu, wheu,' it cried. 'Billy Blood, my son; Billy Blood, my son; wheu, wheu, wheu, and so you are here.' And Billy knew the voice to be the voice of old Captain Morgan,[7] his old captain. And immediately he felt that he too was changing to a gull; he felt that his feet were webbing and his nose growing into spoon shape. Then there came a great cackling and crying, and thither came a swarm of Cape pigeons. 'Wheu, wheu,' they cried, 'here's old Billy Blood, old Bloody Bill, old brandy-bows.' And Billy knew them to be his old shipmates, for one by one he recognized them. There was Ned that they left behind on the Chagres;[8] there was Joe that was shot at Panama; there was Jack that got the fever at St Mary; there were Bill and Dick that the Spaniards hung, and Jimmy that was drowned in the surf. And he felt that his skin was coming out in spots, in black and white mottles like the pigeons. Then there came a busy multitude of penguins, swimming on the waves and slapping at the water with their flappers. They laughed and mewed as they swam, and pecked at anything they saw. And Bill knew them to be the old buccaneers of the past, the men who had sailed with Drake,[9] the men of Algiers and Thelemark[10] – all the old raiders who had died in their shirts since water drowned. And he felt that his arms were shrinking into flappers, that his chest was getting scaly, and that his blood was three-parts oil, like a Valparaiso salad. 'Let me out of this!' he screamed; 'let me out of this!' And immediately he was back in the little room, with the red-cloaked snakes still smoking at the table and laughing in a sort of hissy chuckle.

'Well, Billy Blood,' said the fat black Goat-Snake, 'now you know what's going to be done to you.' 'Oh, sir,' said Billy, 'please, sir, not. Not that, sir; not a bird – not a gulley[11] that the reefers catch with pork fat. Anything but that, sir,' he said. 'Why not?' said the Goat-Snake; 'why shouldn't you be a gul-ley? Haven't you lied and robbed and drunk and killed till your blood is three-parts rum and your soul a thick black blot of guilt? Why shouldn't you be a gulley like your precious com-rades?' Billy didn't find it easy to make an answer. 'Well,' said the Goat-Snake, 'answer me. Why shouldn't you be a gulley? Did you ever do a single good act – one single good act – since you came to be a grown-up man?' So Billy thought for a long time. Then he said, 'Please, sir, I gave a blind beggar a quoit of gold that time I was ashore in Honduras.' 'A lot of good that'll do to you,' said the Goat-Snake. 'Weren't you drunk at the time?' 'Not exactly drunk, sir,' said Billy, 'not drunk exactly. That wasn't it. Only just merry or so.' 'And didn't you do it by mistake?' said the Goat-Snake. 'Didn't you intend to give him the little brass plate you'd stolen from the medicine chest?' 'I did, sir,' said Billy; 'it's true. Only I was the poorer for it. It was a good deed that way.' 'A gulley you must be,' said the Goat-Snake. 'I never heard a paltrier excuse.' 'Please, sir,' said Billy, 'there was a good deed I did when I was a lad at school.' 'Any port in a storm,' said the Goat-Snake. 'What was that?' 'Sir,' said Billy, 'one time they tried to get me to come and rob an orchard. "No," I said. "It's a widow's orchard. I will not rob a widow's orchard with any man." Wasn't that a good deed I'd like to know?' 'A lot of good that'll do to you,' said the Goat-Snake. 'Didn't you pinch the boys' cakes as soon as they were gone to get the apples? Wasn't that why you refused to go – so that you might rob their dinner baskets?' 'You're so hard on a feller,' said Billy; 'you don't give one half a chance.' 'A gulley you must be,' said the Goat-Snake. 'I can't think how you were taught. I never met such a man.' 'There was a good deed I did, sir; really there was, sir,' said Billy, 'when I was a little babe in shorts.' 'Better crust than supperless,' said the Goat-Snake. 'But I must say you run it rather fine. What was that, I wonder?' 'Sir,' said Billy, 'one time when I was teething I kept from yelling in the night, so that my poor mother got a little sleep.' 'I dare say they'd given you a sleeping draught,' said the Goat-Snake. 'But we'll let it go at that. You shall not be a gulley unless you come here again. But you mind your eye, my son. I'm not a jesting person.'

And Billy woke up with a screech on the tavern floor where he had fallen, and he swore off rum from that day. He lived to be churchwarden down to Dartmouth, and was actually buried in the nave.

Ambitious Jimmy Hicks

'Well,' said the captain of the foretop to me, 'it's our cutter today, and you're the youngest hand, and you'll be bowman. Can you pull an oar?' 'No,' I answered. 'Well, you'd better pull one today, my son, or mind your eye. You'll climb Zion's Hill[1] tonight if you go catching any crabs.'[2] With that he went swaggering along the deck, chewing his quid of sweet-cake.[3] I thought lugubriously of Zion's Hill, a very different place from the one in the Bible, and the longer I thought, the chillier came the sweat on my palms. 'Away cutters,' went the pipe a moment later. 'Down to your boat, foretopmen.' I skidded down the gangway into the bows of the cutter, and cast the turns from the painter, keeping the boat secured by a single turn. A strong tide was running, and the broken water was flying up in spray. Dirty water ran in trickles down my sleeves. The thwarts were wet. A lot of dirty water was slopping about in the well. 'Bowman,' said the captain of the foretop, 'why haven't you cleaned your boat out?' 'I didn't know I had to.' 'Well, next time you don't know we'll jolly well duck you in it. Let go forrard. Back a stroke, starboard. Down port, and shove her off.' 'Where are we going?' asked the stroke. 'We're goin' to the etceteraed slip to get the etceteraed love-letters. Now look alive in the bows there. Get your oars out and give way. If I come forward with the tiller your heads'll ache for a week.' I got out my oar, or rather I got out the oar which had been left to me. It was one of the midship oars, the longest and heaviest in the boat. With this I made a shift to pull till we neared the slip, when I had to lay my oar in, gather up the painter, and stand by to leap on to the jetty to make the boat fast as we came alongside. I have known some misery in my time, but the agony of that moment, wondering if I should fall headlong on the slippery green weed, in the sight of the old sailors smoking there, was as bitter as any I have suffered. The cutter's nose rubbed the dangling seaweed. I made a spring, slipped, steadied myself, cast the painter round the mooring-hook, and made the boat fast. 'A round turn and two half hitches,' I murmured, as I passed the turns, 'and a third half hitch for luck.' 'Come off with your third half hitch,' said one of the old sailors. 'You and your three half hitches. You're like Jimmy Hicks, the come-day-go-day. You want to do too much, you do. You'd go dry the keel with a towel, wouldn't you, rather than take a caulk?[4] Come off with your third hitch.'

Late that night I saw the old sailor in the lamp-room, cleaning the heavy copper lamps. I asked if I might help him, for I wished to hear the story of Jimmy Hicks. He gave me half a dozen lamps to clean, with a mass of cotton waste and a few rags, most of them the relics of our soft cloth working caps. 'Heave round, my son,' he said, 'and get an appetite for your supper.' When I had cleaned two or three of my lamps I asked him to tell me about Jimmy Hicks.

'Ah,' he said, 'you want to be warned by him. You're too ambitious (i.e. fond of work) altogether. Look at you coming here to clean my lamps. And you after pulling in the cutter. I wouldn't care to be like Jimmy Hicks. No. I wouldn't that. It's only young fellies like you wants to be like Jimmy Hicks.' 'Who was Jimmy Hicks?' I asked; 'and what was it he did?'

'Ah,' said the old man, 'did you ever hear tell of the Black Ball line?[5] Well, there's no ships like them ships now. You think them Cunarders[6] at the buoy there; you think them fine. You should a seen the *Red Jacket*, or the *John James Green*, or the *Thermopylæ*. By dad, that *was* a sight. Spars – talk of spars. And skysail yards on all three masts, and a flying jib-boom the angels could have picked their teeth with. Sixty-six days they took, the Thames to Sydney Heads.[7] It's never been done before nor since. Well, Jimmy Hicks he was a young, ambitious felly, the same as you. And he was in one of them ships. I was ship-mates with him myself.

'Well, of all the red-headed ambitious fellies I think Jimmy Hicks was the worst. Yes, sir. I think he was the worst. The day they got to sea the bo'sun set him to scrub the fo'c's'le. So he gets some sand and holystone and a three-cornered scraper, and he scrubs that fo'c's'le fit for an admiral. He begun that job at three bells in the morning watch, and he was doing it at eight bells, and half his watch-below he was doing it, and when they called him for dinner he was still doing it. Talk about white. White was black alongside them planks. So in the afternoon it came on to blow. Yes, sir, it breezed up. So they had to snug her down. So Jimmy Hicks he went up and made the skysails fast, and then he made the royals fast. And then he come down to see had he got a good furl on them. And then up he went again and put a new stow on the skysail. And then he went up again to tinker the main royal bunt. Them furls of his, by dad, they reminded me of Sefton Park.[8] Yes, sir; they was that like Sunday clothes.

'He was always like that. He wasn't never happy unless he was putting whippings on ropes' ends, or pointing the topgallant and royal braces, or polishing the brass on the ladders till it was as bright as gold. Always doing something. Always doing

more than his piece. The last to leave the deck and the first to
come up when hands were called. If he was told to whip a rope,
he pointed it and gave it a rub of slush[9] and Flemish-coiled it.
If he was told to broom down the top of a deck-house he got it
white with a holystone. He was like the poet –

Double, double, toil and trouble.[10]

That was Jimmy Hicks. Yes, sir, that was him. You want to be
warned by him. You hear the terrible end he come to.

'Now they was coming home in that ship. And what do you
suppose they had on board? Well, they had silks. My word they
was silks. Light as muslin. Worth a pound a fathom. All yellow
and blue and red. All the colours. And a gloss. It was like so
much moonlight. Well. They had a lot of that. Then they had
China tea, and it wasn't none of your skilly.[11] No, sir. It was tea
the King of Spain could have drunk in the golden palaces of
Rome. There was flaviour. Worth eighteen shilling a pound that
tea was. The same as the queen drunk. It was like meat that tea
was. You didn't want no meat if you had a cup of that. Worth
two hundred thousand pound that ship's freight was. And a
general in the army was a passenger. Besides a bishop.

'So as they were coming home they got caught in a cyclone,
off of the Mauritius. Whoo! You should a heard the wind. O
mommer, it just blew. And the cold green seas they kept coming
aboard. Ker-woosh, they kept coming. And the ship she groaned
and she strained, and she worked her planking open. So it was
all hands to the pumps, general and bishop and all; and they
kept pumping out tea, all ready made with salt water. That was
all they had to live on for three days. Salt-water tea. Very
wholesome it is, too, for them that like it. *And* for them that's
inclined to consumption.

'By and by the pumps choked. "The silks is in the well," said
the mate. "To your prayers, boys. We're gone up." "Hold on
with prayers," said the old man. "Get a tackle rigged and hoist
the boat out. You can pray afterwards. Work is prayer," he
says, "so long as I command." "Lively there," says the mate.
"Up there one of you with a block. Out to the mainyard arm

and rig a tackle! Lively now. Stamp and go. She's settling under us." So Jimmy Hicks seizes a tackle and they hook it on to the longboat, and Jimmy nips into the rigging with one of the blocks in his hand. And they clear it away to him as he goes. And she was settling like a stone all the time. "Look slippy there, you!" cries the mate, as Jimmy lays out on the yard. For the sea was crawling across the deck. It was time to be gone out of that.

'And Jimmy gets to the yard-arm, and he takes a round turn with his lashing, and he makes a half hitch, and he makes a second half hitch. "Yard-arm, there!" hails the mate. "May we hoist away?" "Hold on," says Jimmy, "till I make her fast," he says. And just as he makes his third half hitch and yells to them to sway away – Ker-woosh! there comes a great green sea. And down they all go – ship, and tea, and mate, and bishop, and general, and Jimmy, and the whole lash-up. All the whole lot of them. And all because he would wait to take the third half hitch. So you be warned by Jimmy Hicks, my son. And don't you be neither red-headed nor ambitious.'

The Cape Horn Calm

Off Cape Horn there are but two kinds of weather, neither one of them a pleasant kind. If you get the fine kind it is dead calm, without enough wind to lift the wind-vane. The sea lies oily and horrible, heaving in slow, solemn swells, the colour of soup. The sky closes down upon the sea all round you, the same colour as the water. The sun never shines over those seas, though sometimes there is a red flush, in the east or in the west, to hint that somewhere, very far away, there is daylight brightening the face of things.

If you are in a ship in the Cape Horn calm you forge ahead, under all sail, a quarter of a mile an hour. The swell heaves you up and drops you, in long, slow, gradual movements, in a rhythm beautiful to mark. You roll, too, in a sort of horrible crescendo, half a dozen rolls and a lull. You can never tell when she will begin to roll. She will begin quite suddenly, for no apparent reason. She will go over and over with a rattling clatter of blocks and chains. Then she will swing back, groaning along the length of her, to slat the great sails and set the reef-points flogging, to a hard clack and jangle of staysail sheets. Then over she will go again, and back, and again over, rolling further each time. At the last of her rolls there comes a clattering of tins, as the galley gear and whack pots slither across to leeward, followed by cursing seamen. The iron swing-ports bang to and fro. The straining and groaning sounds along her length. Every block aloft clacks and whines. The sea splashes up the scuppers. The sleepers curse her from their bunks for a drunken drogher.[1] Then she lets up and stands on her dignity, and rolls no more perhaps for another quarter of an hour.

It is cold, this fine variety, for little snow squalls are always blowing by, to cover the decks with soft dry snow, and to melt upon the sails. If you go aloft you must be careful what you touch. If you touch a wire shroud, or a chain sheet, the skin comes from your hand as though a hot iron had scarred it. If you but scratch your hand aloft, in that fierce cold, the scratch will suppurate.[2] I broke the skin of my hand once with a jagged scrap of wire in the main-rigging. The scratch festered so that I could not move my hand for a week. It was a little scratch, the eighth of an inch long. It has left its mark. The sailors used to prophesy that it would cause the loss of my arm.

On the whole we had an easy time of it in the Cape Horn calm. No work was being done about decks. Our rigging was all set up, our blocks all greased and overhauled, our chafing gear in its place, and the heavy-weather sails bent. When we came on deck we had little to do but stand by ready for a call, while the flurries of snow blew past and the ship's planking creaked. The old man was fond of mat-making. I don't know how he made the mats, whether with a 'sword',[3] in the usual way, or by a needle upon canvas. He used the coarse thread of bunting for his material. He made the boys unravel some old signal flags into little balls of thread while we were rolling in the swell. That was nearly all the work we did while the calm lasted.

When we were down below in the half-deck, the little room twelve feet square, where the six boys lived and slept, we were almost happy. We had rigged up a bogey stove, with a chimney which kinked[4] into elbows whenever the roll was very heavy. It did not burn very well, this bogey stove, but we contrived to cook by it. We were only allowed coke for fuel, but we always managed to steal coal enough either from the cook or from the coal-hole. It was our great delight to sit upon our chests in the dogwatch, looking at the bogey, listening to the creaking chimney, watching the smoke pouring out from the chinks. In the night-watches, when the sleepers lay quiet in their bunks behind the red baize curtains, one or two of us who kept the deck would creep below to put on coal. That was the golden time, the time of the night-watch, to sit there in the darkness among the sleepers hearing the coals click.

One of us in each night-watch made cocoa for the others. At about four bells, when the watch was half through, the cocoa-maker would slink below to put the kettle on to boil and to mix the brew in the pannikins. There is an old poet (I think it is Ben Jonson; it may be Marlowe) who asks, 'Where are there greater atheists than your cooks?'[5] I would ask, less rhythmically perhaps, 'Where are there loftier thinkers than your cocoa-makers?' Ah, what profound thoughts I thought; what mute, but Miltonic, poetry I made in that dim half-deck, by the smoky bogey, in the night, in the stillness, amid the many waters. The kings were ashore in their palaces, tossing uneasily (as who would not) upon their purple pillows. Couriers were flogging spent horses along the roads of the world, bringing news of battle, of death, of pestilence. Soldiers were going into action. Prisoners were scraping shot in the chain gang. Women were weeping, and the huntsmen were up in America. Sitting there in the dim half-deck, watching the kettle boil, I saw it all. I was like Buddha under the holy branches. My mind filled with pictures like the magical water in the bowl of a wizard.

Then what a joy it was to take the cocoa tin, containing a greasy dark stuff of cocoa and condensed milk, already mixed. One put a spoonful into each pannikin and then a spoonful of soft, brown, lumpy ship's sugar. Then with a spoon, or with a

sheath knife, one bruised the ingredients together. With what a
luscious crunch they blended! How perfect was the smell of the
crushed mixture! How it covered away, like the smell of incense
at a Mass, the rude, worldly scents, such a star, and stale Negro
Head,[6] and oilskins, and newly greased sea-boots. Then, as one
mixed, one would hear the bells struck. Ting, ting. Ting, ting.
Ting. Five bells – an hour and a half before the watch would
end. One would hear the old men of the sea, the old sailors, as
they shambled along to and fro biting on the pipe-stems, yarn-
ing about ships that were long ago bilged on the coral. One
would hear the scraps of songs, little stray verses, set to old
beautiful tunes. There was one old man who had no better
voice than a donkey. He was for ever walking the deck when I
brewed the cocoa, singing 'Rolling Home', the most popular of
all sailor-songs. I think I would rather have written 'Rolling
Home' than 'Hydriotaphia'.[7] If I had written 'Rolling Home' I
would pass my days at sea or in West Coast nitrate ports[8]
hearkening to the roll and the roar of it as the yards go jolting
up the mast or the anchor comes to the bows.

> Pipe all hands to man the capstan, see your ca–bles
>   run down clear,
> Heave away, and with a will, boys, 'tis to old England's
>   shores we steer;
> And we'll sing in joyous chorus in the watches of the night,
> For we'll sight the shores of England when the grey dawn
>   brings the light.

I used to think that stanza, as the old sailor sang it in the dark
watches, the most beautiful thing the tongue of man ever
spoke.

While he sang, I used to take little tentative nibbles at the
compound in the pannikins. Have you ever been an exile,
reader, at sea, in pr-s-n, or somewhere, where the simple needs
of life cannot possibly be gratified? If you have you will know
how that sweet mush of cocoa tasted. It was like bubbling
water in the desert, like fern fronds above cool springs, like the
voice of the bird in the moonlight, in the green shadows, in

some southern spice garden, drowsy with odours. It was like a
night in June in the forest, by the babbling brook, when the
moon rises, red and solemn, over the hills where the deer feed.
Ah, the taste of it! the scent of it! the hidden meaning of it!

Then as I nibbled, the kettle would come to the boil and the
brew would be made. My watch-mate would come below puff-
ing his pipe, humming his favourite tune of 'The Sailor's
Wives'.⁹ I would fill a pannikin and carry it aft to the boy on
the poop, my watch-mate stationed there, keeping the time.
Round us were the waters, dark and ghostly; the crying sea-
birds; the whales with their pants and spoutings. There were
the masts and the great sails filling and slatting. There were
the sailors lying on the deck, their pipe-bowls ruddy in the
blackness. There was the murmuring and talking sea, full of
mysterious menace. And the sailors' quiet talk, and the smell of
tar from the sail-room, and the man at the wheel abaft all, and
the lame mate limping to the binnacle – it was all beautiful,
solemn, sacred, like a thing in a dream. And then the taste of
the brew, when one settled down in the half-deck. The talk we
had, my sleepy mate and I; talk of work and of ships, of top-
sails and mermaids, the old beautiful talk of youth, that needs
but a listener to be brilliant.

The Yarn of Happy Jack

I once knew an old Norwegian sailor, one of the mildest and
kindest of men, who attracted me strangely – partly because he
was mild and kind, but partly, alas! because he had committed
murder. I cannot remember that the crime weighed heavily
upon him. He spoke of it frankly, as one would allude to a love
affair or to the taking of a drink.¹ It was an incident in life. It
was part of a day's work. That it was exceptional and repre-
hensible not one of his friends, I am convinced, imagined.

We made a voyage together, that old Norwegian and I. We
were in the same watch, and did very much the same duty.
I was very young and green at that time, and he, an old man,

a leader in the forecastle, dignified further by poetical circum-
stance, befriended me in many ways. We used to yarn together
in the night-watches, under the break of the poop, while the
rest of the watch snored heavily in the shadows.

'Hanssen,' I asked him one night, 'who was Davy Jones?'
'Ah, come off with your Davy Jones!' said the boatswain, inter-
rupting. 'Look out he don't get you by the leg.' I repeated my
question. 'Davy Jones,' said the old man. 'I don't know, b' Joe,
who Davy Jones was. I know his locker though, b' gee.' This
was a jest. 'Just the sea?' I asked. 'Dat's one of 'em, b' gee.'
'And what's the other?' 'You want to know too much, you do,'
said the boatswain, interrupting us a second time, 'you and
your Davy Joneses. You're like a Welshman at a fair. "Who
trowned the tuck, Dafy Chones." Come off with you and give
us a breeze.'[2] 'The other one,' said the old man, 'it's up in the
sky, b' gee.' 'Is it a sea too?' I asked. 'Of course it is. Didn't you
never read your Bible?' 'Why, yes, but –' 'Well, then, don't you
know about the waters above the firm-ment and the waters
that are under the firm-ment?' 'If you're going to talk Latin,'
said the boatswain, 'I'm sheering off. I'll not rouse no head
winds by listenin' to you. Bloody Latin they're talking, them
two,' he added, to the third mate, as he walked away. 'They
ought to have been rooks, they'd ought' – by rooks meaning
folk in Holy Orders.

After he had gone I got the old man to give me the whole
story. He told me that up above, in the sky, there was another
sea, of a kind different from our sea, but still fit to carry ships,
and much sailed upon by the people of the sky. He told me that
the ships were sometimes seen in the air – having perhaps heard
from some Greek or Italian of the Fata Morgana,[3] a sort of
mirage, which does verily reflect ships in the sky, though I
believe upside down. He said that he himself had never seen it,
but that it was well-known how the anchors from this upper
sea carried away chimneys and steeples and broke through
roofs in European villages. Such accidents were rather more
common in the hills, he added, because the hills made the upper
sea shallow. In the valleys, where most big towns are, the water
is too deep, and the sky ships do not anchor.

'One time,' he said, 'there was a sailor. His name, b' gee, was Happy Jack, and he was a big man and a sailor (i.e. he was strong of his body and a good seaman). One time Happy Jack got paid off and he tink he go home. So he go along a road, and by and by he come to a town, and he found all hands standing in a field looking up. In the middle of the field there was an anchor, and it was like red-hot gold, and the fluke of it was fast in the ground. It was fast to a cable which went up and up into the sky, so far that you couldn't see the end of it. A great nine-stranded cable it was, with every bit of it shining like gold. It was all laid up of golden rope-yarns. It was a sight to see, that cable and the anchor was. So by and by the parson of the village sings out to get an axe and cut it through, so that they should have the anchor and a bit of the cable to buy new clothes for the poor. So a man goes and comes back with an axe, and he cuts a great chop at it, and the cable just shakes a little, but not so much as a rope-yarn carried away. "You'll never do it that way," says Happy Jack; "you must never have seen a cable, the way you shape at it. What is it you want to do, anyway?" So they said they wanted to get the anchor and the cable to buy new clothes for the poor. "Well," says Jack, "all you got to do is to bury the anchor a fathom deep, and then, when they come to heave in up above, the cable'll carry away, and I shouldn't wonder if you get ten or twenty fathom of it; whereas if you cut it like you're doing you'll not get more'n three feet." So they asked Jack to show them how. "It's as simple as kiss," he says. "Get spades." So they got spades. And then they buried the anchor seven or eight feet deep, with rocks and stuff on the top of it, till it was all covered over like it had a house on top. So when they'd done that Happy Jack thinks he'd earned a supper. And the parson says, "You must be thirsty after all that work." "I am thirsty," he says. So the parson takes him into the town, and gives him a bite of bread and shows him where there's a water-butt. "Nothing like water," he says. "You're right there," says Jack, "there isn't." And so Jack walks out of that town, and back to where the anchor was.

'By and by he began to think that the people in the ship up above might be rather more generous. So he slung his coat off, and began to shinny up the cable, and he climb a great piece; and at last he see the ship.

'And never in his life had he seen a ship the like of that. She was built like of white-hot gold, like a ship built out of the sun – a great shining ship. Her bows was white and round, like a great white cloud, and the air went swirling past them in thin blue eddies. Her ropes were shining, and her blocks were shining, and the sails on her yards were as white as a bow-wash. She had her colours flying at her truck – a long golden streamer that seemed to be white-hot like the hull.

'Now, as he comes up of the sea like, and gets his foot on the cable and his hand on a bobstay, one of the crowd of that ship leans over the rail and looks at him. And he was a queer man, and that's God's truth about him. He hadn't not so much as hair on his head, but instead of hair he had great golden flames. No smoke, mind you, only flames. And he was in a white dress, but the dress was all shining and fiery, and sparks were all over it, like he'd been splashed with them. So Happy Jack kow-tows to this person, and he says, "You'll have a foul hawse[4] when you come to heave in. They been burying your mud-hook," he says. So the fiery fellow says, "Well, Happy Jack, suppose you clear the hawse." So Jack slides down the cable, and he works all night long, and just as it comes dawn he gets all clear. Then he shinnies up and climbs aboard the ship again.

'Now, as soon as he come aboard, the fiery fellows go to the capstan and began to sing, and the song they sang would draw the soul out of the body. It was slow and sweet, and strong and spirited, all in one. And it seemed to Happy Jack that the golden cable was singing too as it came in through the hawseholes. In a few moments the sails were loose and the ship was under way, and she was tearing through it at the rate of knots. All Happy Jack could see was the sails straining, and the ship lying over to it, and the blue air ripping past, and now and then a comet, and a dancing star, and a cloud all red with the sun. So the fiery fellow came up to him, and he says, "You must be thirsty after all that work." "I am thirsty," he says. So the fiery fellow takes him into the cabin – it was all pictures in the cabin, all blue and green – as pretty as you can't tink. And he give

Happy Jack a great golden apple and a bottle of golden wine. And Happy Jack pour out the golden wine and drank it down like it was good for him.

'And the next thing he knew he was lying by the side of the road half-a-mile from where he lived. And he was in a new suit of clothes with shiny buttons – he was all brass-bound like a reefer. And in his hand there was a bag of golden dollars.'

The Bottom of the Well

'Once upon a time there was a sailor named Bill. He was a sea-man, and a hard case. We sailed together in the *Aladdin* barque. She was burnt off Valparaiso[1] a year or two later. Her old man was a son of a gun for style. You should have seen him carry cloth. When Bill was a young man he got a lot of folly – reading them novels. They're a dandy set, them writer fellers. Well, Bill he read them till he got all tied in a knot with it. He got so as he couldn't tell the truth. That's straight. He couldn't call the kettle black.[2] I never heard such lies as he told.

'He was ashore one time, on the beach. That was at Toco-pilla.[3] Was you ever at Tocopilla? No? Well, it's the last place made. It wasn't never finished. It's an open road, Tocopilla is, and when it blows a norther you slip and skip. I was there once, and a norther come, and we was three weeks at sea. Well, Bill was there, on the beach, doing lancher's graft[4] – eight, nine, ten and a tally – tanning his back with nitrate.[5] That's a great graft; two hours' work a day, and a roaring surf twice a week, so as you can't go out.

'So one time Bill was sleeping in his lanch, and he woke up sudden, and he see a little man, all blue and gold like an admiral. He was sitting in the stern of the lanch – and there was all but-terflies round him, great green and blue butterflies, all shining in the sun. So the little man looks at Bill. "Bill, can you spin a yarn?" he says. "I can, sir," says Bill. "Could you spin two, Bill?" "I could, sir," he says. "Could you spin three, Bill?" says the old man again. "Yes, sir," says Bill. "With what I've read,

I could spin three." "Good-oh," says the little man. "Hi. Run-kum. Twit." Them was magic.

'Now, so soon as them magic words was spoken the butter-flies seized the bow-painter. O, thousands of them there were, great green and blue fellers, all shining. And they flapped their wings till they sparkled, giving that hooker a tow. And she forged ahead through the sea – going steady west – and the dolphins come past, all fiery, and the flying fish come past, all bright, and the wind blows kind, and never any sprays come aboard.

'So at last they come to an island, where there was golden flowers on the trees, and a palace of marble, with a Union Jack on the chimney. So they run alongside, and the butterflies goes to the flowers, and the little man takes Bill to the palace.

'So when they come to the palace there was nothing but books, written by them novel fellers. The place was stowed with them, like a ship with dunnage. Heaps and heaps of them, new and old, big and little, Bible books and Deadwood Dick-eys.[6] You never saw such a gash of books. And all along the books there was a sort of row of cells, like in Liverpool Jail, and voices coming out of them, like in Liverpool Jail on Sun-day. "What's in them cells?" says Bill. "Just writer fellers," says the little man. "Now mind, Bill," he says, "you got to spin yarns to the king. Don't you go telling any lies, now. None of your Cape Horn Gospels."[7]

'And with that he shoves Bill through a door, and there he was, in a great big room as big as a church. It was all covered with books – all sorts of books – and at the end of it was a king on a throne, with a sort of soldiers, with axes, standing guard by him. He was a weary-looking man, the king was. Round his throne was all books, written by them novel fellers. They're a gummy lot, them fellers. The king had been reading of them.

'So he sees Bill, and he speaks in a sort of a groan. "I've been looking for truth," he says; "looking for truth in all these books, in all these stories. There's not a rat of truth in one of them. Not a solid rat, there isn't. And some of them I've got, and some of them I've not got, but I've got the biggest liars of them. They're under lock and key, they are. But I've got no

truth. Not a rat of truth have I got. And I've read all these, as
you see."

'So Bill he just bows.

' "Now, Bill," says the king, "tell us them tales of yours. I'm
sick for a true word, and that's the plain fact. Heave and she
goes, now."

'So Bill he pitches him a song and dance. "Once upon a
time," he says, "I was in command of the *Carrowdore* clipper.
And I was bound through the Pal-am-jen-bang Straits,[8] between
Java and Oa-moru.[9] And you may take it from him who dis-
covered them, them Straits is a caution. They're as narrow as
Sunday Lane,[10] and as full of rocks as a barrow is of peanuts.
And I went through on a spring tide, with breakers roaring like
a lot of psalm-singers. And the rocks were all close aboard.
And a mermaid sat on each rock, with golden hair falling over
her. And the mermaids were all playing ball with drowned
men's skulls. It was tough, and I didn't like the looks of it, but
'Starboard,' I says. 'Check in your head brace, Mr Mate,' I
says. 'Heave now,' I says. 'Heave and break your hearts.' And
she ran through, like a calf being chevied by a boys' school,
without so much as starting a yarn."

'And the king looks at his prime minister, and the prime
minister smiles and nods his head. "By James, Bill," says the
king, "you've got the root of the matter in you. It rings true in
every word. Now your second tale. At *once*." So Bill he hands
out another song and dance. "Once upon a time," he says, "I
was in command of the *Euryalus*, forty-gun ship, and I was
cruising off of Cape Tiburon,[11] suppressing them Spanish pri-
vateers. And we come across a raft with old Father Neptune on
it. He was being towed by a lot of porpoise, and he was dead-
oh.[12] And the porpoise was eating shrimps while he slept. So
we slip a bowline over him and hoist him on deck, and I give
him dinner when he wakes. So I fill him to the chin with Navy
rum, and then I pump him. 'Where's them Spanish privateers?'
I says. And he tells me. So then I let her go off, and I put him
aboard his raft again. And I make a general average of the
Spaniards, and the Queen of England made me a knight that
very next Christmas."

'And the king looks at his prime minister, and the prime minister laughs, and they shake hands together, like in the theatre – "Ha, me brother!" Just like that. And the king turns to Bill. "At last," he says, "out of the mouth of a simple person have I heard the truth – the real truth. Oh, your third story. At *once*!" So Bill he just shoves ahead and hands them out another, like they give buns at a school treat.

' "Once upon a time," he says, "I was wrecked on the South Pole – ran bang into it one windy night. I carried away so many splinters from it that we used it for firewood all the time we were on the raft. We were ninety-nine days drifting, and nothing to eat all that while except just whales and that – and one or two flying fish."

' "One or two *what*?" said the king.

' "Flying fish," says Bill; "ordinary flying fish."

' "Flying fish?" says the king. "Flying fish, did you say?"

' "Yes; flying fish, of course," says Bill. "D'you mean to say you're a king and never heard of flying fish?"

'And the king he wept like a child. "I thought you were bringing me the truth," he says. "The truth I have always longed for. And you lie about fish flying like a Portuguese pilot.[13] Here!" he says to the guard. "Remove this person. No, don't kill him. He is not fit to die. Turn him adrift in his boat, with some bread and water. Begone, you and your flying fish! You're the foulest liar I've ever come across!"

'So Bill he was put into his boat and turned adrift, and he mighty near got drowned. And never a lie has he ever told since then. He was that changed by the sight of that old king.'[14]

One Sunday

Ten years ago I was 'in the half-deck' of a four-masted barque. We were lying in Cardiff, loading patent fuel for the West Coast.[1] There were six of us 'in the half-deck'. Saving the cook, the steward, the mate, and the old man, we were the only folk aboard. In the daytime on weekdays we bent sails, or hoisted stores aboard, or shifted topsail sheets. In the evenings we went ashore to flaunt our brass buttons in St Mary Street[2] and to eat sweetstuff in the bun shops. Two of us used to drink 'rum-hot' in a little public-house near the docks. One of us made love to a waitress. We all smoked pipes and cocked our caps at an angle. One of us came aboard drunk one night, in a pretty pickle, having fallen into the dock. Another of our number got kicked out of a music-hall. Youth has strange ways and strange pleasures.

On Sundays we did no work after we had hoisted the house-flag and the red ensign. We were free to go ashore for the day, leaving one of our number aboard to act as boatman. The 'old man' always told us to go to church. Sometimes he asked us for the parson's text when we came aboard again. One of the six, who had been carefully brought up, used to answer for the rest. I think he made up the texts on the spur of the moment. He is dead now, poor fellow. He was a good shipmate.

One Sunday I went ashore with the rest to spend the day in the park, playing cricket with a stick and a tennis ball. In the afternoon we went to a little teashop not far from sailor-town, a place we patronized. It was up a flight of stairs. It was a long room, with oilcloth on the floor and marble-top tables and wicker chairs and a piano. There was a framed text on the piano top. It was all scrawled over on the unprinted part with messages to Kitty, a tall Welshwoman with but one eye, who acted as waitress. The wall was all scrawled over, too, with pencilled texts, proverbs, maxims, scraps of verses.

On this particular Sunday, when I entered, there were half a dozen other apprentices already seated at their teas. They were all West Coast apprentices; that is, they had been one or two voyages to Chile and Peru in 'West Coast barques' engaged in the carriage of nitrates. They were not a very choice lot, as apprentices go, but they knew the West Coast, which we did not, and one of them, a lad named Parsons, was popular among us. He had a singularly sweet tenor voice. He is dead now, too. His ship was burned off Antofagasta.[3] The boat he was in never came to port.

After we had finished our teas we sat about in the teashop,

smoking. One of the third-voyagers – he belonged to a little barque called the *Cowley* – was chaffing Kitty and asking her to marry him. The others were yarning, and holding a Dover Court. One of them was reciting the story of William and Mabel. Another was singing a song popular at sea. Its chorus ends, 'Love is a charming young boy.' It is a very pretty song with a jolly tune. Another was singing 'The Sailor's Wives',[4] a terrible ballad, with a tune which is like a gale of wind. It was regular Reefer's Delight, Dover Court and Seaman's Fancy. That is, there were 'all talkers and no hearers', 'all singers and no listeners', 'all friends and no favour'.[5]

Presently a wild-looking lad whom his mates called Jimmy, got up from his chair and went to the piano. He began to play a dance tune to which I had often danced in the days long before. He played it with a deal of spirit, partly because he was a good player, partly because the tune moved him. Coming as it did (on the top of all that silly chatter), with its memories of dead nights, and lit rooms, and pretty women, it fairly ripped the heart out of me. It stirred every reefer in the room. You could see them stirred by it, though one or two of them laughed, and swore at the player for a dancing-master. After he had finished his tune Jimmy came over to me. I thanked him for his music, and complimented him upon his playing. 'Ah,' he said, 'you're a first-voyager?' 'Yes,' I said. 'Then you're like a young bear,' he said, 'with all your sorrows to come.' I replied with the sea-proverb about going to sea for pleasure. 'Where are you bound?' he asked. 'Junin,[6] for orders,' I answered. 'I was in Junin my first voyage,' he said. 'My hat! I was in Junin. I was very near being there still.' 'Were you sick?' I asked. 'I was,' he said shortly. 'I was that.'

'Ah,' he went on bitterly, 'you're going to sea: your first voyage. You don't know what it is. I tell you, I was sick in Junin. I lay in my bunk, with the curtain drawn, and the surf roaring all the time. It never let up, that surf. All the time I was ill it was going on. One long, long roar. I used to lie and pinch myself. I could have screamed out to hear that surf always going. And then there was a damned patch of sunlight on the deck. It almost drove me mad. She rolled of course, for she was pretty near light. And that patch kept sliding back and to, back and to, back and to. I would see nothing but that patch all day. It was always yellow, and sliding, and full of dust. You don't know what it is to be sick at sea.

'Shall I tell you what it was made me well? I was lying there in my bunk, and there was a crack ship, one of Farley Brothers'[7] – the *Ramadan* her name was. She was homeward bound. She was next but one to us in the tier. You don't know about the West Coast? No? Well, when a ship's homeward bound the crowd cheer – cheer every ship in the port; three cheers for the *Hardy-Nute*, three cheers for the *Cornwallis*, and the ship cheered answers back one cheer. And when a ship sails all the ships in port cheer her – three cheers for the *Ramadan* – and she answers back one cheer. One ship at a time, of course. And every ship in port sends a boat aboard her with a couple of hands to help her get her anchor. Well, the *Ramadan* was sailing, and I was lying in my bunk as sick as a cat. And there they were cheering, "Three cheers for the *Ramadan*." And then the one cheer back. "Hip, hip, hip, hooray." I tell you it did me good.

'And there I was listening to them, and I thought of how prime they must be feeling to be going home, out of that God-forgotten sand-hill. And I thought of how good the cheers must have felt, coming across the water. And I thought of them being sleepy in the night-watch, the first night out, after having "all-night-in" so long. And then I thought of how they would be loosing sail soon. You don't know what it was to me.

'And then I heard them at the capstan, heaving in. You know how it is at the capstan? The bass voices seem to get all on one bar, and the tenor voices all on another, and the other voices each to a bar. You hear them one by one as they heave round. Did you never notice it? They were singing "Amsterdam".[8] It's the only chanty worth a twopenny. It broke me up not to be heaving round too.

'And when they come to get under sail, setting the fore-topsail, and I heard them beginning "There's a dandy clipper coming down the river," I lit out a scritch, and I out of my bunk to bear a hand on the rope. I was as weak as water, and I lay where I fell. I was near hand being a goner. The first words I said was, "Blow, bullies, blow." It was that chanty cured me. I got well after that.'

He turned again to the piano and thumped out a thundering sea chorus. The assembled reefers paid their shot and sallied out singing into the windy streets, where the lamps were being lit. As we went we shouted the song of the sea:

> A-roving,
> A-roving,
> Since roving's been my ru-i-n,
> I'll go no more a ro-o-ving
> With you, fair maid.[9]

A White Night

Sometimes, when I am idle, my mind fills with a vivid memory. Some old night at sea, or in a tavern, or on the roads, or some adventure half forgotten, rises up in sharp detail, alive with meaning. The thing or image, whatever it may be, comes back to me so clearly outlined, under such strong light, that it is as though the act were playing before me on a lighted stage. Such a memory always appears to me significant, like certain dreams. I find myself thinking of an old adventure, a day in a boat, a walk by still waters, the crying of curlews, or the call of wild swans, as though such memories, rather than the great events in life, were the things deeply significant. I think of a day beside a pool where the tattered reeds were shaking, and a fish leapt, making rings, as though the day were a great poem which I had written. I can think of a walk by twilight, among bracken and slowly moving deer, under a September moonrise, till I am almost startled to find myself indoors. For the most part my significant memories are of the sea. Three such memories, constantly recurring, appear to me as direct revelations of something too great for human comprehension. The deeds or events they image were little in themselves, however pleasant in the doing, and I know no reason why they should haunt me so strangely, so many years after they occurred.

One winter night, fourteen years ago, I was aboard a ship then lying at anchor in a great river. It was a fine night, full of stars, but moonless. There was no wind; but a strong tide was running; and a suck and gurgle sounded all along the ship's length, from the bows to the man-catcher. I had been dancing below-decks by lamplight with my shipmates, and had come up for a turn in the air before going to my hammock. As I walked the deck, under the rigging, with my friend, a pipe sounded from below. 'Away third cutters.'[1] I was the stroke oar of the third cutter, and I remembered then that a man had been dining with the captain, and that he would be going ashore, and that he would need a red baize cushion to sit upon, and a boat-rug to cover his knees. I ran below to get these things, and to haul the boat alongside from her boom. As I stepped into her with the gear, I heard the coxswain speaking to the officer of the watch. 'It's coming on very hazy, sir. Shall I take the boat's compass and the lantern?'

I noticed then that it was growing very hazy. The lights of the ship were burning dim, and I could not see a long line of lights, marking a wharf, which had shone clearly but a few moments before. I put the cushion in the stern-sheets and arranged the rug for the visitor, and then stood up in my place, holding the boat to the gangway by the manrope. The coxswain came shambling down the ladder with his lantern and compass. The officer in charge of the boat came after him, with his oilskins on his arm. Then came the visitor, a tall, red-haired man, who bumped his hat off while coming through the entry-port. I could see the ship's side and the patches of yellow light at her ports, and the lieutenant standing on the gangway with his head outlined against the light.

We got out our oars and shoved off through the haze. The red-haired man took out a cigar and tried to light it, but the head of the match came off and burnt his fingers. He swore curtly. The officer laughed. 'Remember the boat's crew,' he said. In the darkness, amid the gurgle of the running water, over which the haze came stealthily, the words were like words

heard in a dream. I repeated them to myself as I rowed, won-
dering where I had heard them before. It seemed to me that
they had been said before, somewhere, very long ago, and that
if I could remember where I should know more than any man
knew. I tried to remember where I had heard them, for I felt
that there was but a vague film between me and a great secret.
I seemed to be outside a door opening into some strange world.
The door, I felt, was ajar, and I could hear strange people mov-
ing just within, and I knew that a little matter, perhaps an act
of will, perhaps blind chance, would fling the door wide, in
blinding light, or shut it in my face. The rhythm of rowing, like
all rhythm, such as dancing, or poetry, or music, had taken me
beyond myself. The coxswain behind the backboard, with his
head nodding down over the lantern, and the two men beneath
him, seemed to have become inhuman. I myself felt more than
human. I seemed to have escaped from time. We were eternal
things, rowing slowly through space, upon some unfathomable
errand, such as the Sphinx might send to some occult power,
guarded by winged bulls, in old Chaldea.[2]

When we ran alongside the jetty, the haze was thick behind
us, like a grey blanket covering the river. I got out with the
stern-fast, and held the lantern for the visitor to clamber out by.
The officer ran up the jetty to a little shop at the jetty head
where the ship's letters were left. The visitor thanked me for my
help, and said 'Good night', and vanished into the mist. His
steps sounded on the slippery stones. They showed us that he
was walking gingerly. Once he struck a ringbolt and swore.
Then he passed the officer, and the two exchanged a few parting
words. I thought at the time that the casual things in life were
life's greatest mysteries. It seemed as though something had
failed to happen; as though something – something beautiful –
had been kept from the world by some blind chance or wilful
fate. Who was the red-haired man, I wondered, that we, who
had come from many wanderings and many sorrows, should
take him to our memories for ever, for no shown cause? We
should remember him for ever. He would be the august thing of
that white night's rowing. We should remember him at solemn
moments. Perhaps as we lay a-dying we should remember him.

He had said good night to us and had passed on up the jetty, and we did not know who he was, nor what he was, and we should be gone in a few days' time, and we should never see him again. As for him, he would never think of us again. He would remember his dented hat, and his burnt finger, and perhaps, if it had been very good, his dinner.

When we shoved off again for the ship the haze was so thick that we could not see three feet in front of us. All the river was hidden in a coat of grey. The sirens of many steamers hooted mournfully as they passed up or down, unseen. We could hear the bell-signals from the hulks, half-a-mile away. Voices came out of the greyness, from nowhere in particular. Men hailed each other from invisible bridges. A boat passed us under oars, with her people talking. A confused noise of many screws, beating irregularly, came over the muffled water. They might have been miles away – many miles – or hard upon us. It is impossible to judge by sound in a haze so thick. We rowed on quietly into the unknown.

We were a long time rowing, for we did not know where we were, and the tide swept us down, and the bells and sirens puzzled us. Once we lay on our oars and rocked in a swell while some great steamer thrashed past hooting. The bells beat now near, now very far away. We were no longer human beings, but things much greater or much less. We were detached from life and time. We had become elemental, like the fog that hid us. I could have stayed in the boat there, rowing through the haze, for all eternity. The grunt of the rowlocks, and the wash and drip of the oars, and the measured breath of the men behind me, keeping time to me, were a music passing harps. The strangeness and dimness of it all, and the halo round the coxswain's lantern, and the faces half seen, and the noises sounding from all sides impressed me like a revelation.

'Oars a minute,' said the coxswain. 'There's the fog-bell.'

Somewhere out of the grey haze a little silver bell was striking. It beat four strokes, and paused, and then again four strokes, and again a pause, from some place high above us. And then, quite near to us, we heard the long, shrill call of a pipe and a great stamp of feet upon hatchways.

'Good Lord! we're right on top of her,' said the officer. 'I see her boom. Ship ahoy!'

'Is that you, Carter?'

We bumped alongside, and held her there while the officer and coxswain ran up the gangway with the letters. We laid in the oars and unshipped the rudder, and a man came down the gangway for the red baize cushion and the rug. 'Hook your boat on,' said the officer of the watch.

That is one of the memories which come back to me, when I am idle, with the reality of the deed itself. It is one of those memories which haunt me, as symbols of something unimagined, of something greater than life expressed in life. Why such a thing should haunt me I cannot tell, for the words, now they are written down, seem foolish. Within the ivory gate, and well without it, one is safe; but perhaps one must not peep through the opening when it hangs for a little while ajar.

Davy Jones's Gift

'Once upon a time,' said the sailor, 'the devil and Davy Jones came to Cardiff, to the place called Tiger Bay.[1] They put up at Tony Adams's, not far from Pier Head,[2] at the corner of Sunday Lane.[3] And all the time they stayed there they used to be going to the rum-shop, where they sat at a table, smoking their cigars, and dicing each other for different persons' souls. Now you must know that the devil gets landsmen, and Davy Jones gets sailor-folk; and they get tired of having always the same, so then they dice each other for some of another sort.

'One time they were in a place in Mary Street,[4] having some burnt brandy,[5] and playing red and black for the people passing. And while they were looking out on the street and turning the cards, they saw all the people on the sidewalk breaking their necks to get into the gutter. And they saw all the shop-people running out and kow-towing, and all the carts pulling up, and all the police saluting. "Here comes a big nob," said Davy Jones. "Yes," said the devil; "it's the bishop that's stopping with the mayor." "Red or black?" said Davy Jones, picking up a card. "I don't play for bishops," said the devil. "I respect the cloth," he said. "Come on, man," said Davy Jones. "I'd give an admiral to have a bishop. Come on, now; make your game. Red or black?" "Well, I say red," said the devil. "It's the ace of clubs," said Davy Jones; "I win; and it's the first bishop ever I had in my life." The devil was mighty angry at that – at losing a bishop. "I'll not play any more," he said; "I'm off home. Some people gets too good cards for me. There was some queer shuffling when that pack was cut, that's my belief."

'"Ah, stay and be friends, man," said Davy Jones. "Look at what's coming down the street. I'll give you that for nothing."

'Now, coming down the street there was a reefer – one of those apprentice-fellows. And he was brass-bound fit to play music. He stood about six feet, and there were bright brass buttons down his jacket, and on his collar, and on his sleeves. His cap had a big gold badge, with a house-flag in seven different colours in the middle of it, and a gold chain cable of a chinstay[6] twisted round it. He was wearing his cap on three hairs, and he was walking on both the sidewalks and all the road. His trousers were cut like windsails round the ankles. He had a fathom of red silk tie rolling out over his chest. He'd a cigarette in a twisted clay holder a foot and a half long. He was chewing tobacco over his shoulders as he walked. He'd a bottle of rum-hot in one hand, a bag of jam tarts in the other, and his pockets were full of love-letters from every port between Rio and Callao,[7] round by the East.

'"You mean to say you'll give me that?" said the devil. "I will," said Davy Jones, "and a beauty he is. I never see a finer." "He is, indeed, a beauty," said the devil. "I take back what I said about the cards. I'm sorry I spoke crusty. What's the matter with some more burnt brandy?" "Burnt brandy be it," said Davy Jones. So then they rang the bell, and ordered a new jug and clean glasses.

'Now the devil was so proud of what Davy Jones had given him, he couldn't keep away from him. He used to hang about the East Bute Docks,[8] under the red-brick clock-tower, looking at the barque the young man worked aboard. Bill Harker his name was. He was in a West Coast barque, the *Coronel*,[9] loading fuel for Hilo.[10] So at last, when the *Coronel* was sailing, the devil shipped himself aboard her, as one of the crowd in the fo'c's'le, and away they went down the Channel. At first he was very happy, for Bill Harker was in the same watch, and the two would yarn together. And though he was wise when he shipped, Bill Harker taught him a lot. There was a lot of things Bill Harker knew about. But when they were off the River Plate, they got caught in a pampero,[11] and it blew very hard, and a big green sea began to run. The *Coronel* was a wet ship, and for three days you could stand upon her poop, and look forward and see nothing but a smother of foam from the break of the poop to the jib-boom. The crew had to roost on the poop. The fo'c's'le was flooded out. So while they were like this the flying jib worked loose. "The jib will be gone in half a tick," said the mate. "Out there, one of you, and make it fast, before it blows away." But the boom was dipping under every minute, and the waist was four feet deep, and green water came aboard all along her length. So none of the crowd would go forward. Then Bill Harker shambled out, and away he went forward, with the green seas smashing over him, and he lay out along the jib-boom and made the sail fast, and jolly nearly drowned he was. "That's a brave lad, that Bill Harker," said the devil. "Ah, come off," said the sailors. "Them reefers, they haven't got souls to be saved." It was that that set the devil thinking.

'By and by they came up with the Horn;[12] and if it had blown off the Plate, it now blew off the roof. Talk about wind and weather. They got them both for sure aboard the *Coronel*. And it blew all the sails off her, and she rolled all her masts out, and the seas made a breach of her bulwarks, and the ice knocked a hole in her bows. So watch and watch they pumped the old *Coronel*, and the leak gained steadily, and there they were hove-to under a weather cloth, five and a half degrees to the south of anything. And while they were like this, just about giving up hope, the old man sent the watch below, and told them they could start prayers. So the devil crept on to the top of the half-deck, to look through the scuttle, to see what the reefers were doing, and what kind of prayers Bill Harker was putting up. And he saw them all sitting round the table, under the lamp, with Bill Harker at the head. And each of them had a hand of cards, and a length of knotted rope-yarn, and they were playing able-whackets.[13] Each man in turn put down a card, and swore a new blasphemy, and if his swear didn't come as he played the card, then all the others hit him with their teasers.[14] But they never once had a chance to hit Bill Harker. "I think they were right about his soul," said the devil. And he sighed, like he was sad.

'Shortly after that the *Coronel* went down, and all hands drowned in her, saving only Bill and the devil. They came up out of the smothering green seas, and saw the stars blinking in the sky, and heard the wind howling like a pack of dogs. They managed to get aboard the *Coronel*'s hen-house, which had come adrift, and floated. The fowls were all drowned inside, so they lived on drowned hens. As for drink, they had to do without, for there was none. When they got thirsty they splashed their faces with salt water; but they were so cold they didn't feel thirst very bad. They drifted three days and three nights, till their skins were all cracked and salt-caked. And all the devil thought of was whether Bill Harker had a soul. And Bill kept telling the devil what a thundering big feed they would have as soon as they fetched to port, and how good a rum-hot would be, with a lump of sugar and a bit of lemon peel.

'And at last the old hen-house came bump on to Terra del Fuego,[15] and there were some natives cooking rabbits. So the devil and Bill made a raid of the whole jing bang,[16] and ate till they were tired. Then they had a drink out of a brook, and a warm by the fire, and a pleasant sleep. "Now," said the devil, "I will see if he's got a soul. I'll see if he give thanks." So after an hour or two Bill took a turn up and down and came to the devil. "It's mighty dull on this forgotten continent," he said. "Have you got a ha'penny?" "No," said the devil. "What in joy d'ye want with a ha'penny?" "I might have played you pitch and toss," said Bill. "It was better fun on the hen-coop than here." "I give you up," said the devil; "you've no more soul than the inner part of an empty barrel." And with that the devil vanished in a flame of sulphur.

'Bill stretched himself, and put another shrub on the fire. He picked up a few round shells, and began a game of knuckle-bones.'[17]

Being Ashore

In the nights, in the winter nights, in the nights of storm when the wind howls, it is then that I feel the sweet of it. Aha, I say, you howling catamount,[1] I say, you may blow, wind, and crack your cheeks,[2] for all I care. Then I listen to the noise of the elm trees and to the creak in the old floorings, and, aha, I say, you whining rantipoles,[3] you may crack and you may creak, but here I shall lie till daylight.

There is a solid comfort in a roaring storm ashore here. But on a calm day, when it is raining, when it is muddy underfoot, when the world is the colour of a drowned rat, one calls to mind more boisterous days, the days of effort and adventure; and wasn't I a fool, I say, to come ashore to a life like this life. And I was surely daft, I keep saying, to think the sea as bad as I always thought it. And if I were in a ship now, I say, I wouldn't be doing what I'm trying to do. And, ah, I say, if I'd but stuck to the sea I'd have been a third in the Cunard,[4] or perhaps a second in a P.S.N.[5] coaster. I wouldn't be hunched at a desk, I say, but I'd be up on a bridge – up on a bridge with a helmsman, feeling her do her fifteen knots.

It is at such times that I remember the good days, the exciting days, the days of vehement and spirited living. One day stands out, above nearly all my days, as a day of joy.

We were at sea off the River Plate,[6] running south like a stag. The wind had been slowly freshening for twenty-four hours, and for one whole day we had whitened the sea like a battleship. Our run for the day had been 271 knots, which we thought a wonderful run, though it has, of course, been exceeded by many ships. For this ship it was an exceptional run. The wind was on the quarter, her best point of sailing, and there was enough wind for a glutton. Our captain had the reputation of being a 'cracker-on', and on this one occasion he drove her till she groaned. For that one wonderful day we staggered and swooped, and bounded in wild leaps, and burrowed down and shivered, and anon rose up shaking. The wind roared up aloft and boomed in the shrouds, and the sails bellied out as stiff as iron. We tore through the sea in great jumps – there is no other word for it. She seemed to leap clear from one green roaring ridge to come smashing down upon the next. I have been in a fast steamer – a very fast turbine steamer – doing more than twenty knots, but she gave me no sense of great speed. In this old sailing-ship the joy of the hurry was such that we laughed and cried aloud. The noise of the wind booming, and the clack, clack, clack of the sheet-blocks, and the ridged seas roaring past us, and the groaning and whining of every block and plank, were like tunes for a dance. We seemed to be tearing through it at ninety miles an hour. Our wake whitened and broadened, and rushed away aft in a creamy fury. We were running here, and hurrying there, taking a small pull of this, and getting another inch of that, till we were weary. But as we hauled we sang and shouted. We were possessed of the spirits of the wind. We could have danced and killed each other. We were in an ecstasy. We were possessed. We half believed that the ship would leap from the waters and hurl herself into the heavens, like a winged god. Over her bows came the sprays in showers of sparkles. Her foresail was wet to the yard. Her scuppers were brooks. Her swing-ports spouted like cataracts. Recollect, too, that it was a day to make your heart glad. It was a clear day, a sunny day, a day of brightness and splendour. The sun was glorious in the sky. The sky was of a blue unspeakable. We were tearing along across a splendour of sea that made you sing. Far as one could see there was the water shining and shaking. Blue it was, and green it was, and of a dazzling brilliance in the sun. It rose up in hills and in ridges. It smashed into a foam and roared. It towered up again and toppled. It mounted and shook in a rhythm, in a tune, in a music. One could have flung one's body to it as a sacrifice. One longed to be in it, to be a part of it, to be beaten and banged by it. It was a wonder and a glory and a terror. It was a triumph, it was royal, to see that beauty.

And later, after a day of it, as we sat below, we felt our mad ship taking yet wilder leaps, bounding over yet more boisterous hollows, and shivering and exulting in every inch of her. She seemed filled with a fiery, unquiet life. She seemed inhuman, glorious, spiritual. One forgot that she was man's work. We forgot that we were men. She was alive, immortal, furious. We were her minions and servants. We were the star-dust whirled in the train of the comet. We banged our plates with the joy we had in her. We sang and shouted, and called her the glory of the seas.

There is an end to human glory. 'Greatness a period hath, no sta-ti-on.'[7] The end to our glory came when, as we sat at dinner, the door swung back from its hooks and a mate in oilskins bade us come on deck 'without stopping for our clothes'. It was time. She was carrying no longer; she was dragging. To windward the sea was blotted in a squall. The line of the horizon was masked in a grey film. The glory of the sea had given place to greyness and grimness. Her beauty had become savage. The music of the wind had changed to a howl as of hounds.

And then we began to 'take it off her', to snug her down, to check her in her stride. We went to the clewlines and clewed the royals up. Then it was, 'Up there, you boys, and make the royals fast.' My royal was the mizzen-royal, a rag of a sail among the clouds, a great grey rag, which was leaping and slatting a hundred and sixty feet above me. The wind beat me down against the shrouds, it banged me and beat me, and blew the tears from my eyes. It seemed to lift me up the futtocks into the top, and up the topmast rigging to the cross-trees. In the cross-trees I learned what wind was.

It came roaring past with a fervour and a fury which struck me breathless. I could only look aloft to the yard I was bound for and heave my panting body up the rigging. And there was the mizzen-royal. There was the sail I had come to furl. And a wonder of a sight it was. It was blowing and bellying in the wind, and leaping around 'like a drunken colt', and flying over the yard, and thrashing and flogging. It was roaring like a bull with its slatting and thrashing. The royal mast was bending to the strain of it. To my eyes it was buckling like a piece of whalebone. I lay out on the yard, and the sail hit me in the face and knocked my cap away. It beat me and banged me, and blew from my hands. The wind pinned me flat against the yard, and seemed to be blowing all my clothes to shreds. I felt like a king, like an emperor. I shouted aloud with the joy of that 'rastle'[8] with the sail. Forward of me was the main mast, with another lad, fighting another royal; and beyond him was yet another, whose sail seemed tied in knots. Below me was the ship, a leaping mad thing, with little silly figures, all heads and shoulders, pulling silly strings along the deck. There was the sea, sheer under me, and it looked grey and grim, and streaked with the white of our smother.

Then, with a lashing swish, the rain-squall caught us. It beat down the sea. It blotted out the view. I could see nothing more but grey, driving rain, grey spouts of rain, grey clouds which burst rain, grey heavens which opened and poured rain. Cold rain. Icy-cold rain. Rain which drove the dye out of my shirt till I left blue tracks where I walked. For the next two hours I was clewing up, and furling, and snugging her down. By nightfall we were under our three lower-topsails and a reefed forecourse. The next day we were hove-to under a weather cloth.

There are varieties of happiness; and, to most of us, that variety called excitement is the most attractive. On a grey day such as this, with the grass rotting in the mud, the image and memory of that variety are a joy to the heart. They are a joy for this, if for no other reason. They teach us that a little thing, a very little thing, a capful of wind even, is enough to make us exult in, and be proud of, our parts in the pageant of life.

In the Roost

There is a saloon in Green Street,[1] New York City, run by a man called Ahrens. The saloon goes by the name of the Roost. It has an ordinary bar, where you can drink and swap yarns with the proprietor; and then, beyond that, it has a sort of parlour, with statues and pictures, and a machine which plays tunes if you feed it with a nickel. On Saturdays a fiddler spends the day there, playing to the guests. On Fridays a club meets there, before and after its visit to a bowling alley. At other times it is a very quiet, old-fashioned, respectable saloon, where I, for one, have passed many pleasant hours. When any of my sailor friends were in New York I used to entertain them there, in the parlour where the pictures hang. It is one of the best places for a yarn in the whole of New York City.

Once it chanced that a friend came to New York aboard a great four-master, and we spent a day together in the Roost, yarning of old times.

'Weren't you in the *Joppa*?' he asked.

'Yes,' I answered, 'I made a passage in her.'

'Had you a man aboard – a man called Ash?'

'Yes; he was painter aboard us.'

'What sort of fellow was he, did you think?'

'A nice quiet fellow. He wasn't following the sea. He was going to be an artist. Did you know him?'

'Yes. He was ordinary aboard the *Terceira*. He was killed.'

'How was he killed?'

'He fell from aloft.'

'He was a nice quiet fellow. They gave him an awful life of it aboard the *Joppa*. Tell me about him. I'm sorry he got killed. He was a plucky chap. How was it? Tell me about it.'

'I didn't see it. I was below. I was at supper. It was in the dogwatch. They were reefing the fore-upper-topsail. It was blowing rather. And we were in the half-deck. We heard them. We heard the sail slat. We heard them singing out. It was blowing rather. Ash was in the watch on deck, of course. There was a good deal of noise, of course. Blocks banging, and then the wind. You know how it is. There's always a lot of noise.

'Then suddenly we heard a great thud. Thud, that was how it was. Just a big thud, as if I'd banged the table. It came from forward. So I turned to Herrick (he was one of the apprentices). So I turned to Herrick: "What was that?" I said. "Oh," he said, "it's a coil of rope flung down." "Yes," said the others. "It was nothing. It was just a coil of rope flung down." So we went on with our suppers. Then suddenly we heard the old man

singing out from the poop: "Holy snakes, Mr Baxter; there's
a — man of your — watch lying on the — deck."

'So then we knew what it was. We'd a fresh-water bucket –
full – on the table; so I grabbed that and ran on deck. It was
Ash. He'd fallen from the upper-topsail yard. He was lying on
his back by the fore-bitts. He was still breathing. Of course it
was hopeless. If it had been the lower-topsail he might have
lived. Of course there was no chance. What's a man to do? It
was hopeless. He was unconscious. That was one good job. He
lived about half an hour. Oh, I don't think he felt it. He just
breathed heavily. Like deep sleep it was. And then the breath-
ing gradually stopped.

'It was very sad for all of us. Death is like that. And none of
the crowd would go aloft again, to the topsail yard. They were
all afraid. You know what a lot they sometimes are.'

'I wouldn't have liked it myself,' I said.

'Ah. It wasn't superstition. It was just that they were afraid
of their own necks. Not one of them would go. We had to
shake out the reef in the middle watch. So I volunteered. And
while I was on the yard, just at the very place Ash fell from, a
rope, a loose gasket or a buntline, I don't know what it was.
Some rope, anyway. It just came ever so soft. So. Ever so soft.
And knocked my cap overboard. I jolly nearly fell myself, and
so I tell you. I'm not ashamed to own it. I jolly nearly fainted.
Scared? I was sick with fear. I couldn't see what it was. I was
never so shaken in all my time. I don't want another turn like
that. I tell you, I thought it was Ash's wraith. And then I saw
what it was.'

'You thought it was Ash's wraith?' I said. 'Now tell me.
What did you think had become of Ash? What did the hands
think?'

'I don't think they felt it after they'd buried him. They kept
him till the morning, and then they sewed him up in some can-
vas and buried him. They'll never bury a corpse at night. They
think the soul stays in the body until the daylight. They think the
soul is afraid of the dark and cannot pass till the day comes.'

'Do you think that?'

'I don't know what I think. I don't think I ever thought about it. I don't fear death. They say that dying people generally die quite peacefully. You see, we never really think of death. We don't know what it is. When you're fit you never can imagine being ill. When you're alive you can't imagine being dead.'

'Yes. But what do you think will happen to you when you die?'

'I don't know what to think. But you remember old Dumbie, the man who saw the visions?'

'Yes.'

'Well. There was that old man. He wasn't really old, of course. He'd knocked around with a pretty tough crowd in his time. And he used to shut his eyes and see things. Things he couldn't have imagined. Angels on fiery horses, and fiery trees that sang songs, and people who were like stars. No, it was stars that spoke like people. Well. What d'ye make of that? There was Dumbie. He'd been a rough and a tough. Anyway he'd been in queer company. And he would talk to you like a poet; like the Prophet Isaiah. He used to point with his finger. So. You've seen him. You've seen him do it yourself. "My finger is on the tree in Eden," he would say. "My body is washed by the four rivers." Well. If you asked Dumbie about death, he used to laugh at you. He didn't believe there was such a thing. If you told him. Well. Suppose a girl had died, and you mentioned her name to him. Well. He would laugh. "She sang to me all last night," he would say. "The sound of her voice was like a sweet fire in my marrow." Ah, he would say, "Death is just going to the Paradise from which this clay shuts us." You've heard him say so yourself. He believes that we are the dead. All the lot of us. He used to say that we were really dead, and that what we call death was really birth. He believed that this life of ours was a sort of asleep, and that all we did right in it was just pleasant dreams. Well. I'm a sailor. I don't hold with dreaming. It's not my job. But, all the same, there you are. Dumbie believed that way, and Dumbie talked like a poet, and Dumbie lived like a prophet, and he died singing like a bird. You judge a thing by its fruit. Well. What are you going to say?'

'I knew an old man once, in Liverpool,' I said. 'He wasn't

like Dumbie, but he'd some queer beliefs. He believed he'd lived before.'

'After Ash died,' said my friend, 'the hands wouldn't fish for the pigeons, or for any of the other birds. They believed that Ash's soul had gone into one of them. They believed that he followed the *Terceira* until we made her fast at Hamburg. But I met a man at Hong Kong once who believed the same as your fellow. He believed he'd lived before. He said he could remember his lives. Ghastly business, I call it. Fancy having another life of soojee-moojee,[2] and soup and bully,[3] and 'lieve the wheel and look-out. Fancy never getting quit of it. Fancy never having a spell-oh.'[4]

'It isn't such a ghastly business. Take Ash, now. There he was. A nice, quiet, decent fellow. And a clever fellow. How old was he? Well, say twenty. He was going to be an artist. He was going to paint ships. So he ships as dauber on the *Joppa*, and goes through seven hells along with a brute of a bo'sun. He was willing to go through twenty hells if he might paint ships when he came to the end. Well. There's pluck for you; fine pluck. Then he ships as ordinary aboard the *Terceira*; and begins to know his business. He was merry, I'll bet, thinking of the ships he would paint, great ships, clippers, junks, galleons, all the whole fleet. Then he falls from aloft; and dies, and never so much as paints a smack. That's a ghastly business, if you like. Well, now. Suppose Ash lives again, and begins where he left off, with the knowledge of this life as a sort of dowry for the next. That wouldn't be so ghastly. And then the women. Think of the women, good women, blessed women, just chucked away on brutes, or never loved at all, or slighted, after all their kindness, by some callous chip[5] or another. Why, man. It would be fine if there could be another life. Think of Ash painting away at whole armadas, and of all the brutes and the chips just eating out their hearts for the love of the women they'd scorned before.'

'You talk like Shakespeare,' said my friend. 'Let's go on to Proctor's,[6] and we'll see the French Eccentric in her gigantic paper-tearing act.'

A Steerage Steward

A few years ago I was in New York City trying to get a passage home aboard some liner, or freight or cattle steamer. I had a little money in my pocket – just enough, in fact, to pay for a steerage ticket to Liverpool; but I preferred to work my way, so that I might not be destitute when I stepped ashore, as I should have been had I taken a berth. It was the Fourth of July when I started on my quest. The weather was extremely hot, and my frequent repulses were depressing. At last I came to a big cattle steamer lying at one of the wharves of West Street.[1] I went aboard her and asked to see the mate, and presently I was passed along an alleyway to his cabin. It was a frowsy little cabin, lit by an electric lamp and a bull's-eye scuttle.[2] It was not over-clean, and it smelt very strongly of the mate's oilskins, which hung behind the door, and of the mate's breakfast, which lay in a tray upon the horsehair settee. It was stiflingly hot; and the cockroaches were running races in their mirth upon all the plane surfaces in reach. The mate, who was a very stout man, lay in his bunk, dressed in his pyjama trousers. He was smoking a cigar and fanning himself with the *Laws of Storms*.[3] He listened very kindly to all that I had to say, and told me that he had nothing to do with the cattlemen, but that one Billy Werke, in one of the streets near the Battery,[4] close to Babbett's Soapworks,[5] was the man to tackle. Lastly he told me to keep clear of the engine-room, and to stow myself away rather than to sign on as a fireman. I asked him if he would recommend me to Mr Billy Werke. He produced the envelope of an old letter and wrote upon it a brief letter of introduction. It ran – 'Give this lad a job. – J. Masters.' When I got to Mr Werke's office I was told that the cattlemen had all been engaged for that trip, but that next week, if I was around, 'he couldn't tell but what he might fix things.' I had a chat with one of the cattlemen in the room. He told me that for the first three days out 'the cattle was just mad', but that afterwards 'you could ride 'em the same as a mu-el', they'd be so gentled.

After that I went back to the ships to look for a passage home, but met with very little luck. Presently I went aboard one of the big liners and got into talk with the man at the gangway. He told me to pass in boldly, and put a good face on it and ask to see the captain. Cheek was the main thing, he said, and if the captain didn't kick me overboard he would surely give me a passage. So I passed aboard, called a steward and sent him to the captain to say that I wished to see him. The captain very politely returned answer that he was engaged at the moment, but that he would wait upon me immediately, so would I mind taking a seat? I took a seat. By and by the captain came to me and heard my request, and seemed much amused at my cheek in sending for him. Then he sent a minion for the head of the steerage stewards, who came hurriedly, brushing the dust from his jacket. The captain asked if he were short of a hand. The steward said he was. The captain said that I was to have the vacancy, and that he hoped that one of the other stewards would lend me a cap and apron for the passage. I signed the ship's articles, got my gear aboard, borrowed a cap and apron, and began my duties. Less than half an hour later the ship's bell was beaten, the gangways were run in, and the ship was homeward bound down New York harbour. My first duty was to assist in the mustering of the steerage passengers at the general collection of tickets.

The steerage passengers over whom I presided were classed as married women, single women, and men. The married women were the dirtiest, for they had children to look after, and when the seasickness began their quarters became very filthy. The single women had a stewardess to look after them. They were always tidy. The men were perhaps cleaner than one would have expected; but the air in all the steerage quarters was very foul and noisome; and the beds and bedding were full of fleas. The stewards, of whom I was one, slept in a small cabin, or glory-hole, pretty far forward. It, too, was full of fleas, so that when we stripped to wash in the mornings we always found ourselves 'stung like tenches'.[6]

After the passengers had been mustered I went below to serve out their crockery. Each passenger received a tin plate, an enamelled tin cup, and a knife, a fork and a spoon. These the recipient was expected to keep clean (if he wished them clean) and to return at the end of the passage. There were one or two tubs in each berth where these things might be washed. At meal-times the passengers gathered at long narrow tables. While they took their seats the stewards went to the galley to fetch from the cooks the kids, or wooden half-tubs, in which the food was served. At dinner some kids were full of sliced meat and others of boiled potatoes. We carried these kids down the tables, flinging slices of meat to all who asked for them. Then we called upon the passengers to 'catch' as we tossed the boiled potatoes to them, or to 'hold out their cups' if they wanted any soup or gravy. After this performance we took great sheets of bread, a yard square, from the bakery. We thrust these into our aprons and carried them down the line of feeders, breaking off little squares or blocks for all who asked. When we had fed the passengers we ate our own dinner at a little reserved table. After dinner we smoked and yarned, and then took brooms and swept up the litter left by the passengers. In the afternoons there was nothing for us to do. Some of us 'turned in' and slept, while others went to the cabin galley to help to wash the plates of the cabin lunch or to help to peel the potatoes for the cabin dinner. At an early hour tea was served. It consisted of bread and butter, or rolls and margarine, with any quantity of bewitched water, tasting of the tin in which it was stored. After tea we again swept the passengers' quarters, and then mustered at a table to clean the 'cabin plate' till 8 p.m. As we polished the knives and forks we used to sing a variety of sea-songs, chanties and others, to beguile the time. One or two of our number had good voices, so that the steerage passengers used to gather round us to listen. At 8 p.m. we served out gruel to those who wanted it (it was much more popular than it deserved), and then, after a final sweep-down, we were free to turn in for the night, unless we were called to help at the washing up of the cabin dinner. We turned out early in the morning to get breakfast ready. After breakfast we had a grand cleaning up of the passengers' quarters, so as to be ready for the daily inspection by the captain and the doctor. We were expected to be 'cleaned' – that is, washed and dressed and in clean aprons – in good time for this ceremony.

The stewards, my comrades, were delightful shipmates, though they suffered very much from the liberality of the passengers. In the cabin the steward gets a tip at the end of the passage, but in the steerage he gets whisky *en route*, and often much more than he can stand. I admired the way in which my shipmates shielded the one who had been 'overtaken' from the notice of his superiors or made excuses for him in the event of discovery. 'Ah, sir,' they would say, 'Tom's had trouble. You don't know what Tom's got on his mind,' and this excuse, for some reason, always passed. Tom was the best of the stewards, and a very kindly fellow. He used to show me the letters he had had from home in the last year or two, and often he would say to me, 'Don't you do a stroke, now. I wouldn't. Why, man, you're a friend of the captain. Don't you do a blooming stroke. You go and turn in.' I did not follow his advice, but I cannot say that I worked with any very passionate fervour. My last task was to clean the cups and plates used in the passage. I soaked them in acid and water, and then scrubbed them with a hand scrubber. The marks of the acid are on my fingers to this day. When the cups and plates had been cleaned I was free to bid my mates goodbye and to pass over the side into Birkenhead.[7]

On Growing Old

The other day I met an old sailor friend at a café. We dined together, talking of old times. He was just home, on long leave, from the Indian Marine, a service in which he is a lieutenant. At first we talked of our shipmates, and of the men we had known at sea or in foreign ports; but that kind of talk was too melancholy; we had to stop. Some had fallen from aloft, and some had fallen down the hold, and a derrick[1] had killed one and a bursting boiler another. One had been burnt in his ship, another had been posted missing. One had been stabbed by a greaser; two or three had gone to the goldfields; one was in gaol for fraud; and one or two had taken to 'crooking their little fingers'[2] in the saloons of the Far West. He and I, we reckoned, were all that remained alive of a group of fifteen who were photographed together only eleven years ago. Before we parted, my friend remarked that I had greatly changed since our last meeting. I had grown quite grey, he said, and I had a drawn, old look about the eyes, and no one (this is what grieved me) would ever think me young again. Then we shook hands and went our ways, wondering if we should have yet another meeting before we died.

I left him thinking of the sadness of life and of a man's folly in not sticking to his work. We had been friends, I thought, intimate friends, comrades, when we had been at sea together. We had shared our clothes, our money, our letters from home, our work, our ease. We had been a proverb and a by-word to a whole ship's company. We were going to stick to each other, we always said, and when we were old, we hoped, we would get a job on a lighthouse, and smoke our pipes and read the papers together, and perhaps write a book together, or invent a safety pawl or a new kind of logship. We had intended all these things. We had hoped never to separate. We had built our lighthouse in the air, and based it in the wash of breakers. Then life, in its strength and strangeness, had swept us apart; and we who had been comrades were now a little puzzled by each other. I was wondering how it was that he could see no beauty in poetry. He was thinking me a little touched by time, an ancient, one grown old prematurely, a fossil, a has-been.

Then I was startled to think that he was right; to think that I was, in sooth, a has-been; that I was grown grey and bent; and that I wore an overcoat. It was shocking to me. I had done with a part of my life, with my youth, with my comrades. I should have no more comrades till I died. I should have friends, and perhaps a wife, and acquaintances to ask to dinner, and people to take a hand at cards with; but of comrades I should have no more. They were things I had done with for ever. I should go a-roving no more. I should never furl a sail again with a lot of men in oilskins. I could hum to myself the chorus –

To *my*
Ay,
And we'll *furl*
Ay
And pay Paddy Doyle for his boots,

but I should never hear it again, as I once heard it, on the great yellow yards, among 'the crowd'. That line of swaying figures on the foot-rope, and the faces under the sou'-wester brims, and the slatting canvas stiff with ice, and the roar and the howl of the wind, and the flogging of the gear. Well; I had done with all that; with that and much else. I was not among 'the crowd' any more, nor could I get back to it. Those places on the map too, those haunting places, those places with the Spanish names, those magical places. Oh, you names, you beautiful names.

Then I thought that, after all, if my youth were gone, the fine flower of it, the beauty, was yet mine. That man, my friend, my old comrade, what had youth been to him? It had been a means to an end, a state of probation, the formula that made his present. Had it any value to him? Did it haunt him? Did it come flooding to his mind in the night-watches? Did it say to him, 'This was life, this was truth, this was the meaning of life'? Could his soul inhabit that past, like a king in a palace? What, of his life, had seemed significant to him? What, in the past, recurred to him? Did anything? I called to mind our first voyage together, with its long, long walks on the deck, under the stars, over the sharp shadows of the sails. I remembered the first whale we saw, and the intense silvery brightness of his spout against the blue water. It had been in a dogwatch, and I had been washing on the booby-hatch, and we spoke[3] a great sailing-ship an hour later. She had come to the wind about half-a-mile away, a noble, great ship, under all sail. I remembered her name, the *Glaucus*, and the extreme stateliness with which she dipped, and then rose, and again dipped, in a slow, swaying rhythm. I remembered the first land we made after our long sailing. We had had the morning watch, and had seen the land at dawn, a faint blue on the horizon, topped with a bright peak

or two that were ruddy with sunrise. The water alongside was
no longer blue, but a dark green, which was not like the seas
we had sailed. As it grew lighter the mist which had lain along
the land was blown away. We saw the land we had come so far
to see, the land we had struggled for, the land we had talked of.
It lay in a line to leeward, a grey, irregular mass, with the sun
shining on it. Over us was a sky of a deep, kindly blue, patrolled
with soft, white clouds, little white Pacific clouds, delicately
rounded, like the clouds of the trade winds. Under us was the
green, tremulous, talking water, and there, towards us, came
the birds of those parts, birds of the sea, flying low, dipping
now and then for fish. Later, as we drew nearer, we saw the
houses, the factory chimneys, the lighthouse, the gleam of a
window. There were the ships in the bay, tier upon tier of them,
their masts like a fence of sticks round a sand-dune. Over the
quiet sea came a little tug, a little wooden tug, with her paint
gone, with blisters on her smokestack. Slowly she came, clang-
ing and groaning, making a knot an hour. Aboard her were the
men we had come so far to see, the strangers, the men with
Spanish names. In a few minutes we were to speak with them,
we were to speak with strangers, the first we had met for four
months. We should hear strange voices, we should see strange
faces, they would have news for us. Eagerly we watched them,
till the heads that had been dots upon her deck were become
human. She drew up to us, clanging and groaning; she came
within hail. We saw them, those strangers. A negro with a red
cap; a little, pale man, smoking a cigar; a tall, brown fellow,
his teeth green with coca;[4] and a boy in a blue shirt teasing a
monkey with a stick. Those were the strangers, the men we had
come to see, the men we had struggled to through the months
of sailing.

That was youth, the flower of youth, the glory of it, the
adventure accomplished. It had been much to me; it is much
still. It had been much to my friend; it was nothing to him now.
I was getting old; yet the thing came back to me, I took a part
in it. The thing comes back to me; the tug, the green water, the
negro with the cap, the masts of the ships at anchor. It is eter-
nal, it is my youth, I am young in it. It is my friend who is old;

it is he who has lost his youth, it has gone from him, it is dead, he has lived his vision.

But when we get to our lighthouse he will have more of such tales to tell me than I to tell him. He has seen so much. He is still seeing so much. He will have a fuller memory to turn over, and arrange, and select from. And when our pipes are smoked out, and it is time for us to go to our hammocks, it is not great poetry we shall sing together. It will be the song we sang when we were comrades, when we sailed the green seas and saw the flying fish. It will be –

> I dreamed a dream the other night,
> Lowlands, Lowlands, hurrah, my John;
> I dreamed a dream the other night,
> My Lowlands a-ray . . .

or some other song that comes with its memory of work done, its suggestion of storm and of stress and of adventure accomplished.

A Memory

In these first frosty days, now that there is mist at dusk into which the sun's red ball drops, one can gather to the fire as soon as the lamps are lit and take the old book from the shelf, the old tune from the fiddle, and the old memory from its cupboard in the brain. Memory is a thing of rags and patches, an odd heap of gear, a bag of orts.[1] It is a record of follies, a jumble of sketch and etching, heaped anyhow, torn, broken, blurred. One can turn it over, and see now a deck scene, with a watch at the halliards, now a woman weeping, now a carthorse tearing down a road, scattering the crowd. That is the common, haphazard, perishing memory, which is what one has to show for the privilege and glory of being man. But among these shadows, these fugitive pictures, these ghosts, there are persistent memories. Besides those angry and wretched faces, and the flaring lights, and terrible suspenses of the common records, there are others.

When those pale faces cease to haunt and the sobs of the woman leave the heart unwrung for a little, then the grander memory comes flooding in, august, symbolic, like the rising of the full moon; like the coming of the tide out of the hollows of the sea. A scene, an event, some little thing, will take to itself a significant beauty. What did this mean, or this, or this? Was it that common thing, was it what we thought? It was a king passing, it was Life going by, it was life laid bare, the tick of the red heart, the face under the veil, the tune's meaning. We thought that it was this, or this; the woman's hand putting back her hair, the haze lifting from the sea. It was a revelation; it was a miracle; it was a sweeping back of Death to his place in chaos.

Now that these frosty days are on us, and the fires are lit, the memory wakens and quickens. Those recurrent images, having the strength of symbols, rise up within me, suggesting their concealed truth. That single memory, which has haunted me so long, persists. It comes to me day after day, charged with meaning, beautiful and solemn, hinting at secrets. The thing was so beautiful it could not be a chance, a mere event, finite, a thing of a day. Like all beautiful things, it is a symbol of all beauty, a hand flinging back the window, the touch bringing the grass blade from the seed, the fire destroying Troy. All lovely things have that symbolic power, that key of release. One has but to fill the mind, and to meditate upon a lovely thing, to pass out of this world, where the best is but a shadow, to that other world, the world of beauty, 'where the golden blossoms burn upon the trees for ever'.[2]

I was at sea in a sailing-ship, walking up and down the lee side of the poop, keeping the time, and striking the bell at each half-hour. It was early in the morning watch, a little after four in the morning. We were in the tropics, not very far from the Doldrums,[3] in the last of the Trades. We were sailing slowly, making perhaps some three or four knots an hour under all sail. The dawn was in the sky to leeward of us, full of wonderful colour, full of embers and fire, changing the heaven, smouldering and burning, breaking out into bloody patches, fading into faint gold, into grey, into a darkness like smoke. There was a haze on the sea, very white and light, moving and settling. Dew was dripping from the sails, from the ropes, from the eaves of the chart-house. The decks shone with dew. In the half-light of the dusk, the binnacle-lamps burnt pale and strangely. There was a red patch forward, in the water and on the mist, where the sidelight burned. The men were moving to and fro on the deck below me, walking slowly in couples, one of them singing softly, others quietly talking. They had not settled down to sleep since the muster, because they were expecting the morning 'coffee', then brewing in the galley. The galley-funnel sent trails of sparks over to leeward, and now and then the cook passed to the ship's side to empty ashes into the sea. It was a scene common enough. The same pageant was played before me every other day, whenever I had the morning watch. There was the sunrise and the dewy decks, the sails dripping, and the men shuffling about along the deck. But on this particular day the common scenes and events were charged with meaning as though they were the initiation to a mystery, the music playing before a pageant. It may have been the mist, which made everything unreal and uncertain, especially in the twilight, with the strange glow coming through it from the dawn. I remember that a block made a soft melancholy piping noise in the mizzen rigging as though a bird had awakened upon a branch, and the noise, though common enough, made everything beautiful, just as a little touch of colour will set off a sombre picture and give a value to each tint. Then the ball of the sun came out of the sea in a mass of blood and fire, spreading streamers of gold and rose along the edges of the clouds to the mid-heaven. As he climbed from the water, and the last stars paled, the haze lifted and died. Its last shadows moved away from the sea like grey deer going to new pasture, and as they went, the look-out gave a hail of a ship being to windward of us.

When I saw her first there was a smoke of mist about her as high as her foreyard. Her topsails and flying kites had a faint glow upon them where the dawn caught them. Then the mist rolled away from her, so that we could see her hull and the glimmer of the red sidelight as it was hoisted inboard. She was rolling slightly, tracing an arc against the heaven, and as I watched her the glow upon her deepened, till every sail she

wore burned rosily like an opal turned to the sun, like a fiery
jewel. She was radiant, she was of an immortal beauty, that
swaying, delicate clipper. Coming as she came, out of the mist
into the dawn, she was like a spirit, like an intellectual pres-
ence. Her hull glowed, her rails glowed; there was colour upon
the boats and tackling. She was a lofty ship (with skysails and
royal staysails), and it was wonderful to watch her, blushing in
the sun, swaying and curvetting. She was alive with a more
than mortal life. One thought that she would speak in some
strange language or break out into a music which would express
the sea and that great flower in the sky. She came trembling
down to us, rising up high and plunging; showing the red-lead
below her water-line; then diving down till the smother bub-
bled over her hawseholes. She bowed and curvetted; the light
caught the skylights on the poop; she gleamed and sparkled;
she shook the sea from her as she rose. There was no man
aboard of us but was filled with the beauty of that ship. I think
they would have cheered her had she been a little nearer to us;
but, as it was, we ran up our flags in answer to her, adding our
position and comparing our chronometers, then dipping our
ensigns and standing away. For some minutes I watched her, as
I made up the flags before putting them back in their cupboard.
The old mate limped up to me, and spat and swore. 'That's one
of the beautiful sights of the world,' he said. 'That, and a corn-
field, and a woman with her child. It's beauty and strength.
How would you like to have one of them skysails round your
neck?' I gave him some answer, and continued to watch her, till
the beautiful, precise hull, with all its lovely detail, had become
blurred to leeward, where the sun was now marching in tri-
umph, the helm of a golden warrior plumed in cirrus.[4]

Ghosts

'Ghosts are common enough,' said an old sailor to me the other
day, 'but they aren't often seen. It's only common ghosts who
are seen.' The finer spirits may only be seen by spirits as fine as

they. The grosser spirits, as of pirates, highwaymen, suicides or of such men as hack and hew each other in the Sagas, these may been seen by ordinary people, in ordinary moods, in daylight, in the public roads. Most of us have known a haunted house; some of us may know of haunted countrysides, of pools, of woods, of quiet valleys, where immortal things still trouble the peace of mortals. For my own part, I know of a little river running through a wood; and the quiet of its dark depth and the stillness of the watching forest give it an abiding horror, a spirit of its own, terrible and malign. I can never pass by that river or among those quiet trees without feeling that about me are a multitude of spirits – some, perhaps, compassionate, but most of them evil – who resent my presence there or would make me one with themselves. The river broadens out into a lake beyond the wood, and the lake is haunted. One has but to look at it to see that it is haunted. Evil is stamped on some scenes as upon some faces; and evil is upon that trembling water and crouched in the reeds beside it and in the darkness of its rocks and deeps. A boy once saw what haunted it, and ran home white with fear and foaming at the mouth. He said he saw 'a kind of a red wirrim[1] watching him', with one pale, passionless eye, cold and blue, like a March heaven or the eye of an octopus.

'Some parts of the sea are haunted,' says the old sailor, 'but some parts aren't. It depends where you go. There's some parts is full of spirits, and others without any. They aren't seen much, but sometimes they come aboard ships, but not to hurt. They wouldn't hurt. They might cause dreams and that – nothing to hurt. Charming young ladies, some of them. They wouldn't do a feller any harm.' He told me that the early morning is the best time to see them, at a little before turn-to time, before the cook has coffee ready. Sometimes – in fact, most frequently – one does not see them, but feels them to be about, in the air, on deck, somewhere. This feeling I have had myself; perhaps most men have had it; a feeling that there is someone present, dodging about on the deck-house, among the boats, on the booms, or in among the bitts. There is an old story of a ship which carried an extra hand who had never signed articles. The crew discovered, when they were in blue water, that one watch had a man too many. 'He was one of them who wanted a passage,' said my friend, 'or perhaps he may have been the devil. There's no knowing.'

These wandering spirits who come aboard to cause dreams are sometimes knavish. I know of a sea captain who dreamed that by altering his course he would pick up a boat of cast-aways. The dream was very vivid, so vivid that he could see the axe marks along the teak of the boat's gunnel where they had cut the cover's lacings. He was much upset by the dream, for he did not wish to spoil a good passage; yet he felt that by keeping to his course he might be responsible for the deaths of his fellow-men. Unlike most captains, he confided in his mate, who was a man of great piety. The mate felt it to be a sign from Heaven. The ship's course was altered, and for the rest of the day she had a man in her topgallant cross-trees, looking out for any boat or raft of the sort seen in the vision. When it grew dark the captain burned occasional blue lights and fired off his pistol and blew his foghorn. The next morning, when it was plain that there were no castaways, he agreed with his mate that he had done all that was in his power. The ship was brought to her course and continued her voyage, and the whisky which had been uncorked ready for the sufferers, consoled the after-guard at dinner.

I once knew a sailor who had sailed in a haunted passenger steamer. She was one of the ships plying between the Plate[2] and Liverpool, but I cannot mention her name, as she is still afloat. She has one peculiarity – a poop as big as the poop of an East Indiaman.[3] On the poop there are many boats, with other clutter, such as skylights and a wheelhouse; but there is free space enough for passengers to play cricket or to dance without breaking their bones. This poop is haunted. The sailor who told me of the ghosts was one of the ship's quartermasters. On one passage, when the ship was in the tropics, he had the middle watch below. The 'fo'c's'le' (which happened to be aft, under the poop) was stiflingly hot, so that he could not sleep, though the windsails were set and the vessel was going through it at a steady clip. At last he turned out of his bunk, took a blanket and a pillow, and went on deck to sleep. He made up his bed on the poop to leeward of one of the boats, and settled down to rest at about three in the morning, just as the dawn had begun to change the colour of the sky. He did not know how long he slept; but he woke up with a start to see a line of men 'brooming down' the poop towards him, with a boatswain in front of them swilling buckets of water on to the deck as they worked aft. He saw them plainly 'as I see my dinner on my plate,' some three or four yards away, all working hard. They were so near that he sprang to his feet at once, grabbing up his gear lest it should be wetted. He had hardly taken his gear in his hand when he thought, with a shock, that he had overslept himself at least an hour and a half; that it was now half-past five, since they were washing decks; that he hadn't been to muster, and that he would get a bee in his ear, if nothing worse, for going on deck to sleep without leaving word where he could be found. As he got up he saw that the boatswain and the hands took no notice of him, though one of the sweepers looked in his direction. 'He was a red-headed fellow,' said the quartermaster, 'and he'd got a scar across one cheek like he'd been hit by a club; an ugly-looking lad he was. So I knew at once he wasn't one of our crowd. And I saw him as plain as I stand here, and he looked at me; and I saw the boatswain as plain too; I saw him tell the red-headed fellow to heave round on his broom and not go dreaming like a God-send-Sunday fellow. No, I didn't hear him say that; I only seen him. And the fellow he went on brooming down directly I seen him get told. I felt queer all over; it was so natural. I wasn't dreaming. I was awake all right. It was a vision. Or if it wasn't a vision, I'll tell you what it was – it was sent. It was sent as a warning. That red-headed fellow was a warning. Sometime I shall meet that red-headed fellow, and, you mark my words, he'll give me a queer push. So I shall stand from under when I come alongside of him. I'd know him again if I saw him all right. Some day I shall see him.' The vision, or warning, or whatever it was kept him awake for the rest of the watch. He went below to the fo'c's'le, having had enough of the poop, and found that he had been asleep hardly more than twenty minutes.

There is something wrong with that poop. It is not a canny place. I know of another queer thing which happened there, and of a man who started up from his sleep beside a boat to prophesy of what should happen to him in a year's time. The prophecy seemed to every one the most crack-brained nonsense; but it was fulfilled exactly, almost to a day, certainly within a week of the time predicted.

But ghosts are common things, commercial things, things which can only squeak and gibber and frighten poor travellers. They are the base ones of the spiritual world. A ship, a beautiful ship, over which the moral virtue of so many men has been awakened, must be peopled by spirits more lovely than red-headed sailors. The lovely bow, which leans and cleaves, slashing the sea into flame, is surely guarded by a presence, erect, winged, fiery, having the eyes and the ardour of one of the intellectual kingdom. At the wheel, the kicking, side-bruising wheel, which takes charge, and grunts, and flings one over the box, there stand for ever those mailed ones, the ship's guides and guards.

Big Jim

One afternoon, many years ago, I was in a Western seaport, with a day's 'liberty' to do what I liked. There were few attractions in the seaport except seamen's dance-houses and drinking dens, so I pushed inland, up some barren sand-hills, into the wilderness. High up among the hills I came to a silver mine, with a little inn or wine-shop close to the shaft, and (more strange in that desert) a sort of evergreen pine tree with some of its branches still alive. There was a bench near the door of the tavern, so I sat down to rest; and I remember looking at the russet-coloured earth from the shaft and wondering whether silver mining were hard work or not. I had had enough of hard work to last me through my time. There was a view over the sea from where I sat. I could see the anchorage and the ships and a few rocks with surf about them, and a train puffing into the depot. A barquentine was being towed out by a little dirty tug; and very far away, shining in the sun, an island rose from the sea, whitish, like a swimmer's shoulder. It was a beautiful sight, that anchorage, with the ships lying there so lovely, all their troubles at an end. But I knew that aboard each ship there were young men going to the devil, and mature men wasted, and old men wrecked; and I wondered at the misery and sin which went to make each ship so perfect an image of beauty. As I sat thinking I heard voices inside the tavern, and a noise of crying – the high, one might almost call it griefless, crying of a native woman. Someone came to the door and looked at me once or twice; but I felt this rather than saw it, for my back was to the door and I did not care to look round. Presently I stood up and went into the tavern, to a curious company.

It was a rather large, bare drinking bar, with an earthen floor and adobe walls. The bar was made of a few deal planks nailed to some barrels. Behind it there were some shelves of bottles and a cask or two, and a few mugs, pannikins and cigar boxes. It was like most low drinking shops; but it was perhaps a shade more bare than the general run. What interested me was the company.

As I entered I noticed that they all looked at me rather hard, and then looked at each other with quick, questioning glances. They were not a difficult crowd to place. They were English and American merchant seamen who had deserted their ships and come mining for a change. But from the way they looked at me it was plain that there was something wrong, and the something was a dead body lying in a corner, half covered by a woman's skirt. By the body, a half-naked woman crouched, wailing in a high, shrill key, which was somehow not at all affecting, as it did not seem to have a passion in it. The body was that of a big, handsome man, evidently the woman's lover. It gave me a kind of awe when I saw that he had a moustache but no beard, for I knew then that the man had been a lover of women; because no man would trouble to shave in such a place without that spur to his vanity. Something told me that the man had died a violent death; but in that country such deaths were common. One of the seamen came up to me and served me with a pannikin of wine: he seemed to be the proprietor. 'It was a fight,' he said simply, seeing me look at the body. 'This morning,' he added, 'a Chilanean done it.' 'Who was he?' I asked. 'They call him Big Jim,' he answered. 'He was a big feller, too; an Englishman, I guess. A miner.' 'He swallowed the anchor,' said another seaman. 'He come here in a barque,' said a third. 'They got scrapping,' said the fourth. 'Over the gell, they got scrapping. Der Chilanean give 'im just one lick, an' Jim quit. There's the knife done it.' He jerked his head towards the corner where the body lay; and there, on the mud floor, was a common vaquero's[1] dagger, with a handle stuck about with silver knobs, and a broad, curving, pointed blade. 'That was the knife done it.'

By and by another miner came loping down the track to the tavern. He rode an old mule, and carried a shovel, which he had borrowed from a friend. He ate some bread, and drank a little wine from the pannikin; and then we all turned out into the air to dig Jim a grave under the forlorn evergreen. It was easy shovelling in that light, sandy earth; the grave was soon ready. We went back to the house to fetch the body. The woman was still wailing there in her passionless thin monotone. I believe she hadn't moved since I entered. We had to lift her from the body, for we could not make her understand; she was cowed or dazed; she made no protest, only wailed and wailed like a hurt negro – exactly like a hurt negro; she must have been part negro, a quadroon,[2] perhaps. One of the men asked if the skirt which covered Jim should be buried with him. 'Ah, no; leave it for the gell,' said one of them; 'it's all the skirt she has.'

When we laid the body in the grave the sun was about to set; and the burial party seemed touched and unwilling to cover the dead with earth. 'I seen him stan' just where he is lying,' said one of them. 'And I seen him. Only yesterday,' said another. 'Funny his being dead now and not seeing nothing,' said the third. 'I guess he didn't think nawthen of dying when he t'r'un out dis morning.' 'It gives one rather a turn,' said the first. 'There was Jim. Look what arms he got. He could do a big day's work, Jim could.' 'Well, he done his last day's work now,

Jim has.' 'Ah,' they said, more or less together, 'he's touched his pay, Jim has.'

Little by little the visitor got some knowledge of Jim as a man and a comrade. He wasn't a drinker, he didn't care for tobacco, didn't use it in any shape. It was girls done Jim. He was a man of education. 'If I'd had the education what Jim had I wouldn't be working down no silver mine' – that was what one or two of them told me. 'He was a hard case with it,' said another; 'he never wear more than his oilskins off the Horn.[3] I seen him stand his look-out with only trousers on. I seen it snowing on his chest.' 'He'd got a fine chest on him, too,' said another; 'I seen him lift 'alf a ton.' 'Go on with your 'alf tons,' said one; 'no man could lift that.' 'He was strong all right, though,' said the first; ''e could carry more than a lanchero.'[4] After this someone wondered if the dead man's spirit could see us; for now that the sun was setting the light was beginning to fade, and I know that we all felt the solemnity of life and death, and the certainty that we, too, in time would lie helpless, even as Jim lay. The thought came to us that it would be strange to the body to lie in a grave after so long roving on the world; and to see no fellow-man, to be shut away from companions, after the long life with companions, after the days of love and unselfish tending. It would be strange to the soul, too, we thought, to be loose at last from the old servant and gaoler, and to be like a wild bird again, flying through the world, nesting in no haunt of men, tortured perhaps, perhaps exultant. The general feeling was that God wouldn't be hard on Jim; and the words (whatever they may seem) were tenderly and reverently spoken. To live hard, work hard, die hard, and go to hell in the end would be hard indeed. 'It would that,' said the others. That was Big Jim's burial service.

We laid a handkerchief over the face, so that the earth might not touch the flesh. Then, with our shovel we covered the body, and heaped the grave with a little pile of earth, and nailed a batten, torn from a packing-case, across the pine tree at his head. We had no pistol for a volley, and it was not for the likes of us to say a prayer, we being still ourselves, and Jim being something beyond us. We stood about the grave a moment, wondering where he came from and whether he had any people.

Then we went back to the tavern, to a meal of bread, red wine and bad dried figs, brought from the sacks and skins[5] which Jim had carried up from town less than a day before.

When I sailed from that port I went aloft to see the last of the silver mine. I could see it, in the clear light, quite plainly; and I could see the one evergreen marking the grave. The chance meetings of life are full of mystery, and this chance adventure, with its sadness and beauty, will always move me. The evergreen must be dead by this time, and perhaps the mine will be worked out and the tavern gone. Big Jim will lie quietly, with the surf roaring very far below him, and no man near him at any time save the muleteers,[6] with their bell-mares and songs, going over the pass into the desert.

El Dorado[1]

The night had fallen over the harbour before the winch began to rattle. The stars came out, calm and golden, shaking little tracks in the sea. In the tiers of ships shone the riding-lights. To the westward, where the Point jutted out, the great golden light of Negra[2] winked and glimmered as it revolved. It was a still night but for the noise of the surf, which beat continually, like the marching of an army, along the line of the coast. In one of the tiers of ships there was a sing-song. A crew had gathered on the forecastle-head, to beat their pannikins to the stars. The words of their song floated out into the darkness, full of a haunting beauty which thrilled and satisfied me. There was something in the night, in the air, in the beauty of the town, and in the sweetness of the sailors' singing, which made me sorry to be leaving. I should have liked to have gone ashore again, to the Calle del Inca,[3] where the cafés and taverns stood. I should have liked to have seen those stately pale women, in their black robes, with the scarlet roses in their hair, swaying slowly on the stage to the clicking of the castanets. I should have liked to have taken part in another wild dance among the tables of the wine-shops. I was sorry to be leaving.

When the winch began to clank, as the cable was hove in, I gathered up my lead-line, and went to the leadsman's dicky, or little projecting platform, on the starboard side. I was to be the leadsman that night, and as we should soon be moving, I made the breast-rope secure, and stood by.

Presently the bell of the engine-room clanged, and there came a wash abaft as the screws thrashed. The ship trembled, as the turbulent trampling of the engines shook her. The bell clanged again; the water below me gleamed and whitened; the dark body of the steamer, with her lines of lit ports, swept slowly across the lights in the harbour. The trampling of the engines steadied, and took to itself a rhythm. We were off. I cast an eye astern at the little town I was so sad to leave, and caught a glimpse of a path of churned water, broadening astern of us. A voice sounded from the promenade deck behind me. 'Zat light, what you call 'eem?'

I could not answer. My orders were to keep strict silence. The point of an umbrella took me sharply below the shoulders. 'What you call 'eem – zat light? Ze light zere?'

I wondered if I could swing my lead on to him; it was worth trying. Again came the umbrella; and again the bell of the engine-room clanged.

'Are you ready there with the lead?' came the mate's voice above me. 'All ready with the lead, sir.' 'What have we now?' I gathered forward and swung the lead. I could not reach the umbrella-man, even with my spare line. Once, twice, thrice I swung, and pitched the plummet well forward into the bow-wash.

'By the deep, eight, sir.'

Again the bell clanged; the ship seemed to tremble and stop. 'Another cast now, quickly.' 'And a half, seven, sir.' As I hauled in, I again tasted the umbrella, and another question came to me: 'What 'ave you do? Why 'ave you do zat?' I swore under my breath. 'Are you asleep there, leadsman?' The mate was biting his finger-ends. I sent the lead viciously into the sea. 'Quarter less seven, sir.' 'Another cast, smartly, now.' Rapidly I hauled in, humming an old ballad to myself. 'We'll have the ship ashore,' I repeated. There was a step on the deck behind me, and again came the voice: 'Ze man, ze man zere, what 'ave he do? Why 'ave 'e go like so?' 'Won't you pass further aft, sir?' said a suave voice. 'You're interrup'in' the leadsman.' It was one of the quartermasters. Once again the lead flew forward. 'By the mark, seven, sir.'

There was a pause; then came the voice again: 'I go zees way?' 'Yes, zees way,' said the quartermaster. The steps of the umbrella-man passed away aft. 'Zees way,' said the quarter-master, under his breath, 'zees way! You gawdem Dago!'[4] I could have hugged the fellow.

'What now?' said the old man, leaning over from the bridge. I cast again. 'And a half, eight, sir.' 'We're clear,' said the voice above me. ''Speed ahead, Mr Jenkins.' I gathered up my line. The engine-room bell clanged once more; the ship seemed to leap sud-denly forward. In a few seconds, even as I coiled my line, the bow-wash broadened to a roaring water. The white of it glim-mered and boiled, and spun away from us, streaked with fires. Across the stars above us the mists from the smokestack stretched in a broad cloud. Below me the engines trampled thunderously. Ahead there were the lights, and the figure of the look-out, and the rush and hurry of the water. Astern, far astern already, were the port, the ships at anchor and the winking light on the Point. A bugle abaft called the passengers to dinner, and I watched them as they went from their cabins. A lady, in a blue gown, with a shawl round her head, was talking to a man in evening dress. 'Isn't it interesting,' she remarked, 'to hear them making the soundings?' The white shirt was politely non-committal. 'Aft there, two of you,' said a hard voice, 'and trice the ladder up. Smartly now.' The lady in the blue dress stopped to watch us.

I did not see the umbrella-man again, until the next day, when I passed him on the hurricane deck. He was looking at the coast through a pair of binoculars. We were running to the north, in perfect Pacific weather, under a soft blue sky that was patrolled by little soft white clouds. The land lay broad to star-board, a land of yellow hills, with surf-beaten outliers[5] of black reef. Here and there we passed villages in the watered valleys, each with its whitewashed church and copper smeltry. The umbrella-man was looking beyond these, at the hills.

He was a little man, this man who had prodded me. He had a long, pale face and pale eyes, a long, reddish beard, and hair rather darker, both hair and beard being sparse. He was a fidgety person, always twitching with his hands, and he walked with something of a strut, as though the earth belonged to him. He snapped-to the case of his binoculars as though he had sheathed a sword.

Later in the day, after supper, in the second dogwatch, as I sat smoking on the fore-coamings, he came up to me and spoke to me. 'You know zees coas'?' he asked. Yes, I knew the coast. 'What you zink?' he asked; 'you like 'eem?' No, I didn't like 'eem. 'Ah,' he said, 'you 'ave been wizzin?' I asked him what he meant. 'Wizzin,' he repeated, 'wizzin, in ze contry. You 'ave know ze land, ze peoples?' I growled that I had been within, to Lima, and to Santiago,[6] and that I had been ashore at the Chincha Islands. 'Ah,' he said, with a strange quickening of interest, 'you 'ave been to Lima; you like 'eem?' No, I didn't like 'eem. 'But you 'ave been wizzin, wizzin Lima, wizzin ze contry?' No, I had not. 'I go wizzin,' he said proudly. 'It is because I go; zat is why I ask. Zere is few 'ave gone wizzin.' An old quartermaster walked up to us. 'There's very few come back, sir,' he said. 'Them Indians –' 'Ah, ze Indians,' said the little man scornfully, 'ze Indians; I zeenk nozzin of ze Indians.' 'Beg pardon, sir,' said the old sailor, 'they're a tough crowd, them copper fellers.' 'I no understan',' said the Frenchman. 'They pickle people's heads,' said the old sailor, 'in the sand or somethin'. They keep for ever pretty near when once they're pickled. They pickle everyone's head and sell 'em in Lima; I've knowed 'em get a matter of three pound for a good head.' 'Heads?' said another sailor. 'I had one myself once. I got it at Tacna,[7] but it wasn't properly pickled or something – it was a red-headed beggar the chap as owned it – I had to throw it away. It got too strong for the crowd,' he explained. 'Ah, zose Indians,' said the Frenchman. 'I 'ave 'eard; zey tell me, zey tell me at Valparaiso.[8] But ah, it ees a fool; it ees a fool; zere is no Indians.' 'Beg pardon, sir,' said the old sailor, 'but if you go up among them jokers, you'll have to watch out they don't pickle you. You'll have to look slippy with a gun, sir.' 'Ah, a gon,' he answered, 'a

gon. I was not to be bozzered wiz a gon. I 'ave what you call
'eem – peestol.' He produced a boy's derringer,[9] which might
have cost about ten dollars, Spanish dollars, in the pawnshops
of Santiago. 'Peestol,' murmured a sailor, gasping, as he sham-
bled forward to laugh, 'peestol, the gawdem Dago's balmy.'

During the next few days I saw the Frenchman frequently.
He was a wonder to us, and his plans were discussed at every
meal, and in every watch below. In the dogwatches he would
come forward, with his eternal questions: 'What is wizzin? In
ze contry?' We would tell him, 'Indians', or 'highwaymen', or
'a push of high-binders'; and he would answer: 'It ees nozzin, it
ees a fool.' Once he asked us if we had heard of any gold being
found 'wizzin'. 'Gold?' said one of us. 'Gold? O' course there's
gold, any God's quantity. Them Incas ate gold; they're buried
in it.' ''Ave you know zem, ze Incas?' he asked eagerly. 'I seen
a tomb of theirs once,' said the sailor; 'it were in a cave, like the
fo'c's'le yonder, and full of knittin'-needles.' 'What is zem?'
said the Frenchman. The sailor shambled below to his chest,
and returned with a handful of little sticks round which some
balls of coloured threads were bound. 'Knittin'-needles,' said
the sailor. 'Them ain't no knittin'-needles,' said another; 'them's
their way of writin'.' 'Go on with yer,' said the first; 'them's
knittin'-needles. Writin'? How could them be writin'?' 'Well, I
heard tell once,' replied the other. 'It ees zeir way of writing,'
said the Frenchman; 'I 'ave seen; zat is zeir way of writing; ze
knots is zeir letters.' 'Bleedin' funny letters, I call 'em,' said the
needles-theorist. 'You and your needles,' said the other. 'Now,
what d'ye call 'em?' The bell upon the bridge clanged. 'Eight
bells,' said the company; 'aft to muster, boys.' The bugle at the
saloon-door announced supper.

We were getting pretty well to the north – Mollendo,[10] or
thereabouts – when I had my last conversation with the French-
man. He came up to me one night, as I sat on the deck to
leeward of the winch, keeping the first watch as snugly as I
could. 'You know zees coast long?' he asked. I had not. Then
came the never-ceasing, ''Ave you know of ze Incas?' Yes, lots
of general talk; and I had seen Inca curios, mostly earthenware,
in every port in Peru. 'You 'ave seen gold?' No; there was never

any gold. The Spaniards made a pretty general average of any gold there was. 'It ees a fool,' he answered. 'I tell you,' he went on, 'it ees a fool. Zey have say zat; zey 'ave all say zat; it ees a fool. Zere *is* gold. Zere is a hundred million pounds; zere is twenty tousan' million dollars; zere is El Dorado. Beyond ze mountains zere is El Dorado; zere is a town of gold. Zey say zere is no gold? Zere is. I go to find ze gold; zat is what I do; I fin' ze gold, I, Paul Bac.' 'Alone?' I asked. 'I, Paul Bac,' he answered.

I looked at him a moment. He was a little red-haired man, slightly made, but alert and active-looking. He knew no Spanish, no Indian dialects, and he had no comrade. I told him that I thought he didn't know what he was doing. 'Ha!' he said. 'Listen: I go to Payta; I go by train to Chito; zen I reach ze Morona River; from zere I reach Marinha.[11] Listen: El Dorado is between ze Caqueta and ze Putumayo Rivers,[12] in ze forest.' I would have asked him how he knew, but I had to break away to relieve the look-out. I wished the little man good night; I never spoke with him again.

I thought of him all that watch, as I kept scanning the seas. I should be going up and down, I thought, landing passengers through surf, or swaying bananas out of launches, or crying the sounds as we came to moorings. He would be going on under the stars, full of unquenchable hope, stumbling on the bones of kings. He would be wading across bogs, through rivers and swamps, through unutterable and deathly places, singing some song, and thinking of the golden city. He was a pilgrim, a poet, a person to reverence. And if he got there, if he found El Dorado – but that was absurd. I thought of him sadly, with the feeling that he had learned how to live, and that he would die by applying his knowledge. I wondered how he would die. He would be alone there, in the tangle, stumbling across creepers. The poisoned dart would hit him in the back, from the long, polished blow-pipe, such as I had seen in the museums. He would fall on his face, among the jungle. Then the silent Indian would hack off his head with a flint, and pickle it for the Lima markets. He would never get to the Caqueta. Or perhaps he would be caught in an electric storm, an *aire*, as they call them,

and be stricken down among the hills on his way to Chito.
More probably he would die of hunger or thirst, as so many
had died before him. I remembered a cowboy whom I had
found under a thorn bush in the Argentine. Paul Bac would be
like that cowboy; he would run short of water, and kill his
horse for the blood, and then go mad and die.

I was in my bunk when he went ashore at Payta, but a fellow
in the other watch told me how he left the ship. There was a
discussion in the forecastle that night as to the way the heads
were prepared. Some said it was sand; some said it was the leaf
of the *puro* bush;[13] one or two held out for a mixture of pepper
and nitrate. One man speculated as to the probable price the
head would fetch; and the general vote was for two pounds, or
two pounds ten. 'It wouldn't give me no pleasure,' said one of
us, 'to have that ginger-nob in my chest.' 'Nor me, it wouldn't,'
said another; 'I draw the line at having a corpse on my tobacker.'
'And I do,' said several. Clearly the Frenchman was destined
for a town museum.

It was more than a year after that that I heard of the end of
the El Dorado hunter. I was in New York when I heard it, serv-
ing behind the bar of a saloon. One evening, as I was mixing
cocktails, I heard myself hailed by a customer; and there was
Billy Neeld, one of our quartermasters, just come ashore from
an Atlantic Transport boat. We had a drink together, and
yarned of old times. The names of our old shipmates were like
incantations. The breathing of them brought the past before us;
the past which was so recent, yet so far away; the past which is
so dear to a sailor and so depressing to a landsman. So and so
was dead, and Jimmy had gone among the Islands, and Dick had
pulled out for home because 'he couldn't stick that Mr Jenkins'.
Very few of them remained on the Coast; the brothers of the
Coast are a shifting crowd.

'D'ye remember the Frenchman,' I asked, 'the man who was
always asking about the Incas?' 'The ginger-headed feller?'
'Yes, a little fellow.' 'A red-headed, ambitious[14] little runt?
I remember him,' said Billy; 'he left us at Payta, the time we
fouled the launch.' 'That's the man,' I said; 'have you heard
anything of him?' 'Oh, he's dead, all right,' said Billy. 'His

mother came out after him; there was a piece in the *Chile Times* about him.' 'He was killed, I suppose?' 'Yes, them Indians got him, somewhere in Ecuador, Tommy Hains told me. They got his head back, though. It was being sold in the streets; his old mother offered a reward, and the Dagoes got it back for her. He's dead all right, he is; he might ha' known as much, going alone among them Indians. Dead? I guess he is dead; none but a red-headed runt'd have been such a lunk[15] as to try it.' 'He was an ambitious lad,' I said. 'Yes,' said Billy, 'he was. Them ambitious fellers, they want the earth, and they get their blooming heads pickled; that's what they get by it. Here's happy days, young feller.'

The Western Islands

'Once there were two sailors;[1] and one of them was Joe, and the other one was Jerry, and they were fishermen. And they'd a young apprentice-feller, and his name was Jim. And Joe was a great one for his pot, and Jerry was a wonder at his pipe; and Jim did all the work, and both of them banged him. So one time Joe and Jerry were in the beer-house, and there was a young parson there, telling the folk about foreign things, about plants and that. "Ah," he says, "what wonders there are in the west."

'"What sort of wonders, begging your pardon, sir," says Joe. "What sort of wonders might them be?"

'"Why, all sorts of wonders," says the parson. "Why, in the west," he says, "there's things you wouldn't believe. No, you wouldn't believe; not till you'd seen them," he says. "There's diamonds growing on the trees. And great, golden, glittering pearls as common as pea-straw. And there's islands in the west. Ah, I could tell you of them. Islands? I rather guess there's islands. None of your Isles of Man. None of your Alderney and Sark. Not in them seas."

'"What sort of islands might they be, begging your pardon, sir?" says Jerry.

' "Why," he says (the parson feller says), "ISLANDS. Islands as big as Spain. Islands with rivers of rum and streams of sar-saparilla.[2] And none of your roses. Rubies and ame-thyses is all the roses grows in them parts. With golden stalks to them, and big diamond sticks to them, and the taste of pork-crackling if you eat them. They're the sort of roses to have in your area," he says.

' "And what else might there be in them parts, begging your pardon, sir?" says Joe.

' "Why," he says, this parson says, "there's wonders. There's not only wonders but miracles. And not only miracles, but sperrits."

' "What sort of sperrits might they be, begging your pardon?" says Jerry. "Are they rum and that?"

' "When I says sperrits," says the parson feller, "I mean ghosts."

' "Of course ye do," says Joe.

' "Yes, ghosts," says the parson. "And by ghosts I mean sperrits. And by sperrits I mean white things. And by white things I mean things as turn your hair white. And there's red devils there, and blue devils there, and a great gold queen a-waiting for a man to kiss her. And the first man as dares to kiss that queen, why he becomes king, and all her sacks of gold become his."

' "Begging your pardon, sir," said Jerry, "but whereabouts might these here islands be?"

' "Why, in the west," says the parson. "In the west, where the sun sets."

' "Ah," said Joe and Jerry. "What wonders there are in the world."

'Now, after that, neither one of them could think of anything but these here western islands. So at last they take their smack, and off they go in search of them. And Joe had a barrel of beer in the bows, and Jerry had a box of twist[3] in the waist, and pore little Jim stood and steered abaft all. And in the evenings Jerry and Joe would bang their pannikins together, and sing of the great times they meant to have when they were married to the queen. Then they would clump pore little Jim across the head, and tell him to watch out, and keep her to her course, or they'd ride him down like you would a main tack. And he'd better mind his eye, they told him, or they'd make him long to be boiled and salted. And he'd better put more sugar in the tea, they said, or they'd cut him up for cod-bait. And who was he, they asked, to be wanting meat for dinner, when there was that much weevilly biscuit in the bread-barge? And boys was going to the dogs, they said, when limbs the like of him had the heaven-born insolence to want to sleep. And a nice pass things was coming to, they said, when a lad as they'd done everything for, and saved, so to speak, from the workhouse, should go for to snivel when they hit him a clip. If they'd said a word, when they was hit, when they was boys, they told him, they'd have had their bloods drawed, and been stood in the wind to cool. But let him take heed, they said, and be a good lad, and do the work of five, and they wouldn't half wonder, they used to say, as he'd be a man before his mother. So the sun shone, and the stars came out golden, and all the sea was a sparkle of gold with them. Blue was the sea, and the wind blew, too, and it blew Joe and Jerry west as fast as a cat can eat sardines.

'And one fine morning the wind fell calm, and a pleasant smell came over the water, like nutmegs on a rum-milk-punch. Presently the dawn broke. And, lo and behold, a rousing great wonderful island, all scarlet with coral and with rubies. The surf that was beating on her sands went shattering into silver coins, into dimes, and pesetas, and francs, and fourpenny bits. And the flowers on the cliffs was all one gleam and glitter. And the beauty of that island was a beauty beyond the beauty of Sally Brown, the lady as kept the beer-house. And on the beach of that island, on a golden throne, like, sat a woman so lovely that to look at her was as good as a church-service for one.

'"That's the party I got to kiss," said Jerry. "Steady, and beach her, Jim, boy," he says. "Run her ashore, lad. That's the party is to be my queen."

'"You've got a neck on you, all of a sudden," said Joe. "You ain't the admiral of this fleet. Not by a wide road you ain't. I'll do all the kissing as there's any call for. You keep clear, my son."

'Here the boat ran her nose into the sand, and the voyagers went ashore.

' "Keep clear, is it?" said Jerry. "You tell me to keep clear? You tell me again, and I'll put a head on you'll make you sing like a kettle. Who are you to tell me to keep clear?"

' "I tell you who I am," said Joe. "I'm a better man than you are. That's what I am. I'm Joe the Tank, from Limehouse Basin,[4] and there's no tinker's donkey-boy'll make me stand from under. Who are you to go kissing queens? Who are you that talk so proud and so mighty? You've a face on you would make a Dago[5] tired. You look like a seasick Kanaka[6] that's boxed seven rounds with a buzz-saw.[7] You've no more manners than a hog, and you've a lip on you would fetch the enamel off a cup."

' "If it comes to calling names," said Jerry, "you ain't the only pebble on the beach. Whatever you might think, I tell you you ain't. You're the round turn and two half hitches of a figure of fun as makes the angels weep. That's what you are. And you're the right-hand strand, and the left-hand strand, and the centre strand, and the core, and the serving, and the marling, of a three-stranded, left-handed, poorly worked junk of a half-begun and never finished odds and ends of a Port Mahon soldier.[8] You look like a Portuguese drummer. You've a whelky red nose that shines like a port sidelight. You've a face like a muddy field where they've been playing football in the rain. Your hair is an insult and a shame. I blush when I look at you. You give me a turn like the first day out to a first-voyager. Kiss, will you? Kiss? Man, I tell you you'd paralyse a shark if you kissed him. Paralyse him, strike him cold. That's what a kiss of yours'd do."

' "You ought to a been a parson," said Joe, "that's what you'd ought. There's many would a paid you for talk like that. But for all your fine talk, and for all your dandy language, you'll not come the old soldier over me. No, nor ten of you. *You* talk of kissing, when there's a handsome young man, the likes of me, around? Neither you nor ten of you. To hear you talk one'd think you was a emperor or a admiral. One would think you was a bishop or a king. One might mistake you for a general or a Member of Parliament. You might. Straight, you might. A general or a bishop or a king. And what are you? What are you? I ask you plain. What are you? – I'll tell you what you are. You're him as hired himself out as a scarecrow, acos no one'd take you as a fo'c's'le hand. You're him as give the colic to a weather-cock. You're him as turned old Mother Bomby's beer.[9] You're him as drowned the duck and stole the monkey.[10] You're him as got the medal give him for having a face that made the bull tame. You're –"

'"Now don't you cast no more to me," said Jerry. "For I won't take no lip from a twelve-a-shilling, cent-a-corner, the likes of you are. You're the clippings of old junk, what the Dagoes smokes in cigarettes. A swab, and a wash-deck-broom, and the half of a pint of paint'd make a handsomer figer of a man than what you are. I've seen a coir whisk, what they grooms a mule with, as had a sweeter face than you got. So stand aside, before you're put aside. I'm the king of this here island. You can go chase yourself for another. Stand clear, I say, or I'll give you a jog'll make your bells ring."

'Now, while they were argufying, young Jim, the young apprentice-feller, he creeps up to the queen upon the throne. She was beautiful, she was, and she shone in the sun, and she looked straight ahead of her like a wax-work in a show. And in her hand she had a sack full of jewels, and at her feet she had a sack full of gold, and by her side was an empty throne ready for the king she married. But round her right hand there was a red snake, and round her left hand there was a blue snake, and the snakes hissed and twisted, and they showed their teeth full of poison. So Jim looked at the snakes, and he hit them a welt, right and left, and he kissed the lady.

'And immediately all the bells and the birds of the world burst out a-ringing and a-singing. The lady awoke from her sleep, and Jim's old clothes were changed to cloth of gold. And there he was, a king, on the throne beside the lady.

'But the red snake turned to a big red devil who took a hold of Joe, and the blue snake turned to a big blue devil, who took a hold of Jerry. And "Come you here, you brawling pugs," they said, "come and shovel sand." And Joe and Jerry took the spades that were given to them. And "Dig, now," said the devils. "Heave round. Let's see you dig. Dig, you scarecrows. And tell us when you've dug to London." '

OTHER PROSE

Autobiography

All day long it had blown salt and fierce from the south-west. The sun had set at last in a moist grey stretch of cloud touched at the top with pale yellow like the colour of weak tea, and since then it had come on very dirty.

Tulip,[1] going to the galley 'to get our supper along', had paused to look aloft a moment, and the sight of the giddy rigging shaking and thrashing in the high wind seemed to him to bode ill for a first-voyager's peace of belly on the morrow.

I stood near the half-deck door, stripped to the waist, and washed myself in a battered tin basin on the top of number three hatch. It was a difficult business, for I was very dirty. I had been coiling mucky hawsers most of the afternoon, and the wet dirt had grimed itself into my face and hands. I was tired, too, very tired: my joints ached, and my arms had a twinge of rheumatism in them that was like rust to the muscles.

Down where I stood I could see the red sparks streaming away to leeward from the galley-funnel, and, low down, hurrying, harried, driven and ripped about, went ever the oily grey clouds tattered into rags at the edges.

The noise of the wind shouting and crying in the shrouds, and the sight of the huddled squalid houses near the dock-side, gave me a dull feeling of disgusted misery, gave me a sense, too, of a bad time coming. A wretched, cold, wet, 'hungry' time soon to make itself felt. I had been aboard for very nearly three weeks, and had already lost the few romantic notions about the sea which two years training on the *Conway* had suffered to remain. Sea-life, I found, was not a life of good blue clothes and brass buttons; not a life of pigtails, cutlasses and lovely Nan. It was a life of dull, rough, dirty work. A life of bad food and brutal usage amid coarse company.

As I washed in the battered tin basin that windy March night, I felt all this, I remember, very keenly. We were to sail next morning, and I was a bit homesick, mammy sick, thinking of home and the fields full of daffodils and all the jolly things one sees in April.

The *Aladdin* lay alongside us. She, too, would sail early on the morrow, and further down the dock lay the *Craigenbannoch*, a sweet little barque bound for the River Plate.[2]

Moored alongside as she was, the *Aladdin* looked strangely tiny. Our great spars dwarfed hers into the merest match-sticks, and I remember wishing that I were James, the *Aladdin* apprentice, so that, on the morrow, poor seasick first-voyager that I should be, I might have lighter sails to wrestle with and a shorter drop should my foot fail me aloft there, on the giddy royal yard.

Though one be as dirty as medieval Paris, in time, by dint of washing, one becomes clean.

I, too, was clean in a little while, and I emptied the tin basin into the dock and slipped my rough blue shirt over my shoulders.

'Jan,'[3] cried Chris[4] from the half-deck, 'come and get your supper before that damn thief Hart[5] has eaten it.'

The half-deck, the apprentices' berth, the hutch where we six lads[6] were kennelled, was an iron deck-house standing perhaps nine feet high.

It measured perhaps fourteen feet each way, though a double tier of bunks to port and starboard, a long narrow black table against the forward bulkhead, and two lockers aft (one on either side of the door) greatly contracted the available inner space.

On the deck, too, were six sea-chests. Black clumsy boxes much knocked about and blunted at the corners, each having the owner's name painted on the side in letters of a dirty white. Four of these were ranged alongside the table and served as seats at meal-times.

The iron bulkheads had been painted in a feeble imitation of polished maple-wood. When skylight and door were closed (as always in foul weather) those iron walls would 'sweat'.

Cold clammy drops would ooze down from beam to deck, each leaving a slimy shiny mark as if a snail had crawled there.

The skylight opened over the table and in wet weather dripped accursedly upon those seated below.

Of the eight bunks two on the port-side were disengaged, and these we had filled with our seamen's bags. (Dirty canvas sacks, bulged most curiously with stout sea-gear and tied at the mouths with tarry scraps of spunyarn.)

The bunk at sea is something more than a kennel. It is drawing-room, boudoir, smoking-room and bachelor's den all in one, and each of us had tried to make his bunk look bright and pretty. Outside we had rigged up curtains of red and green baize, while within them, on the iron bulkheads, we had pasted coloured scraps, blue paper fans, pipe-racks full of cutties,[7] and, in mine at any rate, a little wooden shelf holding an old book or two: Captain Marryat, Captain Chamier,[8] a dog-eared book of Logarithms much thumbed and pencilled, a Barometer Manual in a soiled blue cover, a broken backed copy of *Huckleberry Finn*,[9] and Captain MacNab concerning the Laws of Storms.[10]

The two lockers I have mentioned, one on each side of the door, were painted a dark brown, with the house-flag (in red and blue) on the doors of them. In one of them was a tank which, at sea, held our water allowance. In the other (when not in use) the battered tin basin, and a dirty bucket in which we cleaned our plates.

Inside the half-deck, that night, it was warm and cosy feeling. They had lit the lamp, and Tulip had swept the place out and made it look like a home.

When I entered, the other five lads were already at table amid an array of battered tin pannikins, busy with food and talking between the bites.

Supper consisted of a sodden heavy 'dry-hash' served up in a wooden kid,[11] but we had, in addition, an old brown bread-barge half filled with broken biscuit, and, being still in port, a loaf of soft bread.

At the top of the table stood a tin kettle (I had bought it the week before in a dingy ironmongery up Tiger Bay[12] in sailor-town – I paid sixpence for it). This kettle contained hot ship's tea – a black thin fluid tasting sometimes of tin, sometimes of cheap molasses. Smelling horribly at all times of both.

'Come along, Jan,' shouted Sandy. 'Your bloody tea's getting cold.'

I helped myself to a whack of hash and ate and drank mechanically; I talked little for I still had the homesickness and the aching heart, but the other five talked noisily and much.

'Hart, d'ye think we shall sail tomorrow?'

'Little Billy'll[13] never sail if it blows like this; his wife wouldn't let him.'

'Well, anyway, I heard the mate say we should sail as soon as –'

'That mate isn't half a bad sort; I took his wife ashore in the boat this morning, and after he'd seen her off he stood me a glass of port-wine at a little pub near the station.'

'I wonder whose watch I'll be in.'

'Ay and I. By hell, I'd hate to be in Pyecroft's[14] watch. He's got too big a bloody boot.'

'Well boys, don't you wish you were back aboard the *Conway*?'

'Hart, d'ye think we'll sail tomorrow?'

Now Hart was in his third year at sea and we first-voyagers trusted a good deal to his experience.

'Sail?' he answered. 'Sail? Will Billy Diggory sail? Will he hell – if Billy had had the guts of a cow he'd have sailed this morning – it's only blowing a bit fresh.'

'Why, Captain James, of the *Joppa*, would have danced a bloody hornpipe on his head to get a wind like this to sail with. *He* was the "old man" to sail under. He was a *man*, Captain James was. They called him "Hell or 'Frisco Jimmy" and he would crack on till all was blue. As for this little crawler, by Christ, he makes me sick.'

'Was the *Joppa* as heavily sparred as we are?'

'Heavily sparred? Well – they told me this hooker was heavily sparred. But if you'd seen the *Joppa*'s mainyard, by Christ, you'd have, etc., etc.'

In this world it takes time both to get clean and to learn the truth.

Those words of Hart's stuck in my mind, and I carried them through the world, oh for many a thousand miles, for close upon five years.

And then, one rainy day, my business drew me down to the dingy parts about Deptford, to the docks there.

And I saw the *Joppa* lying at quayside – a little tin ship with toothpick spars – a ship of seven hundred tons at the very outside.

On the poop was a frightened little rabbit of a man, a pale little shuddery ghost who smoked a cigarette and twiddled his thumbs.

He looked a sort of careworn, a sort of pumped on, a sort of half-baked.

There was a watchman at the gangway and I asked him, 'Say! Who's that on the poop? Is it the Captain's steward?'

'No, sir,' said the watchman, 'that's the old man his-self, the Capt'n, Capt'n James 'is name is. Rummy little stick ain't he?'

After supper we rinsed our plates and pannikins in the dirty bucket, dumped the remnants into the dock, and stowed the supper things in the locker, just beneath the water tank.

We slipped off our clumsy boots, and turned into our bunks 'all standing',[15] lighting our pipes while Tulip swept the deck.

Now and again, when the shrill wind ceased singing in the rigging for a second, one heard the dull 'drip – drip' of water splashing on the half-deck floor from sopping oilskins hung from the beams to dry.

It is an oppressive noise that monotonous 'drip – drip' – we all thought it so. Later on, in times of storm, at night, in the cheerless watch-below, I would lie awake, shivering, miserable, in my wet bunk and hear that melancholy noise – 'dropping – a murmurous dropping' – and 'that one sound'[16] would seem to be some hellish water-clock[17] ticking out the seconds to one of the damned.

Hart tapped the ashes from his pipe and commenced to sing a frowsy old song, a dirty sea-ditty, a born-in-the-gutter kind of ballad, which had a dull droning tune, and a chorus in which we were expected to join.

He had just commenced, I say, when the door opened and a voice hailed us from outside.

It was James, the apprentice on the *Aladdin*, the ship lying alongside.

'Phew,' he cried, 'you've made it thick enough.'

He held the door open a little while to let in some fresh air and I got a clear view of him.

He wore a rough old tam o' shanter and a rough blue shirt of serge.[18] As he expected to sail next morning he hadn't bothered to 'dress' and he wore neither collar nor tie.

He was a well-grown kindly lad, very tanned, very freckled, a wholesome, honest, hearty-looking sort, clean-looking, smiling.

He lit his pipe and sat down on the nearest chest.

'Let's have a sing-song boys,' he said.

Chris drew his curtain and peered down from his bunk.

'Yes, my son,' he said, 'let's have a sing-song. It'll cheer us up. Shut up, you other fellows; me and Sandy'll sing you a duet.'

'What the hell duet'll we sing?' asked Sandy.

'Why, "McGilligan".'[19]

'Oh hell, I'm not going to sing that bloody rot.'

'Yes, you are man; why here's James come aboard just to hear you. Shut up, you other fellows. Are ye ready, Sandy?'

'By hell then, alright.'

The duet, or as much of it as sticks like mud in my mind, was as follows.

> I backed a horse the other day, that horse he did not win.
> Before I back that horse again, I'll see him run to
> > Alleluia!
> Keep your seats! I am not swearing.
> > Alleluia!
> The truth I always tell.

Chorus. McGilligan, get your hair cut. Where did you
    get that hat?
    Alleluia. Go to Hell. Whiskers for a cat.
    How d'ye like your eggs done? Could you
    eat a sausage lunch?
    Where'er I go the people cry — — — a penny
    a bunch.

That is as much as I can recollect about 'McGilligan'. It will
be quite enough, I think, for my most curious reader.

When 'McGilligan' came to an end, and the time we sang it
by was singularly quick, Hart sang the ballad of 'Sam Hall'.[20]

Thackeray makes mention of 'Sam Hall', and in a later day,
Mr Kipling also.[21]

I have tried to learn more of 'Sam Hall', for he seems to have
been something out of the common, something of an anomaly,
a good deal of the Barnum Bailey freak.[22]

    My name is Samuel Hall, Samuel Hall,
    My name is Samuel Hall
    And I've –

But there – that's as much about Samuel Hall as can be printed
without fear of prosecution.

It was my turn next, and although I am no singer I can make
a rare noise with my throat, and I rendered 'Spanish Ladies',[23]
an old ballad I know, at least no worse than my audience had
expected.

As Tulip was at all times excused from singing, it was now
McLure's turn. McLure sang a foul fo'c's'le ballad called the
'Sailor's Wives'.[24] It is not a nice song, but the writer had a fine
ear for rhythm and a very intimate knowledge of the sea. I have
often wondered who wrote it.

One night, in the tropics, I was on the poop with the third
mate and he fell to telling me of many things. Ships and women,
wine, ale and voyages, tobacco, pipes, bloody scuffles in dirty
inns, crews with knives going, hittings on the jaws of sailors,
flying belaying-pins, death and hell and blood and foul words

upon the high seas, a piquant, colourable instructive medley much of which has stayed where he spoke it, alas, in the summer night seven years back.[25] 'And then he changed his tune', and set to telling all the blackguard jests[26] and brothel-songs he had learned among the seaport slums. He had learned many. When he had finished, I asked him, 'Who makes up all these beastly things?'

'Why,' he said, 'I dunno, I suppose some — — — of a fine gentleman with nothing better to do.'

But the other day, in a great library, I read an old book of poems. The worst of the songs, the dirtiest tale in all the third mate's batch, I found printed in that old book. The author was a well-known critic.

'Now James,' said Hart, 'you'll sing us something, won't you?'

James doffed his tam o' shanter and tapped ashes of his pipe into a cuspidor.[27]

(The cuspidor was one of two. Hart had made them out of empty mutton-tins. I think they failed rather in their mission. I know I thought so when it was my turn to scrub the house out.)

The song James sang was 'Rolling Home',[28] an old song very dear to me, one of the three good sailor-songs we have.

He sang it well, very touchingly, in a high tenor voice that was singularly clear and sweet. It brought us out of our bunks and the lilt of the chorus must have rung clear, down the wind, for a long sea mile. He had just finished the last stanza when we heard a singer outside.

> 'Miss Tickle Toby kept a school
> For five and twenty boarders.'

'Here's the third mate,' said Chris. 'Open the door there, James, there's a good chap; he may be a bit drunk.'

The door opened as he spoke and the third mate came in.

'Who's drunk, ye rag-tag and bobtail?' he said thickly.

'I was just telling Sandy that his damn pipe smelt, sir.'

'Now, no swearing.'

The newcomer was a handsome fellow rather streaked with the gipsy, thick-lipped, sallow-faced, with a black keen eye and a moustache much burned by cigarette butts.

He backed a little and 'sat' down hurriedly on a chest.

> 'Oh Tommy's dead and gone to hell,
> Oh we say so, and we hope so.
> Oh poor Tommy's dead and gone away to hell,
> Oh poor old Joe.

'Damn it, you fellows, *sing*! You're as glum as if you'd etc.'

'D'ye think we'll sail tomorrow, sir.'

'Dunno! I hope so – this town has about cleared me out. But great snakes, ain't it blowing? Ha, Tulip, my son, you'll be puking your guts out this time tomorrow.'

He banged upon the table with his pipe and broke out with a song:

> 'And all her poor sailors all sick and all sore,
> Away, hay, O hio.
> They'd drunk all their whisky and could get no more,
> Oh a long time ago.

Come now, out with you! Out of your bunk there, Sandy, and we'll have a game of cards.'

'By hell,' said Sandy, 'I've got no money to play cards with.'

'Why, nor have I,' said the third mate. 'That black wench in Mary Street[29] has about cleaned me out. We'll play for matches. Now then . . . Jan – of all the dead-alive swine that ever I saw.'

We sat at the table playing cards until the clock of a church ashore had chimed the hour of midnight. We sat there till the place was so foul with tobacco smoke we could hardly see across the table. The party broke up at last. James bade us good night and passed over the side to the *Aladdin*. Mr Jackson[30] lighted a cigarette and went reeling aft to his bunk, singing, as he went, that 'It was time for us to leave her'.[31]

One by one, we turned-in, looking rather haggard in the dim light. The last man in blew out the lamp.

There was a noise of curtain rings for a second as we drew the red and green baize before settling down to sleep; and then, in the quiet of the little house, one heard more clearly the excessive fury of the wind.

Out at sea that night it must have blown very bitterly. In the grey, pasty morning the dock was noisy with the cries of draggled gulls; poor fishermen that had been blown inland unable to keep the sea.

'Now rouse out, all you sleepers. Hey!'

Looking out of our bunks, our eyes all gummy, our brains all dazed and rusty, we saw that it was Mr Pyecroft, the second mate.

'Now rouse out here. Are ye all dead or what?'

Day had broken – a dull grey day with nothing of last night's uproar to make it bearable. He had opened the door so that I could see the number three hatch and a little piece of deck beyond it. It was all glistening with dull lustre for a drizzling rain, like Scotch mist, had been falling for some hours.

Some seconds passed before I knew rightly what was happening. Then, with a pang, I remembered that I was aboard a tall ship, bound round the Horn,[32] and that we were to sail that morning.

One by one we tumbled out, still half asleep, and sat on our chests, rubbing our eyes, blinking, gaping, yawning like the Lord and Lady in Hogarth's *Marriage à la Mode*.[33] The second mate viewed us with disgust.

'Great snakes,' he said.

'Are we to sail this morning, sir?'

'No. The storm-signal's hoisted. Now, bear a hand there – you look like some of the drowned. D'ye know what time it is? It's nearly eight o'clock. Buck up and get your breakfast.'

The sopping oilskins had dripped themselves dry and now hung cold and yellow above a little pool.

Big drops were splashing from the skylight onto the table, and from the table onto the deck and from the deck, in a dark trickle, to the black crannies behind the chests.

One had a sense of dirty discomfort sitting there in the

puddles, pulling on one's dungarees in the air still stale with yesternight's tobacco smoke. One wanted a wash and a toothbrush to cleanse the night away, but, in a half-deck, a wash and a toothbrush lie fallow till the evening.

'Now, Tulip,' said Hart, 'lay forrard to the galley and get breakfast along. Don't sit gaping there like a ruddy codfish.'

'But Hart, I've not got my pyjamas off. Let Jan go. Jan, you've got your trousers on.'

Hart fetched him a blow on the mouth.

'None of your lip — — you. Do what you're told.'

'Oh, Hart.'

Hart scowled after him as he disappeared with the kettle.

'That swine's turning sulky, b'God. My Christ, *I'll* sulky him if he gives me any more of his jaw.'

Breakfast was pretty much a repetition of last night's supper. Dry-hash and biscuit, a little soft bread, a kettle full of water bewitched, a plate heaped with a sort of butter that the very donkey-engine would have scorned as lubricant, and a tin of ship's marmalade. To add to the discomforts of the meal Tulip was in tears.

'Now stop snivelling, Tulip,' said Hart, 'or I'll give you something to snivel for. What d'ye mean by filling your pannikin before me? Reach me that pannikin you've filled! Now, you ruddy Khitmutgar,[34] get up from table and wait on me. Fetch me a whack of hash!'

As Tulip hesitated, Hart rose.

'By Christ, Tulip,' he snarled, 'if you don't . . .'

Tulip did as he was bid. As he rose he jarred Sandy's elbow, just as Sandy was about to drink, making him spill a little of the hot coffee on his hand and elbow.

Sandy put down his pannikin and smashed Tulip lustily in the short ribs.

'Stop it, Sandy.'

'By Jesus Christ, Tulip.'

A step sounded outside and the second mate appeared.

'What the dickens are ye playing at in here? Great snakes, I've been holloing for the boatman this last half-hour. There's the ruddy postman with the letters on the quay; he's been yelling hell for twenty minutes. One of you drop your grub and take the boat in.'

I was nearest the door and I made a clean spring for it. We all feared the second mate. Sandy was in the right of it. He'd got too big a ruddy boot. Hasten slowly. I cleared the spare spar and raced aft to the gangway, catching my foot in a ring-bolt and coming down on my knees with a cruel welt. I prayed God he hadn't seen me, but no such luck.

'Jesus Christ, Jan, what in hell are ye playing at? D'ye think you're in a ruddy circus or what?'

The second mate, Mr Pyecroft, was, as Hart said, 'A ruddy sarcastic devil'. He had, as Sandy said, 'Too big a ruddy boot'; as the bo'sun told the cook, 'he was a damn fine odds and ends of a sailor.' As the third mate told me, 'he was a bastard's get[35] for style,' and, as I saw for myself, as likely a man as any on the salt seas.

He stood six feet two or six feet three. He had a bitter keen eye and looked vicious. I have never seen an eye like his. It had a hawk-look, a frosty gleam, that burned into one like vitriol.[36]

He was powerfully built, lean, quick and deadly. He seldom swore, and even when he did we did not count him any great shakes as a swearer, but he had a sarcasm[37] that bit into one. When he got around with his spurs on, he said things that sort of turned us sour. If he called me down for anything, I felt colicky till next duff-day.[38]

He was quite the most fearless man I have ever seen, one of the best-tempered, and, when roused, the most horrible abraiser, pulverizer and stiffener-out I have ever come across or stood from under.

The wind had fallen and dropped until there was scarcely enough to blow the wind-vane clear. A drizzling rain fell silently into the water of the dock. A grey squalid misery was every-where about me. There was wretchedness in the dingy houses by the dock-side; in the dock water which gleamed tawdrily in crude colours where oil had fallen; in the decks and dripping spars of the ships; in the stretch of 'dirty' sea seen tossing beyond the dock-gates.

A grey squalid misery was everywhere.

The boat's thwarts were wet. Her well was half full of dirty water and the oar looms had been soaking in the pool, so that when I cast off and pulled for the dock-side I sat on a wet seat and pulled with oars all foul and grimy. In my hurried dressing I hadn't tied the lace of one of my bluchers;[39] the boat's stretcher was half under water, and my boot, being large for me, was half full before I got ashore.

I fetched up at the dock-wall. '*Cairngorm*,'[40] I said. The postman reached down a packet tied with red wool. '*Cairngorm*,' he said. 'That's f'r the *Cairngorm*; you needn't a kept me waitin' in the rain all this time.' I thrust the packet into my belt and shoved off. 'Thank you,' I said. 'Suppose you keep your jaw shut.'

This was the meanest remark I had ever made in my life. I bent to the oars sullenly and pulled back aboard.

As I reached the deck I saw the mate, a little man, with mutton chop whiskers,[41] whose face was much scarred with pock-marks. He was limping to and fro smoking 'the heel out' of his long clay pipe before the steward rang him in to breakfast. I gave him the packet. He broke the red wool and roughly sorted the letters into 'forrard' and 'aft'.

'That's for your lot,' he said, shoving a bunch into my hand. I took them, thanked him, and ran forrard to the house to give them round and to finish my breakfast.

By this time they had finished breakfast, and the coffee in my pannikin was stone-cold. I hurried through my food with little appetite, eating to clear the foul brown taste from my mouth, and hurrying so as to smoke afterwards. Tulip was going about the house, rinsing plates and pannikins: the others sat in their bunks lighting their pipes and reading their home news.

'Jan,' asked Chris, 'what books are those you've got in your chest?'

'Oh, all sorts. D'ye want an exciter?'[42]

'Let's see them. What's that one in the till there? Can I have that? What is it?'

'*Mauleverer's Millions*.'[43]

'My Christ, what a name. Thanks, old man, I'll remember you in my will.'

He flung the book into his bunk and sprang after it, sitting on the blankets and dangling his legs over the edge. He cut himself a quid from a plug of sweet-cake[44] which he kept hidden under his pillow. He had a wide smiling mouth, and, as it worked rhythmically upon the tobacco, he looked like a new sort of sea-calf chewing the cud.

'Tulip,' he said, 'fetch that damn meat-tin, or spittoon (or whatever it is Hart calls it) and put it on top of my chest just beneath me. *That's* more homelike.'

'By Christ,' said McLure, 'you are a dirty beast, Chris. Look at him, you chaps, quidding in his bunk.'

Just then James appeared. 'Have any of you seen our Captain's cat?' he asked.

'Yes,' replied Chris, 'I saw a strange cat forward on the main-hatch yesterday. He was after "Smut" so I banged my cap at him. He hooked it somewhere. I dunno where to.'

'By hell,' said Sandy, 'there was some beast making a bloody noise last night, anyway.'

'You've not seen him this morning, have you?'

'No.'

'They've got the storm-signal hoisted down at the dock-gates. There's dirty weather in the Channel. We're not sailing till tomorrow.'

'Nor are we.'

'Sing out if you see our cat aboard, won't you?'

'Right-oh.'

'Thanks. I must get back aboard and tell the old man.'

He passed through the door and lingered a minute in the gangway, looking at something in the dock.

'I say, you chaps! Look here.'

We all tumbled out pell mell.[45]

'*She's* made heavy weather of it. My hat, look at her smoke-stack.'

Towing past us was a small French steamer, a dirty little tramp just in from the narrow seas. She had been shipping it green for eight and forty hours and her forward well was a dripping cluttered ruin.

Her port bulwarks were gone, torn away flush: nothing

remained of them save only a couple of buckled plates. Over her side a battered davit waggled unsteadily, the dangling tackle still hooked to the remnants of a dinghy.

Her smokestack glistened with a sort of dull whiteness that was like leprosy. It was the salt of the 'sprays' drying and caking into white scurf. A green lazy scum still slipped and settled along her dirty decks, for Channel water must have been coming over her rail until only half an hour before.

As she passed us two weary-looking men, both in oilskins and clumsy wooden shoes, shambled forward from her wheelhouse towards the dingy fo'c's'le. They paused by the galley-door to look at us, and it went to my heart to see them. Their loutish faces were very pinched and haggard, and one poor fellow, I noted, had no stockings; only a wisp or two of straw (pinched from the pigsty probably) to keep his poor toes from the aching cold of a March wind in the Channel.

'*Cairngorm* aho–oy!'

A faint hail came from the dock-side.

'Someone hailing you,' cried James.

The second mate was on deck, and he looked over the rail to pipe the hailer.

'Boat, there, one of you,' he said curtly. 'It's the painter.'[46]

The painter was a slight, delicate, wrung-out rag of a lad. He looked, if I may be allowed the term, a little underdone. He was doomed to pass through several hells in the rough society of the round-house and he bore it all kindly, patiently standing up to his punishment; gentle and clean-minded from first to last. He met with a shocking end, poor fellow, and I mention him because in a way he deserves fuller mention than any shipmate I had that trip.

Of humble origin with a natural bent for painting, he had elected to come to sea for a year or two so as to earn money enough for a course at a good school of art.

Mr Pyecroft knew something of him, and got him his berth as painter. An unpleasant berth, a supernumerary berth[47] – charge of the lamp-room, with sidelights and binnacle-lamps to see to – charge of the paint-room, with paints to mix, oil to dole out. Turps, tar and red-lead.[48]

An encroachment perhaps on the recognized authorities of the bo'sun under whose care these dainties usually rest, and a job, moreover, which left him neither fish, flesh nor good red herring.[49] It made him something of a sailor man, smelling of tar: something of a marine-chandler smelling of paraffin.

In the dogwatches he would bring out his easel and painting gear, and make studies of the mizzen mast from as many points of view as possible. Sometimes he would paint imaginary ships, delightfully spirited sketches which I could never praise sufficiently. Then the bo'sun would loaf around, and do the funny dog, especially if the mate (who had artistic leanings) happened to be within earshot.

'Jesus Christ, Dawber,' he would begin, 'what sort of ruddy hooker's that? That's the ship as never returned, I guess. I guess you never seed a ship, did you? This is what 'e calls paintin', Mr Dalloch![50] By Jesus Christ, 'e's what I call a bloody fool.'

Art criticism is about the easiest business going. Our bo'sun would have done fine on the *Spectator*.

We shambled out into the drizzle with our coat collars turned up.

'Forrard with the lot of you.'

'Sandy,' called the third mate, 'I hear you've got some pills?'

'Yes, sir, by hell, I've got some fine pills.' (I won't go into their merits: Sandy described them picturesquely.) 'Cockle's Little Liver Pills,[51] sir; by hell, they're bloody fine.'

'Nip into your chest and bring me some. I must a been half splashed last night. I feel like one o' the damned.'

Sandy went, returning with a handful.

'How many's a dose? Don't you go playing any o' your monkey-tricks now, Sandy, or I'll put a head on you so as your guts'll ache for a fortnight.'

'Four's a proper dose,' replied Sandy (not a tremor on his solemn Scotch face), 'but if you're really ill, sir, by hell, sir, ye'd better take six.'

Mr Jackson eyed him suspiciously.

'Now, Sandy, none of your damned monkey-tricks.'

'It isn't any monkey-tricks, sir. By hell, they're bloody good.'

The pills were duly swallowed.

'Now away forrard, you rag-tag and bobtail. Spring now, forrard with you. Get onto that handspike and break your back on it.'

He paused a moment.

'Jan! Tulip! Down into the forrard 'tween-decks; I've got a job for you.'

It was a stuffy hole that forrard 'tween-decks. Black with coal-dust, smelling like Hell's mouth, full of odd creaks and groans and sighings. A strange place where rats lived for the most part; an uncanny place at all times. At the foot of the little iron ladder we found a bunch of candles. We lit three or four and stuck them here and there to light us at our work, and then we off-saddled and turned-to.

There were several barrels to be lashed down to the ring-bolts. A cask or two (containing odd lumps of holystone, sand, clouts[52] of old canvas, spare broom-heads, etc.) to be secured in the same way; and in that stifling atmosphere we were both dripping, filthy from top to toe, out of temper, before the job was half through.

Mr Jackson sat on the coamings of the hatch, watching us with some disgust. Now and again he was on his feet blaspheming, aiding us with curse and sinew, then he would loll back to his seat and go on with his scrap of sea-rhyme:

'While crusin' one day down the town for a spree –

You're makin' a damn skew-eyed job of it. Jam it square against the ship's side. Strewth! *That* ain't the way. Oh Jesus Christ, you two, what in hell 'ye playin' at? Dip it *so* fashion. Now make her fast.

I spied a smart craft wid de wind going free
She carried no colours to tell her by which

That ain't no way to wrastle a cask. You get your fingers under a bloody tar barrel an' you'll smash them all to sodomy.

But by her appearance I took her for Dutch.
Singing Fol-di . . .

Very well that. Lay forrard among the coal there and fetch
forrard those sacks.'

'Where will I stow them, sir?'

'Make them up in a roll and stop them with a yarn and
shove 'em in that forrard cask. What the hell d'ye want to
come to sea for, you two? You Jan, you do *try*, an' you've got
some grains of bloody sense, but by your skew-eyed way of
doing things you ought to a been a farmer. As for that come-
day-go-day God-send-Sunday sucker Tulip – God paint my
soul eternal. Put out those candles and bring them on deck
with you.'

On the fo'c's'le-head, heaving at the capstan, Davy (the rig-
ger) with his mates, worked and swore with the four apprentices.
The second mate was with them, swearing and cheering like a
master of hounds.

'Heave now. Heave an' pawl. Heave! Oh, heave like hell
now. Heave an' start her.'

The pawls clocked and clanked and the great hawser came
home.

'What'll we do now, sir?'

A hail from the break of the poop. 'Lay aft there, Jan! Drop
what ye're doin'.'

It was Mr Dalloch, the pock-marked little mate.

'Yes, sir.'

'Get your coat 'n' cap 'n' take the Cap'n's wife ashore.'

'Ay ay, sir.'

I made a dive into the half-deck to get my cap, and shoved it
on as I raced to the gangway. The fine rain was still falling and
the boat was all wet and foul so I took the tin dipper and baled
out her well, working as quickly as I could. I had a big blue
pocket handkerchief, and using this as a clout, I was able to
get the stern-sheets fairly dry before sounds, as of a Rachel
that would not be comforted,[53] warned me that I had better
stand by.

I took off my cap and stood up.

'Now mind your footing, Polly. Help her down there, you boy.'

Mrs William Diggory appeared over the rail. She was a motherly soul, very kind to us boys, and it was a sad sight to see her weeping.

'Help her down there, you boy. Catch her by the leg.'

With my grimy hands I guided Mrs Diggory's feet onto the rungs of the ladder. She flopped down anyhow and collapsed heavily into the stern-sheets. The 'old man' joined her. A hard dry little chip, kindly in a rough sea way, very good to me but a fair terror when rubbed left-handed.[54] He sat cold and stern, and took the tiller.

'Give way, boy,' he croaked.

I made fast at the dock-side and helped Mrs Diggory to land.

'Run and get a four-wheeler[55] in the road there,' said the Captain.

I got a four-wheeler and drove back to them. I got into the boat then so as to be away from a painful scene but Mrs Diggory called me back.

'I want to say goodbye to Jan,' she explained.

'Goodbye, Mrs Diggory.'

'Goodbye, Jan. When Billy comes back I'll ask him, "And how is Jan?" You mustn't forget Mrs Diggory, Jan. When Billy comes back I'll be sure and ask him.'

But here the thought that her Billy wouldn't be back for maybe another two years was too much for her.

'Goodbye, Mrs Diggory.'

'Get into the boat, you boy.'

It was wretched work waiting there in the rain. I heard the four-wheeler rumble off and presently the old man reappeared.

'You, boy. Jan. D'ye drink?'

'No, sir.'

'Well then, I won't ask you to have a glass of wine. Shove off!'

He lit a long black cigar and contemplated the glowing tip of it, as I thought, almost gleefully.

When I got aboard again, work had knocked off and the lads were in the half-deck having a bit of a song.

'All the birds of the air fell a-sighing and a-sobbin'
When they heard of the death of poor Cock Robin.
When they heard of the death
Of poor
Cock Robin.
Totty won't you go? Totty won't you go
Down to the O-hi-O!'[56]

Quite a capital song but lacking in intensity.

'By hell,' said Sandy, when the chorus came to an end, 'I think the third mate won't sleep much tonight. I've given him six little liver pills. Cut me a pipeful, Chris, I do most bloodily want to smoke.'

'The third mate'll put a head on you, Sandy, when he finds out.'

'Ay, by hell. Hart, d'ye think we'll have spell-oh[57] now for the rest of the day?'

There came a shout from the gangway.

'Lay aft there in the half-deck an' get this meat aboard.'

A shore-boat had come aboard with enough fresh meat and vegetables to keep all hands for two or three days. We had rigged up a tackle when the steward appeared, a pale fellow with a thin beard and angular bones. He carried a lot of rough salt and as the raw joints were passed to him he rubbed them with the brine and placed them in pickle in the harness room.

When the provisions were all aboard and the boat 'reported cleaned' we were told to 'Get the canvas-bucket and a couple of coir brooms and clean up this mess here.'

'What shall we do then, sir?'

'Oh, run and play hell.'

But by this time dinner was ready, so we trooped forward for a smoke to give us an appetite. A sumptuous three-course dinner it proved to be. First a huge kid of 'Soap and Bully' – a greasy fluid with rags of meat in it.

'Doughboys in the soup, b'Jesus,' exclaimed Hart. 'Gad boys, we're living.'

Indeed there was a plump doughboy for each of us. Doughboys are dumplings made of flour and fat. They are not nice things, but 'Keep 'em for dessert,' said Hart, so we tore up an old newspaper and made platters of it on which to stand the doughboys while they cooled. Next, in the same huge kid, to be eaten on the same plates, came a piece of boiled beef wondrous bony, garnished with salted cabbage quite black and hard with brine.

'Well, boys,' said Sandy, 'here's for a most bloody good tuck in. If I'm to be seasick, by hell, I'll have something to fall back upon.'

'Jan, you're a Meteorologist – what's the weather going to be?'

'Oh, the wind's getting up. It'll blow hard tonight and rain hard. In the morning it'll be bright and showery – you see if it isn't.'

'Say, Jan,' said Chris, 'how was it you didn't get the Meteorological?[58] Who got it last summer?'

'Cushie.'

'Cushie's dead,' said Sandy, 'I've seen a photograph of his grave. The old chief[59] showed it to me that day we had tea there.'

'Yes, he got yellow-jack[60] in Rio last October.'

'He was a damn good fellow, Cushie was. I used to sling next him on the port-fore.'

'D'ye remember him giving old Strawberry Chops that licking down in the main hold?'

'Ay – poor old Cushie.'

'Hart, what'll we do this afternoon?'

'Oh, it'll be spell-oh this afternoon. Nothing to do except just "broom her down".'

After dinner had been cleared away, Mr Pyecroft came forward, and we asked him: 'Please sir, shall we have to turn-to this afternoon?'

'Yes. Why not? Certainly you will. Why shouldn't you turn-to?'

'I dunno, sir. I thought every job was done.'

'Ah. You "thought". You "thought". You're not here to think, let me tell you. You're here to *work*. No. You can turn-in so long as you're ready for a call.'

'Thank you, sir.'

We turned-in 'all standing'. Most of us read and smoked but Sandy spent an hour or so cutting up a supply of plug tobacco for immediate use. He had a song which he was always singing.

> Paraffin Oil. Paraffin Ale.
> Drink it like tea
> And you'll never be ill
> Of a ban or a bale.

A monotonous song which gar'd[61] us heave boots at him.

'Jan,' said Chris at last, 'suppose you spin us a yarn.'

'Ay, Jan, by hell, one of those yarns you spun aboard the *Conway*. That one about the "Phantom Coach".'

'No. That one about the Powder-ship that had the madman aboard.'

'Oh, let him choose what one he'll tell – a good exciting one, Jan – one with a ghost. That's the sort *I* like.'

'Oh rats, give him a chance to begin.'

I spun them a yarn about a murder, a good meaty case with blood in it.

After tea that evening, Sandy went outside the door, stripped to the waist, to have a clean-up in the tin basin. It was a relief to us all to hear the third mate approaching.

'Where's that devil Sandy?'

There was a noise of a tin basin sent clattering across the deck, a hurry of feet running forward, then wild excited squeals. Prolonged squeals.

Looking out to see the fun, we saw a confused mass some-where by the galley-door. The upper portion, or a part of it, rose and fell swiftly and rhythmically. It was the third mate's right arm plying a stout rope's end to 'I'll give you pills, you young devil.'

Presently Mr Jackson returned to the half-deck dragging
Sandy by the scruff of the neck. Sandy was saying, 'I hope my
pills have done you good, sir?'

As the evening wore on, the wind grew higher and our joking
and yarn-spinning came to an end. I think we were all touched
with homesickness – all genuinely wretched that last night in
dock. Perhaps it was that we were less tired than usual from
having had less work to do. Certainly we were quieter than we
had ever been.

Hart broke the silence.

'You didn't know I was a poet, did you?'

No. None of us had known that. Ship's half-decks don't pro-
duce that breed of cat save once in a blue moon. We let him
understand as much.

'I am, though,' he continued, 'and a bloody fine poet at that.'

'Go on, then. Let's hear some of your bloody fine poetry.'

He read us William Allingham's poem on 'Autumn'.[62]

'I wrote that,' he said.

'I know you didn't,' said I. 'I don't know who wrote it, but I
remember learning that by heart when I was a kid of five.'

'Do you?' he asked. 'That's funny. Perhaps you're thinking
of something like it. Two poets sometimes write exactly the
same thing. That's often been done.'

'Jan,' he continued, 'do you know Longfellow?'

'Yes, pretty well.'

'D'ye know "My Lost Youth"?'[63]

'I've read it.'

'I've got it here in my bunk and I think I'll read it out loud.
Shut up, you other fellows.

> Often I think of the little town
> That is seated by the sea.
> A boy's will is the wind's will,
> And the thoughts of youth are long thoughts.'

He read it movingly. 'Ay,' he said as he came to an end, 'I
always read this the night before sailing. It's the hell of a note
leaving home and this poem comforts me.'

'H'm,' remarked Chris, 'a fat lot of poetry you'd have read, my buck, if you'd had a chance at some of those rum-hots in the "Anchor" pub up Mary Street.'

'Oh, don't talk of rum-hot. You make my mouth water. God if I only had a little.'

Sandy tapped his pipe out and commenced a song:

> 'Strike the bell, second mate, let the watch go below,
> Look away to wind'ard and you'll see its goin' to blow,
> Look at the glass *an'* you'll see its very low,
> Tellin' you to hurry up and strike strike the bell.[64]

Put the light out, Tulip. I vote we sleep.'

There was darkness in the little house, a noise of curtain rings and then deep steady breathings.

On deck the rain was pelting down like shot. The wind was playing old harry[65] up aloft, blowing salt and fierce, blowing great guns. There must have been a fine sea in the Channel that night.

I did not know it then but that was the night I lost my boyhood.

Early, very early next morning there was a noise close aboard of us. Stamping of heavy feet, cries, the rattle of a coil of rope flung on deck from the belaying-pin. There were the cries of sailors singing out at a ship's ropes, then someone giving a curt order and then the dull clucking grunt of a rope moving over a sheave.

'The *Aladdin*'s off,' I thought. None of the others had been awakened, so I stole quietly from my bunk and out on deck, barefooted, in my pyjamas. The night was far spent; a streak of primrose-colour showed faint and delicate in a pale ribbon along the horizon to the east. The wide heavens were all blown clear and clean; all that blue expanse was now filled with a singing fresh wind. The great yellow stars were just paling, giving way to a bright bustling morning. I thought it fine of the spring to have made my last day so fair, and so I looked down the dock and missed the *Craigenbannoch*.

Alongside of us the *Aladdin*'s spars seemed to sway sud-
denly, and, as I looked, I heard the wash of the tug's screws. She
was off.

The little ship slid away from us very gently. I saw James
bent at the wheel, toying with the spokes and thinking himself
Lord Nelson.

'So long, the *Aladdin*,' I cried, 'good luck t'ye.'

'So long, the *Cairngorm*.'

As James turned his head to wave me a goodbye, I shouted
again.

'So long, the *Aladdin*.'

This time he did not reply, being busy with his steering, but
when she was almost out of earshot I heard the last of him in a
faint down-the-wind hail.

'*Cairngorm* aho–oy! You ain't got our cat aboard?'

A month later, when we were running down the trade and the
night-watch dosed on the hatches under the moon, some of the
hands complained of a smell rising, as they said, from the num-
ber three hatch.

'Oh, some rat got his gruel.'

But it was the *Aladdin*'s cat. He had fallen asleep, I suppose,
in some nook among the cargo and the hatches had been bat-
tened down above him. We found him when we unbattened,
and of course his presence accounted for the bad weather we
had off Cape Horn on our voyage.

I went back to my bunk after seeing the last of the *Aladdin*, and
slept till nearly seven bells when the bo'sun roused me out to
the boat ashore.

I shoved on a few clothes and went aft to the gangway. There
the steward met me.

'I want you,' he said, 'to take these two fowls ashore to that
man on the quay there.'

I took the two fowls ashore: they were a gaspy couple, sick
of either the leprosy or the staggers;[66] they'd sky-blue legs to
them and were about the two sickest birds on our side Jordan.
A man who chewed a straw took them from me, and I then

pulled out into the dock to take a last view of England. At the dock-wall was a fat little paddle-tug whose red funnel smoked placidly and whose sides were still wet with the sea. 'She was round in the counter and bluff in the bow',[67] like the lady in the third mate's song, and I recognized her at once. I had seen her on the Mersey scores of times. She was the *Bantam* come to take us down to Mother Carey.[68]

When I got aboard I loafed at the ship's side to look at her. I say loafed because in the past two years I had seen many tugs and my real object in keeping from the house was to let someone else get breakfast along.

As I looked a man came from her galley with a kettle and a platter of herrings. How I envied him.

Chris came to the door of the half-deck, buttoning up his shirt.

'Breakfast, Jan,' he called.

'Here's the *Bantam*, Chris, come and have a look at her.'

'H'm. I suppose she's going to take us out.'

'Yes.'

'She's a rare fine little tug.'

Breakfast was much as usual, but, as we were sailing that day, I opened a tin of 'Desiccated Soup' (Soupe Julienne[69] it was called) which we spread, uncooked, like marmalade, upon our bread. It wasn't at all bad; better than ship's butter anyhow.

Almost before we had finished our first pipes we were 'turned-to'. The last job we had in dock: hoisting the boat, scrubbing her with sand and canvas and stowing her on the top of the half-deck.

We had just finished when the third mate touched my shoulder.

'Look, Jan, here comes the crowds. Jesus Christ, they ain't half-splashed[70] by the look of them.'

Midway across the dock were three or four shore-boats, pulling erratic courses towards us. All were full of men and the bows of all of them were cluttered high with coarse canvas bags, donkey's breakfasts,[71] battered old chests and blasphemy.

The men were nearly all drunk; some sang, some cursed, a

few wrought at the oar. One worthy, a great strapping fellow with a toothless mouth, danced an absurd, drunken hornpipe in the stern-sheets.

One other sucked a whisky bottle and screamed between the sucks.

Somehow they got aboard and somehow they got their gear aboard, and somehow they got forrard, but for the rest of the day the fo'c's'les were two little hells – empty bottles and knives and foul words – 'Like bloody hell afloat,' as the mate said.

One man, a clean lean limber[72] fellow, decently clad, and with a solemn honest face, came aft to where I was loafing and began a conversation.

'You is one of de apprentices?'

'Yes.'

'Dis is a fine ship. What crowd will she have now?'

'Oh,' I answered, 'twenty-one men forrard, six apprentices, six idlers and four in the afterguard.'

'Dat is a fine ship's company! Twenty-one men, you say now? *And* six apprentices? Well, dey is men, dey is men. Dat is twenty-seven. *And* six idlers? What is de sixt now?'

'Oh, the painter.'

'She carry a painter, too? I tell you what, she is a crack ship, dis is, and where is she bound for, now?'

'Oh, Pisagua.'[73]

'Going round de Horn, now, I tell you dat make a big pay-day. And you is a first-voyager?'

I told him 'yes'.

'Well,' he said, 'dere is de t'ird mate (ain't dat de t'ird mate now?). I must get forrard,' and he gave me a queer little sea-nod and bustled forrard to the fo'c's'le.

I liked the man and his way and his voice and the queer accent with which he spoke. He was one of the old breed. 'A Sailorman, every finger a fish-hook, every tooth a marline-spike, every hair a rope-yarn, and his blood right good Stockhollum Tar.'[74]

He was the best man, the best *sailor*, aboard the *Cairngorm* and, as he said to me, 'When I get back from dis cruise I go up again for second mate.'

He called himself Jack Standish and he might have been forty years of age. Sea-life ages one very rapidly so perhaps it was something less. He was quite a remarkable man, brave, trusty, cleanly minded. The only sailorman I have never heard swear.

But long before I had fixed up this conceit of him I was hailed to the fo'c's'le-head to get aboard the tow-rope. Looking aft I could see Hart at the wheel smiling like a horse-collar: looking forward I could see the little squat tug with the red funnel. A man in a blue guernsey was just heaving a bight of the hawser across the bollard. The paddles churned the wrack[75] of the dock into a foam like the froth of working porter;[76] the hawser tautened, I heard the thrash of the engines as the little tug forged ahead. The whole stately fabric of the *Cairngorm* seemed to quiver and sway, and I glanced over the fo'c's'le rail and saw a line of bubbles spreading, spreading, whitening away from her bows. We were off.

Far astern, on the poop, I saw Chris run up a new, clean, red ensign. In the waist McLure guided the blue and red house-flag to its appointed place at the main-truck. From down the docks came a confused noise of cheering.

'So long, the *Cairngorm*. Hip! Hip! Hip! Hooray!'

Very presently we were at the pier-head, passing slowly, slowly through the narrow passage which led to the wide seas – the wide seas I had read about in Marryat. Such a crowd to give us a send off. Dock officials in peaked caps, customs men, boarding house runners,[77] old sailors, lumpers, riggers, stevedores, ship's husbands, crimps[78] and what not.

One man in a glazed silk hat and dirty shirt sleeves ran to the deck's edge and passed a gin-flask to his chum in the fore-shrouds.

'Good bye, Bill,' he shouted.

'Good bye, ol' man, kiss de gells for me. I'll see you dis time nex' year.'

And one poor man there, dressed in thin dungaree slops, barefooted, hatless, sleeveless in that bracing cold wind, stood at the dock's edge ready for what is called 'the pier-head jump'. We were one man short and the mate signed to him and he sprang aboard of us into the fore-chains.

Then all that long-shore company took off their hats and shouted, 'So long, the *Cairngorm*. Three cheers for the *Cairngorm*. Hip! Hip! Hip! Hooray!'

The little pock-marked mate uncovered.

'Three cheers for Pier Head,'[79] he cried, adding, under his breath, 'Three cheers for the bloody stay-at-homes,' and I passed into blue water[80] leaning over the rail, waving a ragged cap and cheering, cheering.

Now we were clear of the docks and busy with the towing-gear on the fo'c's'le-head. Busy getting our port anchor inboard, bustling and heaving and getting my ears singed generally.

I was outside England. England lay astern and to the port hand – stretching ahead, all bright in the sun, screamed over by gulls and kittiwakes – was dancing, tossing Channel.

There was a big American four-master just towing in – green spars she had, I remember, and a skysail yard which made you giddy to look at, and then, ahead of us, was a Norwegian barque just setting sail.

And we were going out in that glowing bright morning, to the south and west, bound for the blue seas and bound for the foreign parts.

Surely a fitting hymn that shout of the men at the pier-head, 'Hip! Hip! Hip! Hooray!'

I danced away aft just as she began to reel and shiver. The *Cairngorm* was feeling the run of the tide, lifting a little, swaying gently as she found her feet.

The third mate was rolling forward on exaggerated sea-legs.

'Way-oh, Jan,' he cried, 'you see that black and white buoy?'

'Yes, sir!'

'Well then,' he cried, taking up the end of a brace and marking time with it upon the fife-rail,

> 'Now you must understand
> That on your starboard hand
> Buoys white and black
> Define your track
> And – keep – you *off* – the – sand . . .

Jesus Christ, I've been ashore so long I've bloody near forgotten how to walk. Give me one of those damn cigarettes of yours, or by Christ I'll put a head on you and log you for bloody mutiny.'

He took a cigarette and swallowed the smoke in great hungry gulps. 'Now, Jan,' he said, 'the first thing *you* got to do is to learn to walk. When she rolls, you just hold yourself same as I do. See? An' in a little while if you're feelin' anyways sick you just drink a pannikin of salt water. That's the very best. Just drink a pannikin from alongside there. It'll fetch you up all standing. And – he continued meaningly – see you puke on the bloody lee-side.'

Sound doctrine which I recommend to all who travel by water, to all sick persons.

An hour or two afterwards, when the *Cairngorm* began to feel the sea, I went as one stricken chilly. A strange deadly feeling, like a cold cloth laid suddenly upon the heart, an uncanny giddiness and lassitude; I was faint, clammy, helpless, weakly wishing for death or dry land.

It was now dinner-time, but the sight and smell of the greasy meat were too horrible.

I remember McLure turning a ghastly face towards me, and I remember wondering whether I looked as he did, and then I went out and sat on the number three hatch letting the fresh wind beat upon my face.

Chris came out after me and put his hand on my shoulder: he had spent his youth on the sea-coast and was broken in, as it were.

'Jan, old man,' he said kindly, 'you must try and eat something. It's a hell of a feeling but it'll be a damn sight worse if you've nothing in you to fall back upon. Let me bring you your whack out here.'

'No thanks, old man. I'll come back to the house.'

I went back to the house and forced myself to feed. I ate ship's biscuit and raw Soupe Julienne. I drank a little vinegar. All the time as I was eating, Chris was talking to me like a nurse coaxing a froward child, and you may laugh and you may sneer but I tell you without shame – that his kindness almost made

me cry. I was the youngest of that ship's company. I was deathly
seasick, and his were the first kindly words I had heard since I
came aboard.

I noticed, too, that he addressed all his coaxings and kind-
nesses to me. McLure went cheerless looked he never so ghastly.
I gave a gulp. 'I'll not look like McLure anyhow,' thought I,
and so the meal came to an end.

'Now, Jan,' said Chris, 'you go out on deck into the fresh
air.'

Indeed the half-deck with its smells of oilskins, ship's food
and ship's tobacco was no good place for anyone in my condi-
tion.

As I picked up my cap the second mate appeared.

'Great snakes, what a face! What! You're not seasick too,
McLure? Why! You make the place look like a deserted — [81]
(not that I was ever in one).' He paused a minute and then con-
tinued with his bitter suavity. 'Why are you turned-in, Hart?
Why aren't you out of your bunk? You're not sick at any rate.
At least you're not going to be.'

'I wasn't feeling very fit, Mr Pyecroft.'

'I thought you'd been three years at sea. Turn out at once.
You'd better stay on deck, Jan. You'll only make a mess of the
floor if you stay in here.'

'Please sir, can you tell me a cure for seasickness?'

'Yes. A piece of fat pork at the end of a bit of spunyarn, and
mind it's *fat*. It's a good cure and damn cheap. You can use it
any number of times,' and aft he marched to his dinner in the
cabin.

Hart turned out grumbling, mighty savage, at being publicly
shamed.

'Never mind,' he said, 'that bloody etcetera thinks himself
the hell of a bloody note. A damn sight better man than he was
seasick every voyage.'

'D'ye mean Nelson?'

'Ay. I'd like to have had that Pyecroft etcetera aboard the
Joppa for a voy'ge or two. By Jesus Christ, Billy Mesham
would've knocked his jaw out of him. I remember one night
it was bloody awful cold, blowing like sodomy, and we were

reefing our main upper-topsail. Billy Mesham and the second mate, an awful little gut's-ache of a fellow, were out at the yard-arm and the second mate said something to Billy (I dunno what it was) so Billy took him by the coat-collar and held him out over the sea (by Jesus) with one hand.

' "Now you etcetera," says Billy, "you give me any more of your gaudy lip and I'll let you drop."

'I tell you the second mate was bloody well etcetera. *He* didn't say much to Billy after that. That's what ought to be done to this fellow once or twice an' he wouldn't be so Hail Columbia.[82] Would he, hell.'

'Billy Mesham must have been most bloody strong,' said Sandy.

'Strong?' said Hart. 'I guess he *was*. He'd a ruddy arm on him had Billy. When he was in Hamburg he got photographed, naked, with a couple of fat Dutch girls. You should have seen his chest.'

'Come along, Jan,' said Chris, 'you and me'll have a mooch around.'

'Do you believe what Hart says, Chris?'

'What!!! Of all the bloody boasting liars. I'll give you a good tip, Jan. Believe half what you see and nothing that you hear. You're looking a damn sight better. My God. Look there at the painter!'

The pale stricken wretch in question held a woebegone and deathly face over the rushing sea. Now and again came an Apocalypse. The sight was too much for me.

As I was leaning over the rail the second mate came along and stood beside me.

'Why, Jan,' he said, 'what's the matter? You don't mean to say you're sick?'

'Yes, sir.'

'Why don't you get a nice piece of fat salt pork at the end of a nice tarry bit of spunyarn?'

I showed him.

'You see that Point?'

'Yes, sir.'

'D'ye know what Point it is?'

'No, sir.'

'It's the "Cow and Calf";[83] when you write home you'll be able to say "I was sick off the 'Cow and Calf'." You'll remember the "Cow and Calf" when you go up for second mate.'

Then the mate came along.

'Now, Jan, why aren't you smoking one of those new pipes o' yours? Eh? What?'

I showed him.

'Have you written any letters home yet for the pilot to take ashore, telling 'em what a nice life the sea is?'

'No, sir.'

'Well, by God, ye'd better get and do it, or maybe the pilot'll leave before you're ready. What're ye sheering off for? Don't you like my tobacco?'

Then the third mate came to have *his* say.

'Jesus Christ, Jan. Now look here! You ain't so much being sick as what I call bloody well retching. What you got to do is *eat*, and then you won't feel it not half so much. You go and lie down for a spell. I'll call you when you're wanted.'

'Thank you, sir.'

I went to my bunk like one going to be flogged. The third mate followed me into the house and sat down on a chest as I turned-in.

'Jan,' he said cunningly, 'if you were to smoke now, it would do you all the good in the world.'

'Oh, don't talk of smoking, sir.'

There was a pause for a minute or two. Then he continued, 'Jan, give us one of those cigarettes of yours.'

'Yes, sir, you'll find 'em in my chest-till.'

He lighted one forthwith.

After a little while, when the smoke had drifted into my bunk, I spoke again.

'Mr Jackson, sir?'

'Yes, Jan.'

'Take all my cigarettes, will you, sir? I'll never want to smoke again.'

'Oh, give us a breeze,[84] in a couple o' days you'll be smoking like the bloody galley.'

He let the words sink in, and then he pocketed the boxes – about three hundred cigarettes altogether.

'Well, Jan, I'll take them, they're better with me than with that etcetera Hart, but when you're through with your sickness you just ask me for them.'

'Thank you, sir.'

A long pause.

'Mr Jackson, sir?'

'Yes, Jan.'

'Were you ever seasick, sir?'

He laughed. 'You should uv seen the bloody half-deck. I sailed in the old *Andalusia*. She's sold now, you saw her lying up in George's Docks.[85] My God though I pity a first-voyager. It's the hell of a bloody note being seasick.'

Another long pause.

'Well, Jan, cheer up! You'll have to turn-out in about half an hour when the watches are picked.'

'Whose watch d'ye think I'll be in, sir?'

'I dunno.'

'D'ye think I'll have to go aloft, sir, when we make sail?'

'Not in your present state. My Christ, no.'

Then he left me, no doubt in a rare good humour at having manoeuvred the transfer of my cigarettes.

By and by the others entered. McLure livid, Tulip yellow, Hart grey, Chris and Sandy boisterous. The thought that for the next two days they would both have double rations was 'riches fineless'[86] to them.

'Hello, Jan,' said Chris, 'how are you now?'

The third mate entered. 'Now out you come here. All hands. Lay aft with you.'

The watches were about to be picked.

All hands were gathering at the break of the poop. The 'growlers' had reeled aft in various stages of drunkenness and were now grouping into strange pictures upon the quarterdeck. Some wore red shirts, some wore blue jumpers, some were barefooted, others were in great knee boots, the only foot gear they possessed. One man's head was broken and the blood kept dripping into his eyes, he brushing it away always with a comical drunken manner that was queer to watch.

Nearly all were drunk, yet none was so drunk as to misconduct himself upon the quarterdeck, and none was so drunk as to keep covered when his name was called. We fell in with them. Sick as I was, this old sea-custom of the picking of the watches had a deal of interest for me. I watched it as I would have watched a play.

To windward of us stood the three mates all eyeing the grumblers with keen critical eyes. They were reckoning up the worth of individuals by the looks in their eyes and the way they carried the drink.

On the poop, Captain Diggory in a long baggy overcoat stumped up and down puffing his cigar.

The ship's articles were called and the company answered their names.

'Johannssen!'

'At the wheel, sir.'

'Müller!'

'Look out, sir.'

Then the picking began.

'I choose you,' said the mate indicating an old burly shellback with brass earrings in his ears and a huge quid in his cheek.

The old man took off his cap and reeled to one side; he was drunker than Davy's sow.[87]

'I choose you,' said the second mate, indicating another drunkard, and so the picking went on till all were picked and till we six lads were picked, and then the mate spoke.

'Well, men, you're at sea now, you know the rules – watch on deck, keep on deck. Watch-below, keep below. Make eight bells there. Relieve the wheel and look out. Go forward.'

By sea-custom, old as Noah's ark, the mate's watch had the 'eight hours out' that night. There is an old sea-proverb, 'the mate takes her out and the captain brings her home'.

As the starboard watch reeled forrard, one drunken jolly
jack commenced a song:

'Now wot's the use of grumbellin', you know it is a fac',
You signed it in the Articles accordin' to the Ac'.
So what's the use of grumbellin' when you know you get
    your whack
Azackly as you signed it by the Merchant Shippin' Ac'.'

Sick as I was I would have learned more: I wanted to follow
the singer till I had his song by heart but I was at sea now and
it was my watch on deck.

I don't know how the dogwatch passed. I fancy McLure and
I sat on the booby-hatch praying for swift shipwreck and oblivion. The wind was getting up. I heard it sing in the shrouds. It
was twilight too by this time and that eerie music and the noise
of the rushing sea put me in a shaking fear of going aloft to
make sail.

Along the horizon a line of black clouds seemed to roll
slowly towards us. We were out of sight of land now by reason
of the dusk, and before us lay 'dirty' sea, and a little squat tug
which belched black smoke and floundered.

It was four bells at last, the wheel was relieved, the starboard watch came on deck again, and I was free to go below to
a ghastly mockery of supper.

In the second dogwatch a sailor takes his ease and his song.
Work about decks is over, so that the 'watch on deck' (save for
the wheel and look-out) are free to lounge forward to smoke
and yarn with the watch-below. Then, when the watch-below
have supped, the pipes are lit, the old yarns spun, and many a
stirring tune goes sweet to the penny whistle. But now!

An hour later the third mate came in to cadge a stamp. In a
little while the tug would cast off and the pilot would go over
the side. He would take letters from us and post them, next
morning, ashore somewhere, giving our friends the latest news
from Mother Carey. But we had no stamps.

Threepence halfpenny in small copper money was our united
wealth.

'Jesus Christ,' said Mr Jackson, 'you're as bad as we are. The second mate and I had a tarpaulin muster[88] this forenoon and we'd only got eleven pence between us.'

I think that after this I must have gone off into a doze and slept for quite a while. I woke up suddenly to hear the following.

'So,' concluded Mr Jackson, 'I just rounded on him quick as a flash. "You're a bloody liar," I said, "you can tell that to the marines. I wasn't born yesterday," I said, "and there's not a man living can say that you've said –" Hey, Jan, how's your poor little guts?'

I shoved a white face through the bunk curtains.

'I feel pretty sick, Mr Jackson.'

'Oh, cheer up,' he said. 'Wait till you get a fat Chileno's arms round your neck. You'll forget all about this. Damn it. What's a little puking?'

Hart took up the broken thread.

'We had one of that sort aboard the *Joppa*, my first voyage. Billy Mesham took him in tow though and — soon made a man of him. He went ashore in Calcutta and he .. .. .. of a .. .. .. for a . . .'

'When I was in the *Andalusia*,' replied Mr Jackson, 'we had some .. .. forward who'd .. .. to half the ship .. .. The West Coast's a tough place. You have to watch it there.'

'Ay,' replied Hart, 'when I was at Junin I saw a growler go ashore to hospital. They're hell-fire places, those West Coast hospitals. Kill or cure the etceteras don't give a — damn.'

'There'll be some trouble turning those fellows to at eight bells by the look of things.'

'Ay, the bo'sun went forrard at four bells to get a hand aft to relieve the wheel an' he got a bottle at him. Smashed just against the bloody door-post.'

Here the conversation lagged. Mr Jackson hummed awhile and then broke into a song.

'As soon as the hooker was clear o' the bar,
    Away hay o hio,
The mate knocked me down with the end of a spar,

Oh a long time ago.
"Lay aft and — — — you, you — — all"
Was everyday language aboard that Black Ball,
A long time ago!'

One bell sounded clear from the poop. The great bell forward echoed it. A minute later Chris entered.

'Now rouse out here, you sleepers, hay.'

His rough cap was cocked back, his black hair was blown from his brow and the wind had put a touch of red to his cheek and made his eyes bright.

'Hey, Jan, old man, out you come there; it'll be eight bells in a minute. How're you feeling now?'

'Oh Lord, Chris, I'm half dead.'

'Cheer up, man, you'll be better on deck; this wind'll do you all the good in the world.'

'Strewth, Jan,' said Mr Jackson, eyeing me with a grin. 'You look like Barney's Bull. I'm etceteraed if you don't.'

I tottered out of the house into the night.

I fought my way aft and answered my name as the watch was called. What happened next I cannot quite call to mind but I remember being on the lee-side of the poop, the mate by me, he telling me to keep the time, bawling in my ear.

'You look inside the chart-house,' he bawled, 'you see that clock there, well – every half-hour you make the bell – make it loud so as the look-out'll hear. 'N' don't you go fallin' asleep or by God I'll pour one o' them buckets on you.'

Looking about me I saw the old man stumping the weather-side. He still puffed a cigar: I could see the red butt glowing, as it were, between his teeth. The shabby brown overcoat kept blowing between his legs, nearly upsetting him.

His was a dreary walk. Forward to the break of the poop for a look aloft, aft to the wheel-box for a squint in the binnacle and a look at the tossing wake. Puffs of smoke at intervals. When he peered into the compass, his face showed pale and ghastly in the light of the binnacle-lamps. He was unshaved and a thick black beard grizzled his hard little chin.

Sometimes a puff of smoke blew towards me and then I was very unwell.

After one such touch the mate limped up to me.

'Now, Jan Errol.[89] Are you consumptive?'

'No, sir.'

'Well, what you're doing now is a grand thing for anyone's got the seeds o' consumption in him.'

'What causes seasickness, sir?'

'Just bile. Maybe you're of a bilious habit and never knew 't. Maybe your father was of a bilious habit before you. What you're doing now's a grand thing for you. Puke all you can. You're all green inside just now; by and by you'll be all red and then we'll hear more o' you.'

So away he limped. I hung on to the jigger-shrouds and like Piers Plowman 'looked on ye water'.[90] Looking on the water, I saw a gull or two blown down the wind, dipping in the foam, screaming.

From my elbow came a hard dry little chuckle: it was the old man.

'Why, Jan, d'ye know what them gulls is saying?'

'No, sir.'

'Why, they're thanking you for all that nice dinner I seed you eat this morning. All that nice beef and cabbage. "Thank ye, Jan," that's what they're saying.'

Then he chuckled his hard dry little chuckle and slapped his thigh and so back to his stumping up and down. Presently he returned.

'D'ye know what all them little fishes is saying now?'

'No, sir.'

'Why, they're askin' arter all them nice cigarettes I seed you smoke. "Where's all them nice buns you brought aboard?" That's what they're askin' about.'

(I should have thought that by this time the fishes would have known with greater certainty than I.)

'An',' that hard dry little voice continued, ' "Thankee, Jan," they're saying. "You *are* a kind boy, Jan, to give us all your nice dinner and all them nice cigarettes." That's what them little fishes is sayin'. Don't you hear 'em?'

'No, sir.'

'What! You don't? Why, I do. I hears 'em sayin' that as plain as plain.'

Then he chuckled and sheered off for another turn or two on the windy side of the deck.

In a little while the binnacle-lamp blew out. 'Boy, there!' came the order. 'Here's this lamp blown out. Take it down to the lamp-room and light it. Maybe the wick wants trimming.'

I slipped the little brass cylinder from its socket (the smell of oil and hot metal bringing me up by the roots) and hurried tremblingly to the lamp-room. The watch (so many as were sober) lay by the sail-room door, smoking and muttering together. The bo'sun was yarning to one of the hands and one big sailor that had a Dutch accent was beating out the tune for a new chanty.

'Ha *Ha!* Come roll him *over*,'[91] in a little muffled voice that was strange to hear.

Once inside the lamp-room my woes redoubled.

The smell of oil and turpentine was death to me. I was giddy with sickness, and the *Cairngorm* was so lively I had a difficulty to keep my feet.

I wedged myself somehow against the bulkhead and trimmed the wick with the blunt scissors I found hanging from a nail. It was very dark, of course, and I had to light wooden matches, one after the other, and work with one hand.

I got it lit at last and hid it under my jacket so that it should not blow out before I got back to the binnacle. I felt that I had passed about a week inside the lamp-room, and was surprised to see the bo'sun still yarning – one of those long sea-yarns, I suppose, which drone through the watch and twist and ramify[92] and never fetch to port.[93] The singer with the Dutch accent was still tapping out his tune: 'O ho. Why don't you *blow*? A ha! Come roll him *over*.'

By and by the little flapping figure fetched up alongside me again. His hard little face was wrinkled in a smile.

'Jan,' he said, 'd'ye see that light astern there?'

I looked in the direction to which he pointed: at each giddy swoop I could see a sort of white brightness which seemed to wink and glimmer and disappear.

'That's little Stag Light,[94] Jan. The last you'll see of England.'

Presently he continued. 'Why ain't you smoking one o' them nice cigarettes o' yourn? Hark at all them little gulls now. "You *are* a kind boy, Jan," they're sayin'. "Thank ye Jan," they're sayin', "for what we've all received, Jan." Ain't that what they're sayin', now?'

Bell by bell the watch wore through. Swoop after swoop, heave after heave, we tossed along into the darkness, churning the sea into a smother. Now it was seven bells and the mate appeared.

'Jan, there!'

'Yes, sir.'

'Strike the bell an' go down an' call the second mate.'

I struck one bell and heard it echoed forrard, and then groped through the alleyway to Mr Pyecroft's cabin.

The place smelt dreadfully of oilskins and paraffin, for his wet-weather gear lay on his chest, and his lamp was turned down and had smoked steadily throughout the watch. I felt that two minutes there would kill me, so I summoned every ounce of strength and let out with a lusty yell: 'Mr Pyecroft, sir. Mr Pyecroft.'

The sleepy giant stretched out a splendid arm and yawned.

'Whas amarrer?'

'Mr Pyecroft, sir. One bell, sir.'

He sat up at once, fully roused.

'Have ye called Mr Jackson?'

'No, sir.'

'Turn up that lamp 'n' go 'n' do it.'

I rushed from the alleyway into the fresh air, there to gather strength for my next effort. A minute or two in the wind refreshed me. I entered the third mate's cabin, struck a match and lit the lamp.

His cabin was in a rare clutter – sea-boots, shore-clothes, balls of spunyarn, oilskins, bunches of marline-spikes, pipes, fids, spare belaying-pins all scattered Hurrah for Joseph,[95] and nearly all scented.

'Mr Jackson, sir. Mr Jackson.'

Deep steady breathing, the fellow slept like one o' the drowned.

I picked up a marline-spike and rapped him pretty sharply on the elbow.

'Mr Jackson, sir, Mr Jackson.'

'Jesus Christ, what the hell's the matter?'

'Mr Jackson, sir. It's one bell, sir' – I paused here for a second. 'Sir, *will* you wake up – I'm going to be sick.'

He was out of his bunk like a shooting star. 'Gerrout o' here – get – get quick.' As I fled on deck – only just in time – I heard him curse me bitterly: his toe had caught pretty sharply against some wreckage. No fear of *him* stealing five minutes more sleep and getting late for muster.

In the half-deck Sandy was calling the watch-below. The lamplight made a bright patch in the waist and I could see a pyjama'd figure yawning in the doorway.

A few minutes later I reported eight bells and made it so; I then crawled forward for a drink of water.

'Here's the pilot,' said Hart. 'He's come for the letters. Good-bye, pilot.'

The pilot was a fine bearded fellow with a face all shiny with salt water. His sou'wester was canted back, his hair was all blown about and rumpled, his oilskins glistened with spray and the wind had made his eyes bright. He shook hands heartily all round in the patch of light outside the half-deck door.

'So long, all you young fellers. So long, young feller-me-lad! Any letters home? So long. A good voy'ge t'ye and a big pay day. So long.'

I was so reeling sick and so careless of all save my own present misery that I hardly know what happened next. I remember getting to the poop again, near the lee jigger-shrouds, with the old man a little forward from me near the poop-ladder. He had lit a new cigar and stood there gazing forward, the high wind scattering his skirts.

'Set the foretopsails,' he shouted. 'Boy there, forrard to Mr Dalloch 'n' tell him to set the fores'l and foretops'ls.'

Running clumsily forward, I found the mate on number two hatch yarning with the bo'sun. I gave him the old man's words and he repeated them.

'Set the fores'l and foretops'l?' he said. 'By God, he didn't say nothing about the tea-things.' (I suppose this was meant for a gibe at me.)

'No, sir,' said I.

'By God, that's strange.' He waddled forrard to a knot of hands gathered in the black shadows of the fo'c's'le.

'Up there, two o' you, and loose the fores'l and foretops. Overhaul y'r gear before you go now.'

Perhaps they didn't hear him, perhaps they were stupid and cross from the blind debauch they had wallowed in since the morning, not a hand stirred.

'God damn it,' he shrieked, 'up there, a couple o' hands, and loose the fores'l.'

I saw a couple of men jump into the weather-shrouds and rattle up aloft, while others overhauled the gear and stood by.

I had not regained the poop when I heard the thunderous slat of a great sail lifting and thrashing in the wind.

I saw the sail beating and backing against the fore-shrouds, and then I heard the click of the pawls as the tack was walked down, and the cries of the men as they scooted aft the sheet.

Presently a hail came from far aloft on the foremast.

'All gone, the fore-upper-tops'l.'

The great halliards, coiled so carefully the night before, were passed aft. I saw a long line of parti-coloured ruffians bousing taut and waiting for the turns to be cast off. Then, but very faintly, I heard a broken wheezy voice crying a tuneless cry:

'Oh whisky is de life of man',[96] followed by a crashing chorus full of rough melody.

'Whiskers! Johnny!'

Every man putting his muscle on, the yard coming up with a jolt at each hoist.

'Tell Mr Dalloch to give her the mainsail.'

I found the mate gazing aloft as the men trimmed the yards. 'The Captain, sir, says give her the mains'l.'

He waddled to and fro for a few seconds and then spoke:

> 'The fores'l for lifting:
> The mains'l for driving
> An' the crojick for making her steer wild.[97]

Up there some o' you an' loose the mains'l.'

'You boy, Jan,' said the old man when I reappeared on the poop, 'go an' have a lie down in y'r bunk. You can't go aloft or you'd go overboard. 'N' in y'r present state you can't work about decks. You couldn't hoist one o' them tops'ls now, could you? Well, you go an' have a lie-down. I'll strike the bells.'

I didn't know how to thank him. Cold and wretched, I stumbled forward. I remember seeing a red light spitting blood, it seemed, along the white of our wash. It was the port-light of the little tug now tossing home. I turned-in all standing and must have fallen asleep almost at once. The last thing I heard with any certainty was the voice of the chanty singer quite close at hand: 'Oh, blow de man down, bullies, blow de man down.'

Followed by the rousing music of the chorus that was worth ten men on the rope: 'Oh, give us a chance fer to blow the man down.'

Sleeping fitfully, I awoke at times to moan; to hear McLure moan; to listen to the wind; to hear the clear bells knelling out the watch; to pray a little while, very wretchedly, for an end to all my going a-fishing and so to sleep again.

One bell at last and Tulip came below to light the lamp.

'Now rouse out, here. Get up, Jan. Sandy, Sandy. McLure.'

The third mate came forrard. 'Now, Jan, how's your poor little guts? Christ, you look like a bloody ghost. Now, out you come. It's bloody near eight bells.'

I had expected that, sick or sorry, sea-usage would keep me on deck standing up to it. Perhaps a brutal usage but, perhaps, in the long run, right.

On the *Conway*, while mooching the deck with a chum, I had often thought of this hard bit of sea-usage, and made sure, in my own mind, that no seasickness would see me quit my duty. I had pictured myself (many a brass-bound young ass has no doubt done the same) as a white-faced hero gripping the wheel with a stern smile, holding her up to the wind, and found dead at his post next morning. Well – here I was – not in blue water yet – a washed-out galley-clout scarce able to crawl.

Nothing of the high-heroic: of the Roman fashion. Nothing but a limp piece of misery: a geck and gull for every ruffian aboard.

'Maybe I was of a bilious habit and never knew 't,' in those days aboard the *Conway*. Maybe I was; but laugh not, gentle reader. In thy Channel steamer, when thou goest to visit foreign parts, in thy Channel steamer be sure that thy bilious habit, even thine, shall find out even thee.

That first night at sea I would have given a hand to be allowed to lie-up for the watch. I was just a walking corpse, the wretchedest-looking creature you ever saw, but I turned-out, and McLure turned-out (and McLure was sicker than I) and the third mate whistled and brought a tinge of blood to our cheeks with, 'By Jesus Christ! You'll make sailors yet. I'll be damned else.'

Being now under sail, the *Cairngorm* was a sight less giddy underfoot.

She was under her topsails, the wind on her quarter, blowing a fresh gale. We were making eight or nine knots and she lay over to it pretty much, for she was being bustled along to clear the Channel. As I went on deck I saw the foot of the cross-jack arching out right over my wobbling head. At each giddy lift and swoop the mate's ditty buzzed in my ears: 'An the crojick, the crojick for makin' her steer wild.'

Good times were in store for us, though. After muster the mate in a few words of supreme disgust sent McLure to his bunk and me to mine.

'I can't have you two dead-and-alive etceteras pukin' around decks,' he said. 'Run and play hell in your bunks and don't let me see you till you're fit for duty.'

We lay in our bunks through all that watch till Sandy lit the lamp and roused the sleepers.

Sometimes I would sleep, sometimes I would moan in a dazed, crazy, light-headed sort of way, sometimes the lamp would be lit and then came a smell of oil, sometimes a pipe and then a smell of tobacco, both smells shaking me core-through.

Now and then, in the darkness, someone crept in for a biscuit

or a drink from the little tank. If Chris came he generally lifted
the curtain of my bunk and passed a word with me. He had a
good heart had Chris.

That's enough about my first night at sea, I think. It was
much more than enough for me.

Next morning, after breakfast had been eaten by the callous
and zinc-lined, by those in fact who were not of bilious habits,
I went on deck, to the lee-side, and looked on the water very
steadily.

When I had looked on the water some little time there was
no need for me to look on the water any longer. We were hum-
ming south, I found, under topgallant sails, ripping through at
ten or eleven knots, a great gale blowing down the Channel
and quite a lively sea all round us boiling up green and
yeasty.

The watch were gathered under the break o' the poop; they
were in oilskins, black and shiny, and yellow and shiny. I saw
Chris by the lamp-room door in a wet suit of amazing yellow-
ness. The yellow sou'wester gave a ghastly look to his face, but
he was happy enough. His hands were tucked inside his belt
(thumbs in his girdle like Master François Villon)[98] and his
great mouth moved smilingly upon the quid.

He was looking up at the mizzen royal yard in a St Cecilia[99]
sort of way, for the wind had blown a patch of sail from the
gasket and he was watching it as it shook itself loose, wonder-
ing I expect why the devil it didn't keep snug when it had the
chance to do so.

I gave the sea a parting glance and went back to my bunk.

By and by, perhaps it was dinner-time.

I asked Hart whether we should see the Scillies. 'I heard the
old man say we'd passed the Scillies in the morning watch,
before it was light,' he answered. 'There's nothing to see in the
Scillies, Jan, they're only bloody islands with gardens on 'em.'

'Have you ever seen them?'

'Ay, I saw one when we were beating up Channel in the
Joppa.'

'Which did you see? St Mary's?'

'No, I think it was St Agnes' but, what the hell, they're all
bloody saints in those parts.'

That was a wretched day; I ate nothing; I was feathery-
headed; I moaned and maundered.[100] I tossed my rough blankets
into valleys and straightened them out into plains. Now and
then I would smell the smell of ship's tea and go and look on
the water. A very wretched, dismal day; quite the worst I could
remember.

The mate came forward and asked after his pair of cripples.
He advised us to smoke all we could and 'Jan,' he said, 'here's
something to put in that diary[101] o' yours: "And the next day
was very much the same but that the wind freshened and blew
the sprays aboard."'

After that second day's misery I woke up and was surprised to
find that the sight of an open cocoa tin was no longer a potent
emetic.

I ate a little raw cocoa, and, behold, it was very good. Break-
fast came along – a tin-can full of burgoo[102] – or thin ship's
porridge. I ate a plateful of it with some brown sugar – greatly to
the disgust of Sandy, who had not reckoned on so speedy a con-
valescence. I washed and spruced myself, and, feeling very weak
but much refreshed, I went on deck when the watch changed.

The old man was on the poop taking a turn or two in the sun
before going below to his breakfast in the cabin.

'Why, Jan,' said he, 'an' where ha' you been this long time?
Come on up here an' have a sit down in the sun.'

I sat down on the wheel-box – to leeward. 'Jan,' he said,
'ain't you got nothin' for them little fishes this mornin'? None
o' them nice cigarettes?'

'No, sir.'

'Why!' he replied. 'Ain't you goin' to give them no break-
fast?'

'No, sir.'

'Why, Jan, what's come to you? You was that generous when
I seed you last. We must find some work for you. Sit there in
the sun an' get your strength, lad. You're noddin' weak. Why,
where's all your colour gone?'

And so on, and so on, in a rough kindly way that was like a strong tonic. I grew to worship that grizzled little joker in time. All of the first-voyagers would have oiled his boots with their weekly whacks of butter.

Hart, pinnacled on his third year at sea, called to mind one Hell or 'Frisco Jimmy, and was silent or condemnatory according to his temper at the time.

At noon, when I went below, I found a kid of salt beef and a string of raw onions. I ate heartily and danced afterwards on number three hatch.

We were four hundred miles from England, we were under all sail, there was a fair wind, we were making eight knots. Routing in my chest I found a tattered yellow-back,[103] one of Captain Chamier's, so I turned-in and read until my watch was through.

That night my watch had the eight hours out.

Going on deck at 8 p.m. I stood the first 'poop', walking the lee-side of the poop until four bells (10 o'clock). This poop-watch was a duty relegated to the boys, a rather useless duty, too, as the only objects in view were the keeping of the time, and the striking of the bell every half-hour.

'Keep on the lee-side and keep awake,' said the mate, the weather-side being, at sea, the sacred side reserved for officers.

It was a fine clear night, a fair wind bowled us along at about eight knots an hour, all sail was set, a few white clouds, ghostly in the moonshine, were blowing through the sky, hanging cobwebs to a few of the stars, and I set myself to walking up and down repeating the Rule o' the Road:[104] 'The lights mentioned in the following Articles, etc., etc., from sunset to sunrise.'

On the weather-side Mr Dalloch limped to and fro smoking his long churchwarden.[105] By and by he leaned over the rail of the break and called me to him.

'Jan,' he said, 'you're at sea now, aboard a crack ship, an' you're a young gentleman; don't you forget it. By God, if I see you or any o' you boys runnin' around with any o' the hands, by God I'll send you to bunk forrard with the men.'

'Very good, sir.'

'What do you gentleman's sons come to sea for?' he asked after a short pause. 'Your sort ought to be parsons or farmers or them bloody sharks called lawyers.'

'I dunno why we come to sea, sir. It's a free an' easy sort of life so people think ashore. Perhaps that's why.'

'See what comes o' readin' novels. It's all them damn novel-writers gives folk them ideas.'

He limped a pace or two to each side, spitting acidly.

'What made you come to sea, sir?'

'Me?' he queried. 'Why I was a poor orphan without any parents an' when I was a boy I went on one o' them old wooden trainin'-ships where I was drilled.'

'Which training-ship was that, sir?'

'Now, none o' your damn business – and there I used to fight with single-sticks. By God, I could break any boy's head aboard. An' after – I shipped thro' the hawseholes – an' now I'm mate aboard the *Cairngorm* commandin' sons o' gentlemen like you and McLure there.'

He limped aft and had a squint at the compass, looked aloft a moment, and then returned.

'Please, sir,' I said, 'when you take a star can you take second magnitude stars as well as first?'

'What d' *you* know about stars?'

'Oh, I know a few, sir.'

'What's that one, then?'

'Vega, sir.'

'And that one?'

'Sirius.'

'And what's that constellation?'

'The Virgin.'

'You ain't supposed to know anythin' about any bloody Virgins at sea, Errol. If you said that to anyone else, by God he'd laugh at you. We call that the "Spanker": "Spica's Spanker".[106] Now, I'll see if you know anythin' else besides stars – what's this rope?'

'Jigger to'gallan' staysail halliards.'

He was fairly taken aback. 'Why by God, Errol, I never thought you'd've known that.'

It was the only rope I knew abaft the mizzen mast and his question had been a lucky one. I grinned and hugged myself. He didn't ask me any more ropes so that I was free to question him about another matter.

'Were you ever in a ship when she got dismasted, sir?'

'Yes,' he answered curtly, 'yes, I was. The bloody skipper knocked every bloody stick clean out of her. Cracking on, that was, with the damn gear not fit to go aloft on. We were runnin' an' she broached-to an' the sea made a clean sweep fore an' aft. Galley, jib-boom, boats, deck-house, every bloody thing. Our rails were gone flush with the decks when we got in to Lisbon.'

'What ship was that, sir?'

'A little wooden barque: the *Burd of Blaines*.'

'Did the owners get anything from the insurance?'

He spat and sucked his pipe into a red glow.

'There's roguery in all trades but ours, Errol. By God, that skipper knew his business. I dunno what he didn't get out of them poor insurance folk. Masts an' gear an' sails all o' the very best, new boats, fresh paint (paint-room flooded o' course), new sidelights, a new galley and range – every bloody thing he wanted. An' a bran' new ship's library too –' he chuckled, 'the old one bein' damaged by the sea. Ah Errol, there's roguery in all trades but ours.'

He leaned over the rail and called curtly to the bo'sun: 'Lee fore brace.'

'Sea sore face,' echoed the watch, getting up noisily from their roost under the break o' the poop and trooping forrard to the braces.

'Now, Jan, forrard with you, an' give McLure a hand on the to'gallan' and royal braces.'

On getting aft again I found that it was two bells so I struck the bell 'two' and went on with my Rule o' the Road: 'Every sea-goin' steamship, when under way,' etc., etc. (Article Three, a long article, which I knew in a parrot fashion and which I have not yet forgotten).

It was then that I noticed, for the first time, the drowsy beauty of the sea in moonlight. Those miles and miles of heav-

ing moonlit water sort of fetched me a jolt over the heart. Very
far away I saw a sailing-ship's green sidelight, the light of some
ship bound home. A block chirped in the jigger-rigging. A
rhythmic murmur came from aloft where the reef-points pat-
tered. Over the side was the wash of water lipping past and,
above everything, the dim skies splashed with cloud and burn-
ing with the intenser stars. I had never seen the stars before.
Those mellow lamps were not the Arcturus, Procyon, Capella,
Bellatrix and Vega I had looked for at night in England.

'Jan.'

'Yes, sir!'

'Oh alright, as long as you're awake.'

Down on deck, in the moonlight, I saw Sandy walking with
McLure and felt sorry for the pair of them.

I knew that Sandy loathed the very sight of McLure. I knew
that my own heart writhed with hatred whenever I came near
McLure. I knew that Sandy and Chris had quarrelled. I knew
that Sandy hated Hart for having caused the quarrel. I knew
that Hart hated Sandy for having divined that he had caused
the quarrel and I knew that all hands hated Tulip.

Here we were, six lads, condemned to live together for
another year and hating each other's company already.

I myself had disliked all hands (Chris of course excepted)
since I had known them. Chris I could chum[107] with; with the
others I was 'an odd fish', 'a bit uncongenial', 'a damned inno-
cent', etc., etc. My one useful gift, that of yarn-spinning, had to
lie fallow because Hart could brook no rival near the throne
and had been mighty sarcastic whenever I had been called upon
to show it.

So, I thought, I will take Sandy's poops[108] and make friends
with Sandy.

At four bells the mate came forward to the rail. 'Relieve the
wheel and look-out,' he called. An old shellback shambled aft
to the wheel, buttoning his reefer as he went. McLure came up
with a nod and took over the lee-side o' the poop. I finished my
Article Three to my own satisfaction and joined Sandy in his
walk.

Sandy took his pipe from his lips and spat into the scuppers.

'It's a bloody ambitious[109] red-headed etcetera, that McLure,' he said, 'by Christ.'

There was no need to malign McLure further. Sandy had expressed my feelings far more finely than I, at that time, could possibly have done.

'It's a pity you and Chris aren't in the same watch,' I said.

'By Jesus Christ,' he went on, 'I didn't think it of Chris. On the *Conway*, by Christ, he promised me. An' now he an' that etcetera Hart' – here he blasphemed a little.

'Well,' said I, 'you'll see Chris and Hart fall out before we cross the Line.[110] Chris won't stand any of Hart's airs and if Hart goes for Chris we'll put him under the pump.'

'By Christ, yes,' said Sandy. 'We'll none of us let that etcetera touch Chris.'

And the subject rested there. As a matter of fact the difference I had prophesied came about within a week and diplomatic relations between Chris and Sandy resumed themselves directly.

'Jan,' said Sandy, 'some bloody fine watch-below will you teach me how to do those bloody Latitudes.'

'What, Sandy, can't you work a meridian?'[111]

'By Christ, I can't.'

'Why, I thought you were in the First when you left the *Conway*?'

'Ay, by hell, so I was but I got into the First by cribbing off that ambi[112] devil Greaser. I couldn't do the bloody things so every exam I used to sit next him. By Christ, it's a wonder I didn't get a prize.'

'McLure did just the same with me,' said I. 'He'd never've got into the Senior if he hadn't cribbed my Navigation papers. Yes, I'll teach you, Sandy, I'll start in the forenoon tomorrow.'

'There's no bloody rally, Jan,' he answered, 'but, by Christ, my father's bloody sick – I don't know more, after being aboard so long.'

'Well, I vote we have a sit down on the booby-hatch an' I'll spin you a yarn.'

'Ay, by hell.'

So I spun him a blood-curdling and ghastly yarn about a murder, and a blood-stain which wouldn't wash out, and a pale lady who gibbered. Quite a twopenny Dread,[113] the details of which are lost to me.

After the yarn was spun and when the pale lady had ceased to gibber, our conversation waned into waxed monosyllables. We were by this time dead sleepy with that heavy cloaking sleepiness which comes of strong sea-air and night sea-watches.

I fought the drowsiness tooth and nail, for, being very young and very green, I had heroic notions about keeping awake in my watch on deck. I was 'nat all asleep ne fully waking',[114] and Sandy, I suppose, was much the same, when the curt solemn voice of the mate spoke from just above us.

'Now, Sandy?'

'Yes, sir.'

'Errol?'

'Yes, sir.'

'Don't let me catch you falling asleep. By God, if I do – I've got a bucket o' water for you.'

'Jan,' said Sandy, 'we must most bloody well keep on walking.'

At last the blessed 'one bell' was struck, our watch was pretty well through.

'Jan,' said Sandy, 'I'll go call that third mate. I'll have some bloody fun with that devil. You call the half-deck.'

There are few things sweeter to a tired mariner than that calling of the sleepers after a weary watch on deck. You go below and light the lamp, and then yell with 'an hideous noise and a ghastful'[115] till sleepy heads protrude from the curtains and drowsily curse your forbears.

Don't think that the curse is a sign that the sleepers are awake. At sea one curses mechanically. Continue to yell till you get them out of their bunks, and then jest with them till they get soured and whang[116] sea-boots at you.

Leave them then, but return in five minutes or they will infallibly fall asleep again.

I have found a watch-below fast asleep on their chests, in their pyjamas, five minutes after they had been pursuing me with curses and the buckle-ends of belts.

On getting below we lost no time in undressing. We flung
our clothes off, not from any keen wish for immediate sleep but
from a disinclination we had for being last man out. The last
man out had to extinguish the lamp, had to grope to his bunk
in the dark.

Sleep, heavy, cloaking, numbing slumber blotted us away at
once. We had scarcely turned-in, we thought, before the door
banged and a match sputtered. Then that accursed yell, 'Now
rouse out here, you sleepers, hey.'

On deck, when we mustered, the air smelt like morning. It
was dark still, but the east was all grey; a cool light, not moon-
shine, made the sea like so much steel.

The stars were paling, a few clouds were sprayed around the
moon and I wondered why the birds were not twittering. It was
all so fresh, so like a dawn at home.

I had arranged to take Sandy's poop, so I went aft and
commenced upon Article Four, turning over Captain Gray's
rhymes[117] when Board of Trade prose[118] became too much for
me.

I watched the quiet colours of the sky changing into faint
yellows and delicate reds. The mate was in the shadows of the
weather jigger-rigging. I could not see him from where I stood
and I was all alone with the quiet, save for the steady figure of
the helmsman above the spokes.

It was Sunday morning, and the day would be a sort of gen-
eral holiday notwithstanding that old sea catechism which
says:

> Six days shalt thou labour and do all that thou art able,
> But the Seventh – holystone the deck and clean-scrape
>   the cable.

On some ships, on nearly all American ships, the hands are
kept busy on Sundays much as on a weekday, but aboard the
Cairngorm, in fine weather, no work was done after the decks
had been washed down in the morning watch. The watch on
deck had indeed to keep on deck so as to do all necessary and
unavoidable work (such as trimming the yards) but until called

to the braces they were free to amuse themselves as they pleased.

Then in the sunlight, on the fore-hatch, on the fo'c's'le-head, the old growlers would loll and bask and take tobacco, yarning of 'the last ship I sailed in'. One or two would get away into the dusk, under the to'gallant fo'c's'le, for a quiet doss, or for a read from such books as they had. Small parties of three or four together would have a washing-day and scour and rinse their parti-coloured gear, hanging it out to dry on the forestay.

One or two would patch their old trews with bits of canvas, and one or two more, having wheedled a little oil or a little paint from the bo'sun, would put a last coating on thin oilskins. And one or two, perhaps more than one or two, would get away snugly somewhere and ply cards for matches, for tobacco, for 'An' if you lose you'll stand my next wheel, b'Jesus.'

At half-past four the 'idlers' were called up (they are called idlers because they stand no night-watches) and at two bells (five o'clock) the cook, coming to the galley-door, drew the watch forward with a cry of 'Coffee!' for, by old sea-custom, coffee is served to the watch on deck at 5 a.m. each morning.

Of all the comfortless meals I have sat down to, and I have sat down to many, none, I believe, for general beastliness and pigstyetude can approach the meals I had aboard the *Cairngorm*. Breakfast, dinner and supper, I hated all three but worse than all three I hated this make-believe of coffee at two bells.

I was not dainty, but I used to sicken at that coffee. It smelt of tin and of ship's molasses and it looked foul, like the sediments of a drain. The surroundings under which it was served perhaps made me hate it more, for we drank it in the dark in the half-deck, quietly lest we should rouse the sleepers, hastily so that we might clear away before turn-to time.

There was no ship's biscuit to eat with it, and ship's sugar to eat with the ship's biscuit, dirty tin pannikins to drink from and two shipmates whom I loathed (and who loathed me) to drink with.

I was all that you may like to think me, gentle reader, but better a tightened belt and dry land (by a long chalk better) than a sea-feast in that society.

After I had been at sea a little while, I used to keep the poop, watch after watch, so as to escape from the society of Sandy and McLure. And especially did I keep the morning poops, partly in order that I might watch the sunrise, partly to escape that comfortless cup of devilled water.

But on this particular morning we will imagine the 'coffee' drunk. In the galley the cook was busy polishing his kettles and kids. The carpenter was at the head-pump. Old Sails aft at the sail-room.

'Jan,' said Mr Dalloch, 'go forrard on the lee-side. McLure, go forrard the weather-side an' coil up any ropes may be on deck.'

Then the head-pump was rigged, brooms and buckets passed along. Washing-down was about to commence so I rolled up my trews and flung my shoes and socks inside the half-deck door.

'B'Jesus Christ,' said the bo'sun, 'b'Jesus Christ, you and Sandy. D'ye know what the old man said to the sky-pilot?'

'No, bo'sun, what was it?'

' "B'Jesus," he said. "Pump, you etcetera, pump," so that's what you do. Heave round on that 'ead-pump.'

We pumped mightily and a mighty splashing of cold water ensued. Every inch of deck was scrubbed religiously. Two men with buckets and brooms scrubbed out the fo'c's'les. Then, when our arms could pump no longer, a hand relieved us at the brakes and we were put to passing buckets to the bo'sun. At every bucket came the formula 'Stand from under', and then – swish – swish – cold water splashing on our bare legs till we were sopping wet and our toes all blue and achey with the cold. While the decks were yet wet, in the first of the sun, just after I had called the watch-below (about 7.30, my diary says), we spoke[119] a little steamer, the *Arabesque*, of London, bound home.[120] I heard the look-out's shout and ran to the little cupboard in the chart-house where the signal flags were kept, and had bent on the numbers long before she was near enough to speak.[121]

'We shall be in the shore-papers by Thursday,' said Mr Dalloch, and after the usual exchange of numbers, etc., I watched her toss away from us, a line of black smoke streaming from her funnel. In half an hour that line of smoke was pretty well all that showed of her.

One bell had been struck and I was lounging about the poop when the old man came on deck for a turn in the sun before he went to breakfast.

With that sailor's second nature he went aft for a squint in the compass, then forrard to the break for a look aloft. Something aloft was not altogether right. 'Jan,' he cried, 'I see you got some nice rope-yarns in your belt.'

'Yes, sir.'

'You see that mizzen to'gallan' yard?'

'Yes, sir.'

'There's a buntline there wants overhaulin' about a fut 'n' a half an' then stoppin'. Now let me see how you kin run aloft arter all them nice pickles I seed you had yesterday.'

'Ay ay, sir.'

I flung the buntlines off the pin and overhauled them through the fair-lead and up I trotted to the swaying topgallant mast! It was the first time I had been aloft since we left dock.

The sea-air and seasickness had freshened me up into a hearty state of health. If this is sea-life, I thought, as I laid out on the yard, I shall do alright after all. Just then the foot of the upper to'gallant sail (being well overhauled and stopped) lifted slightly, and brushed my cap from my head. It fell slowly, hitting the bunts of the topsails, hanging a second in one of the crojick leech lines, then flopping into the sea with a gentle splash.

It was a common sea-incident, but happening just then it came to me like a rebuke. I was as superstitious as any in blue water and I felt that it was a bad omen. The blow fell later on, announced or unannounced, and it knocked the poor tune clean out of me.

In the half-deck, when I got below, I found the table littered with the cold remains of the first breakfast.

Tulip had gone aft to take the poop. Chris was lazily clearing up. Hart, bent awkwardly before a cracked mirror, was shaving. Every Sunday forenoon, in fine weather, Hart wasted a

solemn hour in putting on gorgeous raiment, a white shirt, a
tall collar, a tropic-sunset tie and a blue suit made by a London
tailor.

He shaved with great care and dressed slowly, finickily. His
vanity galled us all because at sea even on Sunday there is no
need for fine apparel. No need for more than the merest rags
consistent with decency. Besides, such a glittering peacock
made us all feel dowdy, dirty, scum o' the earth. Chris, shoving
the shaver aside, as he stowed the dirty pannikins in the locker,
gave vent to his feelings.

'My God my Father, while I stray. What *do* you think you're
doing?' Then, 'My God, you might be going to see your girl the
way you're dressing yourself.'

'We're not all bloody counter-jumpers,[122] even if you are,'
replied Hart, feeling his stubble. 'By Jesus, you fellows haven't
any proper pride.'

'Any proper vanity, you mean.'

'Why it's half your life to put on decent clothes. By Jesus
Christ, it makes you feel like a gentleman. When I'm at home I
spend a couple of hours every Sunday morning dressing myself
for church.'

'You must be damned fond of yourself then.'

To this there was no reply; the shaving came to an end and
then Hart turned royally to the chaste blue trousers.

'Bloody hell, Jan,' he cried, 'you aren't working the lee-
scupper racket still, are you hell?'

'No.'

'You two can count yourselves lucky, by Jesus, in being
allowed to lay-up. When I was seasick aboard the *Joppa*, by
Christ, I had to turn-out and scrape the pigsty, and I was a
damn sight worse than either of you two etceteras.'

'For God Almighty's sake, Hart,' said Chris, 'give us a breeze
about the *Joppa*.'

'What's the matter with *you*?'

'Yes, by hell,' said Sandy, looking down on his plate, 'let's
have no more of the bloody *Joppa*.'

Chris swung to his bunk and burrowed among the blankets.

After a rummage he brought forth *Mauleverer's Millions* and a plug of Lucky Hit.

He cut himself a quid and began to chew.

'Look at the dirty blackguard,' said McLure. 'My Christ, Chris, you're worse than old Gibby aboard the *Conway*.'

'The hell I am. I *can* chuck up chewing. Gibby couldn't.'

'By hell,' said Sandy, 'old Gibby was an etcetera for spitting brown.[123] When he was in Joey's class he used to quid[124] in school and he cut a hole in the deck to quid through. By hell – the bloody deck.'

'The Chief spoke to him once on the lower-deck,' said I. ' "Gibby," he said, "there's a dirty habit some of the boys have; they call it spitting brown."

' "Yes, sir," says Gibby.

' "It's a disgusting, filthy habit."

' "Yes, sir."

' "You never spit brown, Gibby?"

' "No, sir," says Gibby (and all the while he'd got a great quid in his cheek).

' "Open your mouth a minute."

'So Gibby gave a gulp and swallowed his quid and then opened his mouth.'

'Ay, by hell,' said Sandy, 'it damned near killed Gibby, that quid he swallowed. I saw him in his chest in the main-top afterwards and he was most bloody ill.'

'Not so bad as old Herring Bones, though,' said Chris. 'Old Herring Bones swallowed a quid and had to go to the sickbay. He groaned, and, my God, he looked ghastly so they thought he'd been poisoned and sent the cutter in for the doctor. The doctor came aboard and the old nurse told him old Herring Bones had been *eating tea leaves*. She'd a bloody big basinful of tea leaves by that time. My God.'

'By hell. I'd like to be aboard that *Conway* for dinner today.'

'Would I, hell,' said Hart. 'All you first-voyagers think of is what you'll have to eat when you get ashore. When you've been at sea a bit, all you'll think of is what you'll have to drink.'

'What 'u'd you give for a rum-hot now, Hart?'

Someone outside leapt the spare spar and broke out into a song:

> 'In Amsterdam there dwelt a Maid
> Mark well what I do say.'[125]

It was the third mate. 'Where's that etcetera Hart?'

'Here, Mr Jackson.'

'Up on the poop with you, while I go feed my face.'

When Hart had gone, he spoke further.

'Jesus Christ. Is he going to a bloody wedding? Hello, Jan! Where's that devil Sandy?'

Sandy was in his bunk.

'I'm here, Mr Jackson.'

'I'll give you cold water, you young devil. He creeps into my cabin to call me in the first watch and bloody well drowns me. I wish I had you in my watch instead of that dead and alive etcetera Tulip.'

The mate came forrard after breakfast and bade me get out my chessmen. We set the board on the spare spar, which spar we both bestrid. 'I expect you'll beat me at this,' he said, 'I haven't played, not since I joined the ship.'

We sat on the spare spar and began a game. Both of us played with extreme caution, the mate smoking when it was my move, letting his pipe go out when it was his. One or two of the men keeping at a respectful distance watched us curiously. A hushed sentence reached me now and then, 'I t'ink, b'Jesus Christ, dere good players.'

Working my Knights and Queen, I got one or two pieces from him, got him 'going', got him into a fine corner with 'mate', I thought, in three more moves. Then it struck me that it would be unwise to beat him. I was quick in discovering a man's likes and dislikes, and I thought, 'If he dislikes anything he will dislike being beaten by "a gentleman's son".'

I peered at him from under my eyelids. His sallow cheeks were sucked in; his teeth gritted on the pipe-stem. One hand tugged a whisker, the other gripped a knee. He looked vicious.

While I took stock of him he suddenly raised his eyes to mine. He was bitter savage.

'B'Jesus,' came the hushed voice of the audience, 'I t'ink de young feller's winnin'.'

Very cautiously I abandoned my position, the pock-marked face flushed. I saw him chew his pipe to keep the oath in. Now the bo'sun and all the idlers were looking on, half the ship's company were gathered in the waist. Quite a buzz of talk humming down to us.

I raised my Queen slowly, deliberately (I was playing to the gods: it was just boy's swagger). 'Check,' I cried.

'B'God, you do that, do you?' (He too was playing to the gods.) And so the game wore on.

Gradually he fought me into a corner. I lost a piece or two, as I thought, very cunningly.

He had me boxed at last and limped a quick turn or two up and down.

'Mate, by God.'

He turned to the bo'sun. 'By God, bo'sun, he had me fairly on a lee shore once. And by God, Jan, ye never saw it. No, ye never saw it.'

'Thank you, sir,' said I. 'It was a ripping good game.'

'Next Sunday you and I'll have another.'

Going forward shortly afterwards, one of the hands (it was the big toothless sailor I had seen drunk and dancing the day we sailed) stopped me and spoke to me for a minute.

'I t'ink, b'Jesus, you plays chequers[126] pretty good.'

That night, or some nights later, I had the middle watch on deck and spent the first half of it on the poop yarning with the mate. In the dogwatch he had been singing to his banjo under the break of the poop. He played the banjo like a master and he had a good clear tenor voice, though to the half-deck it seemed always a bit high-pitched. He hadn't the art of singing. He had the false music-hall artifice of singing and his songs were the false music-hall songs, cheaply sentimental, vulgarly patriotic. Songs lower by dark degrees than the rude filth of the fo'c's'le: 'Abel Brown',[127] 'In Amsterdam' and 'As I was a going'.[128] One

song of his had closed with the line, 'We want a man like good
Sir Robert Peel',[129] which line McLure had thought to be 'very
true' (on what grounds I know not).

On the poop that night Mr Dalloch was singing himself the
same song.

'Errol,' he said, 'ah Errol, them bloody sharks the
Government'll run old England up a bloody hornets' nest one
o' these days. There isn't a man among 'em: not a man.'

'Well, sir, we've got a good Navy.'

'An' who run the Navy? Who run the Navy?' he queried
bitterly. 'Just them same bloody shop-keepers as don't know a
bloody rope. There's only one man in England as could run the
Navy and him they won't listen to.'

'Who's that, sir?'

'Lord Charles Beresford.'[130]

'He's a good fellow.'

'B'God, he is. B'God, I wish there were a few more like
him.'

I sighed deeply. 'He was to have given away the prizes aboard
the *Conway* last summer, and if he hadn't been suddenly pre-
vented from coming, I'd have got a prize from him and he'd
have shaken hands with me.'

Mr Dalloch growled some irreverent relevance about a dog
and a rabbit and continued.

'I seen him once, Errol, just after that Alexandria.[131] I was
ornery seaman aboard a ship an' I'd been doing somethin' –
never mind what, it don't matter – an' I was doing defaulters'
parade up and down the dock carrying a bloody handspike.
An' Lord Charles come aboard an' he seen me doin' this so he
spoke to the old man 'n' got me off. He's a man that Lord
Charles is. An' a gentleman an', by God, a sailor.'

It was a fine warm night. The watch on deck were under the
break of the poop; some were yarning, some smoking, several
of them, their heads pillowed on their coats, were sleeping
sound sea-sleeps on the bare boards.

I found a vacant place near the door of the alleyway and fell
to considering the pale beauty of the moon. At times I repeated
Article Four. At times I thought of kicking Sandy and having a

mooch with him; I should have slept, I suppose, in a few min-
utes had not an old sailor, the grey brass-earringed man I had
noticed at the picking of the watches, seated himself beside me
and commenced to yarn . . .

Deep Sea Yarns

[Book Review of Conrad's *Youth: A Narrative, and Two Other Stories*]

YOUTH, A NARRATIVE. By Joseph Conrad.
W. Blackwood and Sons. 6s.

Mr Conrad's stories, excellent though they are, leave always
a feeling of disappointment, almost of regret. His is a rare
temperament, an exotic, a poetic temperament, and its artistic
expression, though tense, nervous, trembling with beauty, is
always a little elusive, a little alien, of the quality of fine gum
from Persia, or of a precious silk from Ghilan.[1]

In this volume Mr Conrad gives us three stories, and in each
shows a notable advance upon the technique and matter of his
former work. His manner, indeed, shows a tendency towards
the 'precious', towards the making of fine phrases and polishing
of perfect lines. He has filled his missal-marge[2] with flowerets;
he has planted his forest full of trees; till both prayer and forest
are in some danger of being hid. In the story called 'Youth', and
still more in the story called 'Heart of Darkness' (both of them
stories written as told by one Marlow to a company of friends),
he has set down page after page of stately and brilliant prose,
which is fine writing, good literature and so forth, but most
unconvincing narrative. His narrative is not vigorous, direct,
effective, like that of Mr Kipling. It is not clear and fresh like
that of Stevenson, nor simple, delicate and beautiful like that of
Mr Yeats. It reminds one rather of a cobweb abounding in gold
threads. It gives one a curious impression of remoteness and
aloofness from its subject. Often it smells very palpably of the
lamp, losing all spontaneity and becoming somewhat rhetorical.

An instance of Mr Conrad at his very best is to be found on page 39:

> Between the darkness of earth and heaven she was burning fiercely upon a disc of purple sea shot by the blood-red play of gleams; upon a disc of water glittering and sinister. A high, clear flame, an immense and lonely flame, ascended from the ocean, and from its summit the black smoke poured continuously at the sky. She burned furiously, mournful and imposing like a funeral pile kindled in the night, surrounded by the sea, watched over by the stars. A magnificent death had come like a grace, like a gift, like a reward to that old ship at the end of her laborious days. The surrender of her weary ghost to the keeping of stars and sea was stirring like the sight of a glorious triumph. The masts fell just before daybreak, and for a moment there was a burst and turmoil of sparks that seemed to fill with flying fire the night patient and watchful, the vast night lying silent upon the sea. At daylight she was only a charred shell, floating still under a cloud of smoke, and bearing a glowing mass of coal within.

That is finely said, with a keen feeling for rhythm, and with a subtle appreciation of the musical value of vowel sounds, but it is hardly the sort of thing a raconteur would say across the walnuts. Oil and the file went to the making of it, not the after-dinner glow, the wine-cup and the circle of attentive friends.

The story from which we quote ('Youth') is the best of the three tales the book contains, and is, indeed, a valuable addition to our sea-literature. In 'Heart of Darkness' the author is too much cobweb, and fails, as we think, to create his central character. The third story, 'The End of the Tether', is a more precise piece of creation, though a trifle tedious and diffuse. Prose and scenery cling round the central character like so much ivy, though the picturesqueness of the result is undeniable.

'Youth' is, without doubt, the best thing Mr Conrad has done. Tales of just that quality are rare, and the book should establish Mr Conrad in the high position he already holds, even if it should fail to add to his laurels.

On the Sea and Sailors

It keeps eternal whispering about us, singing in our ears like a
tune, crying in our hearts like a lure, but no ear has caught the
tune, and the lure has lured men too completely for them to
strive to expound its magic. Watching it at night, when the tide
is coming in with a long slow swirl, lapping among the rocks
with a suck and gurgle, and the soft burst of bubbles, one
catches, or seems to catch, that message ever whispering in the
spun filaments of an eddy. There is the old mystery, the imme-
morial sorrow of many waters. There is the old passionate
heart forever grieving. The wash of it, and the scent of it, and
the variant beauty of its strength a mystery and a passion for all
time. You may study the great waters for a life-time, but they
will remain inscrutable, as mysterious as God, as strong as
Death, and as eternal as the stately pageant of the stars. The sea
will teach much, but of itself nothing. It will hint at much while
withholding all things. No one can sing of it, it is too full of
beauty. No one can think of it over-long, for it is still brooded
over by the Spirit of God, and its great secret heart is too full of
His terror. It remains about us like a great shining and uncoil-
ing snake, a menace, a delight and a lure. It keeps its eternal
whisper and laughs at the puny pageant of the ships that pass.
It is a trackway of the wandering, the errant and the unhappy.
It is a home for nothing but the bones of drowned ships and
men.

Something of its mystery lies upon its waif children, the sail-
ors. For their lips have been sealed since the beginning or only
opened for the brief utterance of lies. Men put out in ships
from a longing they have for seeing the world beyond the sky-
line, from a joy they have in going to a place, for gain or to find
an enemy, for any reason, almost, save a desire to know the sea.
They fulfil their heart's longing and come home, but it is no
longer a home, the lure lies upon them like a coil of magic on
the heart and they go out on the quest again, not knowing what
they seek, but as wanderers and vagabonds as little at peace as
the gulls.

Of the men who have known the sea, who have looked into the water and seen inhuman beauty, who have spelled out the riddled runes upon the herring, there are but two whose words are of the spirit and not of the lips. These are Herman Melville, a man of great depth of vision, but with an expression uncertain in its beauty, a style tending in its inspiration towards incoherence, and Mr Joseph Conrad, a man of lesser vision but with a beauty of craft like the delicate beauty of rare gems. To these names might be added that more glorious name of Coleridge, though Coleridge's vision was either too profound or too broken, and the mystery and terror of his rime either too earthly or too accidental. He heard the voice of many waters when he made his poem,[1] but feverishly, like the buzzing in the ears during the exhibition of opium. To him the sea was incidental and subordinate. His poem has more the strangeness of fever than the strangeness of a perfect beauty.

Nearly all men have known the sailor, for the sailor, even the old sailor, is an elemental type and has grown but slightly in complexity since Homer saw him on his oar-bench, ploughing the wine-dark water to an old tune. Chaucer knew him, and saw in him a knavish alien with the vices of a strong man, with a merry heart and a foul tongue, and a body made comely by the sun and the salt air. Shakespeare knew him, and saw in him a boisterous irreverent brute with a sense of duty. Cervantes knew him and thought him a pleasant person with a somewhat low sense of humour. An old writer of the time of Queen Anne has painted him in the manner of Hogarth as 'a rare Dog, whose thoughts reach not much above the top-mast Head', though the same dog's-eared pamphleteer continues that:

> this poor composition of beef and oatmeal views all things, as Sheep do the Stars, or a Carthorse what passes in Cheapside, without any after-thought or Reflexion.[2]

And more recent writers, such as the excellent Marryat,[3] the good Dana,[4] the wise and scholarly Scott,[5] have not found in him either sign of change or operation of improvement. He has had his poets to sing him, has poor Jack, but his taste in poetry is still that of the eighteenth century. He will recite Falconer,[6] at odd times, often attributing the famous couplet about the 'lee-yard arm' to Shakespeare. He will still sing Dibdin,[7] but only such poems as can be sung to the tunes of familiar hymns.

The only poet who has seen the sailor in the dingy intimacy of his fo'c's'le, and sung him in verse which is more clarion than doggerel, is Mr E. J. Brady, an Australian, whose book of poems, *The Ways of Many Waters*,[8] was published in Sydney a few years ago. Mr Brady writes in ballad-metres, much as Adam Gordon[9] wrote, and Kingsley[10] and Macaulay[11] before him. He writes movingly and convincingly without putting an undue accent upon that 'plea for escape', or submission to a certain idea which mars most modern English ballads, and without subordinating his talent to realistic effect. He has a certain manly frankness about certain masculine shortcomings, which one admires, because man is a frank creature naturally and not a whit the nicer for being hypocritical in print. He knows the vagabond and the steward, and the stevedore,[12] and that pitiful hero the sailorman. He knows them perfectly:

> May you never be a syler of the mercantile marine,
> Or you'll always be a syler, an' you'll never 'ave a bean.
>
> But it's round the world a-goin'
> With the ebbin' an' the flowin',
> An' you needn't fear the bailiff, an' you needn't pay no rent;
> There's a month or two at sea,
> Then a rattlin' roarin' spree . . .
> *An' I dunno if I left it that I'd ever be content.*[13]

But the curious thing is that he knows the blue-jacket[14] quite as well as his poor relation, and 'The Passing of Parker', a long ballad of the death of a blue-jacket in a China Squadron battle-ship, is perhaps the best narratival ballad in dialect that we have. We like Mr Brady less as a serious poet, because his assertion in that métier is mere violent rhetoric, and comes from a very windy tradition. Though he can be suggestive and moving in some of the images he uses, as in:

> The penguin, standing lonely
> 'Neath weird, snow-darkened skies,

which conjures up a vision of the no-man's-land somewhere south of the Magellan Straits.

Someday, perhaps, when the golden age has returned, and all clipper-ships and liners are rusted nests for the tunnies[15] somewhere beyond the reach of lead, the oarsmen of the world's galleys will have a poesy and a drama. They will have an elaborate ritual of beautiful songs. They will sing hymns to the sea when the riding lantern goes up at dusk. They will invest their affection for the elements with the attributes of deity, and they will act little plays about the under-water and the white goddesses that haunt the weeds there. Sailors have done this in historic times, and though with us they have acted rather differently it is only because we have looked upon the sea as a trackway and not as a great water brooded over by the Spirit of God.

The Rose of Spain

[Book Review of Conrad and Hueffer's *Romance*]

ROMANCE. By Joseph Conrad and Ford Madox Hueffer.
London: Smith, Elder. 6s.

Some books are like old music, or old magic, in their power upon the brain that reads them. A few notes quavering upon a spinet,[1] or some little burning of gums within the five-angled star,[2] will bring a beauty into the mind, but always a transitory beauty. When the delicate hands have turned from the keys, and when the emerald has been put away, the smoking circle quenched, and the bright immortal faded, the shaken soul becomes again tranquil, the light pales and the fire dies down. It is as though there had been no music and no vision, for the enchantment only lingers for a little while, 'and when it is gone we are dead',[3] like leaves collapsed after a blowing along a road. But some books have always a great enchantment, having always that power of making the heart like a song. And these books, though they may be no grand creations, are always wonderful to us, like golden latch-keys into Heaven.

Since Mr Conrad published *Youth* (in the autumn of last year) we have looked upon him as the bearer of such a magic key, though its gold wards turn only in the lock of one door and open only to one vision. It may be that to Mr Conrad one story is ever in the telling, like the dominant in a fugue,[4] and this story is of a young man, and of the sea and the ships sailing, and of the golden times when the earth, to the young man, was a green jewel to the sight, and the very air an intoxication. His vision is always the vision of a young man, because to him trouble is not so much a weariness as a battle beautiful with swords. And it is always, in some measure, a vision of the sea because the sea leads one to the south and west, to the haunted countries of the young, where the very blossoms are languorous with passion, where the star of youth burns the most strongly. The sea has that fascination for the young that the lantern has for the moth. Youth will always desire water, even as it desires beauty, or swiftness, or strength, or battle, or any sane activity of the limbs. But youth desires the sea, as Mr Conrad has observed, rather as the path to beauty than a thing lovely in itself. It is so much melancholy water, a noisy medley of so many waves, but beyond it are the green islands, where the queen lives, where none can grow old nor weary.

In this new book, *Romance*, Mr Conrad has collaborated with Mr F. M. Hueffer,[5] and the collaboration has been salutary in some respects, but in others, if not baneful, at least of doubtful benefit. In his other writings Mr Conrad has wrought upon his subject with a multitude of touches, as though the central gold were hidden with cobwebs, as though the etcher, after giving his depth to the shadows, had continued to ply the burin.[6] One or two of his tales have been, like tapestries, made almost meaningless by the thick implication of the coloured silks. But in this book his touch is more certain, more sharply to the point, less cunning in its approach. The story is a definite story, lying before one like a road across a valley, and one has not to try this footpath, or that stile, before gaining the highway. In this respect, we think, the collaboration has been a definite gain, for one can sacrifice cheerily much metaphysics to a greater clearness. But in another respect we think it has been something of a loss, because the narrative attempts to make up, by a certain violence of assertion, that which its excised subtlety has taken from it. It is always a little violent, this story, as though its folk were actors upon a stage, as though the limelight were glistening and the folk in coloured gear, with wigs, and the tragic manner. There is something almost pantomimic in the way they kill each other, as though the blood were but red ink at so much the quart; as though the victim, after dying horribly, would watch the villain from the wings, and jest with him at his exits. It is towards the end that the tale becomes most pantomimic, with the false lights and false emotions of the modern stage. It ends like a play, where an old judge, it may be an old harlequin, speaks solemnly an epilogue while the feet shuffle off towards the doors. It is just this taint of the rouge-box and the footlight which keeps the book from the first rank.

The story is of a young man of Kent, the son of an earl of a ruined fortune, who has Spanish relatives connected dimly with the West Indies. These relatives are of great wealth, and one of them, a pale, brilliant youth, visits England, and falls in love with the young man's only sister. His suit does not prosper, and complications arise, which make it necessary for him to fly the country, his relative, John Kemp, the hero, with him. They are helped to a ship, by the moonlight, by a gang of smugglers, who ride the tubs nightly on the coast of Kent. They reach Jamaica, where their ways separate; Carlos, and his Spanish servant Castro, vanishing darkly to some mysterious port of pirates, a place called Rio Medio, where the English frigates cannot go by reason of shoal water. After a year or two strange circumstances bring John Kemp there, to rescue Carlos's sister from the subtle villain of the tale, a man called O'Brien. After a good deal of gun-firing, knife-play and blackguard attack from the rabble, with some infinitely tender and noble passages on the death of Carlos, John Kemp contrives to escape, with Carlos's sister, by this time his affianced lover. By the craft of O'Brien he is arrested in Havana, as the captain of the pirates. He is sent home to England for trial, in the British flagship, on the ballast, manacled, his wrists chained, the reek of the bilges just below him. He is tried, with a somewhat unnatural violence of rhetoric, as it seems to us, and is only saved by the sudden arrival of a West Indian friend able to speak in his interest.

The tale is a beautiful thing, beautiful like the daybreak or a sailing-ship, with much noble prose in it, and much brilliant writing. When one has read it through it still shows us the blue seas of the south, the green trees in the island, the white of the romantic houses, the wine-shops, the crime, the mournful Spanish swagger. It has that fascination that is in all Spanish things. It is so full of the sea, and of the beauty in the sunny islands to the south, that it catches one at the heart like a sight of Rio, like a memory of Brazil, like the memory of a boat of negroes coming alongside, in the glow of the sun, with the rare fruits of the tropics.

The Sea Writers

Captain Frederick Marryat

Frederick Marryat, our most entertaining marine writer, was born at Westminster, of good Huguenot stock,[1] in the year 1792. He was educated at private schools, where he was noted, among his schoolmates, for the strange relative largeness of his skull. By his masters he was noticed for a boisterous temper, and for an intolerance of discipline which led him to run away to sea several times during the few years he was with them. When he was fourteen years old he was sent to sea in the

midshipman's berth of the *Imperieuse* frigate, at that time com-
manded by Lord Cochrane,[2] one of the most fiery captains in
the service. He kept a brief journal of the cruise of this frigate
(she was in the Mediterranean), a journal which consists of
single-line entries, but is yet eloquent of the busy life on board.
Elsewhere he speaks of the perpetual hurry from one port to
another; the constant lowering of the boats to attack anchored
ships; the scanty sleep; and the daily firing of the great guns.

In the second year of the cruise he was one of the defenders
of the Fort of Rosas,[3] when that stronghold was attacked by
the French and Italians. He received three wounds, one of them
severe, in this affair, and was specially mentioned for good
behaviour in his captain's despatch. A year later he was invali-
ded home from the swamps of Walcheren[4] with a bad bout of
fever. In 1810 he was at sea again with Sir Samuel Hood,[5] after-
wards going to the West Indies and to North America with
Captain E. P. Brenton,[6] in the *Spartan*. He became Commander
in 1815, a few days before the battle of Waterloo, his first com-
mand being the *Beaver* sloop, of, I believe, fourteen small guns,
which vessel he commanded at St Helena, as a guarda-costa,
from 1820 until the death of Napoleon. He returned to Eng-
land in 1826, was made C.B.,[7] and given the command of a
beautiful frigate, the *Ariadne*, which he commanded until his
resignation in 1830.

When he left the Navy he commenced author, writing one,
two or three books a year, besides doing a considerable mass of
journalism. He travelled on the Continent, in Canada and in
the United States from 1836 to 1838, finally settling down at a
little farm near Langham, in Norfolkshire. In 1847 he tried to
obtain employment afloat, for he had had heavy money losses
owing to the failure of some West Indian property. The Lords
of the Admiralty refused his application in a manner more than
usually tactless, and his rage at their reply caused him to break
a blood vessel. While still weak from this mishap the news was
brought to him of the loss of his eldest son, then lieutenant
aboard the *Avenger*. He never recovered from the shock, but
sank slowly, dying in August, 1848, at his home at Langham.
His gamekeepers and farm labourers carried him to his grave at

Langham churchyard, mourning him much as the Irish Kernes[8]
may have mourned their dead chiefs of old. One of the coffin-
bearers was an old poacher who figures as the hero of one of
the less familiar books.

Captain Marryat began his literary career with an able tract
against the press-gang, a work which won him the enmity of
King William,[9] and may have delayed his promotion in the Ser-
vice. His second book was the *Amended Code of Flag Signals*,
on which is based the present International Code. This work
gained for him the decoration of the Legion of Honour[10] from
the French king. His first venture in fiction, *Frank Mildmay*,
was written on board the *Ariadne*, in 1829, mostly from per-
sonal reminiscences. It had an immediate success with the
public, and was followed, in quick succession, by the novels
which have made him famous. In 1832 he succeeded 'silly Tom
Campbell'[11] as editor of the *Metropolitan Magazine*,[12] to which
paper he contributed many essays and short stories.

Towards the end of his life he took to writing books for chil-
dren, and the last books he published were all of this kind. He
wrote several manly ballads of the sea, and a number of delight-
ful letters, so that his range, as a literary man, is unusually
wide. He was also a capable draughtsman, and an excellent
caricaturist. Only one or two of his caricatures were published,
in colour, but several others were circulated in the Fleet, to the
great prejudice of his reputation.

Of his books I have always liked that best which I have read
last, so that at the present moment I prefer *Peter Simple*. I have
not read them all, but of those I know I remember *The Priva-
teersman* with the least pleasure, though it contains several
stirring chapters to redeem it from positive badness. As a bal-
lad writer I rank him above everyone in his own class, though
I would not say that that class is a very important or significant
class. As a sailor and a gallant officer, I feel that he deserves
greater fame than he has, for he introduced one or two noble
changes in our naval system, and saved, at one time or another,
some twenty lives at the imminent peril of his own.

As a writer he is delightful, and, in his own way, without
peer. He makes alive for us that old world of the wooden

man-of-war, then changing from the squalid world that Smollett[13] knew to the trim world, all brass and clean canvas, which sailed for the Baltic in 1854.[14] When Marryat knew it, it had already lost something of its grimness, and his characters, therefore, are seldom truculent, seldom unrelieved, like those of Smollett. But it was yet a strange world, for even then 'a man-of-war, like a gallows, refused nothing',[15] and the crew of one of Marryat's ships was raised from nineteen nations, and contained workers in fifty-seven different trades. By reading Marryat one can realize that ship's company, just as the mention of the company helps us to realize Marryat. Inventive I do not think he was, though the plot of *Japhet* is certainly a fine piece of invention. But he was observant, and had a good memory, so that he could stuff his books with transcripts from real life, and make them alive with real people.

Whole chapters of his books, like the delicious press-gang yarn in *Peter Simple*, or the midshipman's berth vignettes in *Midshipman Easy* or *Frank Mildmay*, are as actual as the real events. Many of his characters, especially his subordinate characters, are real flesh and blood, as vivid as when Marryat knew them. Sixty or seventy years ago, I make no doubt, his readers, walking the Portsmouth streets, might have met the rosy-gilled Sir Hurricane, or the obese Mr Oxbelly,[16] and chatted with the one upon his peculiar hobby, and with the other upon his peculiar grace. They might have seen those matchless boats' crews at the landing-place; the merry bumboat wenches,[17] with their crates of red herrings and soft bread; and the little pinched middies[18] with their dirks. Had they taken a boat at the wharf, among the drunkards chaffing with the boatmen, and gone out on a sunny day to the anchorage, they might have stepped aboard the real *Diomede*, or the real *Harpy*, and walked the white decks, past the rows of sea cannon, with the real Captain Wilson or Mr Sawbridge.[19]

Marryat's folk are still alert and bustling, and their broad, hearty humour still engaging, for though one tires of art and wearies of intensity, 'the music of the thing that happened'[20] is a music as continual as the sunrise, and as pleasant to men's ears as Pan-pipes. Few of us are so married to dry land that they cannot go afloat in his company, hearing the piping of Mr Biggs,[21] the roar and groaning of the cannon, the salt winds of the sea, and the white sails straining to the braces. Such a cruise need not take one out of soundings,[22] while the company it offers is of a sterling quality, even though it use with undue frequency 'the language used in ships', against which Mr Coleridge[23] protested.

Herman Melville

Herman Melville, one of the two excellent writers that America has produced, was born in New York City on the 1st of August, 1819. The same year gave birth to Walt Whitman, the second of the aforementioned two, and to James Russell Lowell, author of the *Biglow Papers*. Melville's father, Allan, was a merchant of the Empire City,[1] who passed his evenings with old books, chiefly metaphysical, in the library of his home, now long destroyed, in the suburb of Greenwich village, now a populous, noisy and rather mean quarter of the city. He was a travelled man, this American merchant, and came of good stock, so that his little son grew up among cultured people, and heard strange tales, throughout his childhood, of the sea and ships, and of the seaports far away, and of the sailors, bronzed and earringed, whom he saw by the West-street saloons. Especially did he hear tales of Liverpool, that most magical of seaports, for his father had been thither in a sailing-ship, and had brought back one or two books, with engravings in them, representing the docks, or St Nicholas Church,[2] or Bidston Tower,[3] which the young Herman would pore upon for hours. I do not know whether they determined him to go to sea, for a New York boy has many calls to salt water without looking for them in cheap engravings. But it is certain that they left a strange impression on him, as though, in some other life, he had lived amid those scenes, and known them as a man knows his home. When he did go to sea (and that going had some elements of 'running away' about it), it was in a Liverpool-bound vessel, as 'able' seaman (surely his biographers mean 'ordinary'), in the year 1837, when he was eighteen years of age.

On his return to America he stayed ashore for a while,

making a precarious living as a school teacher, and subduing
refractory pupils with his fists. In 1840 Dana[4] published his
Two Years Before the Mast, a book which set Melville hunger-
ing for the sea (it will seem strange to a landsman, but such was
the effect it had), and led to his second voyage a year later. He
sailed from 'good old Nantucket' in a whale ship called the
Acushnet, which name Melville has shortened into *Dolly*. Life
on board a whale ship is at all times horrible, but off the Horn[5]
it must be more horrible than elsewhere. Melville was a fore-
castle hand, the *Dolly* was a leaky old tub, and her captain a
'Down-East Johnny-Cake'.[6] They tumbled round the Horn
together, in such ice and green water as one may picture, and
arrived in time, short-handed, ill found and discontented, in
the warm cruising grounds of the South Pacific. Here the *Dolly*
visited the port, or haven, of Nukahiva, in the Marquesas
Islands, in order to refit and to ship fruit and natives. Melville
had had as much whaling as he needed at the time, and, there-
fore, took the opportunity of stealing ashore with a friend.
With great difficulty they contrived to cross that part of the
island in which they might have been discovered. They pene-
trated to a hidden valley, inhabited by cannibals, where dusky
warriors made them captives, and guarded them, though kindly,
for several months. Melville's imprisonment was longer than
that of Bob, his shipmate; but he escaped at length, after a
bloody fight, on board an Australian whaling barque, short-
handed as usual, whose captain had heard of white prisoners
among the natives, and had hoped to ship them.

Melville did not stay very long with his deliverer, but seems
to have 'gone among the islands', a charming sea-gipsy, for
rather more than a year. Afterwards he shipped as a top-man
on board the American frigate *United States*, then an old ship,
which thirty years before had taken HMS *Macedonian* from
the English. He sailed round the Horn in her, touching at Rio
de Janeiro, and arrived at Boston in 1844. He spent a year or
two ashore, writing *Typee*, the story of his life among the can-
nibals, which was published in New York and London in 1846.
It had a wide sale in both countries, so that he felt justified in
devoting himself to a life of letters. He married a Miss Shaw, a

Massachusetts lady, in 1847, and lived for a while at Boston, afterwards moving to New York, where he obtained employment in the Customs. He went round the Horn in his brother's ship in 1860, in order to lecture at San Francisco. Being a married man, he took no part in the Civil War, saving the utterance of various poems. He lived to a happy, quiet, old age among his books and etchings and pleasant literary friends, and died at New York in 1891, aged a little over seventy-two.

His writings are like nothing else in the language, for they express a nature strangely rare, which lived strangely, and came to strange flower. He has been compared to George Borrow,[7] but it will not do to push the parallel too far, for Borrow's prose, at its best, is like a picture by Crome[8] – simple, manly and full of broad light and blowing wind. Melville's prose, at its best, is something which I cannot estimate, for it takes one from the common world to some rarer place, where strange seas are breaking, strange blossoms growing on the trees, and strange folk talking wisdom in the sun. His books may be divided into two classes – the reminiscent and the imaginative – and both classes have their admirers. In the one class are *Redburn*, the story of his boyish voyage to Liverpool; *Typee*, the story of his life among the cannibals; *Omoo*, the tale of his life in the islands; and *White Jacket*, his life in the American Navy. Of these, *Typee* and *Omoo* are the most charming, and I doubt if anyone has read them without longing to be on blue water, on some reeling fabric of a ship, swaying in, under white strained sails, to some sweet coral island's haven. Personally, I am very fond of parts of *Redburn*, though one must know New York and the haunted sailor-town of Liverpool to appreciate that gentle story thoroughly. *White Jacket* is an excellent piece of work, telling of a strange kind of life, now extinct, as it was lived on a strange kind of ship, now gone. It is the best book on that old sailor life; and perhaps one should not read Marryat, nor Chamier, nor Lord Dundonald[9] until one has *White Jacket* and a few pages of Smollett[10] at one's fingers' ends.

In the other class of his writings are his best book, *Moby Dick*, and his worst book, *Mardi*, which latter, I imagine, few have ever read through. It is written in a fantastic, fanciful, tentative manner which aims high, as one can see, but is too boyish and too wayward to be readable. When he wrote it he was playing with his material, trying to learn his art. It is written in exactly the inspired boy style, and has all the folly, but yet a little of the beauty, and much of the eagerness, of youth. *Moby Dick* shows us what the same writer could do when he had developed his instrument, and it is not too much to say that that noble story is the best sea book in the English language. Of its quality as prose I hope to speak elsewhere and at greater length,[11] but I cannot close this article without testifying, however briefly, to the lofty beauty of its story. In that wild, beautiful romance Herman Melville seems to have spoken the very secret of the sea, and to have drawn into his tale all the magic, all the sadness, all the wild joy of many waters. It stands quite alone; quite unlike any book known to me. It strikes a note which no other sea writer has ever struck. And when, in one unforgettable chapter, his crew of old sailors gathers on the fo'c's'le to talk by the light of the moon of life, and man, and the sorrows of man's making, he rises to a pitch of mournful beauty such as one might find in Webster, in Middleton, or some other Elizabethan, if not in Shakespeare himself. One may say of *Moby Dick* what Melville in that tale says of the ship which bears his characters. One may call it 'A noble tale, but a most melancholy; all noble things are touched with that.'[12]

R. H. Dana

Richard Henry Dana, the son of the poet of that name, was born at Cambridge, Massachusetts, in August, 1815. He was educated at Harvard, where he was noted, as his father had been noted before him, for his intolerance of all authority. His father, I believe, is still spoken of at Harvard with awe as the 'Rotten Cabbage Rebel'. His son, our hero, was merely rusticated. On apologizing for his misdeeds he was allowed to graduate, thus finishing his education in 1837. It had been his intention to study law on leaving college, but his eyesight was giving way, and study was out of the question. He decided to go for a long sea voyage, and preferred to go as a common

sailor, for, as he said, he was 'a boy who could not be pruden-
tial, and caught at all adventure'. He had been reading Ames's
Mariner's Sketches,[1] a bright little volume, lively with the ways
of the sea, and it was this book which made him ship before the
mast. He sailed in the brig *Pilgrim*, from Boston, a few weeks
after leaving college. On his return, two years later, he pub-
lished his *Two Years Before the Mast*, and settled down to the
study of his profession. He was admitted to the Bar in due course
and became in time an authority on international law, a subject
on which he wrote several learned volumes. He went round the
world in 1859, suffering shipwreck (his ship being burned)
near the Sandwich Islands. He also visited Cuba, and wrote a
rather dull chronicle of the visit. He died in 1882, in his sixty-
eighth year, at his home at Cambridge, Massachusetts.

His book stands by itself in sea-literature, for though many
have tried to write of life at sea, not one has succeeded in quite
such a startling manner. *Two Years Before the Mast* is a real
piece of life, an actual and vivid transcript. It gives the reader
just that impression of reality which one gets from a novel of
Defoe,[2] such as *Colonel Jack* or the *Journal of the Plague*. Any-
one anxious to know what life in the merchant service is (for it
has not changed materially since Dana wrote, as far as sailing-
ships are concerned) must go to Dana, for in no other writer
will he find a picture equally vivid and true. In Dana he will
find the whole craft and mystery revealed, nothing withheld,
nothing overstated. Apart from its veracity as an account of
human event it is remarkable, this sailor's log, for the beauty of
much of its description. I know of hardly any printed passage
so moving in its dignified pathos as that in which the young
sailor describes the flogging of his shipmates. One has but to
read it to see the whole scene; the little brig's deck, the six sail-
ors, and the flushed, screaming savage with the rope's end.
Then the passage immediately following, where the men are
down in the forecastle, under the slush-lamp,[3] with hell in
their hearts, and miseries before them on the morrow. It is
all told most masterly, without one touch of weakness or
over-emphasis. The whole matter is before the reader. There
are the men, brooding on their wrongs, some of them bleeding

from wounds. There is the ship, dipping her nose in green
water, on a lonely coast, where she will stay for many months.
The misery is there, and will be there till the ship reaches home.
And there is the young college graduate, sick with pity, vowing
silently that, 'if God should ever give him the means, he would
do something to redress the grievance and relieve the suffering.'
All the book is alive and human, but at this point Dana writes
with all the tenderness and compassion of a woman. It is impos-
sible for one to read the passage without making some such a
vow as he made, and feeling thankful, however wrongly, that
the savage, with 'the face as red as blood', who did the crime
died evilly but a few months later.

    One does not have to be a sailor to enjoy Dana; indeed, he
is less popular with sailors than with landsmen. But then sail-
ors read nothing but the Bible and Miss Braddon,[4] and have
forgotten what a stunsail is – a fact which makes Dana's sea-
manship a dubious matter to them. A landsman can follow
Two Years Before the Mast without reference to Nares' Epit-
ome.[5] For though there is much talk of ropes and sails, there is
yet much poetry, moving and delicate, and many precise pic-
tures simply coloured. What could be brighter and more alert
than this record of a meeting on the seas?

> She came down to us, backed her main-topsail, and the two ves-
> sels stood 'head on', bowing and curvetting at each other like a
> couple of war-horses reined in by their riders. It was the first ves-
> sel that I had seen near, and I was surprised to find how much she
> rolled and pitched in so quiet a sea. She plunged her head into the
> sea, and then, her stern settling gradually down, her huge bows
> rose up, showing the bright copper, and her stern and breast
> hooks dripping, like Neptune's locks, with the brine.

    Later on in the book, in the record of his homeward passage,
Dana describes most admirably the 'driving' of a ship by a cap-
tain who longed for home. It was blowing hard from the
southward, and the captain was pressing his ship to get her
clear of the Horn.[6] He gave her the topsails, which buried her
in a smother from the bows to the gangway. 'What she can't

carry she may drag,' he cried, and he bade set a foretopmast stunsail, on a boom which 'bent like a whalebone', so that she shook to the core. 'She seemed actually jumping from sea to sea', running eleven knots, and steering 'as wild as a colt'.

> For more than an hour she was driven on at such a ferocious rate that she seemed actually to crowd the sea into a heap before her, and the water poured over her spritsail yard as it would over a dam.

More sail was piled on her, till she swooped and plunged like a hawk, spinning the wheel round whenever a sea struck the rudder. 'She had more on her than she could bear', yet it was useless to try to take it in, so the skipper 'held on', letting her go 'gloriously', 'with a clear sea, and as much wind as a sailor could pray for'. Dana is full of spirited things like this, for his run home is nothing more than a pæan in praise of hurry. The skipper, a newly married man, had been away two years, and was eager for home. The mate was 'not to be beaten by anybody'; while the second mate, though he was afraid to press sail, 'was afraid as death of the captain', and 'carried on longer than any of them'. When one reads the closing chapters one longs to be afloat, hanging on to a ship's weather-shrouds, while the seas go roaring aft, and the white drift flies scattering. There is misery and wretchedness in a sea-life, and Dana says so very clearly; but none who has been to sea may read his account without longing to be hauling on a rope, or leaning over a yard, fisting at a topsail. His book, in this, is like the sea itself, for though the sea may be the bleakest memory in a life, as it is with me, it recurs always as something magical, something to thrill the soul. Dana's two years were years of roughness, years of savagery, years of leanness. But he remembered them always, as we remember them, as a part of youth, a holy time, when the wind went singing in the sky, and life was a little work done gaily with some comrades. In his old age he made that voyage of his again, and in California his old wits brim with memories, and he writes touchingly of old shipmates, and of the old fair ships he had sailed in, as though those two years were years of romance, years of blessedness, perhaps the only real years he had ever been fated to know.

Chanties

A chanty is a song sung by sailors when engaged in the severest of their many labours. The word chanty is generally mispronounced by landsmen. It is not pronounced as spelt, like the word chant with an added *y* final. It is pronounced shanty, to rhyme with scanty,[1] the *ch* soft and the *a* narrow. The verb to chanty is frequently used, as in the order 'Chanty it up, now', or the injunction 'Heave and chanty'.

There are three varieties of chanty, each kind adapted to its special labour. There is the capstan chanty, sung at the capstan when warping, or weighing anchor, or hoisting topsails with the watch. There is the halliard chanty, sung at the topsail and topgallant halliards, when the topsails and topgallant sails are being mastheaded. And there is the sheet, tack and bowline chanty, used when the fore, main and cross-jack sheets are hauled aft, and when the tacks are boarded and the bowlines tautened. Formerly, in the days when ships were built of wood, and leaked from an inch or two to two or three feet a day, there used to be pumping chanties, sung by the pumpers as they hove the brakes[2] round. Now that ships are built of steel or iron, which either leak not at all or go to the bottom, there is no pumping to be done aboard, save the pumping of fresh water from the tanks in the hold for the use of the crew, and the daily pumping of salt water for the washing-down of the decks. I have passed many miserable hours pumping out the leaks from a wooden ship, but I was never so fortunate as to hear a pumping chanty.

Strictly speaking, there is a fourth variety of chanty, but it is a bastard variety, very seldom used. The true chanty, of the kinds I have mentioned, is a song with a solo part and one or two choruses. The solo part consists of a line of rhyme which is repeated by the solo man after the first chorus has been shouted. The bastard variety which I have just mentioned has no solo part. It is a runaway chorus, sung by all hands as they race along the deck with the rope. You hear it in tacking ship. It is a good song to sing when the main and mizzen yards are being swung simultaneously. All hands are at the braces straining taut, and at the order they burst into song and 'run away with it', bringing the great yards round with a crash. It is a most cheery kind of chanty, and the excitement of the moment, and the sight of the great yards spinning round, and the noise of the stamping feet impress it on the mind. The favourite runaway chorus is:

What shall we do with a drunken sailor? What shall we do with a drunken sailor? What shall we do with a drunken sailor, early in the morning? Way, hay, there she rises; way, hay, there she rises; way, hay, there she rises; early in the morning.

Chuck him in the long-boat till he gets sober. Chuck him in the long-boat till he gets sober. Chuck him in the long-boat till he gets sober. Early in the morning. Way, hay, there she rises; way, hay, there she rises; way, hay, there she rises; early in the morning.

It is sung to a vigorous tune in quick time. It is the custom among sailors to stamp with their feet at each 'Way, hay'. The effect is very spirited.

Of the chanties proper, the capstan chanties are the most beautiful, the halliard chanties the most commonly heard, and the sheet, tack and bowline chanties the most ancient. In a capstan chanty the solo-man begins with his single line of verse. Before he has spoken the last word of it the other men heaving at the bars break out with the first chorus. Immediately before the chorus has come to an end the solo man repeats his line of verse, to be interrupted at the last word by the second chorus, which is generally considerably longer than the first. It is a glorious thing to be on a forecastle-head, in heaving at a capstan bar, hearing the chain coming clanking in below you to the music of a noisy chanty sung by a score of sailors.

[The Solo, or Chanty-man]	In Amsterdam there dwelt a maid.
[The Sailors]	Mark well what I do say!
[The Solo, or Chanty-man]	In Amsterdam there dwelt a maid,
	In Amsterdam there dwelt a maid.
[The Sailors]	And I'll go no more a-ro-o-ving
	With you, fair maid.
	A-roving, a-roving.
	Since roving's been my ru-i-n,
	I'll go no more a-ro-o-ving with
	you, fair maid.

That is the most beautiful of all the chanties. It is sung to an old Elizabethan tune which stirs one's blood like a drum-tap. The song, or solo of it, is strangely like the song in one of Thomas Heywood's plays. Several of the couplets are identical. The curious will find the song in *Lucrece*, in the fifth act.[3] I cannot quote it here.

A halliard chanty is begun by the solo-man in the manner described above. It has generally two choruses, but they are of the same length – not short and long, as in the case of the anchor chanty. The solo-man is always a person of some authority among the crowd. He begins his song after the first two or three pulls upon the halliards. There are countless halliard chanties, and new ones come into use each year. Those which one hears occasionally ashore are nearly always old ones, little used at sea. The sailors have grown tired of them. I do not know what chanties are most used now at sea. In my time we used to get the yards up to

[The Chanty-man]	A long, long time and a long time ago,
[The Sailors]	To me *way* hay *o-hi-o*.
[The Chanty-man]	A long, long time and a long time ago,
[The Sailors]	A *long* time *ago*.
[The Chanty-man]	A smart Yankee packet[4] lay out in the bay,
[The Sailors]	To me *way* hay *o-hi-o*;
[The Chanty-man]	A smart Yankee packet lay out in the bay,
[The Sailors]	A *long* time *ago* (etc.)

The pulls upon the rope are delivered during the choruses upon the words I have italicized. Another very popular chanty was

[The Chanty-man]	Come all you little nigger-boys,
[The Sailors]	And roll the cotton down.
[The Chanty-man]	O come all you little nigger-boys,
[The Sailors]	And roll the cotton down (etc.)

The tune to this is bright and merry. It puts you in a good temper to be singing it. Another strangely beautiful chanty is that known as 'Hanging Johnny'. It has a melancholy tune that is one of the saddest things I have ever heard. I heard it for the first time off the Horn,[5] in a snowstorm, when we were hoisting topsails after heavy weather. There was a heavy, grey sea running and the decks were awash. The skies were sodden and oily, shutting in the sea about a quarter of a mile away. Some birds were flying about us, screaming.

[The Chanty-man]	They call me Hanging Johnny.
[The Sailors]	Away-i-oh.
[The Chanty-man]	They call me Hanging Johnny.
[The Sailors]	So hang, boys, hang.

I thought at the time that it was the whole scene set to music. I cannot repeat those words to their melancholy wavering music without seeing the line of yellow oilskins, the wet deck, the frozen ropes and the great grey seas running up into the sky.

Of the sheet, tack and bowline chanties the oldest is 'Haul the Bowline', which was certainly in use in the reign of Henry VIII. It is still very popular, though the bowline is no longer the rope it was. It is a slow, stately melody, ending with a jerk as the men fall back with the rope.

[The Chanty-man]	Haul on the bowline, the fore and maintop bowline.
	Haul on the bowline.
[The Sailors]	The bowline *haul*.

Another excellent chanty in this kind is the following:

[The Chanty-man]	Louis was the King of France afore the Revolu-ti-on.
[The Sailors]	Away, haul away, boys; haul away toge-e-ther.
[The Chanty-man]	But Louis got his head cut off, which spoiled his consti-tu-ti-on.
[The Sailors]	Away, haul away, boys; haul away O.

The chanty is the invention of the merchant service. In the navy they have what is called the silent routine, and the men fall back upon their ropes in silence, 'like a lot of soldiers', when the boatswain pipes.[6] It must be very horrible to witness. In the merchant service, where the ships are invariably under-manned, one sings whenever a rope is cast off the pin. You haul a brace to the cry of 'O, bunt him a bo', 'O rouse him, boys', 'Oho Jew', 'O ho ro, my boys' and similar phrases. You clew up a sail to the quick 'Lee-ay', 'Lee-ay', 'Ho ro', 'Ho', 'Aha', uttered in a tone of disquiet or alarm. You furl a course to the chant of 'Paddy Doyle and his Boots'. Without these cries and without the chanties you would never get the work done. 'A song is ten men on the rope.' In foul weather off the Horn it is as comforting as a pot of hot drink. A wash and a song are the sailor's two luxuries.

I did not hear the chanties sung last week at the Salford Hippodrome,[7] but I have heard chanties sung upon the stage both in this country and in America. They were not in the least like the real thing. They were too slow, bowdlerized and too much tinkered by that abomination the musical composer. I gather that the Salford artists were much more happy. Those who wish to obtain the music of the commoner chanties will find Miss Laura Smith's *Music of the Waters*[8] and the anthology of Dr Ferris Tozer[9] of use to them. Several may be found in the songbook of the Guild of Handicraft.[10] I have also seen a collection of them published (I believe) by Messrs Metzler.[11] The files of the *Boy's Own Paper*, *The Cadet*[12] and the publications of the Folk-Song Society may also be consulted with advantage.

Those who wish to learn the words of the solos sung by the chantymen must go to sea in sailing-ships. They are nearly always unsuited for publication. The opening lines (such as I have quoted) are generally the least objectionable.

New Novels: Joseph Conrad

[Book Review of Conrad's 'Twixt Land and Sea]

'TWIXT LAND AND SEA. By Joseph Conrad.
Dent and Co., 6s.

'Twixt Land and Sea, by Joseph Conrad [. . .] contains three stories, written in the new and handy form (about a third the length of the ordinary novel), which will perhaps be the usual literary form in the decade after this. Mr Conrad has always used this form with fine effect, and he uses it again here finely, with a complete mastery of his art and with his old colours of mystery, romance and the strangeness of life. His three new stories illustrate the three kinds of creative writing for which he is best known. The first tale, 'A Smile of Fortune', is another study in the manner of 'Heart of Darkness'. The suggestion of a strange and rather great character through a veil of mystery, which is plucked away, as it were, thread by thread, by a multitude of clever pickings, till the character behind it stands out, bigger perhaps than we had expected, but also stranger although revealed. The second story, 'The Secret Sharer', is a new romance of the sea, a second 'Youth', beautiful like that fine tale, with the suggestion that something done with difficulty and perhaps unavailingly has, after all, brought something into life, bigger than one thought, something to count as significant later on when the play is considered as a whole. The third story, 'Freya of the Seven Isles', ends the symphony of the book with a study of a blindness, mental this time, not physical, as in the tale at the end of 'Youth', but not less tragical, being the blindness of an old, kindly father to the depths of emotion in his tragically placed daughter.

Of the three tales the first two have most of that particular art and personal way of looking at life which give Mr Conrad's books their new and fine flavour in the mind. All three are written in a firm and beautiful prose, at once precise and supple, good both in dialogue and in description. There is quality in the prose as in the subjects, difficult to define exactly, except as a personal quality of the kind sometimes got in loneliness by a strong and strange temperament who is more sensitive to impressions than his way of life gives warrant for. This quality in the choice of subjects and in the way of handling them is Mr Conrad's own special quality. There is not and has never been anything in the least like it. Given an unusual temperament placed in a rough-and-ready way of life which leads men into those unusual places where unusual traits in character are called out, a quality of this kind is likely to develop; a quality of great mental sensitiveness, which is the real man, hidden behind the mask of the activity of the occupation. Having this special gift of sensitiveness, and having as a master mariner little occasion to use it in his daily work, it seems to have developed in Mr Conrad a deep, never-sated curiosity about life, mostly about the life known to him, the life of sailors and of the men who deal with sailors, as traders, charterers, consignees, consuls and ship's chandlers, natives of various colours, and so on, and his main achievement is this – that he has brought these people into the imaginative kingdom in all the sincerity of their simplicity. His is not a vision of the world, like Shakespeare's, nor of a society, like Chaucer's; but of unusual people outside the settled orders, and his vision is all the more intense from being focussed on individuals.

His power of focussing upon the out-of-the-way gives an uncanny flavour to the first of those three tales, told in the first person of a sea captain newly arrived at an island, where he is served by a profound and single being with a kind of elemental greatness in his singleness, who has an inexplicable daughter and a home like a private madhouse. Little by little one is made more intimate with the man and his home, one comes almost to dread him and it, then one changes to dislike him or despise him, and ends by thinking him rather great, rather sinister, but quite mysterious one way or the other, in the end (like life itself, sanely looked at). The second story is not less wonderful in its atmosphere: a captain newly come to a ship in a far-away Eastern road, with the masts of another ship (waiting to be towed up the river) just visible over an island, and night coming down, and a murderer, flying from the law, in the water alongside, having swum out on a last chance. This tale, made perhaps a little petty by some of its intrigue, gets a great lift of romantic beauty towards the end, and finishes with what musicians call a full close. The third tale, wonderful throughout for its colour, strikes one as having its movement rather clogged, and its complications made a little slow, until the tragedy is at its height, when, after a few swift moments, we are taken from direct contact with the characters.

Sailing-Ships

For the last generation the numbers of square-rigged sailing-ships have been declining. It has become less and less easy to run them at a profit, steamers have ousted them from one carrying trade after another, fewer and fewer are built, to replace those wrecked or destroyed, and most sailors realize that their day is done. For many years they have had but one traffic in which they can profitably compete with steamers, and this traffic, that of carrying nitrates from Chile and Peru, to the United States or Europe, will be done by steamers as soon as the opening of the Panama Canal[1] makes the long passage round Cape Horn or through the Straits of Magellan unnecessary. It is possible that thirty years hence the great square-rigged sailing-ships of this generation will have vanished from the seas, as utterly as the three-decker.

It is natural that what has served its turn should disappear and few who know her will regret the passing of the sailing-ship, but at the same time her case is interesting and unusual. Often an art dies gradually, through a long and painful decline from pride to vanity and so to idiocy, but in this case, as in so

many others, in an age of competitive commercialism, the art is
not declining, but ceases at the moment of its greatest develop-
ment, from being superseded by something else. As we have her
at present, a steel structure of from five hundred to three thou-
sand tons, the sailing-ship is the best known achievement of a
kind of art at which every generation from the time of Noah
has worked, and to which each has added. For a few years
more she will be with us, beautiful with the thought of many
millions of men, then she will cease and be forgotten, like the
velocipede,[2] the high bicycle[3] and the hansom-cab.[4]

Many causes led to the great development of the sailing-ship
by which her tradition is perfected and ended. The coming of
the steam-ship drove the builders to design a type of ship which
could compete in speed with steam over long routes. They
designed the clippers of the sixties and seventies, which were
certainly the fastest sailing-ships ever built, though too fine to
be profitable cargo-carriers, and only of service while the way
to the East was round the Cape of Good Hope. When the Suez
Canal[5] was cut their occupation was gone. The builders then
tried to design a type of ship which could compete with steam
in cheapness as a cargo-carrier over long routes. They designed
and gradually perfected the two types of sailing-vessel now
most in vogue, the small, cheap easily handled barque, and the
enormous four- or five-master, which would carry three or four
thousand tons of cargo with a crew of perhaps twenty or
twenty-five fo'c's'le hands. These two types have held their own
fairly successfully though under increasing pressure. They are
the last to die, and anyone who has seen them will say that they
are noble things worth recording for future times. Things so
beautiful and so complex with the triumph of man's intellect
and ingenuity, ought not to be allowed to pass unrecorded; but
the marine nations are commercial, and the last century has
shown them to be careless in recording their great achieve-
ments.

There is very little authentic artistic record of the ships of the
past; hardly any of the life on board them. There is no worthy
drawing of the lower-deck of one of Nelson's ships, nor of her
men; the clippers of the sixties are only recorded formally, if at

all, by artists of little power; no one has drawn their crews. There must be many photographs of the more recent types of sailing-ships, but they are all in private hands, untabulated and inaccessible, and among them all there are perhaps very few showing how life was lived aboard them. It is a pleasure to welcome Mr Coburn's[6] pioneer attempt to record the beauty and dignity of these passing types, and to show something of the hardness and roughness of the life by which they are kept going.

EXTRACTS FROM NOVELS

From *Lost Endeavour*

There was a great deal of confusion in the *Marie Galante* that afternoon. Half a dozen hands had been wounded by the posse,[1] two very seriously, including the drunken doctor. With these out of action, as well as those hurt in the fight with the Indians, we were desperately short-handed. It ought not to have been so; for she was a small and handy ship, under hardly any sail; but the leak was a serious matter, keeping six hands always at the pumps in twenty-minute spells. With a hand steering, a hand looking out aloft, a hand taking charge and keeping the rest to their work, we were as short-handed as the Ark, as Dick said. The hands made a sort of a meal on deck, with a good allowance of spirits. I noticed that Dick kept a careful eye on them as they ate. He checked the least appearance of rudeness and discontent, with what seemed to me to be unnecessary bitterness. He seemed uneasy during the meal. He kept glancing at the water from the pumps. 'Why,' he said, in a surprised tone, 'ain't them pumps sucking yet? Sing out when they suck.' Then he turned to the next spell, who were standing by to take their turn. 'I'll give a ten-dollar mess-treat to the spell which sucks her.' (By sucking he meant making the pumps to 'suck', or draw up air, showing that they had emptied the well.) 'What are you staring at?' he said to me. 'You want some work to do. You've eaten as much as you're worth. So. You see that fore-hatch. Go down it into the 'tween-decks, and from there into the fore-hold. At the foot of the ladder you'll see a cask lashed abaft the stanchions of the hatch. In the cask is some soft-brick and some old sail-rag. You get some of that, and clean the brass on the cabin-windows. Down with you, now.' I left my food, and ran away to do what I was bid.

Down in the fore-hold below the water-line it was very dark. I groped all about the fore-hatch for the cask which Dick had mentioned, but I could not meet with it anywhere. I was just going to go on deck again, to tell Dick that I could not find the cask, when I saw a light, like a lantern light, moving about above the bales and casks of the stowed cargo, in the narrow space between their tops and the 'tween-deck beams and planks. I did not know what it was at first. It frightened me. Enough wickedness and violence had gone on in that ship for it to be haunted by evil things, such as they say walk in old castles at night. It is all nonsense, of course; no one ever sees such things; one fears darkness because one cannot see what is in it. But you go down into a dark hold, full of gurglings and groanings, after a day and night of wildest nervous strain, and see a globe of light coming slowly towards you out of the darkness, and you will remember all the ghost stories you ever read, and believe them, and quake all down your marrow at them. After ten seconds of horror I saw that a man was scrambling over the bales towards me with a lantern in his hand. 'Don't cut,' said Dick's voice. 'Hold on; I want you.' He slid himself down some packs of vicuna wool,[2] and brought to alongside me. 'Here,' he said. 'Come on here, and don't make a noise.' He pulled me over to the ship's port-side. 'See this,' he said, showing a small earthen-ware pot. 'Watch me.' He placed it against one of the great ribs of the ship and laid his ear to it. 'Quiet,' he said. 'Don't stir. Quiet a minute.' He listened intently for a while, and then moved to the rib further forward, where he listened again. Then he went right up to the bows of her and listened again at the foremost rib of all, in a space so dark that I could only grope my way with one hand on the ship's side. The lantern, being of thick horn, gave little more light than a rushlight. He sighed a little at the foremast rib, and bade me come aft again to one of the after ribs. 'Be careful of the ring-bolts,' he said. 'We had the slaves down here three trips back, and some of the irons are still about. There. Now, quiet again.'

We listened together intently in that central darkness. It was unreal there. It was strange. It was wonderful. I felt that we were two conspirators down below, plotting something; or if you like, two doctors testing the ship's heart-beats, two little thoughts in a brain, two dim figures from a dream.

'Now,' said Dick. 'Come here, boy. Put your ear to the pot here and listen carefully.' I stepped up to him, and laid my ear to the pot; and instantly, as though I had laid a shell to my ear, a noise of water came to me – not as it comes with a shell, though; nor as it comes from a tap. It was a peculiar noise. There was a gurgling and a bubbling sound, as though a brook were running at a little distance. All sorts of noises were mixed up with it, of course. There was the piping, groaning noise of a ship's side straining at every roll, and the noise of rats scuffling and squeaking; but very plainly, through all the noises, there came the noise of water gurgling and bubbling. At first I thought that it might be the water creaming away from the bows as we drove along; but I soon found that that noise was distinct. 'Well,' said Dick at last, 'what do you make of it? What do you hear?'

'Water,' I answered, 'water gurgling.'

'Yes,' he said. 'Water gurgling. About how much water? A good big brook of water?'

'Yes,' I said. 'A pretty good swift brook of water.'

'Yes,' he answered. 'A pretty good swift brook. Well, it's coming into us, that brook. There's two feet of it in the well. I tell you, boy, it will be a close call for us this trip. She's knocked a big hole in herself.' I was aghast at this. I didn't know what to answer. At last I asked him what they would do, and whether they could get to the island.

'No,' he said. 'No, no. With a hole like that in her, and a crew of hangbacks like them on the deck there, that's out of the question. We shan't smell Boca Drago[3] this trip.'

'No?' said I. 'And you can't put in to James Town[4] nor into the creek here, for the country's raised on you. And by this time the frigate will be after you, and you won't be able to get away from her. You've got no sails.'

'Yes,' he said, in a gloomy voice. 'We may look to be chased

in less than an hour. I wonder what we could do. One thing is
sure, we are in a bad way all round. But, listen, you. Do you
hear the pump going?'

'No,' I answered, after a pause. 'They've stopped pumping.'

'Well,' said he, 'I'll dye my hair. Do they want her to sink?'
He ran up on deck, muttering angry words; I followed him.

When we got to the deck we found the hands quarrelling
round the pump, some part of which had broken internally,
choking it. Some were maintaining that the thing could be
mended; the others, by far the larger body, were saying that
they would break the head of anyone who mended it; for why,
said they, should they want to mend a pump which would keep
them hard at work all day, short-handed as they were? Dick
was never a patient man. He flung them aside angrily, so that
he might examine the damage. 'See here,' he said, after a short
examination. 'One of you fools has been monkeying with this.
Which of you was it?'

Nobody answered; but the tone of Dick's voice troubled
them a good deal; they hung their heads, and looked as school-
boys look between the lecture and the flogging. 'Where is
Theo?' said Dick, sucking in his lower lip and biting on it.

'Gone asleep,' said one of them. 'His wound's broke out
again, so José gave him a sleeping draught, and he's just off,
quiet as a lamb. He'll sleep till night, I guess.'

'Well then,' said Dick, rounding on them fiercely. 'I com-
mand here, I guess. And I'll tell you something. Virginia,[5] there,
is death to you. See? You fired on the posse, even if you didn't
kill anybody. And, even without them counts, our cargo here is
enough to hang the lot of us. That ticks off Virginia. In one of
them creeks, getting ready to come after us, is the station frig-
ate, which we thought was at James Town. She'll be after us at
any minute. So much for her. We're at sea without sails and
without stores. We're short-handed, and a lot of our hands are
hurt. And a pretty rotten lot the sound ones are. Lastly, we've
got two foot of water in the well, and one of you beauties has
gone and wrecked the pump. That ticks off us. Now then, you
may chew on that for a while; I'm going to have a smoke.'

He lit a seaman's short pipe, and walked up and down to

windward of them, giving them contemptuous glances from time to time. I never saw a sorrier lot of men than those crestfallen pirates. At first they stood dumbfoundedly looking at each other. Then one of them went to the place abaft the mainmast where the sounding-rod hung, to measure the leak for himself. The rod was no longer there; Dick had dropped it overboard privily. They had to accept his word for the leak's presence; and since they could not disprove it, they did so. One or two of them bent down in a faint-hearted way as though to repair the pump. The others stared stupidly at Dick, and then looked at each other, each hoping that somebody else would pipe up an answer or suggest a remedy. At last one of them, more frightened than the others, asked 'what would become of them, please,' which was just the question which Dick wanted.

'Why,' he said, 'if you are not hanged you'll be drowned, which is what I hope from my heart you will be.' This crushed any little show of mutiny which might have been left in them. It made them realize that they were in a pretty tight place. One of them said that the best thing would be to run the ship ashore, or take her humbly into James Town and submit to the king's mercy.

'Yes,' said Dick. 'The posse are following along the shore, hoping that that is what you'll do. As for the king's mercy, you've just defied it. Find another answer. Guess again, my Toro.' Toro did not guess again, nor did anybody else guess again. 'Well,' said Dick, 'you are all fallen dumb, are you? You were talkative enough just now. Now perhaps you'll listen to me, before she sinks on you, as she will if you leave her to herself much longer. Up there, some of you, and rip that awning off her. It's a bare chance. Two of you bring up blankets from below – twenty or thirty, and any mattresses you may run against. Stop, no. A bale or two of that vicuna wool, down in the fore-hold. That's a thicker kind of stuff. Be lively with it. Don't stand looking on, the rest of you. Fetch out the handpump and get her started. The rest of you get a chain of buckets ready, in case it comes to that. I'll keep this ship alive as long as there's any sense in it. Stamp now. Jump.'

In a few minutes the awning came down from the main-yard. Dick stretched it out on the deck, and sent some hands to get two tackles passed round the ship from without (under her keel), one on each side of the site of the supposed leak. While they were doing this, he put other hands to the work of sewing thick handfuls of wool, or rolls of blanket, on the inside of the awning, so as to make it resemble a furry mat. I helped at this work by tearing out the wool from the bale and hand-ing it to those who had sail-needles. We worked at a feverish rate. As we worked, a man came up from the 'tween-decks to say that the little hand-pump, which would at least have held the leak in an even balance, was out of order in some way. A hole had been knocked in the shaft, letting in the air. There was no working it. It wouldn't draw water. Dick didn't say much to this.

'Some more of you beauties' handiwork,' he muttered. 'Well. If I get you out of this mess,' he added, 'perhaps you'll be wiser another time.' They certainly looked as though they had made up their minds to be a great deal wiser another time. For my part I doubted whether that other time would ever come. When I thought of that gurgling water down in the hold, I began to think of what would happen if this contrivance of Dick's came to nothing. What would happen? The water would come creep-ing, in little runnels, over the 'tween-decks, sliding across with a nasty rush at each roll. And each roll would be smaller than the one before. And each pitch would be deader, and 'more soggy' (as they said) than the one before. Till at last she would be a log on the sea, settling, settling, settling, the swing-ports awash, the hatchway a brimming well, the bitts an island. Then we should waver to one side, and lurch, and go down, like a dropping stone; and I should smell the sea-floor, as Dick called it, and lie rolled about by the ground swell, with the little white sea-snails and the coral-plants and the shadows of big ships passing.

'Now,' said Dick, when we had finished the work. 'The sooner we get this joker over the side the better. There's three foot inside the lower hold by this time. So heave now, hearties. Over with her.' We adjusted the tackle to the corners of the

awning, and then hauled it under the ship's keel, till we had got
it, as we judged, over the hole. Dick took me down below from
time to time to try the leak by the method of the pot. After
the fourth readjustment of the tackle I found that the noise of
the running brook had ceased, but that in its place there was a
dull swashing noise, just below our feet as it seemed. The rats
were in great numbers, running about excitedly, without any
fear of us.

'See those rats?' said Dick. 'They're flooded out from the
lower hold. We've got as much sea down below us as would
float a Campeachy sloop.[6] Hark at it swishing around. Ugly
noise. It gives you a grue,[7] I think. But we've checked the leak
for the time, that's certain. That gives us time to look around
us, anyhow. We'll get the pumps rigged.'

But getting even the hand-pump rigged was no easy job to
men left practically without tools. Dick was a marvel of adap-
tive skill and patience, the craftsman's two qualities, but even
he found it hard to get anything done.

'Well,' he said at last, when the pump sent its first wavering
jet of water over the side, 'she works at last. I pity Doggy Sam
if I ever come across him in the future. He's given me the time
of my life getting this pump rigged. Heave gently, boys. She
may burst on you at any minute. Now we'll tackle the big one.'
All this time we were dragging slowly along on a course about
S.E., holding slantingly away from the land, now distant from
us about four miles. We were crawling, because we had no fit
sails to set. What we should do in foul weather, or if the wind,
freshening and drawing ahead, should force us back, I could
not imagine. I supposed that we must be driven inevitably into
James Town.

'Aloft there,' shouted Dick. 'Any sign of the frigate? Come
down for a glass and see if you can make her out inshore there.'

A careful examination of the coast-line through a spy-glass
showed the mouth of Myngs' Creek, but no sign of the frig-
ate.

'Good,' said Dick. 'There'll be no moon tonight. We shall
get away after all, boy. Does anyone here know about Myngs'
Creek?'

From *The Bird of Dawning*

When this was done the night was beginning to close in. There
was no sign of any bettering in the weather; it promised to be a
night of storm. Cruiser tried to think only of the good things in
their condition: that they were alive, in a seaworthy boat, with
some food and drink, that they had made some thirty miles of
easting,[1] and had lain-to without mishap. Yet he did not feel
happy. Where would they be if they had to lie-to often? And
what was going to happen about water? And how was he to
bring cheer to all these men when he had no cheer within him-
self? He was not cheerful: he was as wet and cold and cramped
as any of them, and had worked harder and had had more dis-
appointments.

He thought, 'This is so beastly a night that I must give them
something to cheer them; not brandy, they had a nip of brandy,
and once a day is all we can afford of that. We might perhaps
each have three raisins.'

Three raisins with the pips in them can be made to last a
long time. He contrived that all hands should compete to see
who should make a raisin last the longest; they got through an
entire hour thus; and were still sucking or chewing raisins when
Fairford suggested that as it was the second dogwatch they
should have a sing-song.

As it happened he had a good tenor voice and many songs
which the crew had not yet heard. He sang very touchingly the
ballad of 'The Fair Pretty Maid'; and then at the general request
his own favourite of 'We met, 'twas in a Crowd', in which all
hands could join in the refrain of:

> And thou wast the cause of
> This anguish,
> My mother.

The tune had been for many years popular, the sailors had long
known and loved it: what did the words and the meaning mat-
ter? The song made all of them forget their troubles in a delight

which all shared. They were warming up to the singing of it a
second time in unison when one of the two men forward, keep-
ing the anchor watch, gave a loud cry. Cruiser leaped up,
thinking that the drogue's painter had parted. He had only time
to sing out, 'What is it?' when he saw for himself what it was,
and all hands saw and said, 'My God.'

Ahead, to windward, they had been accustomed to seeing
the slow hills of the sea lumping up, collapsing at the top,
advancing and roaring and seething by. A big sea was running,
to themselves so near to the surface it seemed much bigger than
it would have seemed from a ship's deck.

Now out of the darkness of the storm ahead, such a sea was
lifting as they had never seen. The first sight of it was to them
as though a low range of hills was moving bodily forward; then
the effect changed in their minds to that of a line of crags. It
was dark, toothy at the top with fangs, like the body of night
below, and moving with a life of its own from somewhere. All
there had at once the dreadful feeling that it was alive. How
high it was they could not guess, but higher certainly than any
wave that any of them had ever seen. It was not like a wave; it
was like the Judgment Day advancing, wolfing up all the sea
into its power and licking out the sky with its tongue. Cruiser
could only gasp to himself, 'My God, that's got us.' But he had
two thoughts: one for his crew, one for his boat. He cried,
'Hold on, all,' and contrived to get to the steering oar, and hove
on it, to keep her bows on to it. It seemed to them that it crack-
led as it advanced as though it was breaking the air to shreds.
It sent out fore-boilings and up-bubblings that broke and wrin-
kled about them; all the sea seemed to know beforehand of it
and to laugh and to writhe. No one of them doubted that it was
the end. Perhaps it was the end of the world as well.

'Heave out that spare drogue,' Cruiser called.

Dreadful as it was they could not keep their eyes off it.
Marching swiftly as it was it seemed that it would never come.
Cruiser felt oddnesses, unevennesses and hardnesses rubbing
under the boat's keel and plucking at it: all the sea's surface
went stiff suddenly with eddies; his oar blade seemed to plunge
in steel springs. A power slued the boat to one side: he let it

take her: when it passed, he hove on his oar and forced her back. She shoved her snout towards it. He bent with all his strength to hold her there. She bowed down: then instantly, the mountain was on them: they were going up, up, up, the darkness which was a living thing growling and snarling at them and moving with a force and speed so awful that Cruiser caught a joy from the instant. He shouted to the boat, 'Good old girl, you'll do it yet.'

The boat went up, up, up into a hush: then rose so that Cruiser could just gasp to himself, 'She'll toss us end for end.' He saw the two forward hands crouched in the bows high up above himself, as it were on the top rungs of a ladder about to fall backwards. Then the air and the boat were both forgotten, being changed suddenly and utterly into a rush and blinding power of water, trembling below, furious above, and a weight on the bodies pressing down.

This passed. Cruiser knew that he was not dead, but that the boat very nearly was. She was full of water and trembling on the brink of collapse.

'Get to it. Bale her,' he cried. 'Take anything you can and bale her.'

They had three buckets, three dippers and a fetch-bag with which to bale. The men had these out and at work at once. No one in her thought that they could save her: she was full to the gunwale, they were over their waists in water, and the boat moved under them as though about to go bodily down. All the teak rubbing-piece of the gunwale was torn loose, and her three topmast straiks were spouting like freeing ports: this and her buoyancy chambers had saved her.

'A few more like that,' Cruiser said, 'and we shan't have a dry rag left on board.'

'No, sir.'

No one was badly hurt, yet all had something to show for it, a bruise or cut or scrape. However, there was the boat to bale; that kept them working hard for more than an hour, by then it was eight bells and pitch dark: all were very weary and depressed. They had no light save the baleful glimmering of the sea-bursts: all the rest of their world seemed now to be swallowed up in the storm; the loose straiks were working and grinding; the drogue cables kept surging and yanking; there was a weeping leak coming in at the stem, and no sign of mend in the weather.

From *The Box of Delights*

'Well, that's a jolly good thing,' Kay said, and being much cheered by the news, he went upstairs to get his catapult and some bullets. He kept these in a little secret hiding-place underneath his bed. After he had put them in his pocket he looked out of the window towards King Arthur's Camp, and there in the fields below the Camp he saw the gleam of water. He ran down at once to the others. 'I say,' he said, 'it's splendid. The floods are out. We'll go for a mud-lark. We'll get out all our ships and sail them on the floods.'

Both Peter and he had received ships from the Bishop's Christmas Tree. Kay had a ship called the *Hero* which went by methylated spirit, Peter had a ship which he called the pirate ship, the *Royal Fortune*, which went by clockwork, and Kay, in addition to these, had an old cutter which he called *Captain Kidd's Fancy*. 'We'll launch these and christen them properly,' they said.

'It's perfectly lovely,' Kay said, 'that the floods are out. We'll pretend that these ships are real ships, and we'll provision them with almonds, raisins and chocolates and we'll all take long sticks so as to poke them off if they get stuck anywhere. And we'll take sandwiches, cakes and hard-boiled eggs and we won't come back till teatime.'

'I've got some lovely little things that would do for the ships,' said Susan. 'In the stocking which they gave me from the tree there were those little tiny wooden barrels filled with Hundreds and Thousands.[1] They were just the sort of barrels to go in the ships.'

She fetched the little barrels and they divided them up among the three ships, and they put raisins and currants and bits of biscuits in each barrel.

'I vote,' Jemima said, 'that the other barrels shall be filled with ham, which we will pretend is salt pork.'

'They don't take salt pork any more,' Peter said. 'They take pemmican, which is beef chopped up with fat and raisins and chocolate and beer and almonds and ginger and stuff. It must be a sickening mess, but it's very nourishing. It's supposed to be what the ancient Britons had. They could take a piece as big as a currant and live on it for a week.'

As there weren't enough barrels to provision the ships, Kay got some matchboxes and egg-collector's pillboxes, which they filled with food. Jemima produced some drapers' patterns of woollen goods.[2] 'The ships ought to have these,' she said. 'They'd be exactly the size of thick blankets for the little sailors.'

'I tell you what we might do,' Susan said. 'When we get to the water we might take a little plank and make a landing-stage of it, and take some of those little flags that we've got, and we'll pretend that these ships are Christopher Columbus's ships going out to discover. We'll tie the ships to the landing-stage and then Jemima shall be the Queen of Spain and Kay had better be the King of Spain, and we will all be monks and nuns and people and sing to Columbus, and then we'll push him out into the Atlantic.'

'That would be a good idea,' Kay said. 'And then, presently, we could be Sir Francis Drake,[3] and some of us could be Indians and some of us could be Spaniards. And then one of us will be going to be burnt by the Inquisition, and, just at the end, we'll rush in and kill all the Spaniards, and take all their treasure and sail away to Plymouth. And we could fire red-hot shot, to tell the truth, if we didn't get the cannon too wet. You see, we can't fire gunpowder, but we could get the caps from toy pistols and load the guns with those, and then, if you put a match to the touch-hole they sometimes go off with quite a bang.'

'You'd better have some anchors,' Jemima said. 'All ships have anchors, otherwise they wouldn't be able to stop.'

'You've got to be jolly careful with anchors, with ships so little as these,' Kay said. 'Very often, if you try anchoring little ships like these, the anchor will pull them right underneath the water.'

They made ready the ships. Peter found a plank and rigged up some flags upon it for the landing-stage. Ellen brought sandwiches, cake, boiled eggs, fruit and ginger-beer. Kay had a bottle of methylated spirit for the engine. Then they went out to the woodshed to Joe, who gave each one of them a long wand or stick for poking off the ships if they got stuck. Then away they went in bright, sunny, clearing weather, with the noise of running water everywhere. When they came to the meadows there were pools in all the hollows and many of the molehills were bubbling up water like running springs. When they came to a suitable place on the mill stream they fixed the landing-stage and the children poked about among the banks with their sticks, while Kay and Peter got the methylated spirit furnace to make steam in the boiler.

Kay had the Box of Delights[4] in his inner pocket and sometimes poked his hand inside to be sure that it was there.

Presently all was ready. The King and Queen of Spain, with the monks and nuns and people, sent off Christopher Columbus on his voyage, and away the ships went downstream with the children following, shouting and cheering and poking them clear of the banks with their sticks.

When they had gone about half-a-mile down the stream, Susan, who was looking up at the sky, said, 'There's an aeroplane: no; two.' The others didn't see the aeroplanes at first but then saw them like two bright specks against a dark cloud. 'It's odd we didn't hear them,' Susan said. They hadn't heard them.

They went on with their ships, paddling in the water, getting very wet and enjoying themselves so much that they forgot about all other things, till Kay suddenly saw a shadow running across the field in front of him, and, looking up, saw two aeroplanes circling silently overhead. 'I say,' he said, 'look at the aeroplanes, absolutely silent.'

He didn't say so, but the thought flashed through his mind that the aeroplanes were there after them, but the other thought also flashed that no aeroplane would dare to land on ground so rotten with springs as that low-lying field. 'They'd stick in the mud if they tried that,' he thought.

'They're going to land,' Susan said. 'They're coming down by the copse there.'

'I'll bet they're after us,' Kay said to himself. 'Bring the ships in to the banks.'

They saw the two aeroplanes come down onto the big dry open field near the copse on the other side of the stream. There were some old willow trees where Kay was standing. He climbed up one of them. 'There are four men getting out of the aeroplanes,' he said. 'They've got pistols and ropes and they're coming this way. I think it would be wise to get out of the way.'

'Do you think they're after us?' Susan said.

'I shouldn't wonder,' Kay said.

'But it's all tommy-rot,' Jemima said. 'Who'd be coming after us with pistols and ropes? They're probably mole-catchers coming to set traps over these fields now that the moles are working in the soft earth.'

'That's a champion remark,' Peter said. 'When did you ever hear of mole-catchers coming in aeroplanes with pistols?'

'They're the men who kidnapped the Punch and Judy man,' Kay said. 'That's the man who was in the front of that attack: the tall one with the white splash of paint on his leggings. I'll bet they're after us.'

'What shall we do?' said Susan. 'Shall we run to the mill or the farm?'

'They'd beat us to either of those,' Kay said.

'Could we get down into the gully there?' Susan said.

'The gully's full of water in this flood,' Kay said.

'Well, what can we do?' Susan asked.

'Well, I've got here,' Kay said, 'a sort of magic dodge. If we all hold hands while I touch a button on it, we shall all shrink into little tiny creatures, and then we'll pop on board our ships and go down the stream.'

They held hands, and he twiddled the little button, and, instantly, each one of them felt lighter and brighter than ever before. The earth seemed to shoot up and to become enormous, and there they were, clambering on board their gigantic ships. They cast loose the strings which tied them to the bank and away they sailed downstream, round a bend and on. 'All very well,' Kay thought, 'as long as we can keep in mid-stream, but in a flood like this if we jam against some wreckage or fallen tree we shall be sucked right under.'

Just as the ships went round the bend, Kay saw the four men coming in sight close to the bank. It was plain that each man had two long pistols stuck in his belt and they were coiling lassoes ready for a throw. The ships went gaily down the mill stream into the mill-race. At the mill-race came a roaring and terrible torrent, down which the ships plunged so swiftly that they were through it before they had time to be afraid. In an instant they were in quiet water out of all the currents, gently rubbing the ships' sides against the roots of an elm tree, which grew in the high bank. Kay and Peter hooked the anchors onto some of the roots of the tree. They secured all three ships alongside each other.

From *Victorious Troy*

Suddenly, the foresail just behind them flogged backward at them with a thundering slat. Dick saw the leech of the topsail quake as the sea took the wind out of it. He knew that the sails would go; but that was nothing now. Something flashed in the sky above; something shook the ship, as though she were a rat, worried by a dog; something cracked and collapsed far aft, but this last he could not be sure of, it may have been the top of the wave blotting out all that part of the ship. He felt the ship become a stone under his feet and begin to sink like a stone. There was to be no ship now, only an enormous, raging, grey-black, red-black, glimmering, corpse-lit, awful water, bigger than the downland, that hissed and cackled and slid in little horrid laughs, and spat itself forward at the top and moved like a mountain crumpled forward by an earthquake. All hands were in the fore-rigging or fore-bitts, crouched against it, ducked to

it, gripping with all their might, catching turns round them-
selves. Some said, 'God,' some said, 'Hell, boys.' Dick caught
four of the biggest breaths he could. Then, very suddenly, and
with appalling weight and speed the mountain of water was
over them all, shutting out all knowledge and all sense.

Dick felt that the weight would break in his chest, and that
things would be a great deal pleasanter if he let it. He opened
his eyes; he was in deep blackness of water. No ship could live
under such a weight. He felt that the ship was sinking with
him; down, down, down, never to see the light again. No ship
could rise from such a blow. No deck, no hatch could stand
that weight of water. This was no doubt Death, a great pressure
on the chest and a smarting on the eyes, weight, pain, black-
ness. Then that changed to something quite pleasant and pretty,
of a cornfield bright in the sun and ripe to the harvest, with a
clear swathe already cut in the corn, so that he could walk
uphill, always uphill, in the light, to something well worth
going to. Then this suddenly changed to something purple
across the eyes, then red in the eyes, then golden, while the
roaring in his ears whirled and whirled into something that was
not roaring. Suddenly his head was out of the water; he gulped
a couple of breaths and then was splashed by a cold spray in
the face.

The deck was full of water; he was in water up to the chin; a
wallow of water went over him again. He felt the ship to be with-
out hope, settling like a stone beneath him. He had never felt that
hopelessness in her movements before: it was unlike anything
that he had ever felt. She had so plainly given up the ghost; she
was beaten to death. The water passed from his face; he got a
good gulp of breath, two or three together, though the ship was
full to the rails with enormous seas toppling about her.

'She must go down, now,' he thought. 'She can't get up from
this.'

But then there came a kind of stirring beneath his feet, a
kind of labouring effort in the fabric which gave him the lie.

Once, a year or two before, on a Saturday night when in
port in London, he had gone to see a boxing contest in
Whitechapel. He had seen the boxer of his choice put down,

rise, sorely hurt, having been punched over the heart, and then again go down from a second punch in the same place. He remembered the count going against his man – five . . . six . . . seven . . . while he lay on the floor, and then, at eight, he had slowly risen, contrived to get into a clinch and hung on, and covered up and got out of the way, perhaps not knowing in the least what he was doing, and so fought out the bout, avoiding the knock-out. Even so, now, in the stricken ship, a life stirred. Very, very slowly she lifted with the monstrous weight upon her. She rose spouting and streaming.

'God, she'll do it . . . the good old slut,' the man Suckley said.

'I do believe she will,' Dick answered.

'The mizzen topgallant's gone,' Suckley said. 'Where the hell's the man at the wheel?'

They did not see any man at the wheel: there was none. The mizzen topgallant mast had gone at the cap, taking both yards with it. Dick could not see them: they were gone.

A darkness of water and wind came down together upon the ship, so that she seemed to lie down and beg to be spared. Dick had seen beaten horses and cattle act in just that way. The poor thing seemed to be pleading with something that might perhaps be moved. While he crouched there, hanging on, still over the waist in water, he saw the mainsail, that lay stowed in storm gaskets along the mainyard, fling itself out of the gaskets into tatters. It was exactly as if the poor thing had put out hands in supplication, waving, piteous, ineffectual baby hands, stretched for mercy. There was not going to be much mercy.

The gust that had put them down suddenly deepened so as to pin them down, while a new cataract, full of gleams and fury, swept them off their feet and soused them. They rose from it as it passed, all out of breath, expecting another. It had seemed nothing of a sea to the big one, but it finished what that had begun.

As Dick got his chest and then his waist out of it he saw that foresail and foretopsail had gone from above him without his knowing it. All that was left of them were these pitiful, flopping and flogging hands, still flying from the yards, and two cloths, in rags, spinning round and round the foretopmast stay, with a piece of the chain tack that had tied itself in knots.

'God,' Suckley suddenly said, 'it's got the mainmast.'

What one of all the countless strains had been the last unbearable strain they could not tell. Suckley could not tell afterwards what it was that had made him speak. Some sudden movement, no doubt, that told of a backstay gone. As Dick looked, at Suckley's sudden cry, he saw that the mainmast was nodding its assent to its own death.

'Look out,' he cried. 'Stand from under, all hands.'

All who had been watching had already scattered 'from under' to the shelter of the fo'c's'le-head; Dick leaped after them, and there turned, to see what was to happen next.

The mast staggered a little: it waggled. With a snapping, stripping, splitting noise, unlike anything that any of them had ever heard, yet plain above all the roaring, it seemed to drop and shorten itself. Then it seemed to hesitate or waver (it only seemed) as the roll changed and began to gather. Then with a rising rush of noise, with its two steel lower yards, each weighing over three tons, its doublings, its topmast, its upper-topsail yard, its topgallant mast with the two topgallant yards, and all their weight and tracery of wire shroud, backstay and batten, gear, lifts, braces, halliards and tackle, its countless blocks, fairleads and cringles and flying tatters of sail, fell as a tree in a wood falls with a splittering, thunderous crash, which carried all before it, snapping the lee foretopsail yards and carrying the ruins with it to a shower of sparks, splinters and collapsing mess from the port main-bitts to the fore-rigging.

Probably not one man of the crew saw more than the first blow or shock as the foretopgallant yards were flung flying and the foretopsail yards snapped at the slings. When the final collapsing crash came they were all back behind the windlass, crying 'O God Almighty', while the flying fragments of wire, chain, iron and wood whizzed, clanged and settled.

That was only for a moment. A minute later they were out 'from under' to see what remained of the ship. The mainmast was gone. It had snapped off its topgallant mast at the cap and flung it overboard, where it now dragged.

From *Live and Kicking Ned*

On leaving Massa,[1] with great difficulty, I got the slaves the
afternoon privilege of a quarter-pint of water, and begged that
this mercy might be continued every afternoon, in the worst of
the heat. It was only granted when I said that the men would
surely die of heat-stroke without it, and then only on the con-
dition that I myself pumped the water and served it. Pegg
thought that I should be too proud to do this, but I did it. He
mocked me for doing it.

'Here's one of these Friends of Africa, going round bottle-
holding to a lot of stinking savages. This is the way to keep the
white man's Face, I must say.'

However, on the next day, the slave-guards, the trusty, tough
boatswains' mates, reported while we were at breakfast, that
the slaves had got the 'sullens', that is, they were in a conspir-
acy, not to eat or drink.

Pegg asked, 'Are you sure? It ain't their religion coming
out?'

'No,' the mates replied, 'it's the sullens. They took their chop
and slabber[2] last night; but this morning we found it all spat
out.'

I said, 'Very likely they're seasick.'

'Seasick,' Pegg said with much contempt. 'We know when a
slave's seasick, I hope. No. It's the sullens; their cursed black
froward natures.'

'It's certainly the sullens,' one of the mates said. 'I seen 'em
doing it; spitting it out; we tried 'em with some slabber just
now; just to see.'

'Right,' Pegg said, 'that'll be their chief. He sends round the
word and they all take it from him, and starve 'emselves dead.
Never neglect sullens. You get up the three who seem to be
chiefs; we'll start Jouncer on 'em at once. Christianity says you
ain't to kill yourself, nor let another kill hisself. I'll give 'em
good Christianity from Jouncer.'

He went to a locker and produced some grim iron appli-
ances.

'These are Jouncers,' Pegg explained. 'Put one of them in Juba's mouth, with the spikes and that, then you've only to turn this screw to heave his jaws apart, and then the chop has to go down and the slabber on the top. If they don't know their good, I do. We'll have up the two or three what get the respect. When they've had nicee chop, we'll see if we can't persuade 'em to dance a little to show they like it.' He was watching me, and saw my disgust. 'We don't go to college,' he said 'to learn how to doctor slaves. If they lose appetite with us, we make 'em eat, and if we find 'em sullen, we make 'em dance. A good cut or two with a cat'll make a big black Mantacaw[3] dance like Harriet Lane,[4] and a turn with the Jouncer'll make a rabbit eat like a wolf. Sense is what we go by here, let me tell you.'

I said that from what I had seen of the men in the hold, his methods wouldn't succeed. 'They'll die,' I said. 'Those men are a tough lot. You won't bend them; they'll die.'

'You'd like 'em to die, wouldn't you?' he said.

'Yes,' I answered, 'I'd rather they died than live to be slaves.'

'They're not going to die, nor are you going to let 'em die,' he said.

'I am under medical oath,' I said, 'not to let anyone die if I can prevent it. I warn you, that those men'll die if you try your methods with them. They've got something in them that's stronger than you.'

'We'll see that,' Pegg said. 'I rather think we'll win. Iron is stronger than most things. Iron and pain'll make a lot of difference to even the proudest Juba. You might remember that, too, for your own good.'

'If that be a threat,' I said, 'let me warn you, for your own good, not to threaten me. I have some very good friends who may make it exceedingly uncomfortable for you.'

He knew that I referred to the Governors to whom I had letters, and to those unknown, but doubtless powerful friends who had caused me to be received at a moment's notice.

'I can't stay jawing here,' he said. 'I've got my duty to do.'

I, too, had my duty to do. I had to examine every member of the crew for marks of fever or disease. While I was doing this (and there were four in need of treatment), Pegg applied his methods to three whom the mates said were the chiefs. They were not the chiefs: they were the three most easily brought on deck. After this was over (and I saw nothing of it, or I would have protested), it fell to me to make my first examination of the slaves in the shelves. One of the boatswain's mates attended me with a lantern. I may say that after my little tussle with Pegg, I had some fear that he might chain me with the slaves, for sale later. However, I judged that he needed me as a surgeon at present; my turn would come later.

I went with my lantern-bearer along the 'tween-decks to the little man-hole which led to the tiers. The 'tween-decks was as hot as any closed space under a wooden roof in the tropics can be. But when I came to the man-hole to the hold the heat of that lower place was something that one could lean against. It had been shut in all night, save for the slender pipe of one windsail and two little barred holes.

The heat was but a small part of the terror of that darkness.

I had often been told in conversation round the cabin table that all ships stank below the water, even in the colder climates. They said that water would seep in, by one way or another, and accumulate below and swiftly rot into something that stank like skunks, the 'bilge-water' which so many have mentioned. This smell hung about the lower parts of the ship at all times, and mixed with other smells, of dry-rot, and wet-rot, ship's canvas, new tar, not very fresh provisions, cargo, paint, rope and the presence of rats and mice. Now to all these rank and rancid stinks was added the reek of seventy prisoners, chained prone upon the shelves. The boatswain's mate noticed that the smell affected me.

'It come up very ripe this morning, sir,' he said. 'You'll get used to it. Use is second nature. It gets thicker than this in a busy season. This is nothing. I've known men faint, going round with the chow,[5] but that was in the lower tiers, when we were running full.'

'How can men live in air worse than this?' I asked.

'Why,' he said, 'they do live, the most of 'em. The aim of

most folk is to live; even though it mayn't be fun, they'd rather live than not live. But these fellas aren't like Christians. They get something like this from their own choice in the villages where they're at home. If you'll let me go first, sir, I'll hand you down; this ladder is very steep. Hold the lantern, will you, Bill?'

Bill held the lantern, and I came down into the space of the hold, in a heat and stench such as made even Newgate[6] seem a Paradise.

'It's these lads we believed were the ring-leaders,' the man explained. 'They seem took very bad.'

I could not at once make out where I was, for the hold was very dark. Bill's lantern cast a yellowish glow about the place. I could see gleams upon chains and upon stanchions. I did not see the slaves at the first look, only stood, trying not to be sick in the fog of stench in which I was. Bill's lantern burned dimly unless he held it up. The place was full of noises, mostly uncanny, as a ship's hold always must be. The water went lamenting past as we slipped along; down below me the water gurgled and splashed in the bilges; the planks creaked and whined; little slow, stripping, progressing cracklings ran along the beams as she rolled now one way, then back; there was a kind of drumming noise of wind coming down the windsail flapping the edge which secured it. Above all these noises, I was aware of the presence of the misery of many men, who were lying close to me, breathing heavily, moaning now and then, in rage or stupor, and shifting about, with many clinkings of chain. Gradually I came to see in the darkness a sort of long, low shelf or slab on which dark figures were packed, heads towards me. A long line of heads was on each side of my ankles. The men had been packed there as close as they would lie.

'We put 'em low down,' Bill explained, 'for if we have a good buy down Coast, we'll have room for two or three tiers above these. And we stick them heads nearest so as they can't kick, and we can drag 'em out easier if they up and die on us.'

'Let me see the men who are sick,' I said. 'Hold the lantern so that I can see.'

He held the lantern in turn over three faces; all three were close to the hatchway. Being the easiest to come at, they had been chosen for Jouncer. The three men had all been cut with the cat-of-nine-tails, and all three mouths were bloody from the Jouncer. The three presented the same symptoms, which were new to me. They were unconscious; they did not respond to voice or touch; their eyes were inverted and their pulses very slight, so slight that I knew that they were in an extreme of weakness. I did not understand it. I asked the men if they had been flogged with great severity. 'No,' they said, 'they only give 'em a dozen or so, more in fun than anything, just to make 'em dance. We always touch 'em up to make 'em dance. It was nothing.' I said that they were scored and cut with the lashes and that didn't look like fun. To this they repeated, 'That a sea-man would have thought nothing of it; just nothing at all.'

However, these men were not seamen, and did think of it. For all that I could do, all three died before noon, and were flung overboard.

'That's one of their tricks,' Pegg said. 'That's their sullen spite.'

I said, 'I told you that these men would die if you tried your methods on them. They have died. These men have something in them that will beat you every time you pit yourself against them.'

To my astonishment, Tulp spoke up. He was a little drunk, having somehow found some rum. Whenever he was a little drunk, strange knowledge shone from Tulp; it shone now. 'The Doctor's right, sir,' he said. 'These leeward warrior tribes can all will themselves dead. They're taught the trick young, in case they're caught in battle. Old Captain Quoin told me he'd seen a hundred will themselves dead at once, "all to be dead by day-break", and they were. They just settle down and die. You'll have all these Matas dead the same way if you try.'

'I'll give 'em something to die for,' Pegg said savagely.

Notes

This section provides full details of sources, including notes on first publication, and annotates phrases or terms for which I feel some explanation may be useful.

Unless otherwise stated, the copy-text for each poem or piece of prose is its first publication in book form. Significant differences between versions of a poem or piece of prose are noted. I have, however, stopped short of providing full variorum information.

Given the number of seafaring terms that are used throughout the book, I have provided a 'Glossary of Nautical Terms' (see p. 350) for some of the more common words (including a few that are not strictly nautical but reappear throughout the texts). Explanations of less repetitious phrases are noted below. I would, naturally, be grateful to learn of any omissions or errors.

Masefield included glossaries to a number of his books and it seems appropriate to use his definitions whenever possible, both here and in the 'Glossary of Nautical Terms'. References to *Salt-Water Ballads* (London: Grant Richards, 1902), *Dauber* (London: William Heinemann, 1913), *The Conway* (London: William Heinemann, 1933) and *The Bird of the Dawning* (London: William Heinemann, 1933) therefore relate to those volumes. Other definitions are gleaned from a variety of sources, including: R. H. Dana, *The Seaman's Friend* (Boston, MA: Charles C. Little and James Brown, fourth edition, 1845); W. H. Smyth, *The Sailor's Word-Book* (London: Blackie and Son, 1867); W. Clark Russell, *Sailors' Language* (London: Sampson Low, Marston, Seale and Rivington, 1883); the *Oxford English Dictionary* and Eric Partridge, *A Dictionary of Slang and Unconventional English* (London: Routledge, eighth edition, 1984).

There is a perceptive article by Anton A. Raven of Dartmouth College entitled 'A Study in Masefield's Vocabulary' (*Modern Language Notes*, March 1922, pp. 148–53). The article notes that 'the most casual reader of the poems of John Masefield must notice the number of uncommon words that the poet uses.' Raven concludes that, although meaning may be elusive, Masefield's diction has 'connotative values'. I have attempted to explain unfamiliar terms, but leave words with 'connotative values' to the reader.

POETRY

Nicias Moriturus

First published in *The Outlook*, 3 June 1899. Present as the twelfth poem in *Salt-Water Ballads* (London: Grant Richards, 1902). There are many differences between the two versions. The third stanza, for example, was originally printed:

> I shall hear 'em hilly-hollyin' the weather crojick brace;
> Hear the sheet-blocks jiggin' hornpipes all achafe;
> Hear the tops'l halyard chanty – feel the salt spray sting my face –
> I'll be seaward though my body's anchored safe.

The final line of the last stanza appeared as 'For it's time to go aloft when Jack is dead'. In November 1899 the poem was included in *Naval Songs and Ballads*, an anthology selected by Frank Rinder (London: Walter Scott, 1899), and that volume constituted the first appearance in book form of any Masefield work. Masefield re-titled the poem 'The Turn of the Tide' for the second edition of *Salt-Water Ballads* (London: Elkin Mathews, 1913).

1. *Nicias Moriturus*: The Latin title includes the ancient Greek name, Nicias. It can be translated as 'Nicias when about to die'.
2. *hilly-hollying*: Stan Hugill in *Shanties from the Seven Seas* (London: Routledge & Kegan Paul, revised edition, 1979) notes that the earliest stage in the development of a hauling chanty was probably the line 'Hey, holly, hilly, oh! Hey, ro, ho, yu!' The verb 'hilly-hollying' therefore presumably refers to the singing of chanties. Of additional note is 'The East Indiaman' chanty. This includes a chorus of which 'Hilly, holly, hilly, holly ho' is one of its earliest forms.
3. *catspaw*: Ruffled surface of the water caused by a light air, generally before a steadier breeze.

Trade Winds

First published in *The Outlook*, 5 October 1901. Present as the twenty-fourth poem in *Salt-Water Ballads* (London: Grant Richards, 1902). There are no substantive differences.

1. *soughing*: Moaning, whistling or rushing sound. In a letter to his sister, Norah, dated 19 November 1901, Masefield notes that he wished he had burned 'Trade Winds'. He continues: 'It is a limp attempt and the last stanza is hateful to me. The sough in soughing rhymes with the feminine of boar. Is pronounced the same . . . It derives from a Norse word signifying to murmur.'

Cardigan Bay

First published in *The Outlook*, 23 November 1901. Present as the twenty-seventh poem in *Salt-Water Ballads* (London: Grant Richards, 1902). There are a number of minor variants, including the lengthening or contraction of words. In *The Outlook* the poem is provided with a date of October 1894, which is not, presumably, the date of composition. At this time Masefield was returning to England as a 'Distressed British Sailor' and by the end of the month he had arrived back home in Ledbury.

1. *billows*: Waves caused by the wind (noted by Smyth as 'a term more in use among poets than seamen').
2. *seventy-four*: A two-decked ship carrying seventy-four guns, common between the mid eighteenth and early nineteenth centuries.

Bill

First published in *The Outlook*, 21 December 1901. Present as the fifth poem in *Salt-Water Ballads* (London: Grant Richards, 1902). The earlier version has greater use of phonetic spellings and contracted words ('Jest' for 'Just', ''im' for 'him' and ''is' for 'his', for example). The third line of the second stanza reads: ' "An', blame ye, get a gait on ye. Ye're slower'n a blushin' snail." ' This example demonstrates that Masefield's diction for *The Outlook* was less coarse than that submitted to Grant Richards.

1. *clout*: Piece (of cloth).
2. *gait on*: Move on.

[Bidding Goodbye]

Hitherto unpublished and adapted from a working draft (Bodleian Library, Dep.c.313). The title is editorial and insertion at this point in the chronological sequence is conjectural.

Sea-Fever

First published in *The Speaker*, 15 February 1902. Present as the twenty-fifth poem in *Salt-Water Ballads* (London: Grant Richards, 1902). The earlier text is as follows:

> I must down to the seas again, to the lonely sea and the sky,
> And all I ask is a tall ship and a star to steer her by;
> And the wind's song, and the wheel's kick and the white sail's shaking,
> And a grey mist on the sea's face and a grey dawn breaking.
>
> I must down to the seas again, for the call of the running tide
> Is a wild call and a clear call that may not be denied.
> And all I ask is a high wind and white clouds flying
> And green seas and blown spume, and the sea-gulls crying.
>
> I must down to the seas again, to the vagrant gipsy life,
> To the spindrift and the whale's spout and wind like a whetted knife,
> And all I ask is a merry yarn from a laughing fellow rover,
> And quiet sleep and a sweet dream when the long trick's over.

1. *must down*: 'must go down' first appears in *Ballads and Poems* (London: Elkin Mathews, 1910). The word 'go' is also present in *Selected Poems* (London: William Heinemann, 1922) but omitted from *Collected Poems* (London: William Heinemann, 1923). It reappears in *Poems* (London: William Heinemann, 1946). When questioned, in 1927, about the first line of the poem, Masefield replied: 'I notice that in the early edition, 1902, I print the line "I must down". That was as I wrote the line in the first instance. Somehow the word "go" seems to have crept in. When I am reciting the poem I usually insert the word "go". When the poem is spoken I feel the need of the word but in print "go" is unnecessary and looks ill' (see Linda Hart, 'A First Line Mystery', *Journal of the John Masefield Society*, Vol. 2 (Ledbury: John Masefield Society, 1993), pp. 11–14). The working manuscript of the poem is in the Berg Collection, New York Public Library. It reveals drafts both with and without the additional word. Two extant audio recordings of Masefield reading the poem, from 1941 and 1960, include 'go'.

Burial Party

First published, as 'Burying at Sea', in *The Speaker*, 12 April 1902. Present as the fourth poem in *Salt-Water Ballads* (London: Grant Richards, 1902). There are a number of minor variants. The first version includes a prefatory quotation:

> ''N' don't you go buryin' no corpses arter dark, acos, if you do, the sperrit don't get quit o' the corp till the dawn. That's acos sperrits are mortal afraid o' the dark 'n' sticks in the dead 'uns' throats till it grows light agen.'

1. *corp*: Corpse.
2. *neap*: The highest point of a 'neap tide', being the tide with the least difference between high and low water, just after the first and third quarters of the moon.
3. *rummy rig of a guffy's yarn*: Strange construction of an idiot's tale.
4. *juice of a rummy note*: Essence of a singular or odd note.
5. *bloody*: Originally 'blushin''.
6. *Will o' the Wisp*: Phosphorescent light.

Sorrow o' Mydath

First published in *The Speaker*, 31 May 1902. Present as the thirty-eighth poem in *Salt-Water Ballads* (London: Grant Richards, 1902). There are a number of minor variants.

1. *Mydath*: With no entry for Mydath in George C. Chisholm's *Longmans' Gazetteer of the World* (London: Longmans, Green and Co., 1895) or J. G. Bartholomew's *The Survey Gazetteer of the British Isles* (London: George Newnes, 1904), the name may be a rendering of 'My Death'. In a letter to John D. Gordon, *c*. March 1953, Masefield helpfully wrote 'Mydath was the name of a place in an early poem: it was supposed to be near the sea somewhere: but is now mercifully just about extinct' (Berg Collection, New York Public Library).
2. *Weary the heart and the mind*: Originally 'Weary the mind and the spirit'.
3. *spindrift*: Sea spray blown along the surface of the water.

Mother Carey

First published in *The Speaker*, 7 June 1902. Present as the nineteenth poem in *Salt-Water Ballads* (London: Grant Richards, 1902). There are a number of minor variants.

1. *rips*: Rascals.
2. *norred*: Northward.
3. *forred*: Forehead.
4. *kin*: Can.
5. *rip*: In contrast to the earlier use of 'rips' (see note 1 above), this may refer to rough water caused by the meeting of currents.
6. *gristly*: Presumably Masefield's rendering of 'grizzly'.
7. *lairy*: As Masefield noted in *The Conway*, the word can mean 'slow, slack; also cunning'. In this context, where the line originally read: 'You're smart, you thinks, 'n' you're lairy', he evidently means the latter.

Fever-Chills

First published, as 'Coast-Fever', in *The Speaker*, 12 July 1902. Present as the seventh poem in *Salt-Water Ballads* (London: Grant Richards, 1902). There are a number of minor variants.

1. *tottered*: Originally 'stumbled'.
2. *clout*: Piece (of cloth).
3. *lick*: Touch.
4. *quinine*: A bitter drug used to reduce fever.
5. *if they gets fever-chills*: The word 'they' is italicized in *The Speaker*.
6. *Chief*: First mate, in this context.
7. *Cape Horn fever lays*: A malingerer's tricks or lies. The version in *The Speaker* reads 'Cape Horn fever tricks'.
8. *rags o' duds*: Delicate weakling's clothes or ragged clothes.
9. *bloody coal*: Originally 'blushin' coal'.

'Port o' Many Ships'

First published in *The Speaker*, 16 August 1902. Present as the sixteenth poem in *Salt-Water Ballads* (London: Grant Richards, 1902). There are no substantive differences.

1. *wrack*: Seaweed which, here, is growing on sunken ships.

D'Avalos' Prayer

First published, as 'A Last Prayer', in *A Broad Sheet*, October 1902. Present as the thirty-fifth poem in *Salt-Water Ballads* (London: Grant Richards, 1902). There are a number of minor variants.

1. *D'Avalos*: Presumably from the family who were prominent in Renaissance Italy, including Fernando d'Avalos (1489–1525) and Alfonso d'Avalos (1502–46). Both were military, rather than naval, commanders.
2. *to drown and roll me under*: Originally published as 'to whelm and roll me under'.
3. *tunny-fishes*: Tuna fish.
4. *thresh*: Originally 'thrash'.

One of the Bo'sun's Yarns

First published as the eighth poem in *Salt-Water Ballads* (London: Grant Richards, 1902).

1. *a-bluin'*: Squandering.
2. *landed me 'n' bleached me fair*: Brought or positioned me and made me pale with fear.
3. *Hook*: The Hook of Holland on the North Sea coast.
4. *one o' the brand o' Cain*: A murderer; Cain, the first son of Adam, murdered his brother, Abel, in Genesis 4: 1–16.
5. *chin*: Talk.
6. *dodderin'*: Foolish meddling.
7. *heeled*: Lurched to one side.
8. *D.B.S.'d*: Masefield notes 'D.B.S.' as a 'Distressed British Sailor. A term applied to those who are invalided home from foreign ports' (*Salt-Water Ballads*).

Sea-Change

First published as the tenth poem in *Salt-Water Ballads* (London: Grant Richards, 1902). Subsequently published, as 'Jimmy the Dane', in *The Speaker*, 13 December 1902.

1. *Sea-Change*: Presumably an allusion to Ariel's song in *The Tempest* (Act I, scene ii).
2. *Goneys an' gullies*: 'Albatrosses' and 'Sea-gulls, Cape Horn pigeons, etc.' (*Salt-Water Ballads*).
3. *mollies*: 'Molly-hawks, or Fulmar petrels. Wide-winged dusky

sea-fowls, common in high latitudes, oily to taste, gluttonous. Great fishers and garbage eaters' (*Salt-Water Ballads*).

4. *snorter*: Violent gale.
5. *copper-bound*: The hull of a ship was often sheathed in copper to preserve the timbers. An albatross that is 'copper-bound' may be a metaphor for a bird about to travel large distances. Alternatively, a copper was a ship's boiler used for cooking. The albatross may be travelling towards the ship's kitchen for scraps.

One of Wally's Yarns

First published as the thirteenth poem in *Salt-Water Ballads* (London: Grant Richards, 1902).

1. *Wally*: An instructor on board HMS *Conway*, Wallace Blair (1840–97) was described by Masefield in *So Long to Learn* (London: William Heinemann, 1952) as 'a most gifted story-teller, a yarn-spinner of the old dogwatch kind, famous for it throughout the ship'.
2. *swiggin'*: Pulling on a rope which is attached at one end to a fixed object and at the other end to a movable one.
3. *live*: Survive.
4. *Barney's Bull*: A favourite expression of Masefield's. In the Glossary to *Salt-Water Ballads*, Masefield unhelpfully includes 'Bull of Barney' as 'a beast mentioned in an unquotable sea-proverb'. Partridge suggests the expression 'like Barney's bull' is to be extremely fatigued or physically distressed. He also notes, and quotes Masefield, that blowing like Barney's Bull is to blow a full gale.

Cape Horn Gospel – I

First published as the seventeenth poem in *Salt-Water Ballads* (London: Grant Richards, 1902).

1. *shored*: In naval terminology 'to shore' is usually to hold an object in position (with stout timbers). Evidently usage here is different.
2. *sogered*: Skulked. Masefield describes a 'soger' as 'a laggard, malingerer, or hang-back. To loaf or skulk or work Tom Cox's Traverse' (*Salt-Water Ballads*).
3. *Jan*: Masefield's nickname, later reserved only for family and close friends.

Cape Horn Gospel – II

First published as the eighteenth poem in *Salt-Water Ballads* (London: Grant Richards, 1902).

1. *Dago . . . chin*: 'Dago' is a pejorative term for a foreigner, especially a Spaniard, Portuguese or Italian; 'chin' is literally 'talk', but evidently here used to indicate rude or cheeky comments.
2. *corp*: Corpse.
3. *chips in clouts*: 'Chips' presumably, here, indicate pieces of his body; 'clouts' are pieces (of cloth).
4. *Line*: The Equator.
5. *calenture*: Delirium of sailors, associated with the tropics.
6. *Plate*: River Plate, the widest estuary in the world, formed by the Uruguay and Parana rivers on the south-east coast of South America.
7. *snugged her down . . . cuss*: To 'snug down' is to make all ship-shape; 'cuss' means 'creature', although, in this context, it refers to the ship.
8. *Started a plate*: To have a plate, in the ship's construction, spring or break away from its proper position.
9. *reskied*: Rescued.
10. *looted duds*: Stolen clothes.
11. *D.B.S.*: 'Distressed British Sailor. A term applied to those who are invalided home from foreign ports' (*Salt-Water Ballads*).
12. *Prince's Stage*: Princes Landing Stage in Liverpool Docks, constructed around 1850.

A Ballad of John Silver

First published as the thirty-first poem in *Salt-Water Ballads* (London: Grant Richards, 1902).

1. *John Silver*: R. L. Stevenson's pirate, Long John Silver, appeared in *Treasure Island* (serialized 1881–2 and first published in 1883).
2. *rakish . . . lissome*: 'Rakish' means 'fast-looking and smart'; while 'lissome', from a combination of 'lithe' and 'some', means 'full of supple agility'.
3. *quidding*: Tobacco-chewing (from 'quid', a lump of chewing tobacco).

Lyrics from *The Buccaneer*

The first three lyrics were first published as the thirty-second, thirty-third and thirty-fourth poems in *Salt-Water Ballads* (London: Grant Richards, 1902). The fourth lyric is included within manuscript fragments of *The Buccaneer* (Berg Collection, New York Public Library). When Masefield sent these fragments to Elizabeth Robins, on 1 April 1910, he noted: '*The Buccaneer* (play) was written to amuse Yeats in 1901, WBY being then melancholy' (Berg Collection, New York Public Library).

1. *gold doubloon*: A Spanish gold coin.
2. *Cain*: See note 4 to 'One of the Bo'sun's Yarns' above.
3. *Spanish Main*: Historically, the Spanish-occupied north-eastern coast of South America between the Orinoco River and Panama, and the adjoining parts of the Caribbean Sea.
4. *skuas*: Large predatory sea birds.
5. *rollers*: Long, swelling waves.
6. *snickersnees*: Knives or daggers.

Spunyarn

First published as the forty-first poem in *Salt-Water Ballads* (London: Grant Richards, 1902).

1. *Spunyarn*: See 'Glossary of Nautical Terms'.
2. *slather*: Move in a sliding manner, or to coat the rope with tar.
3. *moil*: Drudgery.
4. *brace*: Stiffen or reinforce.

Personal

First published as the forty-third poem in *Salt-Water Ballads* (London: Grant Richards, 1902).

[An Inscription for *Salt-Water Ballads*]

Hitherto unpublished and adapted from a working draft (Bodleian Library, Dep.c.313). The poem presumably dates from the publication of *Salt-Water Ballads* in November 1902. The title is editorial. In 1927, writing to the Society of Authors, Masefield referred to 'a poem which I wrote in about a dozen copies of *Salt-Water Ballads* for various friends' (British Library, Add. Ms. 56584, ff. 123–4). Three examples have been traced: Jack B. Yeats's copy (Houghton Library, University of Harvard), a copy with the bookplate of Madeline Jones (Berg Collection, New York Public Library) and a copy with the book-plate of Kevin O'Duffy inscribed 'to the writer's unknown (and sole) admirer' (George Houle Rare Books).

1. *Skipper*: Here used as a commendatory term for the reader, rather than 'Captain'.
2. *avick*: Colloquial term from the Irish *a mhic* meaning 'my son, my boy'.
3. *footle*: Foolishness.
4. *tinker's D*: Not caring at all (from 'tinker's damn').
5. *Compass Card*: A compass in the form of a card, showing the thirty-two principal bearings, which rotates to point to magnetic north, or, more simply, part of a compass on which bearings are marked.

Cargoes

First published in *A Broad Sheet*, May 1903. Present as the third poem in *Ballads* (London: Elkin Mathews, 1903). There are a number of minor variants.

1. *Quinquireme of Nineveh from distant Ophir*: A quinquireme is a galley ship from the Hellenistic era with five banks of oarsmen on each side; Nineveh was the capital of the biblical Assyrian Empire, on the Tigris River; while Ophir was a biblical port or region, famous for its wealth.
2. *Palestine*: Region on the eastern coast of the Mediterranean, historically an area including the modern-day Israel, the Israeli-occupied Palestinian territories and parts of Lebanon and Syria. In *A Pamphlet Against Anthologies* (London: Jonathan Cape, 1928), Laura Riding and Robert Graves noted that 'the route from the land of Ophir to Palestine before the days of the Suez Canal was one no quinquereme [*sic*] could take unless it first casually circumnavigated Africa.' Challenged in 1930, Masefield responded: 'it has often puzzled myself that a quinquireme owned in Nineveh should be rowing to Palestine, but perhaps before the Flood fully subsided such things were possible' (Letter to Stuart Fawkes, 23 January 1930, Archives of the John Mase-field Society, CBS Archives 6/213).
3. *ivory, / And apes and peacocks*: See 1 Kings 10: 22.
4. *Sandalwood, cedarwood*: Sandalwood is the scented wood from

sandalwood trees of the genus *Santalum*, found in India and
South-east Asia; cedarwood is the hard-wearing and scented
wood from cedar trees.
5. *Isthmus*: The narrow strip of land in Panama, connecting North and
South America.
6. *gold moidores*: Portuguese gold coins. The line originally
appeared as 'Topazes, and silverlings, and bright moydores.'
7. *Butting*: Pushing.
8. *Tyne coal*: Coal mined near the River Tyne in north-east England.
9. *pig-lead*: Blocks of crude lead, direct from a smelting furnace.

Blind Man's Vigil

First published in *A Broad Sheet*, May 1903. Present as the fifteenth
poem in *Ballads* (London: Elkin Mathews, 1903). There are a number
of minor variants.

1. *lilt ... Main*: A 'lilt' is a light and springing musical rhythm;
'Main' is the Spanish Main, historically the Spanish-occupied
north-eastern coast of South America between the Orinoco River
and Panama, and the adjoining parts of the Caribbean Sea.
2. *Reach*: A stretch of river between two bends.
3. *dance in hemp*: Hanging.

Spanish Waters

Stanzas five and six only first published, untitled, in *A Broad Sheet*,
May 1903. A different version was published, as 'Blind Man's Vigil',
in *The Green Sheaf*, No. 7 (1903). Present as the second poem in
Ballads (London: Elkin Mathews, 1903) and, subsequently, heavily
revised for the second edition of *Ballads* (London: Elkin Mathews,
1910). Different versions are discussed in my article '"Spanish
Waters": A Process of Revision', *The Journal of the John Masefield
Society*, Vol. 6 (Ledbury: John Masefield Society, 1997), pp. 4–9.

1. *Spanish waters, Spanish waters, you are ringing in my ears*: The
version published in *The Green Sheaf* commences with an
entirely different first stanza, as follows:

> I'm a tattered starving beggar fiddling down the dirty streets,
> Scraping tunes from squeaking catgut for a plate of broken meats,
> Scraping tunes and singing ballads: old and blind and castaway,
> And I know where all the gold is that we won with L'Ollonay.

2. *Muertos*: Spanish for '(the) dead'. Possibly Caja de Muertos, an uninhabited island off the coast of Puerto Rico.

3. *spit*: Narrow strip of land projecting into the sea.

4. *colibris*: A variety of humming-bird. The line in *The Green Sheaf* reads: 'The home of gaudy humming birds and golden colibris.'

5. *Key*: A reef or low-lying island.

6. *carracks ... Lima Town*: Carracks are galleons, often fitted for warfare, formerly used by the Portuguese in trading with the East Indies; Lima is the capital city of Peru.

7. *Gold doubloons and double moidores, louis d'ors and portagues*: All types of gold coin, 'doubloons' and 'louis d'ors' from Spain and France respectively, 'double moidores' and 'portagues' from Portugal.

8. *Clumsy yellow-metal earrings*: Originally 'Heavy yellow-metal earrings' in *A Broad Sheet*.

9. *ouches ... Rio ... Guayaquil*: 'Ouches' are clasps or buckles for fastening pieces of clothing; Rio is Rio de Janeiro, the city in Brazil; and Guayaquil is a seaport city in Ecuador.

10. *Silver cups and polished flagons*: Originally 'Silver sacramental vessels' in *A Broad Sheet*.

11. *mattocks*: A 'mattock' is a similar tool to a pickaxe.

12. *Execution Dock*: Located on the Thames, in Wapping, and in use over four centuries for hanging pirates, smugglers and mutineers. The line in *The Green Sheaf* reads: 'In the clanking chains at Wapping Stairs where thieves and such are hung'.

13. *L'Ollonais*: François l'Olonnais (*c.*1635–*c.*1668), the French pirate known as the 'Bane of the Spaniards'.

Roadways

First published in *The Speaker*, 2 May 1903. Present as the sixteenth poem in *Ballads* (London: Elkin Mathews, 1903). There are a number of minor variants.

1. *Wales*: The original couplet reads: 'One road runs to London, / One road leads to Wales'. Writing in *So Long to Learn* (London: William Heinemann, 1952), Masefield describes 'terrible Wales' as a place 'where anything might happen to you. (Men might sing very sweetly to you, or even speak poetry to you; one had to mind out in Wales.)'

2. *God put me here to find*: Originally 'God sent me here to find'.

Captain Stratton's Fancy

First published in *The Speaker*, 9 May 1903. Present as the fourth poem in *Ballads* (London: Elkin Mathews, 1903). There are a number of minor variants, including the reversal of stanzas four and five.

1. *dancing*: Originally 'courting'.
2. *Henry Morgan*: Welsh pirate captain (*c*.1635–88), and later Lieutenant Governor of Jamaica.
3. *tay*: Tea.
4. *Jamaica*: Jamaican rum. The British changed the naval issue of brandy to rum upon capture of Jamaica in 1655.
5. *bung*: A stopper for a cask.
6. *puncheon*: Large cask, holding 72–120 gallons (327–545 litres).
7. *troll*: Roll or trundle.
8. *mort*: A large number (of).

St Mary's Bells

First published as the sixth poem in *Ballads* (London: Elkin Mathews, 1903).

1. *Holy Mary / By San Marie Lagoon*: Possibly an intentionally vague geographical location, although it could be the area around Cadiz in Spain. Cadiz is located at the extremity of a sandy point, with the ocean on one side and a lagoon on the other. At the far side of the bay the town of El Puerto de Santa Maria is situated.
2. *sonsie*: Robust and comely with a suggestion of 'lucky' (the word deriving from the Gaelic *sonas*, 'good fortune').

The Emigrant

First published as the eighth poem in *Ballads* (London: Elkin Mathews, 1903).

1. *lilts*: Tunes or songs marked by a light springing rhythm.

Christmas, 1903

First published as 'Coming Into Salcombe – A Christmas Chanty' in *A Broad Sheet*, December 1903. Present as the forty-second poem in *Ballads and Poems* (London: Elkin Mathews, 1910). There are a number of minor variants.

1.   *Start Point light*: The lighthouse at Start Point, in Devon, built in 1836.
2.   *rime*: Frost.
3.   *Prime*: The second canonical hour of prayer for the first hour of the day at 6 a.m.
4.   *bar of Salcombe*: A 'bar' is a shoal or sandbank at the mouth of an estuary or harbour; Salcombe is a port on the south Devon coast.
5.   *The belfry rocks ... homeless long*: Within *A Broad Sheet* the poem concludes:

> The belfry rocks as the bells ring; the chimes go merry like a song.
> So a long last pull,
> And a strong last pull –
> Good-bye, old hooker, and so-long.

An Old Song Re-sung

First published in the *Manchester Guardian*, 28 May 1904. Present as the fifth poem in the second edition of *Ballads* (London: Elkin Mathews, 1910). There are a number of minor variants.

1.   *With emeralds and rubies and sapphires in her hold*: The original cargo was 'emeralds, and laces and satins'.
2.   *Skins*: Containers for liquid, made from animal skin.

A Song

First published, as 'A Song', in the *Manchester Guardian*, 26 October 1904. Present as an untitled prefatory poem in *A Mainsail Haul* (London: Elkin Mathews, 1905). There are a number of minor variants.

1.   *chalking up the score*: Recording the charge.
2.   *brooked*: Tolerated.
3.   *the music was life and life's romance*: The original line concludes: 'the dancing was youth and youth's romance.'

The Gara Brook

First published, and sole appearance, in the *Manchester Guardian*, 18 November 1904.

1.   *Gara Brook*: A river forming a boundary between Slapton and Strete in south Devon. Masefield and Jack B. Yeats constructed

toy boats and sailed them on the Gara in April 1903. Their
exploits were recorded by Jack B. Yeats in *A Little Fleet* (London: Elkin Mathews, 1909).

2. *acres in stook ... stubbles*: 'Acres in stook' indicates fields with
groups of sheaves of corn stood on end; 'stubbles' – usually in
the singular, 'stubble' – are short cut stalks left in the ground
after the harvest.

3. *kine*: Cows.

A Whaler's Song

First published, and sole appearance, in *The Speaker*, 14 January
1905.

1. *spindrift*: Sea spray blown along the surface of the water.
2. *tatter the seas into drift*: Tear the sea into spray.
3. *red-coats*: British soldiers, known by their scarlet uniforms.
4. *swarthy sea-dogs*: Literally 'sun-burned old sailors', but here
unnamed pirates.
5. *rollers*: Long, swelling waves.
6. *blue-jackets*: Seamen in the navy.
7. *harry*: Harass.
8. *scurfed to the tops with the brine*: Covered to the tops with scaly
deposits of salt.
9. *squatters ... sends*: 'Squatters' indicates a crouching movement
(i.e. going down into the waves) and 'sends' making way on the
sea with much splashing.
10. *Medway*: The River Medway, mostly in Kent, flows into the
Thames estuary.

The Greenwich Pensioner

First published, and sole appearance, in *The Speaker*, 15 April 1905.

1. *Greenwich Pensioner*: The Royal Naval Hospital for sailors was
founded in 1694 as a residential home in Greenwich. It closed in
1869.
2. *I'll go no more a roving by the light of the moon*: cf. Lord Byron's
'So we'll go no more a-roving' (1817) and, later, W. E. Henley's
'We'll go no more a-roving by the light of the moon' (1908).
Masefield included Byron's poem in *My Favourite English Poems*
(London: William Heinemann, 1950).
3. *under sod*: Buried.

Posted as Missing

First published in the *Pall Mall Magazine*, September 1906. Present as the twenty-fourth poem in the second edition of *Ballads* (London: Elkin Mathews, 1910). There are a number of minor variants.

1. *shark-weed*: An unidentified marine plant. Possibly a reference to shark egg cases (also known as mermaid's purses).
2. *mangle*: Squeeze wet clothes in a machine with two rollers, turned by hand.

Campeachy Picture

First published in *A Broadside*, June 1908. Present as the tenth poem in *King Cole and Other Poems* (London: William Heinemann, 1923). There are no substantive differences.

1. *Campeachy*: The coast of south-east Mexico, Bahía de Campeche (Bay of Campeche), was a haunt of pirates from the seventeenth to the nineteenth century.
2. *rusk*: Roll of bread.
3. *pipe*: Make a whistling sound.

A Pleasant New Comfortable Ballad Upon the Death of Mr Israel Hands, Executed for Piracy

First published, and sole appearance, in *A Broadside*, September 1908, signed by 'Wolfe T. MacGowan'. A letter from Elizabeth C. Yeats to an unknown recipient (Houghton Library, University of Harvard, Autograph file) identifies Masefield as the author. See also my article 'McGowan's Code: Deciphering John Masefield and Jack B. Yeats', *Yeats Annual* 13 (London: Macmillan, 1998), pp. 308–16.

1. *Mr Israel Hands*: An eighteenth-century pirate, and second in command to Blackbeard (*c.*1680–1718). The manner of his death is unknown.
2. *'I Wail in Woe'*: In *Eastward Ho!* (1605), a comedy by George Chapman, Ben Jonson and John Marston, the character of Quick-silver sings his 'excellent ditty' 'to the tune of "I wail in woe, I plunge in pain"' (see Act V, scene v). The song was the original goodnight ballad, to the tune of 'Labandala Shot', written for George Mannington, executed at Cambridge Castle in 1576.
3. *prigs and cullies*: 'Prigs' are thieves and 'cullies' those who are

easily deceived, or the latter could simply be a derogatory term
for a man.

4. *Tyburn tree*: Gallows. Tyburn, formerly a village west of the City
   of London, close to where Marble Arch is now, was where pris-
   oners were executed until the eighteenth century. The 'Tyburn
   Tree' was a new type of gallows erected there in 1571 that ena-
   bled several prisoners to be hanged simultaneously.

Third Mate

First published, as 'A Young Man's Fancy', in *A Broadside*, June 1910,
signed by 'R. E. McGowan'. Present as the thirty-ninth poem in *Bal-
lads and Poems* (London: Elkin Mathews, 1910). There are a number
of minor variants.

1. *clacking*: Making a hard, sharp noise.
2. *spindrift*: Sea spray blown along the surface of the water.

Truth

First published in the *English Review*, June 1911. Present as the fourth
poem in *The Story of a Round-House and Other Poems* (New York:
Macmillan, 1912) and also included in *Philip the King and Other
Poems* (London: William Heinemann, 1914). I have used the punctu-
ation from the later version.

Ships

First published in the *English Review*, July 1912. Present as the third
poem in *The Story of a Round-House and Other Poems* (New York:
Macmillan, 1912). First included by Masefield in an English publica-
tion within *Philip the King and Other Poems* (London: William
Heinemann, 1914). I have chosen the latter as the copy-text. There are
a number of minor variants.

1. *nourish*: Volume publications include 'flourish'. I have chosen
   the earlier reading here.
2. *Helen*: Helen of Troy, wife of King Menelaus, was abducted by
   Paris and thus precipitated the Trojan War.
3. *my city*: Liverpool.
4. *St Nicholas' bells*: The bells of the Church of Our Lady and Saint
   Nicholas in Liverpool.
5. *coulters*: A 'coulter' is the blade fixed in front of the share on a

plough. Masefield's imagery is therefore of ship's bows slicing
through the sea (cf. note 2 to 'The Wanderer' below).

6. *Wanderer*: A four-masted barque, launched in 1891 and sunk in
    1907. The ship had a profound influence on Masefield. In 1962
    he described her as 'a ship of splendour whose image for years
    haunted me and made me write' (*The Fortune of the Sea and The
    Wanderer's Image*, Argo LP RG230 (London, 1962)). (See also
    the poem 'The Wanderer' in this volume.)

7. *Cutty Sark*: The original line read 'The *Copley* swift'.

8. *Redgauntlet*: The ship originally named here was the *John
    Lockett*.

9. *Fernie Fleet*: The Fernies were an important ship-owning family
    in the nineteenth century. William James Fernie managed the
    Merchant's Trading Company and the National. His brother,
    Henry Fernie, was also a ship-owner.

10. *spoken*: Signalled.

11. *McVickar Marshall's . . . Fernie Brothers*: 'McVickar Marshall'
    is an incorrect rendering of the shipping company of Macvicar,
    Marshall and Co. In the first issue of *Liverpool's Shipping: Who's
    Who* (Liverpool, Journal of Commerce, 1909) the company's
    entry is under 'Palace Shipping Co., Ltd.', with Macvicar, Mar-
    shall and Co. listed as managers; the 'Fernie Brothers' were
    William James and Henry Fernie (see note 9 above).

12. *roller-tops*: Crests of long, swelling waves.

13. *Alfred Holt's blue smokestacks*: Alfred Holt and Company,
    founded in 1866, was better known as the Blue Funnel Line.

14. *Arabian*: The ship originally named here was the *Loanda*.

15. *Booth liners, Anchor liners, Red Star liners*: Ships of the Booth
    Steamship Company (1881–1986), the Anchor Line of steam-
    ships, founded in 1856 and acquired by Cunard in 1911, and the
    Red Star Line, founded in 1871 and amalgamated into the Inter-
    national Mercantile Marine Company in 1902.

16. *back-stayed into rake*: A mast supported by long ropes (stays)
    extending from the upper mastheads to both sides of the ship
    so that it inclines slightly from the perpendicular towards the
    stern.

The Gara River

First published, and sole appearance, in *A Broadside*, August 1913,
signed by 'Wolfe T. MacGowan'. I have added punctuation where
necessary.

1. *Gara River*: See note 1 to 'The Gara Brook' above.
2. *Monte*: The first vessel created by Masefield and Jack B. Yeats in
    their 'Gara Fleet' (see note 1 to 'The Gara Brook' above). Yeats
    states in *A Little Fleet* (London: Elkin Mathews, 1909) that the
    ship 'was made out of a flat piece of wood about five inches long,
    shaped at one end for the bow. She had two masts . . . and was
    rigged as a fore and aft schooner with paper sails.'
3. *beaks*: A 'beak' is the projection at the prow of a warship.
4. *combes*: Short valleys running up from the coast.

The Pathfinder

First published within the text of *Sard Harker* (London: William
Heinemann, 1924). The fictional ship is introduced, in prose, as
follows:

> The *Pathfinder* was the last and finest of Messrs. Wrattson & Willis's
> sugar clippers. She made some famous passages in the sugar and wool
> trades before she went the way of her kind.

1. *benison*: Blessing.

The Wanderer

First published, privately, as the first poem in *Poems of The Wanderer.
The Ending* (Oxford?: John Masefield, 1930). Present as the fourth
poem in *The Wanderer of Liverpool* (London: William Heinemann,
1930). I have used the latter as my copy-text.

1. *Wanderer*: See note 6 to 'Ships' above.
2. *coultered the ungarnered*: Masefield's use of ploughing imagery,
    from 'coulter' (the blade fixed in front of the share in a plough),
    evokes the ship slicing through the sea (cf. note 5 to 'Ships'
    above); 'ungarnered' literally means 'uncollected' or 'not stored',
    but here indicates the sea.

The Crowd

First published, privately, as the sixth poem in *Poems of The Wan-
derer. The Ending* (Oxford?: John Masefield, 1930). Present as the
ninth poem in *The Wanderer of Liverpool* (London: William Heine-
mann, 1930). I have used the latter as my copy-text.

Posted

First published, privately, as the ninth poem in *Poems of The Wanderer. The Ending* (Oxford?: John Masefield, 1930). Present as the twelfth poem in *The Wanderer of Liverpool* (London: William Heinemann, 1930). I have used the latter as my copy-text.

1.   *The cuttle mumbles*: 'Cuttle' is 'cuttle-fish', while 'mumbles' means to chew or bite with toothless gums, or turn over and over in the mouth.

If

First published, privately, as the tenth poem in *Poems of The Wanderer. The Ending* (Oxford?: John Masefield, 1930). Present as the thirteenth poem in *The Wanderer of Liverpool* (London: William Heinemann, 1930). I have used the latter as my copy-text.

1.   *If*: Rudyard Kipling's better-known poem of the same title was written in 1896 and first published in 1910.

I Saw Her Here

First published, privately, as the eleventh poem in *Poems of The Wanderer. The Ending* (Oxford?: John Masefield, 1930). Present as the fourteenth poem in *The Wanderer of Liverpool* (London: William Heinemann, 1930). I have used the latter as my copy-text.

After Forty Years

First published as a prefatory poem to the second part of *The Conway* (London: William Heinemann, 1933).

1.   *After Forty Years*: Masefield left HMS *Conway* in March 1894 and is therefore short of his fortieth anniversary by one year.
2.   *hasting*: Speeding.
3.   *Wally Blair*: See note 1 to 'One of Wally's Yarns' above.

A Seaman's Prayer

First published in the *Pall Mall Magazine*, July 1934 (illustrated by W. Heath Robinson) and reprinted as the first poem in Masefield's Christmas card for 1935.

Number 534

First published in *The Times*, 25 September 1934. Also present in the souvenir programme for the launching of the *Queen Mary* and included within Masefield's poetry Christmas card for 1935 (see Philip W. Errington, *John Masefield – The 'Great Auk' of English Literature – A Bibliography* (London: British Library, 2004), p. 790).

1. *Number 534*: RMS *Queen Mary* (launched on 26 September 1934) was, during her construction, known as 'Hull Number 534'.
2. *masst*: With masts.
3. *wester*: A gale or wind blowing from the west.

The Eyes

First published as the twenty-fifth poem in *A Letter from Pontus and Other Verse* (London: William Heinemann, 1936).

Canal Zone

First published as the twenty-ninth poem in *A Letter from Pontus and Other Verse* (London: William Heinemann, 1936).

1. *Canal Zone*: Panama Canal Zone. Sir Francis Drake (see next note) died off the coast of Portobelo in Panama in 1596.
2. *Francis Drake*: (1540–95) Seaman, pirate, circumnavigator and protector against the Spanish Armada.
3. *the bonnet and the bee*: In contrast with the aeroplane, Masefield notes two nautical terms presumably to suggest that sailing-ships are now outdated. A 'bonnet' was an additional piece of canvas attached to the foot of a sail in order to catch more wind. A 'bee' was a ring or hoop of metal. There is no apparent reference to the phrase 'a bee in one's bonnet'.

To the Seamen

First published as the second poem in *The Nine Days Wonder* (London: William Heinemann, 1941). The poem is from Masefield's account of the 1940 Dunkirk evacuation. The book was originally entitled *The Twenty-Five Days*, and proof copies were distributed in 1940 before the censor prevented publication. Masefield therefore produced a revised and truncated version entitled *The Nine Days Wonder*, which includes this poem for the first time.

1.   *Zuydecoote*: More usually spelled 'Zuydcoote', a village approximately five miles to the east of Dunkirk on the coast of northern France.

Crews Coming Down Gangways

First published as the thirteenth poem in *A Generation Risen* (London: William Collins, 1942).

Give Way

First published as the eighteenth poem in *In Glad Thanksgiving* (London: William Heinemann, 1967).

1.   *Sloyne*: An anchorage on the River Mersey.
2.   *dissever*: Divide.

SHORT STORIES

Sea Superstition

First published in the *Manchester Guardian*, 5 December 1903. Present as the third story in *A Mainsail Haul* (London: Elkin Mathews, 1905).

1.   *Horn*: Cape Horn, at the tip of South America, considered one of the most dangerous navigation routes.
2.   *comber*: A long and curling wave.
3.   *halt*: An archaic term for crippled or lame.
4.   *Tagus*: The River Tagus, which flows across Spain and Portugal for 626 miles before jointing the Atlantic Ocean near Lisbon.
5.   *red-lead*: A red oxide of lead, used as a pigment.

A Sailor's Yarn

First published in the *Manchester Guardian*, 23 January 1904. Present as the fourth story in *A Mainsail Haul* (London: Elkin Mathews, 1905).

1.   *Black Ball line*: A fast nineteenth-century packet service ship running between Liverpool and New York.

2. *A.B.*: 'An "able-bodied" seaman; formerly one who had served five or seven years at sea' (*The Bird of Dawning*).

3. *rastle*: A variant of 'wrestle'.

4. *blue*: Squander; a variant of 'blow'.

5. *sombre-airers*: Sombreros.

6. *silver dollars*: British 'silver dollars' were trade coins mostly used in the Far East in the late nineteenth and early twentieth centuries.

7. *Mole*: A structure, usually of stone, that serves as a pier or similar construction.

8. *Johnny Dago*: Pejorative term for a foreigner, especially a Spaniard, Portuguese or Italian.

9. *puncheons*: Large casks, holding 72–120 gallons (327–545 litres).

10. *calavances*: Certain varieties of bean.

11. *donkey's breakfasts*: Bundles of straw used for bedding. Later used as a term for straw mattresses.

12. *Crimee shirts*: Presumably 'Crimean Shirts', very large garments with straight sides and multi-pleated sleeves that were narrow at the wrist but then significantly widened at the shoulders.

13. *coir-brooms*: Brooms made using fibre manufactured from the outer husks of coconuts.

14. *lanchero*: Spanish word for a boatman.

15. *Horn*: Cape Horn, at the tip of South America, considered one of the most dangerous navigation routes.

Port of Many Ships

First published in the *Manchester Guardian*, 2 April 1904. Present as the second story in *A Mainsail Haul* (London: Elkin Mathews, 1905).

1. *man rope . . . Flemish point*: Masefield's listing includes both practical knots (a 'man rope' is a knot at the end of a rope used to create a hand hold) and decorative knots (a 'Matthew Walker' is, for example, a decorative knot that prevents fraying to the end of a rope).

2. *Black Ball clipper*: Ship from the Black Ball line (see note 1 to 'A Sailor's Yarn' above).

3. *'Stockhollum tar'*: Swedish Stockholm tar is a dark brown or black viscous pine tar. Used during ship building to treat wood, it was also applied to ropes and fixtures for weather-proofing.

4. *cirro-cumulus*: A bank of high-altitude small white clouds.

5.   *boatswain pipes*: A boatswain would use a high-pitched pipe, known as the 'boatswain's call', to bugle commands to the crew to make them quiet so that they could hear his orders.

6.   *sperm-whales . . . thrasher*: A catalogue of whales, dolphins and porpoises. The inclusion of the 'forty-barrel Jonah' presumably acknowledges the 'great fish' of the Old Testament as an unknown type of whale and the old sailor adds it to his list to give a sense of drama (from the biblical overtones) and for apparent completeness. Reference to 'forty-barrel' relates to the quantity of oil which the whale would produce. The 'thrasher' and the 'grampus' are common names for the killer whale. Herman Melville includes the 'Killer' and the 'Thrasher' in his listing of whales in Chapter 32 of *Moby-Dick* (1851) and, noting the chaos of classification that Melville presents (and which Masefield echoes), we should, perhaps, accept Masefield's character's listing simply as a non-inclusive and often repetitious catalogue.

7.   *Callao to Rio*: From Callao in Peru to Rio de Janeiro in Brazil and, therefore, semi-circumnavigating South America.

8.   *seventy-fours*: Two-decked ships carrying seventy-four guns, common between the mid eighteenth and early nineteenth centuries.

9.   *White Star boats*: Vessels of the White Star Line, founded in 1845 (and merged, in 1934, with the Cunard Line). The Line's most infamous ship was, of course, the *Titanic*.

10.   *Mr Blair*: See note 1 to 'One of Wally's Yarns' above.

A Spanish Sailor's Yarn

First published in the *Manchester Guardian*, 19 May 1904. Present as the eighth story in *A Mainsail Haul* (London: Elkin Mathews, 1905).

1.   *Wine of the Sea*: Possibly a reference to the Chilean coastal city of Viña del Mar ('Vineyard of the Sea'), which is within the Greater Valparaiso area (see note 1 to 'The Yarn of Lanky Job' below).

2.   *piracqua*: A two-masted barge or narrow canoe made from a single tree-trunk (also 'piragua').

3.   *turtlers*: Small boats used when hunting for turtles.

4.   *Whydah*: A kingdom on the coast of West Africa and a major slave-trading post.

5.   *four ships cruising at a time*: I have reverted, for this sentence, to

the text from the *Manchester Guardian*, which provides a better
explanation of the exploits of the ships.

6. *steering-crutch*: Support or prop for the tiller.
7. *tarpon*: A large silvery fish.
8. *stretcher*: Usually the board in a rowing boat against which a
    rower presses his feet. Here it apparently refers to part of the
    steering-crutch.

The Yarn of Lanky Job

First published in the *Manchester Guardian*, 16 July 1904. Present as
the fifth story in *A Mainsail Haul* (London: Elkin Mathews, 1905).

1. *Valparaiso*: Masefield was a patient at the British Hospital at Val-
    paraiso, the seaport city in Chile, around August and September
    1894. He had been discharged from the crew of the *Gilcruix*.
2. *Coquimbo*: A port city in Chile.
3. *Aconcagua*: The highest mountain in the Americas.
4. *fever*: The text in the *Manchester Guardian* here reads 'sun-
    stroke'.
5. *caul*: The membrane enclosing a foetus, which, if a section is still
    present on a child's head at birth, is thought to bring good luck.
6. *bluff-bowed*: Having bows that are nearly vertical.
7. *starn*: Stern.
8. *Avonmouth*: The large Bristol port at the mouth of the River
    Avon.

In Dock – I

First published, and sole appearance, in *The Speaker*, 5 November
1904.

1. *Cairngorm*: The ship in which Masefield was apprenticed was a
    four-masted barque named the *Gilcruix*. She belonged to the
    White Star Line and had been built in 1886. Later renamed the
    Barmbek and then the *Pacifique*, she was broken up in 1923.
    Throughout his autobiographical writing and several short sto-
    ries Masefield uses the fictitious name of the *Cairngorm*.
2. *duds*: clothes.
3. *Pisagua*: A 'nitrate' port in the Iquique region of Chile. For more
    on this, see note 2 to 'In Dock – II' below.
4. *'McGilligan'*: Not the Irish song 'Mick McGillian's Daughter
    Mary Ann', although possibly a parody. The song alludes to

'Where Did You Get that Hat?', which was popular after 1880.
There is also reference to the cartoon character of Ally Sloper,
who first appeared in print in 1867.

5. *'Sam Hall'*: A popular ballad, known in a variety of versions.
The opening stanza of one version (evidently sanitized) reads:

> Now my name is Samuel Hall, Sam Hall
> Oh my name is Samuel Hall
> Oh my name is Samuel Hall, and I hate you one and all
> You're a bunch of muckers all blast your eyes.

6. *'Spanish Ladies'*: Commencing 'Farewell and adieu to you, fine
Spanish ladies'. Roy Palmer in *Boxing the Compass* (Todmor-
den: Herron Publishing, 2001) notes it was frequently used as a
capstan chanty. Masefield was, it seems, especially fond of the
ballad. In 1903, citing his source as 'Words and Music given to
John Masefield by Wally Blair, A.B.', he included it in the period-
ical *The Green Sheaf*. It is also printed, with music, in *Sea Life
in Nelson's Time* (London: Methuen, 1905) when Masefield
describes it as 'a beautiful old song, long popular at sea'.

7. *'The Long, Long Time Ago'*: Masefield included the chanty 'A
Long Time Ago' in *A Sailor's Garland* (London: Methuen, 1906).
The first line is given as 'A long, long time, and a long time ago'.

8. *Marryat*: Captain Frederick Marryat (1792–1848), novelist (see
'The Sea Writers: Captain Frederick Marryat' in this volume).

Don Alfonso's Treasure Hunt

First published in the *Manchester Guardian*, 7 December 1904. Pres-
ent as the first story in *A Mainsail Haul* (London: Elkin Mathews,
1905).

1. *Now in the old days*: The yarn, as first printed in the *Manchester
Guardian*, commences with a paragraph that was subsequently
deleted. It reads:

> I once met a sailor who had one eye, one tooth, and one ear. His
> face was the colour of old parchment, with streaks of red in it deep-
> ening into purple about the eyes. He had a sort of longshoreman's
> job when I knew him, hiring out boats by the hour or taking small
> children for a row. He spun me this yarn one slack season while we
> fished for lithe together over the stern of a dinghy.

2. *Dagoes*: Pejorative term for foreigners, especially Spaniards,
Portuguese or Italians.

3.   *licker*: Within his miscellany column in the *Manchester Guard-ian*, the day after publication of the tale, Masefield provided further detail about this particular liquor:

> A correspondent writes to ask us the name of the 'licker' mentioned in 'Don Alfonso's Treasure Hunt', printed in our issue of yesterday. The author of that tale refuses to reveal the name of the drink, for it is an extremely cheap liquid the introduction of which would be fatal to the British Empire. It is more deadly and much cheaper than the 'pink gin', at 4s. the dozen, which the wily Belgian trades for tusks and gold-dust in the Upper Congo. It costs about 2d. a gallon in the unhappy countries where it is drunk. It is said to be the direct cause of more than thirty of the fifty-two revolutions that have disturbed Ecuador since 1854. Travellers in Chili or in Argentina, if they ride abroad soon after the spring sheep shearings, are unlikely to meet anybody untainted by the poison. The roads are peopled by drunken guachoes, each carrying a bottle of the stuff, and riding by the guacho instinct and by a little of that providence which keeps drunkards from mishap. There is another 'licker' in those parts known as 'anisow', which is as strong but more expensive. It finds favour among the sailors in the ports, who lower buckets at night over the bows for its reception. In the darkness a bumboatman puts off in a boat with a good supply of bottles. He places these in the buckets, and receives cash in payment. If the mates of the ships are not old hands it sometimes happens that an entire crew will be helpless when called in the morning. The vino, or vin ordinaire, is very sour, but J.M. has seen men overcome by it after a day's continual drinking. It is as cheap as water in many parts of South America. There is also a very pleasant native beer, called chica, which is drunk largely. Temperance people in those parts drink the famous pampas drink 'maté', a sort of tea, which is a comforting, diffusive stimulant, though rather tasteless.

4.   *play*: Possibly the pantomime of *Aladdin*.
5.   *chewing the rag*: Yarning or chatting.
6.   *Blue Nose ship*: A Canadian ship from Nova Scotia.
7.   *Tortugas*: Tortuga, a Caribbean island and part of Haiti, was a major centre of Caribbean piracy. La Tortuga Island, part of the islands that include the Tortuguillas, was also notorious as a refuge of pirates.
8.   *Chagres*: The main Atlantic port of the Isthmus (of Panama, connecting North and South America), discovered by Christopher Columbus in 1502.

9.   *Samballs*: Untraced, although evidently islands in the Caribbean.
10. *blunt*: Money, especially coins.
11. *silver dollars*: British 'silver dollars' were trade coins mostly used in the Far East in the late nineteenth and early twentieth centuries.
12. *Deadwood Dicky books*: Deadwood Dick was the hero of Edward L. Wheeler's 'dime novel' series from 1877. After Wheeler's death, a second series ran until 1897.
13. *calaboosa*: A Southern or Western American term for a jail, this may also carry the move nautical sense of 'caboose' the house on deck where cooking is done.
14. *'Salve'*: The *Manchester Guardian* text suggests healing or salvation with 'Salve', which I prefer, here, to the mere salutation which appears in *A Mainsail Haul* as 'Salue'.
15. *scripters*: The exact sacred writing is unidentified, although note 'the fire shall devour thy bars' (Nahum 3: 13) as a suggestion entirely out of context.
16. *pully-hauly*: Using all one's strength, from the action of pulling and hauling.
17. *red wheft*: The red ensign (familiarly known as a red duster) of the merchant navy.

In a Fo'c's'le

First published in the *Manchester Guardian*, 9 March 1905. Present as the eighteenth story in *A Tarpaulin Muster* (London: Grant Richards, 1907). In a letter to Harley Granville Barker, dated 30 March 1907, Masefield revealed his sources for the contents of *A Tarpaulin Muster* (British Library, Add. Ms. 47897, f. 13). Of this story Masefield notes it was based on 'memory'.

1.   *out of soundings*: Taking a sounding is to measure the depth of water; therefore a ship 'out of soundings' is in deep water.
2.   *'a bloody coxcomb'*: There are three references to Sir Toby's bloody coxcomb in *Twelfth Night*, Act V, scene i.
3.   *'sent to Coventry'*: To refuse association or speech with a person.
4.   *'Arion on the dolphin's back'*: Arion was a poet and accomplished musician in ancient Greek myth who is said to have created the dithyramb (a type of hymn to the god Dionysus). He was kidnapped by pirates but, faced with drowing, sang a song which attracted a dolphin that rescued him. This image of a musician, or one who survives drowning, recurs through literature (see *Twelfth Night*, Act 1, scene ii).

5. *Ishmael*: Eldest son of Abraham, who was expelled with his
    mother to wander in the desert; therefore a term for a person
    rejected from home or society (as famously used by Herman
    Melville for his narrator in *Moby-Dick*).
6. *chew*: A quid of tobacco.
7. *'Spanish Ladies'*: See note 6 to 'In Dock – I' above.
8. *'Bunclody'*: After the town in County Wexford, the song (also
    known as 'The Streams of Bunclody') begins: 'Were you ever at
    the moss house where birds do increase'.
9. *'The tide is flowing'*: Probably the song titled 'Just as the Tide was
    Flowing', which commences 'As I walked out one morn in May'.
10. *Horn*: Cape Horn, at the tip of South America, considered one
    of the most dangerous navigation routes.
11. *Canton River*: China's third-longest river, flowing into the South
    China Sea.
12. *slush*: Melted fat or grease discarded from the ship's galley.
13. *worriting*: Worrying or distressing.
14. *Barney's bull*: See note 4 to 'One of Wally's Yarns' above.
15. *'when my mother's cows come home'*: A variant of the familiar
    phrase meaning a long, but indefinite time.
16. *chows*: Pejorative term for Chinese.
17. *Yankee packet*: An American ship.

Anty Bligh

First published in the *Manchester Guardian*, 15 March 1905. Present
as the ninth story in *A Tarpaulin Muster* (London: Grant Richards,
1907). In a letter to Harley Granville Barker, dated 30 March 1907,
Masefield revealed his sources for the contents of *A Tarpaulin Muster*
(British Library, Add. Ms. 47897, f. 13). Of this story Masefield notes
it was based on 'actual reminiscence. Story suggested by a sailor, and
by a drawing of Jack Yeats's.'

1. *Ha! Ha! . . . Come, roll him over*: From the chanty entitled 'One
    More Day' that begins 'Only one more day, me Johnnies'.
2. *one or two to spare*: In a letter to Elizabeth Robins, dated 29 March
    1910, Masefield wrote:

    > I also thought of a fine Scandinavian sailor named Kruse, who was an
    > A.B. [able seaman] in the *Gilcruix* with me. He was a splendid man . . .
    > He wanted to buy a towel from me, and he was the nicest man aboard,
    > so I gave him one, a very good one, and would not take his money (i.e.
    > sea-money, 2 lbs of plug tobacco). He used to meet me in the night
    > watches, after that, to teach me seamanship, and yarn to me . . .

(Berg Collection, New York Public Library). W. Kruse can be iden-
tified in the 1894 *Gilcruix* crew list as a 22-year-old from Hamburg
(National Archives, BT.100/98B).

3.   *Fernando Noronha, where the prison is*: Fernando de Noronha
     is an archipelago of twenty-one islands in the Atlantic, about
     two hundred miles from Brazil. The islands housed a prison from
     1737 to 1942.

4.   *neck*: Presumptuous behaviour. Note also that Masefield explained
     about large necks in a letter to Elizabeth Robins, dated 29 March
     1910 (Berg Collection, New York Public Library):

> Sailors and others who go barefoot a good deal get big feet and
> ankles. And the constant use of the arms and shoulders makes them
> thick in the neck. When you are a mate, and have to pick your
> watch from a roaring gang of drunkards just flung on board, out of
> the gutters, by the crimps, you pick your men by the thickness of
> their necks. The chances are that a thick-necked man will be
> immensely strong, and at sea, if you can't have seamanship (which
> is about as rare as good lyric verse) you go for strength.

5.   *gait on*: Move on.

6.   *six water dollops*: Presumably a particularly watered-down ver-
     sion of grog.

7.   *foul block*: A block is a wooden pulley containing a metal wheel
     through which a rope runs. The wheel (also known as a sheave)
     was greased to allow it to run freely. Without grease the block
     became dry, the sheave failed to turn properly, and was known
     as a 'foul block'.

8.   *Mole*: A structure, usually of stone, that serves as a pier or simi-
     lar construction.

9.   *perry-acks*: 'Perry-ack' is slang for 'periagua' (or 'piragua'), com-
     prising a narrow canoe made from a single tree-trunk.

10. *catch a crab*: To fail to pull an oar cleanly from the water at the
     end of a stroke. The blade turns inwards and sinks, causing the
     oarsman to lose control of the oar.

11. *beef*: Nautical slang for strength or effort.

12. *skyoot*: A variant of 'skyhoot', which, itself, is a fanciful version
     of 'scoot'. The perry-ack therefore moves suddenly and swiftly.

13. *Bull Point Light and der Shutter Light*: The first Bull Point light-
     house, off the North Devon coast, was built in 1879. (Following
     damage in 1972 a new lighthouse was built in 1974.) The
     'Shutter Light' refers to a lighthouse close to Great Shutter Rock
     on Lundy Island. There are three lighthouses on Lundy: the first,
     built in 1819, was abandoned in 1897; new lighthouses were

built in 1897 on the North and South extremities of the island. In his article 'Sea Songs', published in *Temple Bar* (January 1906) Masefield notes that he 'first heard [the chanty 'Whisky, Johnny'] in the Bristol Channel, off Bull Point, with the Shutter Light glimmering in the distance'.

14. *cutty pipe*: Short tobacco pipe.
15. *chinning*: Talking.

The Devil and the Deep Sea

First published in the *Manchester Guardian*, 23 March 1905. This was Masefield's second version of the yarn. *The Green Sheaf*, No. 6 (1903), included 'A Deep Sea Yarn'. The tale is also present as the twelfth story in *A Mainsail Haul* (London: Elkin Mathews, 1905) and it commences:

> Up away north, in the old days, in Chester, there was a man who some-how never throve. Nothing he put his hand to ever prospered, and folk came to look upon him as an unchancy fellow, one of the better-dead and so forth . . .

1. *Spoon*: Slang for a simple or foolish person.
2. *red cent*: An American one-cent coin named after its red copper colour.
3. *jalap*: A purgative drug.
4. *slush*: Melted fat or grease discarded from the ship's galley.
5. *hurrah for Joseph*: Evidently an expression for being haphazard or disorganized. The origin is unknown although it may be of relevance that Royal Marines on Royal Navy ships were known by the nickname 'Joseph'.
6. *Barney's bull*: See note 4 to 'One of Wally's Yarns' above.

In Dock – II

First published, and sole appearance, in *The Speaker*, 6 May 1905.

1. *wrastle out*: A variant of 'wrestle'.
2. *nitre*: Potassium nitrate (saltpetre). The South American nitrate market was one of the last trades to use sailing-ships, which travelled from Europe to Chile via Cape Horn. After loading nitrate in Iquique, these returned home eastwards around Cape Horn. Constance Babington Smith notes that Masefield's first voyage, in the *Gilcruix*, was from Cardiff to Iquique with a cargo

of 'blocks of compressed coal-dust' or 'patent fuel' (*John Masefield – A Life* (Oxford: Oxford University Press, 1978, p. 23)). The return trip would presumably have been with a cargo of nitre.

3.   *red cent*: An American one-cent coin named after its red copper colour.
4.   *red-lead*: A red oxide of lead, used as a pigment.
5.   *manilla*: Or 'manilla hemp', comprising a strong fibre often used for rope.

A Port Royal Twister

First published in the *Manchester Guardian*, 30 May 1905. Present as the seventeenth story in *A Tarpaulin Muster* (London: Grant Richards, 1907). In a letter to Harley Granville Barker, dated 30 March 1907, Masefield revealed his sources for the contents of *A Tarpaulin Muster* (British Library, Add. Ms. 47897, f. 13). Of this story Masefield notes it was 'invention'.

1.   *Port Royal*: City at the mouth of Kingston Harbour in Jamaica.
2.   *burnt brandy*: Brandy that has been heated and flamed to burn off the alcohol.
3.   *pole-axed steer*: A young bull killed by a butcher's axe.
4.   *water-clock*: A clock which measures time by the flow of water.
5.   *zips*: Originally capitalized as 'Zips' and presumed to relate to the sound of the birds rather than a specific type of bird. The capitalization may reflect a trade name for a zip fastener. Desfayes notes 'Zip' as linked to German and Italian names for the Song Thrush, Cirl Bunting and Yellow-Hammer (which seem inappropriate in this context – see Michel Desfayes, *A Thesaurus of Bird Names* (Sion: Musée Cantonal d'Histoire Naturelle, 1998)). The name 'Zip' is not included in H. K. Swann's *Dictionary of English and Folk-Names of British Birds* (London: Witherby & Co., 1913).
6.   *Diego Ramirez*: The Diego Ramirez islands are located about sixty miles south-west of Cape Horn.
7.   *Captain Morgan*: Welsh pirate captain (*c.*1635–88), and later Lieutenant Governor of Jamaica.
8.   *Chagres*: The main Atlantic port of the Isthmus (of Panama, connecting North and South America), discovered by Christopher Columbus in 1502.
9.   *Drake*: Sir Francis Drake (1540–95), seaman, pirate, circumnavigator and protector against the Spanish Armada.

10. *Algiers and Thelemark*: Algiers was an infamous stronghold for
     pirates; 'Thelemark' is an alternative spelling for 'Telemark' in
     Norway (and therefore invokes Viking raiders).
11. *gulley*: Singular of 'gullies'. Masefield defines gullies in his
     glossary to *Salt-Water Ballads* as 'Sea-gulls, Cape Horn pigeons,
     etc.'.

Ambitious Jimmy Hicks

First published in the *Manchester Guardian*, 16 June 1905. Present as
the eighth story in *A Tarpaulin Muster* (London: Grant Richards,
1907). In a letter to Harley Granville Barker, dated 30 March 1907,
Masefield revealed his sources for the contents of *A Tarpaulin Muster*
(British Library, Add. Ms. 47897, f. 13). Of this story Masefield notes
it was based on 'actual reminiscence. Story told me by Wally Blair,
now dead.'

1.   *Zion's Hill*: The name given to the old forecastle-head of the
     Conway (see the Introduction), with reference to the hill in Jeru-
     salem.
2.   *catching any crabs*: To fail to pull an oar cleanly from the water
     at the end of a stroke. The blade turns inwards and sinks, caus-
     ing the oarsman to lose control of the oar.
3.   *quid of sweet-cake*: A small lump of tobacco.
4.   *caulk*: Afternoon nap.
5.   *Black Ball line*: A fast nineteenth-century packet service running
     between Liverpool and New York.
6.   *Cunarders*: Ships of the Cunard Line (Cunard Steamship Com-
     pany), founded in 1839.
7.   *Sydney Heads*: The entrance to Sydney Harbour in Australia.
8.   *Sefton Park*: A public park in Liverpool and, therefore, the scene
     for parading Victorian Sunday finery.
9.   *slush*: Melted fat or grease discarded from the ship's galley.
10. *Double, double, toil and trouble*: *Macbeth*, Act IV, scene i.
11. *skilly*: An insipid brew of tea or coffee. Masefield notes 'skilley'
     as 'tea or coffee supplied to messes' (*The Conway*).

The Cape Horn Calm

First published in the *Manchester Guardian*, 18 July 1905. Present as
the sixteenth story in *A Tarpaulin Muster* (London: Grant Richards,
1907). In a letter to Harley Granville Barker, dated 30 March 1907,

Masefield revealed his sources for the contents of *A Tarpaulin Muster* (British Library, Add. Ms. 47897, f. 13). Of this story Masefield notes it was based on 'memory'.

1. *drunken drogher*: A drogher was a small West Indian vessel that carried passengers and trades among the ports of those islands. A 'drunken drogher' was, presumably, an inebriated person in charge of such a vessel.
2. *suppurate*: Fester.
3. *'sword'*: The manufacture of mats usually employed a piece of wood shaped like a sword, and named as such.
4. *kinked*: Twisted.
5. *'Where are there greater atheists than your cooks?'*: In Jonson's *The Alchemist* (1610) Tribulation Wholesome asks, 'Where have you greater atheists than your cooks' in Act III, scene i.
6. *Negro Head*: Nautical slang for a brown loaf of bread.
7. *'Hydriotaphia'*: Sir Thomas Browne's *Hydriotaphia* was first published in 1658.
8. *West Coast nitrate ports*: Ports on the western coast of Chile, including Valparaiso (see note 1 to 'The Yarn of Lanky Job' above), engaged in the South American nitrate trade (see note 2 to 'In Dock – II' above).
9. *'The Sailor's Wives'*: A song which begins: 'The first one was the gunner's wife and she was dressed in green'. Roy Palmer in *Boxing the Compass* (Todmorden: Herron Publishing, 2001) notes this as 'very much a Royal Navy song'.

The Yarn of Happy Jack

First published in *The Speaker*, 2 September 1905. Present as the twenty-fourth story in *A Tarpaulin Muster* (London: Grant Richards, 1907). In a letter to Harley Granville Barker, dated 30 March 1907, Masefield revealed his sources for the contents of *A Tarpaulin Muster* (British Library, Add. Ms. 47897, f. 13). Of this story Masefield notes it was 'founded on a tale a sailor told me'.

1. *the taking of a drink*: The text in *The Speaker* adds 'or the buying of a red silk handkerchief'.
2. *give us a breeze*: Give us a rest.
3. *Fata Morgana*: A complex form of mirage that distorts objects on the horizon, causing them to appear elevated and elongated.
4. *foul hawse*: When a ship's hawse is neither clear nor open, i.e. the chains are entangled or twisted or otherwise caught.

The Bottom of the Well

First published in the *Manchester Guardian*, 7 September 1905. Present as the nineteenth story in *A Tarpaulin Muster* (London: Grant Richards, 1907). In a letter to Harley Granville Barker, dated 30 March 1907, Masefield revealed his sources for the contents of *A Tarpaulin Muster* (British Library, Add. Ms. 47897, f. 13). Of this story Masefield notes it was based on 'invention and very bad at that'.

1. *Valparaiso*: See note 1 to 'The Yarn of Lanky Job' above.
2. *kettle black*: From the proverb 'the pot calls the kettle black arse'.
3. *Tocopilla*: Province, and city, in the north of Chile which, translated, means 'the devil's corner'.
4. *lancher's graft*: Probably meaning a boatman's hard work (derived from the Spanish word, *lanchero*, for a boatman).
5. *tanning his back with nitrate*: probably shovelling saltpetre (potassium nitrate) into a ship's hold. See also note 2 to 'In Dock – II' above.
6. *Deadwood Dickeys*: See note 12 to 'Don Alfonso's Treasure Hunt' above.
7. *Cape Horn Gospels*: Extravagant lies, derived from tall stories of Cape Horn, and claimed as fact. See the poems 'Cape Horn Gospel – I' and 'Cape Horn Gospel – II' in this volume.
8. *Pal-am-jen-bang Straits*: The Strait of Malacca is one of the most important shipping lanes in the world connecting the Pacific and Indian Oceans. Palembang is one of the coastal towns.
9. *Oa-moru*: Town in the South Island of New Zealand.
10. *Sunday Lane*: Probably a slang term for a specific location in Cardiff, near the Pier Head.
11. *Cape Tiburon*: On the south-west coast of Haiti in the West Indies.
12. *dead-oh*: Naval slang for an advanced stage of drunkenness.
13. *Portuguese pilot*: Presumably suggesting that all foreign pilots were deceitful, since the term 'Portuguese' referred to any foreign officer or seaman (other than a Frenchman).
14. *He was that changed by the sight of that old king*: The original version of the text ends:

> 'So Bill he was put into his boat and turned adrift, and he mighty near got drowned. And he told me all that himself. And never a lie has he ever told since them. He told me that. Yes, sir. He told me that. He was that changed by the sight of that old King.'

One Sunday

First published in the *Manchester Guardian*, 15 September 1905.
Present as the twenty-first story in *A Tarpaulin Muster* (London:
Grant Richards, 1907). In a letter to Harley Granville Barker, dated
30 March 1907, Masefield revealed his sources for the contents of *A
Tarpaulin Muster* (British Library, Add. Ms. 47897, f. 13). Of this
story Masefield notes it was based on 'memory'.

1. *loading patent fuel for the West Coast*: See note 2 to 'In Dock –
    II' above.
2. *St Mary Street*: Major street in Cardiff on which a large number
    of pubs and hotels were located.
3. *Antofagasta*: A port city in northern Chile.
4. *'The Sailor's Wives'*: See note 9 to 'The Cape Horn Calm'
    above.
5. *'all friends and no favour'*: Masefield omits the final two sen-
    tences of this paragraph in *A Tarpaulin Muster*.
6. *Junin*: A small nitrate port, approximately thirty miles north of
    Iquique in Chile.
7. *Farley Brothers*: Untraced. It is feasible that Masefield provides
    a fictionalized name for the Fernie Brothers (see notes 9 and 11
    to 'Ships' above).
8. *'Amsterdam'*: The chanty 'The Maid of Amsterdam'.
9. *A-roving ... fair maid*: The refrain from 'The Maid of
    Amsterdam'.

A White Night

First published in the *Manchester Guardian*, 3 October 1905. Present
as the second story in *A Tarpaulin Muster* (London: Grant Richards,
1907). In a letter to Harley Granville Barker, dated 30 March 1907,
Masefield revealed his sources for the contents of *A Tarpaulin Muster*
(British Library, Add. Ms. 47897, f. 13). Of this story Masefield notes
it was based on 'actual reminiscence'.

1. *Away third cutters*: Those rowing the third of the small boats
    carried by a larger ship.
2. *old Chaldea*: Winged bulls were closely identified with ancient
    Chaldean mythology as followed by the eleventh dynasty of the
    kings of Babylon (around the sixth century BC).

Davy Jones's Gift

First published in *Country Life*, 11 November 1905. Present as the sixth story in *A Tarpaulin Muster* (London: Grant Richards, 1907). In a letter to Harley Granville Barker, dated 30 March 1907, Masefield revealed his sources for the contents of *A Tarpaulin Muster* (British Library, Add. Ms. 47897, f. 13). Of this story Masefield notes it was 'invention'.

1. *Tiger Bay*: The name for the general area around Cardiff Docks and Butetown. Murders and red-light districts contributed to a dangerous reputation.

2. *Pier Head*: Location in Cardiff at the end of Bute Street and commanding a view of the entrances to both West and East Bute Docks.

3. *Sunday Lane*: Probably a slang term for a specific location in Cardiff, near the Pier Head.

4. *Mary Street*: St Mary Street was a major street in Cardiff on which a large number of pubs and hotels were located.

5. *burnt brandy*: Brandy that has been heated and flamed to burn off the alcohol.

6. *chinstay*: Band that fastens a hat or cap under the chin.

7. *Rio and Callao*: The usual journey was from Callao in Peru to Rio de Janeiro in Brazil, semi-circumnavigating South America. Bill Harker picks up love-letters in the opposite direction.

8. *East Bute Docks*: There were two Bute Docks in Cardiff: the West Bute Dock (opened in 1839) and the East Bute Dock (opened, in two phases, in 1855 and 1859).

9. *Coronel*: The name of the barque appears as the *Coronet* in *Country Life*.

10. *Hilo*: Coastal town in Hawaii.

11. *off the River Plate, they got caught in a pampero*: The River Plate is the widest estuary in the world, formed by the Uruguay and Parana rivers on the south-east coast of South America; a 'pampero' is a River Plate gale.

12. *Horn*: Cape Horn, at the tip of South America, considered one of the most dangerous navigation routes.

13. *able-whackets*: A sailors' card game, described by Masefield in *Sea Life in Nelson's Time* (London: Methuen, 1905) as 'a pastime in which cards, blasphemy, and hard knocks were agreeably mingled'. The loser in the game is beaten over the palms of the hands with a rope or twisted handkerchief.

14. *teasers*: Short lengths of rope with a 'hangman's knot' at the end, used for chastisement.
15. *Terra del Fuego*: Archipelago (Tierra del Fuego) off the southern-most tip of South America, of which the southern point forms Cape Horn.
16. *jing bang*: Group.
17. *knucklebones*: A game, also known as dibs, jacks or huckle-bones, involving five small objects which are thrown up and caught in different ways.

Being Ashore

First published in the *Manchester Guardian*, 20 February 1906. Present as the twentieth story in *A Tarpaulin Muster* (London: Grant Richards, 1907). In a letter to Harley Granville Barker, dated 30 March 1907, Masefield revealed his sources for the contents of *A Tarpaulin Muster* (British Library, Add. Ms. 47897, f. 13). Of this story Masefield notes it was based on 'memory'.

1. *catamount*: An American name for a panther or puma; also a pun on King Lear's 'cataracts' (see next note).
2. *blow, wind, and crack your cheeks*: *King Lear*, Act III, scene ii.
3. *rantipoles*: Rude or unruly people.
4. *Cunard*: The Cunard Line (Cunard Steamship Company), founded in 1839.
5. *P.S.N.*: The Pacific Steam Navigation Company, founded in 1838 to carry mail by steamship to the Pacific.
6. *River Plate*: The widest estuary in the world, formed by the Uruguay and Parana rivers on the south-east coast of South America.
7. *'Greatness a period hath, no sta-ti-on'*: From John Donne's 1601 poem 'The Progress of the Soul'.
8. *rastle*: A variant of 'wrestle'.

In the Roost

First published, and sole appearance, in the *Manchester Guardian*, 16 March 1906.

1. *Green Street*: There is a Green Street in Brooklyn, New York. A more likely location is Greene Street one block away from Washington Square Park in Greenwich Village, New York.
2. *soojee-moojee*: To scrub and scour.

3. *soup and bully*: A soup including preserved meats and vege-
    tables. W. Clark Russell states it is 'usually horribly nauseous'.
    Masefield venders the meal as 'Soap and Bully' in 'Autobiog-
    raphy' (p. 186).
4. *spell-oh*: A rest. Masefield includes the term 'spello' in his 'Gloss-
    ary of *Conway* Slang' as 'allotted work, or a rest from same'
    (*The Conway*).
5. *chip*: A cheating man, derived from 'a chip off the block of
    Adam'.
6. *Proctor's*: Assuming this tale to be set around the time that
    Masefield was a bar-hand in New York in 1895, 'Proctor's Pleas-
    ure Palace' was located at 58th Street (between Lexington and
    3rd Avenue) while 'Proctor's Theatre' was located at 23rd Street.
    Contemporary newspapers reveal that Proctor's often advertised
    as being 'Always Cool'. The attraction Masefield specifically
    mentions has not been identified.

A Steerage Steward

First published, and sole appearance, in the *Manchester Guardian*, 21
June 1906.

1. *West Street*: The long street on the extreme west of Manhattan
    from which wharves or piers grant access to the Hudson River.
2. *bull's-eye scuttle*: The 'cabin' is presumably lit by two sources of
    light: an electric bulb and a window which resembles a porthole
    and includes a bulbous glass feature known as a 'bull's-eye'.
3. *Laws of Storms*: Presumably *Catechism of the Law of Storms* by
    J. Macnab (first published in 1884). Masefield refers to the work
    again in his 'Autobiography' (see note 10 of 'Autobiography'
    below).
4. *Battery*: The southern tip of New York City facing the harbour.
    Named after the artillery battery.
5. *Babbett's Soapworks*: The factory of the soap manufacturer B. T.
    Babbitt (1809–89), who was the first to market individual bars
    of soap.
6. *'stung like tenches'*: *Henry IV, Part 1*, Act II, scene i.
7. *Birkenhead*: The earliest extant letters from Masefield to his sis-
    ter Ethel are dated July 1897 and addressed from New Charter
    Road, Rock Ferry (an area of Birkenhead). HMS *Conway* was
    moored in the immediate vicinity. Masefield did not remain long
    in Birkenhead and had found lodgings in London before the end
    of the year.

On Growing Old

First published in the *Manchester Guardian*, 17 August 1906. Present as the tenth story in *A Tarpaulin Muster* (London: Grant Richards, 1907). In a letter to Harley Granville Barker, dated 30 March 1907, Masefield revealed his sources for the contents of *A Tarpaulin Muster* (British Library, Add. Ms. 47897, f. 13). Of this story Masefield notes it was based on 'actual reminiscence and vanity'.

1. *derrick*: Either tackle used at the outer quarter of the mizzen mast, or a crane for moving heavy weights.
2. *'crooking their little fingers'*: Evidently an expression for drinking, origin unknown.
3. *spoke*: Here, signalled.
4. *coca*: The dried leaves of a South American shrub, frequently chewed as a stimulant.

A Memory

First published in the *Manchester Guardian*, 4 October 1906. Present as the eleventh story in *A Tarpaulin Muster* (London: Grant Richards, 1907). In a letter to Harley Granville Barker, dated 30 March 1907, Masefield revealed his sources for the contents of *A Tarpaulin Muster* (British Library, Add. Ms. 47897, f. 13). Of this story Masefield notes it was based on 'actual reminiscence'.

1. *orts*: Worthless odds and ends (in Herefordshire dialect).
2. *'where the golden blossoms burn upon the trees for ever'*: I have been unable to find the exact source of this quotation, although there is more than a passing connection to a passage in Pindar's second *Olympian Ode*. Masefield, it seems, was fond of it, however. In his introduction to *The Travels of Marco Polo* (London: J. M. Dent, 1907) he writes that 'Columbus . . . half expected to sight land "where the golden blossoms burn upon the trees forever".'
3. *Doldrums*: Nautical term for the region near the Equator in which winds are light and variable.
4. *cirrus*: A form of wispy white cloud, especially at high altitude.

Ghosts

First published in the *Manchester Guardian*, 5 November 1906. Present as the seventh story in *A Tarpaulin Muster* (London: Grant Richards, 1907). In a letter to Harley Granville Barker, dated 30 March

1907, Masefield revealed his sources for the contents of *A Tarpaulin Muster* (British Library, Add. Ms. 47897, f. 13). Of this story Masefield notes it was based on 'reminiscence and sailor's gossip'.

1.   *wirrim*: Probably a phonetic rendering of 'worm'.
2.   *Plate*: River Plate, the widest estuary in the world, formed by the Uruguay and Parana rivers on the south-east coast of South America.
3.   *East Indiaman*: A large ship of the various East India companies, generally as large as any built, with carved embellishments and highly gilded.

Big Jim

First published in the *Manchester Guardian*, 22 January 1907. Present as the third story in *A Tarpaulin Muster* (London: Grant Richards, 1907). In a letter to Harley Granville Barker, dated 30 March 1907, Masefield revealed his sources for the contents of *A Tarpaulin Muster* (British Library, Add. Ms. 47897, f. 13). Of this story Masefield notes it was 'a mixture of dream, fact and invention'.

1.   *vaquero*: Spanish for 'cowboy'.
2.   *quadroon*: A person with one grandparent of dark skin.
3.   *Horn*: Cape Horn, at the tip of South America, considered one of the most dangerous navigation routes.
4.   *lanchero*: Spanish word for a boatman.
5.   *skins*: Containers for liquid, made from animal skin.
6.   *muleteers*: Drivers of mules.

El Dorado

First published in *Macmillan's Magazine*, February 1907, as 'The Gold-Seeker'. Present as the fourth story in *A Tarpaulin Muster* (London: Grant Richards, 1907). In a letter to Harley Granville Barker, dated 30 March 1907, Masefield revealed his sources for the contents of *A Tarpaulin Muster* (see British Library, Add. Ms. 47897, f. 13). Of this story Masefield notes it was 'mostly invention, based on fact, and on a story a sailor told me'.

1.   *El Dorado*: A South American city or country which, in legend, is rich in gold.
2.   *Negra*: Evidently a lighthouse on the west coast of South America.
3.   *Calle del Inca*: A specific street name ('the street of the Inca').
4.   *Dago*: Pejorative term for a foreigner, especially a Spaniard, Portuguese or Italian.

5. *outliers*: The outlying parts.
6. *Santiago*: The capital city of Chile.
7. *Tacna*: City in southern Peru, on the border with Chile and inland from the Pacific Ocean.
8. *Valparaiso*: See note 1 to 'The Yarn of Lanky Job' above.
9. *derringer*: Small large-bore pistol (after the American inventor H. Deringer).
10. *Mollendo*: Town bordering the Pacific Ocean in southern Peru.
11. *Payta . . . Marinha*: Payta is a seaport city in north-west Peru, also known as 'Paita'; 'Chito' would appear to be Quito, the capital city of Ecuador; the Morona River flows from Ecuador into the Amazon in Peru – the most western of the rivers mentioned here by the character Paul Bac; while 'Marinha' is presumably Marinilla, a town in Colombia.
12. *ze Caqueta and ze Putumayo Rivers*: The Caqueta rises in the Andes in Colombia. It flows into Brazil, where it is called the 'Japurà', and enters the Amazon. The Putumayo is a tributary of the Amazon bordering Colombia with Ecuador and then Peru. It runs west of and parallel to the Caqueta.
13. *puro bush*: 'Puro' was a common name for tobacco. In addition to its common use, tobacco also has preservative properties.
14. *ambitious*: Slang, used on the *Conway*, defined by Masefield as 'zealous, with a view to personal advantage; also foolishly zealous, asking for more work, etc., etc.' (*The Conway*). (See also 'Ambitious Jimmy Hicks' in this volume.)
15. *lunk*: A slow-witted person. The *Oxford English Dictionary* suggests the word to be of American origin.

The Western Islands

First published in the *Pall Mall Magazine*, December 1907. Present as the eighth story in the revised *A Mainsail Haul* (London: Elkin Mathews, 1913).

1. '*Once there were two sailors . . .*': The yarn, as first printed in the *Pall Mall Magazine*, begins with a paragraph subsequently deleted. It reads:

    In New York City there is the most wonderful street in the world. It runs along the beach, or edge, of Manhattan Island. On one side of it you have the ships, with their bows pointing at you. On the other side of it there is a long row of shops, mostly liquor-shops, where you can get great 'schooners' of lager for your five-cent piece or 'nickel'. When you come out of a saloon, you kick your feet against the lintel, to free your boots of the sawdust of the floor. As you pause to do this, you see the bows of the ships, with their names in gold above the hawseholes, and beyond them you see the bay, with the sun upon it; and if ever a sight makes you sick to be ashore, the sight of that bay, in the sunshine, is the one. In the summer there you get prickly heat all over you, and within you a thirst for lager, such as nothing but a schooner will allay. I used to go down to this street in the summer evenings, for it was cooler there, near the sea, than in the avenues. And I used to long to be at sea, in one of the ships at the wharf; yet I had always just sufficient sense to stick ashore, at the work I was doing. There was a barque I used to go aboard. Her name was the *Pactolus*, but the 'P' had been broken off her bows, and everybody called her the *Actolus*. She was a wooden vessel, American owned. I knew her caretaker very well. He was an old Liverpool sailor. He used to tell me strange yarns, as we smoked together, in the little caboose or galley. He told me this one.

2. *sarsaparilla*: A preparation of the dried roots of various plants used as a flavouring for some drinks and medicines. Once used as a tonic.

3. *twist*: Tobacco stored in twists of paper.

4. *Limehouse Basin*: A link between the Thames and Regent's Canal and used by ships when offloading cargo to barges.

5. *Dago*: Pejorative term for a foreigner, especially a Spaniard, Portuguese or Italian.

6. *Kanaka*: South Sea Islander, especially one formerly employed in forced labour in Australia.

7. *buzz-saw*: Circular saw.

8. *Port Mahon soldier*: Presumably a version of 'Port Mahon Soger' (see note 2 to 'Cape Horn Gospel – I'). This term, together with 'Port Mahon Baboon', is included in the Glossary for *Salt-Water Ballads*. Masefield states:

> I have been unable to discover either the origin of these insulting epithets or the reasons for the peculiar bitterness with which they sting the marine recipient. They are older than Dana (*circa* 1840).
>
> An old merchant sailor, now dead, once told me that Port Mahon was that godless city from which the Ark set sail, in which case the name may have some traditional connection with that evil 'Mahoun' or 'Mahu', prince of darkness, mentioned by Shakespeare and some of our older poets.
>
> The real Port Mahon, a fine harbour in Minorca, was taken by the French, from Admiral Byng, in the year 1756.

I think that the phrases originated at the time of Byng's conse-
quent trial and execution.

9.   *turned old Mother Bomby's beer*: Some Elizabethan dramatists
     refer to Mother Bomby as a fortune-teller or witch. William
     Hazlitt noted of John Lyly's play *Mother Bombie* (published in
     1585) that it was 'very much what its name would import, old,
     quaint, and vulgar'. John Gerard in his *Herbal* (1597) makes
     reference to 'Mother Bombies rules'. Masefield, in *The Bird of
     Dawning*, gives Coates the recollection of 'a chop and chow
     joint' in Pagoda called Mother Bomby's 'where the reefers
     went'.
10. *drowned the duck and stole the monkey*: Probably an expression
     signifying idiotic behaviour. Given a choice between a duck and
     a monkey, the first was presumably considered edible while the
     second was a more accomplished thief. Origin unknown.

OTHER PROSE

Autobiography

Hitherto unpublished and adapted from the author's original manu-
script in five quarto notebooks (private collection). The title is editorial.
There are many pages (or segments of pages) which have been pasted
in and these suggest that Masefield carefully revised several sections.
The account of the voyage is incomplete, however, and Masefield sud-
denly abandons his narrative to provide daily reports under date
headings. I have chosen to present, here, the majority of the text before
Masefield's change in style. The original manuscript is lightly punctu-
ated and I have added punctuation where necessary.

1.   *Tulip*: See note 6 below.
2.   *River Plate*: The widest estuary in the world, formed by the
     Uruguay and Parana rivers on the south-east coast of South
     America.
3.   *Jan*: Masefield's nickname, later reserved only for family and
     close friends.
4.   *Chris*: See note 6 below.
5.   *Hart*: See next note.
6.   *six lads*: Masefield names Tulip, Sandy, Hart, Chris and McLure
     as his companions in the half-deck. The 1894 *Gilcruix* crew list
     cites John E. Masefield (aged fifteen), George S. Christopher
     (aged seventeen), Hamilton Hely (aged seventeen), Robert Shaw

(aged sixteen) and Cyril A. Connorton (aged seventeen), all engaged in the capacity of 'boys' and straight from HMS *Conway*. The final member of the apprentices' berth appears to be Samuel B. Hurst (aged nineteen), who is the only entry in the 'Account of Apprentices on Board' (National Archives, BT.100/98B).

7. *cutties*: From 'cutty pipe', a short tobacco pipe.

8. *Captain Marryat, Captain Chamier*: Captain Frederick Marryat (1792–1848), novelist (see 'The Sea Writers: Captain Frederick Marryat' in this volume), and Captain Frederick Chamier (1796–1870), naval captain and novelist.

9. *Huckleberry Finn*: Judith Masefield, in 'Some Memories of John Masefield' ('Introduction' to Corliss Lamont, *Remembering John Masefield* (London: Kaye & Ward, 1972)), notes Mark Twain's novel as one of her father's favourite books. Writing to Cyril Clemens (1902–99), a cousin of Mark Twain's, in September 1965 (Columbia University (Ms/Masefield)), Masefield stated:

> I call *Huckleberry Finn* more than a novel. It is like a story by Dickens but by a younger and more rousing man than Dickens, from a younger and more rousing society. The sense of the River and of the wild and generous souls near it, makes the book unique; there is nothing like it, and all must bow down to it.

10. *the Laws of Storms*: J. Macnab's *Catechism of the Law of Storms* (first published in 1884).

11. *wooden kid*: Defined in 'A Steerage Steward' as a wooden half-tub, in which food was served.

12. *Tiger Bay*: The name for the general area around Cardiff Docks and Butetown. Murders and red-light districts contributed to a dangerous reputation.

13. *Little Billy*: The 1894 *Gilcruix* crew list names G. M. Dixon (aged thirty-nine), from Hastings, as the captain of the ship (National Archives, BT.100/98B). He is renamed William Diggory for this narrative.

14. *Pyecroft*: Pyecroft is later identified as the second mate. Masefield's original text, however, names Pickford at this point and therefore the crew member's actual name. George F. Pickford is listed on the 1894 *Gilcruix* list as aged twenty-three.

15. *'all standing'*: A term for a fully rigged ship and, by extension, used of a person fully dressed.

16. *'dropping – a murmurous dropping ... that one sound'*: See Yeats's 'The Wanderings of Oisin' (1889), in which, in Book III, appears the line 'Dropping; a murmurous dropping; old silence and that one sound'.

17. *water-clock*: A clock which measures time by the flow of water.
18. *tam o' shanter and a rough blue shirt of serge*: James wears a cloth or woollen cap of Scottish origin in addition to a shirt made from a twilled and durable fabric.
19. *'McGilligan'*: See note 4 to 'In Dock – I' above.
20. *'Sam Hall'*: See note 5 to 'In Dock – I' above
21. *Thackeray . . . and in a later day, Mr Kipling also*: 'Sam Hall', as adapted by the singer C.W. Ross, is presented as the song of 'The Body Snatcher' sung by Mr Hodgen in Chapter 30 of Thackeray's *Pendennis* (1848–50). In a letter to the Reverend William Brookfield, from October 1848, Thackeray notes: 'I have been to the Cyder Cellars since again to hear the man sing about going to be hanged' (see Gordon N. Ray (ed.), *The Letters and Private Papers of William Makepeace Thackeray*, Vol. 2 (London: Oxford University Press, 1945), p. 442). Kipling makes reference to the song in his story 'The Mutiny of the Mavericks', published within *Life's Handicap* (London: Macmillan, 1891).
22. *Barnum Bailey freak*: Circus freak, after Phineas Taylor Barnum (1810–91) and James Anthony Bailey (1847–1906), the American circus partners.
23. *'Spanish Ladies'*: See note 6 to 'In Dock – I' above.
24. *'Sailor's Wives'*: See note 9 to 'The Cape Horn Calm' above.
25. *seven years back*: This would suggest that Masefield first started this narrative in 1901. On the inside of the upper cover of one notebook he provides a postal address, which indicates that Masefield was still working on the text during 1903.
26. *blackguard jests*: Lewd jokes.
27. *cuspidor*: A spittoon.
28. *'Rolling Home'*: See references within 'The Cape Horn Calm'. Stan Hugill refers to the song as 'the most famous homeward-bound song of them all' (see Roy Palmer, *Boxing the Compass* (Todmorden: Herron Publishing, 2001), p. 243). Writing of 'Rolling Home' in his article 'Sea-Songs', Masefield noted that 'I think that on the whole it has given me more pleasure than any song I have ever heard' (see *Temple Bar*, January 1906, p. 79).
29. *Mary Street*: St Mary Street was a major street in Cardiff on which a large number of pubs and hotels were located.
30. *Mr Jackson*: The third mate can be identified as George W. Baxter (aged twenty), in the 1894 *Gilcruix* crew list.
31. *'It was time for us to leave her'*: Adapted from the chanty 'Leave her, Johnny' with the first line 'Oh the times was hard and the

wages low'. Roy Palmer in *Boxing the Compass* (Todmorden: Herron Publishing, 2001) notes it was sung at the end of a voyage. The correct line is 'And it's time for us to leave her'.

32. *Horn*: Cape Horn, at the tip of South America, considered one of the most dangerous navigation routes.

33. *Hogarth's Marriage à la Mode*: William Hogarth's series of six paintings and engravings from around 1743. Scene two ('The Tête à Tête') shows the Lord and Lady seated on either side of a fireplace, the Lady stretching sleepily and the Lord slumped as if exhausted.

34. *Khitmutgar*: An Indian male servant who waits at table.

35. *get*: Offspring.

36. *vitriol*: Sulphuric acid.

37. *sarcasm*: This would suggest that the second mate may be an inspiration for Masefield's character of Sard Harker. In Masefield's novel of that name (London: Heinemann, 1924) it is explained that 'he was called "Sard" Harker (though seldom to his face) because he was judged to be sardonic.'

38. *colicky till next duff-day*: Literally to have pains in the stomach until the next occasion duff, a flour pudding boiled in a bag, is served.

39. *bluchers*: Heavy-duty leather half-boots, named after Gebhard von Blücher (1742–1819), the Prussian general who fought alongside the Duke of Wellington at the Battle of Waterloo.

40. *'Cairngorm'*: See note 1 to 'In Dock – I' above.

41. *mutton chop whiskers*: Facial hair with a narrow top at the ears, then wide and rounded towards the chin. The chin itself is clean shaven.

42. *exciter*: A volume likely to produce excitement.

43. *Mauleverer's Millions*: The novel *Mauleverer's Millions: a Yorkshire Romance* by Sir Thomas Wemyss Reid (1842–1905) was first published in 1886. The copy in the British Library suggests it was first issued in blue wrappers, priced at one shilling.

44. *quid . . . of sweet-cake*: A small lump of tobacco.

45. *pell mell*: In a disorderly or confused fashion.

46. *painter*: Pre-dating Masefield's short story 'In the Roost' (included in this volume), this is Masefield's earliest traced reference to his tale of a painter that would become *Dauber* (see the Introduction, pp. xix and xxx). It demonstrates that 'Autobiography' is not strictly autobiographical since the ill-fated painter was not on board the *Gilcruix*.

47. *supernumerary berth*: A berth in excess of the regular number.

48. *red-lead*: A red oxide of lead, used as a pigment.

49. *neither fish, flesh nor good red herring*: Proverbial expression
     meaning 'fit for neither one thing nor another'.

50. *Mr Dalloch*: The mate can be identified as M. Bullock (aged
     twenty-eight), in the 1894 *Gilcruix* crew list.

51. *Cockle's Little Liver Pills*: Presumably Masefield's rendering of
     'Carter's Little Liver Pills'. These pills, first produced by Samuel
     Carter in 1868, were frequently advertised 'for a sick stomach
     and headache'. They contained Bisacodyl, known as a laxative,
     and the result of taking more than the recommended dose would
     surely have taken the third mate's mind off a hangover.

52. *clouts*: Pieces (of cloth).

53. *Rachel that would not be comforted*: The favourite wife of Jacob
     in the Old Testament, known for weeping for her children. See
     Matthew 2: 18.

54. *rubbed left-handed*: Presumably a variant of being rubbed up the
     wrong way.

55. *four-wheeler*: A four-wheeled hackney carriage.

56. *'All the birds of the air . . . Down to the O-hi-O!'*: This song
     incorporates, or is based on, the English nursery rhyme 'Who
     Killed Cock Robin'.

57. *spell-oh*: A rest. Masefield includes the term 'spello' in his 'Gloss-
     ary of *Conway* Slang' as 'allotted work, or a rest from same'
     (*The Conway*).

58. *Meteorological*: The 1893 Meteorological Prize on the *Conway*
     was awarded to James Ewart Kershaw. He achieved 94 per cent
     in his exam and was presented with an aneroid barometer.

59. *old chief*: Here, the captain of the *Conway*, Lieutenant A. T.
     ('Lippy') Miller, RN. He was captain from 1881 and died in his
     cabin in 1903.

60. *yellow-jack*: Also known as 'yellow fever', a viral disease trans-
     mitted by mosquitoes.

61. *gar'd*: Presumably connected with 'gar', used in oaths, as a cor-
     ruption of 'God', or from 'gared' (in Scottish or Northern dialect),
     meaning to cause, compel or make.

62. *William Allingham's poem on 'Autumn'*: The 'Autumnal Sonnet'
     by William Allingham (1824–89) begins: 'Now Autumn's fire
     burns slowly along the woods'. It was first published in *Flower
     Pieces* in 1888.

63. *'My Lost Youth'*: Henry Longfellow (1807–82) published 'My
     Lost Youth' in 1855. It begins 'Often I think of the beautiful town'
     and was collected in *The Courtship of Miles Standish* in 1858.

64. *'Strike the bell, second mate . . . strike the bell*': 'Strike the Bell'

was a sailors' song, popular in the latter part of the nineteenth
century. Roy Palmer notes within *Boxing the Compass* (Todmor-
den: Herron Publishing, 2001) that is was based on Henry Clay
Work's 'Ring the Bell, Watchman', written to salute the end of
the American Civil War (1861–5).

65.   *playing old harry*: Playing the devil.
66.   *staggers*: A disease in animals affecting the brain and spinal cord,
marked by confusion and staggering.
67.   *'She was round in the counter and bluff in the bow'*: From the
third stanza of the chanty 'Blow the Man Down'.
68.   *Mother Carey*: See 'Mother Carey' in this volume. The supernat-
ural figure personifies the cruelty of the sea.
69.   *Soupe Julienne*: A type of vegetable soup.
70.   *splashed*: Evidently slang for 'drunk', origin unknown.
71.   *donkey's breakfasts*: Bundles of straw used for bedding. Later
used as a term for straw mattresses.
72.   *limber*: Supple and nimble.
73.   *Pisagua*: A 'nitrate' port in the Iquique region of Chile. For more
on this, see note 2 to 'In Dock – II' above.
74.   *'A Sailorman . . . right good Stockhollum Tar'*: See note 3 to
'Port of Many Ships' above.
75.   *wrack*: Seaweed and other rubbish in the dock.
76.   *working porter*: Fermenting black or dark brown beer, bitter in
flavour.
77.   *boarding house runners*: Those employed to solicit custom for a
boarding house.
78.   *lumpers . . . stevedores, ship's husbands, crimps*: Lumpers are
employed to load and unload cargoes; stevedores usually oversee
lumpers; ship's husbands are agents who attend to the require-
ments of a ship while in port, usually relating to stores, repairs
and equipment; and crimps are procurers of seamen by doubtful
means not recognized by the Board of Trade.
79.   *Pier Head*: Location in Cardiff at the end of Bute Street and com-
manding a view of the entrances to both West and East Bute
Docks.
80.   *blue water*: The open sea.
81.   *a deserted —* : In Masefield's manuscript he chooses to omit a
word and merely leaves a space.
82.   *Hail Columbia*: Evidently intended as a reference to the second mate
in offensive terms. He is presumably to be regarded as self-import-
ant or domineering, hence the reference to the unofficial national
anthem of the United States. Masefield's early writing, prior to the
First World War, is frequently critical of America and Americans.

83. *'Cow and Calf'*: An unidentified position, presumably comprising two rocks of different sizes.

84. *give us a breeze*: Give us a rest.

85. *George's Docks*: A dock within the Port of Liverpool, opened in 1771. The dock was filled in during 1899.

86. *'riches fineless'*: *Othello*, Act III, scene iii.

87. *Davy's sow*: From the expression 'as drunk as David's sow', meaning an advanced state of drunkenness.

88. *tarpaulin muster*: The pooling or collection of money by seamen (especially to buy liquor). Money was thrown on to a tarpaulin. Masefield's second collection of short stories was published as *A Tarpaulin Muster* in 1907.

89. *Errol*: Apparently an unrecorded nickname for Masefield during this voyage.

90. *'looked on ye water'*: The ninth line of the Prologue to William Langland's *The Vision of Piers Plowman* (*c*.1360–87) reads: 'And as I lay and lenede and loked on the watres'.

91. *'Ha Ha! Come roll him over'*: From the chanty entitled 'One More Day' that begins 'Only one more day, me Johnnies'.

92. *ramify*: Separate into related or component parts.

93. *never fetch to port*: Here, meaning 'never end'.

94. *Stag Light*: Possibly slang for 'Hartland Point', a lighthouse off the coast of north Devon. Another possibility is that Masefield uses the unofficial term given to isolated lighthouses in the United States Lighthouse Service. The term was applied to stations so remote that only a bachelor, or 'stag', would be assigned to them.

95. *Hurrah for Joseph*: See note 5 to 'The Devil and the Deep Sea' above.

96. *'Oh whisky is de life of man'*: Masefield included the chanty 'Whiskey! Johnny!' in *A Sailor's Garland* (London: Methuen, 1906). The first line is given as 'O whiskey is the life of man'.

97. *'The fores'l for lifting . . . steer wild'*: A few lines from the penultimate stanza of 'The North Country Collier', which commences: 'At the head of Wear Water, about twelve at noon'. Masefield included the verse in *A Sailor's Garland* (London: Methuen, 1906).

98. *François Villon*: (1431– after 1463), the fifteenth-century French poet and vagabond is often represented by a woodcut in the 1489 edition of *Grand Testament de Maistre François Villon* in which one hand is close to, but not tucked into, his girdle.

99. *St Cecilia*: The patron saint of musicians and church music who, when being put to death, raised her head and sang to God.

100. *maundered*: Muttered.

101. *diary*: Masefield's manuscript diary from this voyage is preserved in the Berg Collection, New York Public Library. In March 1910 Masefield sent it to Elizabeth Robins together with a letter:

> . . . You asked me if I ever kept a diary. Yes, dear. I did once, sixteen years ago, for a few days. Bad weather off the Horn brought it to an end untimely. But here it is, dear. The only relic of my sea days, I do verily believe. It was with me round the Horn, and in hospital in Chile; it has been in a ship's half-deck, and in a London attic . . .

The volume comprises a Letts 'Rough Diary' with one week per opening. The entries run from 4 April through to 30 June 1894 and a number of page openings still have flakes of tobacco in the gutter. The diary of a fifteen-year-old tells a different tale from this 'autobiography' and Masefield exhibits a less mature grasp of language. On seasickness, for example, the entry for 25 April concludes:

> . . . Was sick while passing Bull Point and felt very ill indeed until I went below about 9 p.m. Coming on deck at 12 p.m. I took the poop watch and was very sick all the watch. Captain and the mate were very kind. We set sail about 12 and the tug then left us. Was very glad to get below again.

102. *burgoo*: A term for oatmeal porridge in use from the early eighteenth century.

103. *yellow-back*: From cheaply produced novels bound in yellow wrappers and later meaning any cheaply issued or reprinted novel.

104. *Rule o' the Road*: A highway code for the sea comprising a set of rules governing the conduct of vessels at sea in order to avoid collisions.

105. *churchwarden*: A clay pipe with a very long stem.

106. *Spica's Spanker*: The four principal stars within the Corvus constellation.

107. *chum*: To be on friendly terms. First-term boys on HMS *Conway* were called 'new chums' and Masefield's account of this period of his life was published as *New Chum* (London: William Heinemann, 1944).

108. *poops*: Watches on the poop deck.

109. *ambitious*: Slang, used on the *Conway*, defined by Masefield as 'zealous, with a view to personal advantage; also foolishly zealous, asking for more work, etc., etc.' (*The Conway*). (See also 'Ambitious Jimmy Hicks' in this volume.)

110. *Line*: Equator.

111. *work a meridian*: Part of calculating a ship's position at sea. Meridians are lines of longitude. When the sun crosses an observer's meridian, the local time is noon. Time was, of course, vital for calculating the position of a ship.

112. *ambi*: See 'ambitious' in note 109 above.

113. *twopenny Dread*: A cheap thriller.

114. *'nat all asleep ne fully waking'*: From 'The Cuckoo and the Nightingale', once attributed to Geoffrey Chaucer.

115. *'an hideous noise and a ghastful'*: Probably a variation on 'a ruthful noise and ghastful' (referring to the noise made by fighting cats) in *De Proprietatibus Rerum* ('On the Properties of Things') by the thirteenth-century monk Bartholomew the Englishman.

116. *whang*: Violently throw.

117. *Captain Gray's rhymes*: A reference to Thomas Gray, of the Board of Trade (see also next note), and his *Rule of the Road ... with Aids to Memory in Four Verses* (London: J. D. Potter, 1867). The work provided steering and sailing rules together with verses, for example:

> Meeting Steamers do not dread
> When you see three Lights ahead –
> Port your helm, and show your RED.

This single-leaf work was expanded in 1878 into a pamphlet, *Observations on the Rule of the Road at Sea*, and enjoyed numerous reprints. Gray's contributions to marine poetry would also be reprinted within other texts. W. R. Williams in his *Practical Hints and Suggestions for the Young Fisherman* (Hull: Edwin Ombler, 1896) included, for example, Gray's 'Aids to Memory (in four verses)' at the conclusion of the volume.

118. *Board of Trade prose*: The Board of Trade issued regulations governing shipping, conditions aboard ships, etc. Their prose was heavy and bureaucratic. For a text-book on the subject of Board of Trade regulations, including extracts from various Shipping Acts, I can recommend David Wright Smith's *The Law Relating to the Rule of the Road at Sea* (Glasgow: James Brown and Son, 1910) as a volume of soporific splendour.

119. *spoke*: Here, signalled.

120. *a little steamer, the Arabesque, of London, bound home*: In Masefield's manuscript diary the incident with the 'little steamer' appears to have occurred on 29 April:

Sighted and spoke a steamship, the *Arabian Prince* of North Shields, at about 7.30. We shall be reported in the papers in a week or less. No work in particular to do but was passed as a sort of holiday . . .

121. *speak*: Here, to signal.

122. *counter-jumpers*: Draper's assistants, who jumped over the counter in their eagerness to serve customers. The term therefore carried the insult of one who was obsequious and fawning.

123. *spitting brown*: Chewing tobacco.

124. *quid*: Here a shortened version of 'quidding' or chewing (and spitting) tobacco.

125. *'In Amsterdam . . . what I do say'*: From the chanty 'The Maid of Amsterdam'.

126. *chequers*: The game of draughts. This sailor evidently doesn't know the difference between draughts and chess.

127. *'Abel Brown'*: The chanty 'Abel Brown the Sailor'. The name Abel Brown probably signifies 'A.B.', the abbreviation for 'able seaman'.

128. *'As I was a going'*: Untraced, and a phrase that occurs in a vast number of songs.

129. *'We want a man like good Sir Robert Peel'*: Possibly the song 'Sir Robert Peel', which begins 'In the pleasant month of May, 'twas in the year thirty-eight'.

130. *Lord Charles Beresford*: (1846–1919) British admiral and Member of Parliament, later 1st Baron Beresford.

131. *Alexandria*: During the Egyptian war of 1882, part of the Urabi Revolt, Beresford was captain of HMS *Condor* and took part in the bombardment of Alexandria. He earned considerable fame for taking his ship further inshore to bombard at closer range.

Deep Sea Yarns

First published, and sole appearance, in *The Speaker*, 31 January 1903.

1. *Ghilan*: The Persian province of Ghilan produced fine silk in large quantities.

2. *missal-marge*: Derived from 'missal', a book containing the service of the Mass for an entire year; 'missal-marge' is here intended to indicate an extravagant volume. Robert Browning includes 'his lady's missal-marge with flowerets' in *Men and Women* (1855).

On the Sea and Sailors

First published, and sole appearance, in the *Academy and Literature*,
25 July 1903.

1. *his poem*: Samuel Taylor Coleridge's 'The Rime of the Ancient
   Mariner' was first published within *Lyrical Ballads* in 1798.
2. *a rare Dog . . . without any after-thought or Reflexion*: From *The
   Wooden World Dissected* (1706) by the satirist Edward Ward
   (1667–1731). Masefield quotes, presumably from memory, from
   part fourteen, entitled 'A Sailor'. The sentence first quoted actu-
   ally begins: 'His Thoughts reach not much above the
   top-mast-head . . .'
3. *Marryat*: Captain Frederick Marryat (1792–1848), novelist (see
   'The Sea Writers: Captain Frederick Marryat' in this volume).
4. *Dana*: Richard Henry Dana (1815–82), American lawyer and
   politician (see 'The Sea Writers: R. H. Dana' in this volume).
5. *Scott*: Presumably, given the epithet, Sir Walter Scott (1771–
   1832). Masefield was, however, an admirer of Duncan Campbell
   Scott (1862–1947), who, by the time this article was written,
   had published two volumes of poetry. Masefield includes work
   by Duncan Campbell Scott but not Sir Walter Scott in his anthol-
   ogy *A Sailor's Garland* (London: Methuen, 1906).
6. *Falconer*: William Falconer (1732–69) published *The Shipwreck*
   in 1762. It contains the couplet 'And he who strives the tempest
   to disarm, / Will never first embrail the lee-yard arm'. Masefield
   includes a section of *The Shipwreck*, incorporating the couplet,
   in *A Sailor's Garland*.
7. *Dibdin*: Charles Dibdin (1745–1814), dramatist and song writer,
   wrote numerous nautical songs, including 'Tom Bowling'.
8. *The Ways of Many Waters*: First published by the Bulletin News-
   paper Company of Sydney in 1899.
9. *Adam Gordon*: The poet Adam Lindsay Gordon (1833–70) pub-
   lished *Sea Spray and Smoke Drift* in 1867. Masefield does not
   include any of his work in *A Sailor's Garland*.
10. *Kingsley*: Better known as a novelist, Charles Kingsley (1819–
    75) is represented in *A Sailor's Garland*.
11. *Macaulay*: The historian, poet and essayist Thomas Babington
    Macaulay (1800–1859) is represented in *A Sailor's Garland*.
12. *stevedore*: An overseer of one employed to load and unload car-
    goes.
13. *May you never be a syler . . . ever be content*: The verse is from

the poem 'Sailor-Man' and Masefield quotes, presumably from memory, rendering some of Brady's contracted words in full. The text from Brady's 1899 edition is as follows:

> May y'u never be a syler of the mercantile marine,
> Or y'u 'll always be a syler, an' y'u 'll never 'ave a bean ...
>
> But it's round the world a-goin,
> With the ebbin' an' the flowin',
> An' y'u need n't fear the bailiff, an' y'u need n't pay no rent;
> There 's a month or two at sea,
> Then a rattlin' roarin' spree ...
> *An' I dunno if I left it that I'd ever be content!*

14. *blue-jacket*: A seaman in the navy.
15. *tunnies*: From 'tunny-fishes', alternative name for tuna fish.

The Rose of Spain

First published, and sole appearance, in *The Speaker*, 14 November 1903.

1. *spinet*: A musical instrument similar to the harpsichord only with one string per key. Masefield, it seems, was fond of the name and included 'A withered wire, / Moves a thin ghost of music in the spinet' in his poem 'On Growing Old' (1920).
2. *five-angled star*: The five-angled star, or pentagram, is a symbol of mystical and magical significance.
3. *'and when it is gone we are dead'*: A line from Yeats's poem 'The Blessed' (first published in 1897 within *The Yellow Book* and collected by the author within *The Wind Among the Reeds* in 1899).
4. *dominant in a fugue*: A fugue, a type of contrapuntal musical construction, begins with a statement of the subject in the tonic (or primary) key. This is followed by the entry of a second voice providing the subject transposed to another key, which is usually the dominant. This is known as the answer. Since the Baroque era in music the construction of fugues has been seen as evidence of compositional expertise.
5. *Mr F. M. Hueffer*: Ford Madox Ford (1873–1939), author and editor.
6. *burin*: A sharp implement used to engrave.

The Sea Writers
Captain Frederick Marryat

First published, and sole appearance, as 'The Salt Winds of the Sea', in the *Daily News*, 12 August 1904. This, the first of nine previously unknown articles on sea writers, was a review of new editions of *Peter Simple* and *Mr Midshipman Easy* with introductions by W. Clark Russell. It was not until the second article that Masefield appears to have retrospectively decided his article on Marryat was the first in the series. I omit here the final paragraph which makes reference to the W. Clark Russell editions.

1.   *Huguenot stock*: French Protestant stock.
2.   *Lord Cochrane*: Admiral Thomas Cochrane, 10th Earl of Dundonald (1775–1860), the British naval flag officer and politician.
3.   *Fort of Rosas*: Spanish fort in Catalonia.
4.   *Walcheren*: An island in the Netherlands. During the Napoleonic Wars the Walcheren Campaign of 1809 was a disaster.
5.   *Sir Samuel Hood*: Vice-Admiral Sir Samuel Hood, 1st Baronet (1762–1814), officer of the Royal Navy.
6.   *Captain E. P. Brenton*: Captain Edward Pelham Brenton (1774–1839), officer of the Royal Navy.
7.   *C.B.*: Companion of the Order of the Bath.
8.   *Kernes*: From the poorer class of the 'wild Irish'.
9.   *King William*: William IV (1765–1837), who had served in the Royal Navy in his youth.
10. *Legion of Honour*: The *Légion d'honneur*, the highest decoration in France, awarded for distinguished civil or military conduct.
11. *'silly Tom Campbell'*: Thomas Campbell (1777–1844), the Scottish poet.
12. *Metropolitan Magazine*: Founded by Thomas Campbell as *The Metropolitan* in 1831, the periodical became the *Metropolitan Magazine* in 1833. It ceased publication in 1850.
13. *Smollett*: Tobias Smollett (1721–71), the Scottish novelist and one-time naval surgeon.
14. *sailed for the Baltic in 1854*: The Baltic campaign of the 1853–6 Crimean War.
15. *'a man-of-war, like a gallows, refused nothing'*: Probably an expression, rather than a quotation. Masefield used the phrase

again when describing press-gangs in *Sea Life in Nelson's Time* (London: Methuen, 1905), p. 53.

16. *Sir Hurricane . . . Mr Oxbelly*: Sir Hurricane Humbug is a character within *Frank Mildmay* while Lieutenant Oxbelly is second in command of the *Rebiera* in *Mr Midshipman Easy*. He is described as having 'an uncommon protuberance of stomach'.

17. *bumboat wenches*: Women who sold their wares from bumboats, the vessels that conveyed provisions to ships which were lying off port. The most famous example of a bumboat wench is Little Buttercup in Gilbert and Sullivan's *HMS Pinafore*.

18. *little pinched middies*: Midshipmen wearing loose blouses with a sailor collar.

19. *Captain Wilson or Mr Sawbridge*: Captain Wilson, described as 'a sort of cousin to the [Easy] family', is a character in *Mr Midshipman Easy*; Mr Sawbridge is, initially, the first lieutenant of the *Harpy* in *Mr Midshipman Easy*.

20. *'the music of the thing that happened'*: Untraced.

21. *Mr Biggs*: Mr Biggs is boatswain aboard the *Harpy* in *Mr Midshipman Easy*.

22. *out of soundings*: Taking a sounding is to measure the depth of water; therefore a ship 'out of soundings' is in deep water.

23. *Mr Coleridge*: S. T. Coleridge does not appear to use this exact phrase. It is surely Masefield's rendering of one of Coleridge's ideas on poetic diction. The 1798 'advertisement' to *Lyrical Ballads* noted that 'the author [of "The Rime of the Ancyent Marinere"] believes that the language adopted in it has been equally intelligible for these three last centuries.' The rejection of contemporary literary diction was, of course, part of the creation of *Lyrical Ballads*, although Coleridge was to attack 'low and rustic life' (and, by association, low and rustic language) as a source of poetic idiom in his *Biographia Literaria* (1817).

Herman Melville

First published, and sole appearance, in the *Daily News*, 20 August 1904.

1. *Empire City*: An early nineteenth-century name for New York City.

2. *St Nicholas Church*: The Church of Our Lady and Saint Nicholas in Liverpool is known, locally, as the 'Sailor's Church'.

3. *Bidston Tower*: Bidston is in the centre of Birkenhead on the Wirral. There are three landmarks visible from a distance: the

windmill, the observatory and the lighthouse. Masefield refers to either the windmill (the present 'tower mill' was built around 1800) or the lighthouse (the first Bidston lighthouse was in operation 1771–1872). The observatory was built in 1866 and is, therefore, too modern for an engraving from Melville's youth.

4.   *Dana*: Richard Henry Dana (1815–82), American lawyer and politician (see 'The Sea Writers: R. H. Dana' in this volume).

5.   *Horn*: Cape Horn, at the tip of South America, considered one of the most dangerous navigation routes.

6.   *'Down-East Johnny-Cake'*: 'Johnny-Cake' is a cornmeal flatbread. The expression originates from R. H. Dana's *Two Years Before the Mast* (1840) in which the captain of the *Pilgrim* states in Chapter 8:

> I'm Frank Thompson, all the way from 'down east'. I've been through the mill, ground, and bolted, and come out a regular-built down-east johnny-cake, good when it's hot, but when it's cold, sour and indigestible; – and you'll find me so!

7.   *Borrow*: George Henry Borrow (1803–81), author of *Lavengro* (1851).

8.   *Crome*: John Crome (1768–1821), the artist from Norwich known as 'Old Crome'.

9.   *Marryat, nor Chamier, nor Lord Dundonald*: Captain Frederick Marryat (1792–1848), novelist (see 'The Sea Writers: Captain Frederick Marryat' in this volume); Frederick Chamier (1796–1870), naval captain and novelist; and Admiral Thomas Cochrane, 10th Earl of Dundonald (1775–1860), the British naval flag officer and politician who wrote several volumes of memoirs.

10. *Smollett*: Tobias Smollett (1721–71), the Scottish novelist.

11. *I hope to speak elsewhere and at greater length*: This hope was, apparently, unrealized.

12. *'A noble tale, but a most melancholy; all noble things are touched with that'*: Melville describes the ship *Pequod* in Chapter 16 of *Moby-Dick* as 'A noble craft, but somehow a most melancholy! All noble things are touched with that.'

R. H. Dana

First published, and sole appearance, in the *Daily News*, 27 August 1904.

1.   *Mariner's Sketches*: Nathaniel Ames (1805–35) published his non-fictional *A Mariner's Sketches* in 1830.

2. *Defoe*: Daniel Defoe (*c*.1659–1731), writer and journalist, author of *Robinson Crusoe* (1719). In 1909 Masefield was to edit a volume of Defoe selections (*Masters of Literature: Defoe*), which included a biographical introduction together with an appreciation of the writer.

3. *slush-lamp*: A crude lamp that burns melted fat or grease.

4. *Miss Braddon*: Mary Elizabeth Braddon (1837–1915) was the author of *Lady Audley's Secret* (1862) and seventy-four similarly sensational novels.

5. *Nares' Epitome*: A reference to *The Naval Cadet's Guide*, later titled *Seamanship*, by Admiral Sir George Strong Nares (1831–1915) and first published in 1860.

6. *Horn*: Cape Horn, at the tip of South America, considered one of the most dangerous navigation routes.

Chanties

First published in the *Manchester Guardian*, 16 August 1905. Present as a sectional introduction in *A Sailor's Garland* (London: Methuen, 1906). There are a number of minor variants. Publication in the *Manchester Guardian* caused an exchange in the 'Correspondence' section. On 17 August the paper published a letter from Edward West, who described himself as 'a "shellback" of the past'. He wrote that he wished to take exception to Masefield's remark that chanties were unsuited to publication. He noted: 'I have pulled and hove to many a chanty, and, although the words were often improvised, memory recalls very few that can be spoken of as vulgar or in bad taste.' Masefield responded on the same day, with his answer published on 19 August:

> . . . With reference to Mr West's letter in your issue of the 17th inst., I wish to state that I have carefully considered the words of twenty of the Chanties most popular in the merchant service some nine or ten years ago. The words of seventeen of the twenty are quite unsuited for publication. I do not call them vulgar nor in bad taste. They are merely frank and Chaucerian. I do not know what Mr West's experience may have been. I wrote the article to which he takes exception from my own knowledge; and I will not withdraw a single statement . . .

1. *scanty*: In the *Manchester Guardian* Masefield suggested that the word rhymed with 'Dante'.

2. *brakes*: Handles of pumps.

3. *Lucrece, in the fifth act*: Masefield, it appears, was confused
    about the source. Here he cites the fifth act of Thomas Hey-
    wood's *The Rape of Lucrece* (1607). A few months later, in his
    article 'Sea-Songs' (published in *Temple Bar* in January 1906),
    Masefield notes John Fletcher's *The Tragedy of Valentinian*
    (1610–14) as the source. By October 1906 in *A Sailor's Garland*
    he identifies Act IV, scene vi of *The Rape of Lucrece* (and is
    therefore inconsistent with this essay, which is included as a
    prefatory introduction in the volume). The song, which charts
    the conquest of Lucrece, 'Did he take fair Lucrece by the toe,
    man?', in *The Rape of Lucrece*, Act IV, scene vi, is only slightly
    similar in sentiment.
4. *Yankee packet*: An American ship.
5. *Horn*: Cape Horn, at the tip of South America, considered one
    of the most dangerous navigation routes.
6. *boatswain pipes*: See note 5 to 'Port of Many Ships' above.
7. *Salford Hippodrome*: Opened in 1906 to a design by the archi-
    tect J. J. Alley, the Salford Hippodrome in Cross Lane, Salford,
    was a variety and music-hall theatre. It was demolished in 1962.
    The act to which Masefield refers has not been identified.
8. *Music of the Waters*: Laura Smith's *The Music of the Waters. A
    Collection of the Sailors' Chanties, or Working Songs of the Sea,
    of All Maritime Nations* was published in London by Kegan
    Paul, Trench in 1888.
9. *Dr Ferris Tozer*: *Sailors' Songs or Chanties* by J. Frederick Davis
    and Ferris Tozer was published in London by Boosey in 1887.
10. *songbook of the Guild of Handicraft*: Published by Charles and
    Janet Ashbee's Essex House Press between 1903 and 1905, *The
    Essex House Song Book, Being the Collection of Songs formed
    for the Singers of the Guild of Handicraft* was, according to a
    bibliography produced by the press, a 'collection of some 200
    representative songs of England, together with their music, from
    the Middle Ages to our own day'.
11. *Metzler*: A change of music publisher from the text in the *Man-
    chester Guardian*, which cites Messrs Chappell.
12. *The Cadet*: The school magazine of HMS *Conway*. The period-
    ical was first published in 1889.

New Novels: Joseph Conrad

First published in the *Manchester Guardian*, 16 October 1912.

Sailing-Ships

Hitherto unpublished and adapted from a working draft (Bodleian Library, Dep.c.314). The article was originally intended to accompany examples of Alvin Langdon Coburn's photographs and these descriptive sections have been excluded here. In his autobiography, published in 1966, Coburn notes that he was approached by Masefield 'in the spring of 1914 . . . to make [i.e. photograph] a series of sailing ships . . . The final result was several hundred negatives of which about fifty were worth printing. Seven of them were published in *Harper's Magazine* for Christmas 1914 with a poem by Masefield, who also wrote captions and descriptions of the illustrations.' It appears that Masefield and Coburn may originally have planned a book before deciding on a magazine article for the material. The *Harper's Magazine* piece comprises the poem 'Ships' together with seven photographs by Coburn, each with a two-line caption by Masefield. The working draft from which the present piece is adapted is presumably part of Masefield's work for the aborted book and includes expanded captions.

1. *Panama Canal*: The canal that connects the Pacific Ocean to the Caribbean Sea opened in 1914 and replaced the need to sail via Cape Horn.
2. *velocipede*: An early form of bicycle invented in the 1860s, known more familiarly as the 'boneshaker'.
3. *high bicycle*: A bicycle with a large front wheel and much smaller rear wheel, dating from around the 1870/80s and known as the 'penny-farthing'.
4. *hansom-cab*: A horse-drawn carriage seating two passengers with a driver on an elevated seat behind the passenger's compartment and the reins positioned over the roof.
5. *Suez Canal*: The canal that connects the Mediterranean and the Red Sea opened in 1869 and allowed travel between Europe and Asia avoiding navigation around Africa.
6. *Mr Coburn*: Alvin Langdon Coburn (1882–1966), photographer and mystic.

EXTRACTS FROM NOVELS

From *Lost Endeavour*

Extracted from the first English edition, published by Thomas Nelson and Sons, on 25 November 1910 in an edition of 12,000 copies. It is an adventure novel set in Virginia and the Spanish Main (historically, the Spanish-occupied north-eastern coast of South America between the Orinoco River and Panama, and the adjoining parts of the Caribbean Sea) during the late seventeenth century.

1. *posse*: Here a body of armed Virginian planters seeking to prevent the departure of the smugglers' ship *Marie Galante*.
2. *vicuna wool*: A fine silky wool from the South American vicuna, which is closely related to the alpaca and llama.
3. *Boca Drago*: English name for Bocas del Toto, a province of Panama.
4. *James Town*: A settlement in the Virginia Colony, founded in 1607.
5. *Virginia*: The Colony of Virginia was the first English colony in the New World.
6. *Campeachy sloop*: A small vessel used on the Campeachy coast of south-east Mexico (see note 1 to 'Campeachy Picture' above).
7. *grue*: A feeling of terror or horror.

From *The Bird of Dawning*

Extracted from the first English edition, published by William Heinemann on 6 November 1933 in an edition of 15,000 copies. The novel recounts a strange event during the China-Tea-Race in the late 1860s.

1. *easting*: A nautical term for gaining on a course to the east.

From *The Box of Delights*

Extracted from the first English edition, published by William Heinemann on 30 August 1935 in an edition of 7,500 copies. This classic children's novel of the fantasy genre tells of Kay Harker and his efforts to keep a magic device from the evil clutches of Abner Brown.

1. *Hundreds and Thousands*: Small pieces of confectionery sprinkled as decoration on cakes, ice-cream and other deserts.
2. *drapers' patterns of woollen goods*: Presumably, here, specimen books providing small samples of woollen material.
3. *Sir Francis Drake*: (1540–95) Seaman, pirate, circumnavigator and protector against the Spanish Armada.
4. *the Box of Delights*: The magic device in Masefield's fantasy novel that enables the possessor to 'go small', 'go swift' and 'enter the past at will'.

From *Victorious Troy*

Extracted from the first English edition, published by William Heinemann on 31 October 1935 in an edition of 15,000 copies. The novel concerns a ship that is hit by a cyclone in the South Pacific and tells of the unlikely saviour of the vessel.

From *Live and Kicking Ned*

Extracted from the first English edition, published by William Heinemann on 30 October 1939 in an edition of 7,500 copies. The novel, a continuation of *Dead Ned* (London: William Heinemann, 1938), recounts the adventures of a young doctor who is wrongly convicted of murder and hanged. The hanging is unsuccessful and the doctor flees England aboard a slave-ship bound for Africa.

1. *Massa*: Masefield's port of Little Massa on the African slave coast. The name probably derives from the term for 'master' in representations of Caribbean speech.
2. *slabber*: A slush of food.
3. *Mantacaw*: Presumably a generic term for a black person. In *Dead Ned* (1938) the character of Old Black Mantacaw is introduced as Captain Ashplant's mistress:

    > She's a slave ... and one day she'll be treated like a slave and be kicked from Hell to Hackney and back again and then again the long way round. Then the next day she'll be the Old Man's fancy girl; and then she's the queen of this good ship; and we never know which she's going to be from day to day – the queen or the door-mat.

    At this juncture in the *Ned* trilogy, however, Captain Ashplant has died and the Mantacaw has been left behind in the port of Great Momboe. The name is therefore adopted by Pegg in a different context.
4. *Harriet Lane*: Sailor's term for canned meat. There appear to be two sources: a woman called Harriet Lane was said to have been caught in the machinery of a tinned-meat factory. Secondly, the murderer Henry Wainwright was executed in 1875 for the killing of Harriet Lane, his mistress and mother of his two illegitimate children. Both appear anachronisms for this tale of the late eighteenth century.

5. *chow*: Food.
6. *Newgate*: Newgate prison in London was in use between 1188 and 1902. In *Dead Ned* (London: William Heinemann, 1938), the narrator writes of Newgate:

> Of all the fearful places man had made for man, I know none more awful than a Christian prison ... I had seen hospitals in times of epidemic with many dying, but some there had hope of cure, and were cured. In Newgate the expectation was of death; none hoped; none admitted the possibility of hope ...

Glossary of Nautical Terms

For information on the sources for some of the glosses provided here –
frequently drawn from Masefield's own works – please see the
introduction to the Notes.

abaft 'Towards the stern of a vessel' (Dana)

abaft the beam 'That half of a ship included between her amid-ship
section and the taffrail' (*Salt-Water Ballads*)

afterguard Ordinary seamen and landsmen in the ship's crew. They
are stationed on the quarterdeck and poop to work the after sails

barque Generally a small ship or sailing vessel of a small size; also
applied to three-masted ships with the foremast and mainmast
square-rigged and the mizzen mast fore-and-aft-rigged

barquentine A small barque with the foremast square-rigged, and
the mainmast and mizzen mast fore-and-aft-rigged

beam Horizontal cross-timber that runs from the sides of the ship to
support the deck; also used to refer to a specific side of the ship (e.g.
'sighted on the port beam')

belaying-pin Bar 'of iron or hard wood to which running rigging
may be secured or *belayed*. Belaying pins, from their handiness and
peculiar club-shape, are sometimes used as bludgeons' (*Salt-Water
Ballads*)

bells 'Two bells (one forward, one aft), which are struck every half-hour
in a certain manner to mark the passage of the watches' (*Dauber*)

bend A variety of knot used to join two ropes together, or one rope
to another object; also used as a verb

binnacle 'The case in which the compass is held' (*The Bird of
Dawning*)

bitts 'Strong wooden structures (built round each mast) upon which
running rigging is secured' (*Dauber*)

block   Wooden pulley containing a metal wheel through which a rope runs

boatswain   Officer in charge of a ship's rigging, anchors, cables and deck crew

bobstay   The rope or chain which holds down a ship's bowsprit

booby-hatch   Raised covering over a small hatchway

boom   Spar along the foot of a fore-and-aft-rigged sail

bo'sun   See *boatswain*

bouse/bowse   To haul with tackle

bowline   Rope attaching the weather-side of a square sail to the bow; or a knot which forms a non-slip loop at the end of a rope

bowman   Rower positioned nearest the bow in a rowing boat

bowsprit   A spar running from the ship's bow and to which the fore-stays are secured

brace   Rope 'by which the yards are inclined forward or aft' (*Dauber*)

brails   Small ropes attached to the edge of a sail to truss it up before furling

brig/brigantine   'A square-rigged vessel, with two masts' (Dana)

bumpkin   'An iron bar (projecting out-board from the ship's side) to which the lower and topsail brace blocks are sometimes hooked' (*Salt-Water Ballads*)

buntlines   Ropes attached to a sail and used to turn part of it up and out of the wind in order to reduce pressure on the sail

bunts   'The central portions of square sails' (*The Bird of Dawning*)

capstan   A large revolving cylinder with a vertical axis, for winding ropes or cables

careen   After beaching a ship, to turn it on each side in turn for cleaning, caulking or other repairs

cat   Cat-o'-nine-tails; or 'the tackle used to hoist the anchor up to the cat-head' (Dana)

cat-head   The supporting wooden beam on the bow of a ship – angled outwards so that the raised anchor doesn't damage the side of the ship

catted   'Said of an anchor when weighed and secured to the "cat-head"' (*Salt-Water Ballads*)

caulk/caulking   To seal/sealing the seams of a boat with waterproof matter to make it watertight

chafing gear   Material placed around rigging to prevent wear

clew   (noun) The lower corner of a square sail, or the lower aft corner of a fore-and-aft sail, to which a rope is attached for controlling the sail

clew   (verb) 'To clew up' is to draw the lower corner (clew) of a sail up to the yard or mast in order to furl it; 'to clew down' is to let down a sail by the clew to unfurl it

clewlines 'Ropes by which the lower corners of square sails are lifted' (*Dauber*)

clipper 'A title of honour given to ships of more than usual speed and beauty' (*Dauber*)

clue See *clew* (verb)

coaming 'The raised rim of a hatchway; a barrier at a doorway to keep water from entering' (*Dauber*)

coaster A small vessel that sails along the coast, or moves from port to port of the same country

cobble Flat-bottomed fishing boat

courses 'The large square sails set upon the lower yards of sailing ships' (*Dauber*)

coxswain The person on board ship in charge of a small boat and crew, and of which he has command unless a superior officer is present

crank 'Crank-wheel' used for spinning rope and fixed on a spindle

cringled 'Fitted with iron rings or cringles, many of which are let into sails or sail-roping for various purposes' (*Dauber*)

crojick See *cross-jack*

cross-jack 'A square sail set upon the lower yard of the mizzen mast' (*Dauber*)

cross-tree Two horizontal beams fixed partway up a mast, used for spreading the shrouds that extend higher up the mast and to provide a standing-place for sailors

cutter A small boat carried by a large ship

davit A small crane, usually for suspending or lowering lifeboats

deckhouse A room (or 'house') erected on the deck

dipper Utensil for ladling water

dogwatch The dogwatches comprised two short watches, 4–6 p.m. and 6–8 p.m. (see *watch*)

donkey engine Auxiliary steam engine used to drive a winch or windlass

donkeyman Man in charge of a donkey engine

drogue A piece of equipment, usually constructed like a parachute, which is pulled behind a boat to reduce its speed. Masefield describes it as 'a floating sea-anchor, to which a ship or boat may ride in foul weather' (*The Bird of Dawning*)

dunnage Material such as brushwood or mats stowed with cargo to prevent chafing or wetting; also a term for miscellaneous baggage

fair-leads 'Rings of wood or iron by means of which running rigging is led in any direction' (*Dauber*)

fid A square bar of iron or wood used to support the weight of the topmast or topgallant mast; or a conical pin made from wood used to open the strands of a rope when splicing

fife-rails 'Strong wooden shelves fitted with iron pins, to which ropes may be secured' (*Dauber*)

fo'c's'le See *forecastle*

fore-and-aft (Of sails or rigging) set lengthwise and not on the yards

forecastle 'The deck-house or living-room of the crew. The word is often used to indicate the crew, or those members of it described by passengers as the "common sailors"' (*Salt-Water Ballads*)

fore-course Lowest sail on the foremast of a three-masted ship

futtock One of the middle timbers in a ship's frame between the floor and top timbers

gaskets 'Ropes or plaited lines used to secure the sails in furling' (*Salt-Water Ballads*)

grog Mixture of rum and water

guarda-costa Spanish coastguard vessel

gunnel/gunwale 'The upper edge of a boat's planking' (*The Bird of Dawning*)

half-deck 'A cabin or apartment in which the apprentices are berthed. Its situation is usually the ship's waist; but it is sometimes further aft, and occasionally it is under the poop or even right forward under the top-gallant fo'c's'le' (*Dauber*)

halliards More usually spelled 'halyards' and comprising 'ropes by which sails are hoisted' (*Dauber*)

handy billy Another name for the 'watch tackle', consisting of one double block and a single block with a hook, used to help haul a sail or other heavy objects

hank A coil of rope; or a ring for securing the staysail to the stay

hawseholes Holes in the side of a ship through which a cable or anchor-rope passes

hawser A thick rope or small cable primarily used in towing or mooring a ship; the hawser passes through a hawsehole

head The projecting end of a pier; or the fore part of a ship or boat

holystone Soft sandstone used for scouring decks

hooker Derogatory or affectionate slang for a ship; Masefield notes 'hooker' as 'a periphrasis for ship, I suppose from a ship's carrying hooks or anchors' (*Salt-Water Ballads*)

house-flag Flag flown by a merchant ship to show which company owns the vessel

hoy Small vessel used for short distances

jack Abbreviation for 'jack-cross-tree' (see *cross-tree*); or a small flag flown at the bow of a ship

jib A variety of staysail that, in large ships, stretches from the outer end of the jib-boom to the foretopmasthead; in smaller ships the jib stretches from the bowsprit to the masthead

jigger Small sail at the stern of a ship

jolly-boat A ship's boat, with external planks overlapping downwards, normally hoisted at the stern of a ship and used for light work

kites 'Light upper sails' (*The Bird of Dawning*)

knot Unit of speed equivalent to one nautical mile per hour

lain-to See *lie-to*

lazarette 'A strong-room in which provisions are stored' (*The Bird of Dawning*)

lee/lee-side Sheltered side of the ship, away from the wind

leech Border or edge of a sail

leeward 'Pronounced "looard." That quarter to which the wind blows' (*Salt-Water Ballads*)

lie-to To apply oneself vigorously and steadily to a task; or 'to stop the progress of a vessel at sea' (Dana)

log Apparatus for determining the speed of a ship; or, from 'log-book', an account of events on board ship

logship A piece of wood or canvas bag at the end of a log line for catching water when the log is lifted; also noted by Masefield as 'a contrivance by which a ship's speed is measured' (*Dauber*)

mainyard Lower yard on the mainmast

man-catcher Safety net below the bowsprit

marline Thin two-stranded rope

marline-spike 'A steel spike, about fifteen inches long, used in splicing ropes, etc.' (*The Bird of Dawning*)

midshipman Naval officer with a rank between naval cadet and sub-lieutenant

mizzen The principal sail on the mizzen mast

mizzen mast The mast astern of the mainmast

mouse To put turns of rope around the end of a hook to secure the rope

oar loom   The long shaft of an oar
old man   Nautical slang for the captain of the ship

painter   The rope attached to the bow of a boat for securing it to a
   mooring
pannikin   'A tin cup containing nearly half a pint' (*The Bird of
   Dawning*)
pawl   See *safety pawl*
point   Short piece of cord at the lower edge of a sail for tying up a reef
poop   Highest deck of a ship and the one nearest the stern

quarter   One side or other of the stern of a ship

reef   (noun) A section of sail rolled up to reduce the amount of sail
   exposed to the wind; also an abbreviation for *reefer*
reef   (verb) To roll up or take in part of a sail to reduce its area and
   hence the amount of sail exposed to the wind; or to shorten a mast
   or bowsprit, etc., by taking part of it in
reefer   A midshipman or person who reefs sails; also a thick jacket or
   coat
reeve   To pass a cable or rope through a hole, pulley, ring or block
resheath   To renew the metal on the bottom of a ship
riding-light   A light, usually white, which is displayed by a vessel
   when riding at anchor
royals   'Light upper square sails; the fourth, fifth, or sixth sails from
   the deck according to the mast's rig' (*Dauber*)

safety pawl   Short bar used to lock a capstan, windlass, etc., to pre-
   vent it from recoiling
scantling   'Planks' (*Salt-Water Ballads*)
screws   Screw-propellers
scupper   'Channel at the ship's side [leading to a hole] for the carry-
   ing off of water' (*The Bird of Dawning*)
sheet   (noun) Rope attached to the lower corner of sail (see *clew*) to
   control it
sheet   (verb) Abbreviation for 'to sheet home', to extend the sheets (of
   the topsails in a square-rigged ship) to the tips of the yards below
shellback   Nautical slang for a sailor of advanced years, especially if
   tough and knowledgeable
shrouds   'Wire ropes of great strength, which support lateral strains
   on masts' (*Dauber*)
skysails   'The uppermost square sails; the fifth, sixth, or seventh sails
   from the deck according to the mast's rig' (*Dauber*)

slat/slatting 'The noise made by sails flogging in the wind' (*Dauber*)

sling 'To set a cask, spar, gun, or other article, in ropes, so as to put on a tackle and hoist or lower it' (Dana)

slip A 'slipway' is the inclined surface from which ships are launched

smack Single-masted sailing boat for fishing or coasting

sounding Measuring the depth of water

sounding-rod Device used to measure the depth of water under a boat or in a ship's hold

spar Stout pole used as a mast or yard

spill-way Slope or channel constructed to carry away surplus water

spunyarn 'A three-strand line spun out of old rope-yarns knotted together. Most sailing ships carry a spunyarn winch, and the spinning of such yarn is a favourite occupation in fine weather' (*Salt-Water Ballads*)

square-rigged A variety of rigging and sail arrangement in which the primary sails are carried on horizontal spars which are perpendicular (or square) to the ship's keel and masts

stair Landing stage

stanchion An upright bar or support

stay Rope supporting a mast

staysail Triangular sail set along the line of the keel rather than at right-angles to it

steamer-tramp Steamer ship (see *tramp*)

stirrup Rope with an eye at one end

stop Tie up with thin rope

straik 'A streak or line of planking' (*The Bird of Dawning*)

stretcher Piece of wood positioned at the bottom of a boat against which a rower presses his feet when rowing

stroke Rower sitting nearest the stern of a rowing boat who sets the time for the other rowers

studdingsail 'A sail set at the extremity of a yard to increase the area of a ship's canvas' (*The Bird of Dawning*)

stunsail See *studdingsail*

swab Pejorative term for an officer

swing-ports 'Iron doors in the ship's side which open outwards to free the decks from water' (*Dauber*)

tack 'To stay or 'bout ship. A reach to windward. The weather lower corner of a course' (*Salt-Water Ballads*)

taffrail 'The rail or bulwark round the sternmost end of a ship's poop or after-deck' (*Salt-Water Ballads*)

thwart Crosspiece in a boat forming a seat for a rower

topgallant Square-rigged sail set immediately above a topsail

topmast 'The second mast above the deck. Next above the lower
  mast' (Dana)

tops'ls See *topsails*

topsails 'The second and third sails from the deck on the masts of a
  modern square-rigged ship are known as the lower and upper top-
  sails' (*Dauber*)

tramp A cargo vessel, without a fixed trading route, which takes
  cargoes for any port as opportunity allows

trick 'The ordinary two-hour spell at the wheel or on the look-out'
  (*Salt-Water Ballads*)

trucks 'The summits of the masts' (*Dauber*)

turn-to/turning-to Set/setting to work

waist 'That part of the upper deck between the quarter-deck and
  forecastle' (Dana)

watch 'A division of time on board ship. There are seven watches in
  a day, reckoning from 12 midnight round through the twenty-four
  hours, five of them being of four hours each, and the two others,
  called dog watches, of two hours each, viz., from 4 to 6, and from
  6 to 8 p.m. Also, a certain portion of a ship's company, appointed
  to stand a given length of time. In the merchant service all hands are
  divided into two watches, larboard and starboard, with a mate to
  command each' (Dana)

well Enclosure protecting a ship's pumps

whack 'An allowance' (*The Bird of Dawning*)

wheel The ship's wheel; also the period of time spent at the wheel

winch 'A purchase formed by a horizontal spindle or shaft with a
  wheel or crank at the end. A small one with a wheel is used for mak-
  ing ropes or spunyarn' (Dana)

windlass 'The machine used in merchant vessels to weigh the anchor
  by' (Dana)

windsail A canvas wind catcher fitted with a tube to lead fresh air
  below

yard-arms 'The extremities of a yard' (Dana)

yards 'The steel or wooden spars (placed across masts) from which
  square sails are set' (*Dauber*)

Index of Poem Titles

Index of First Lines
to the Poems